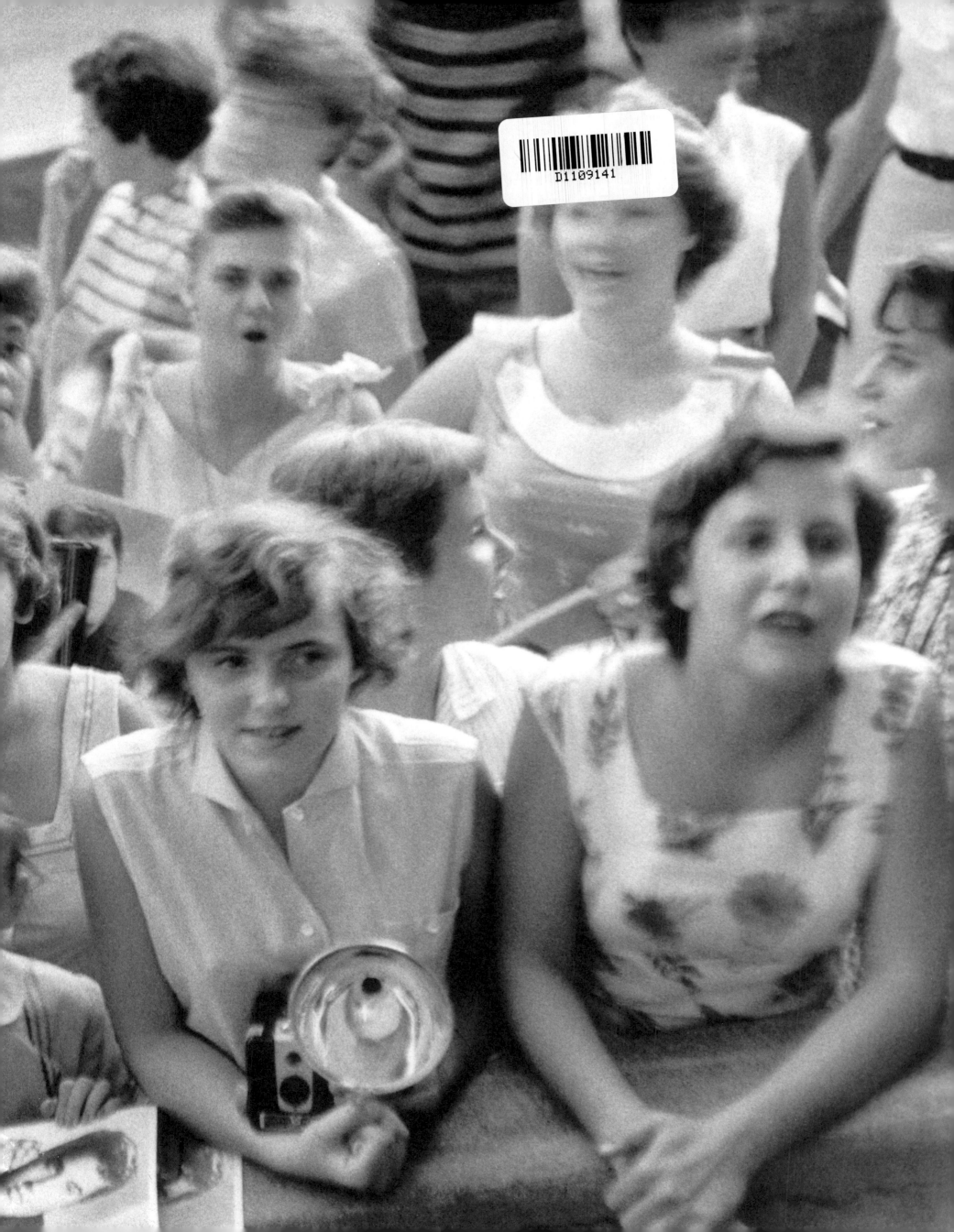

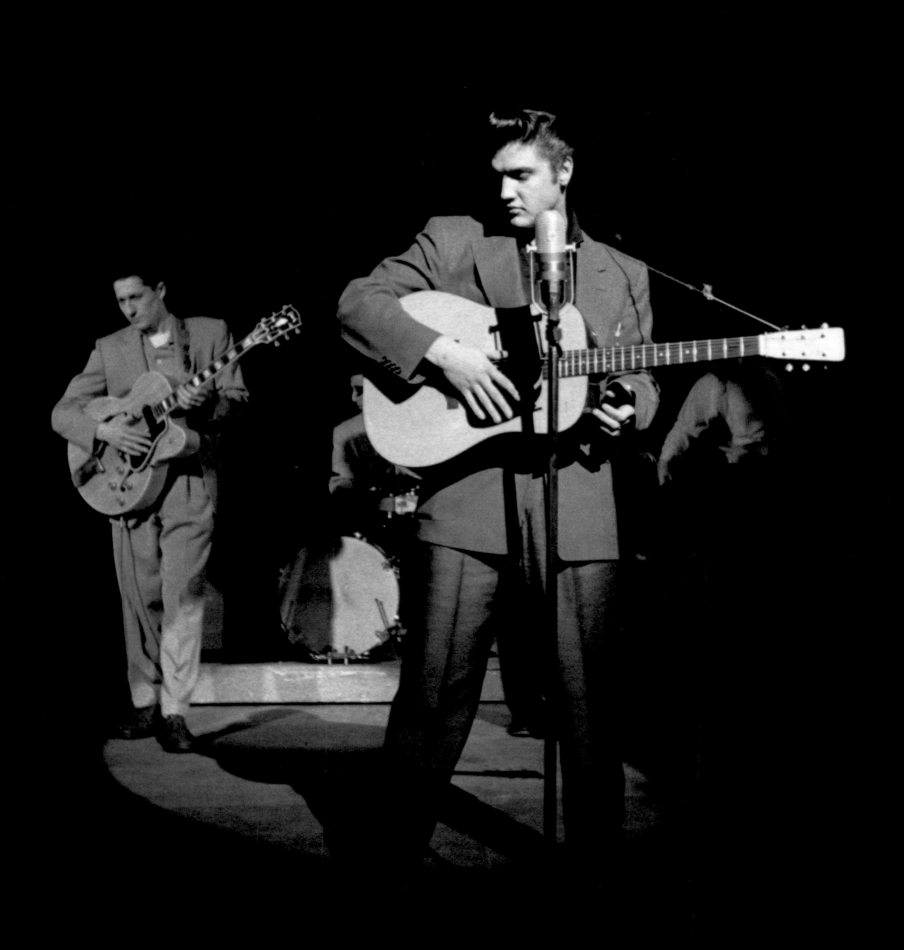

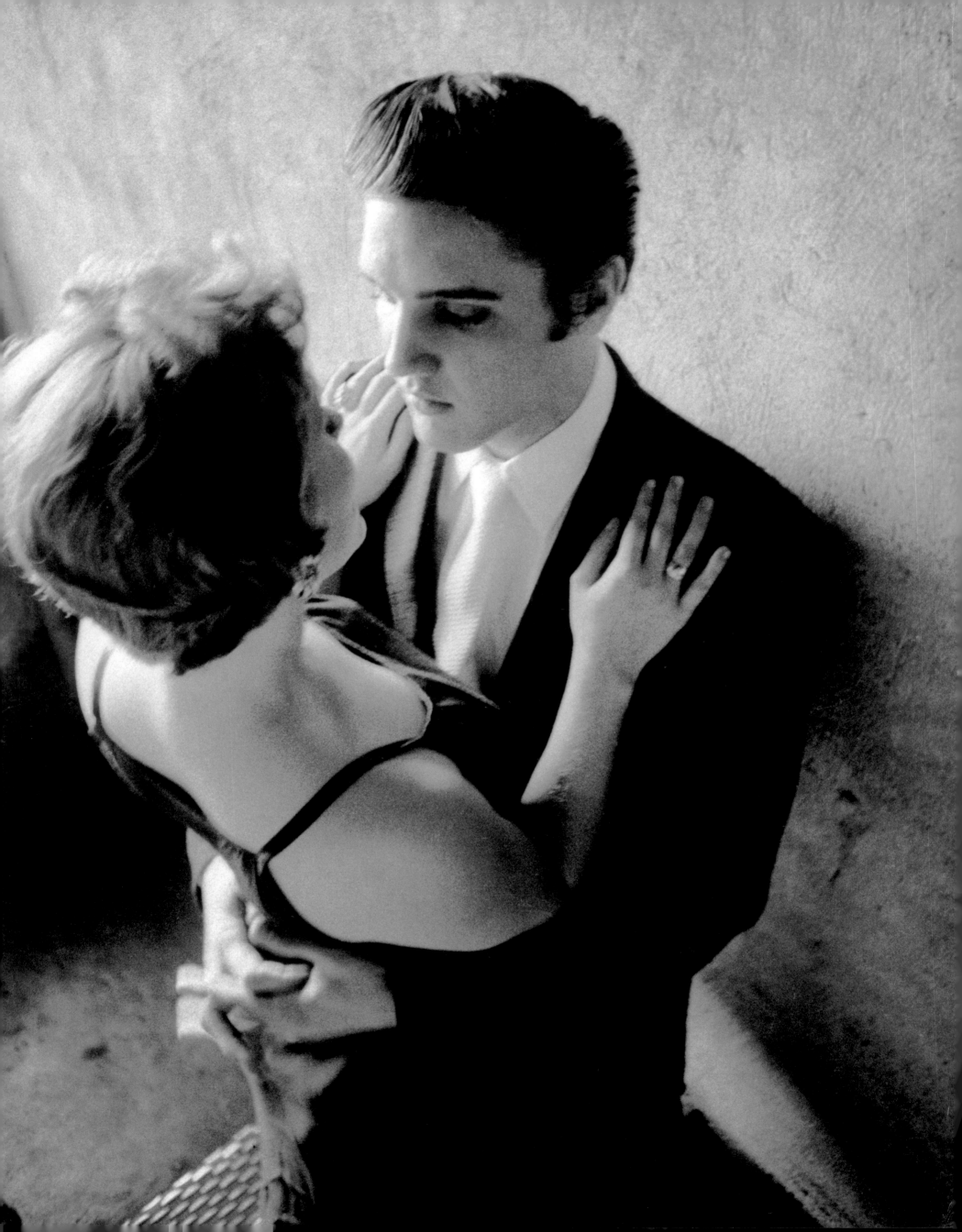

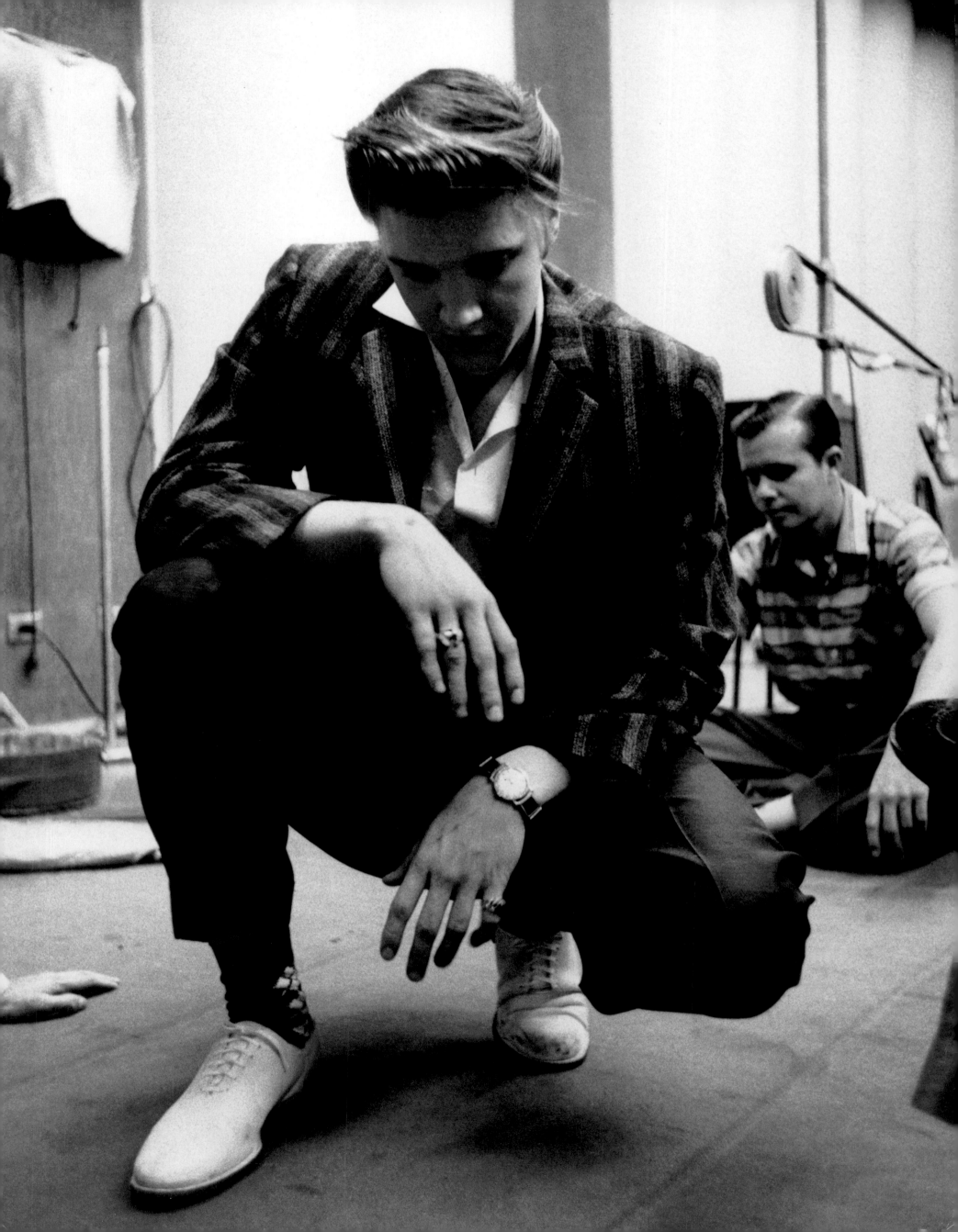

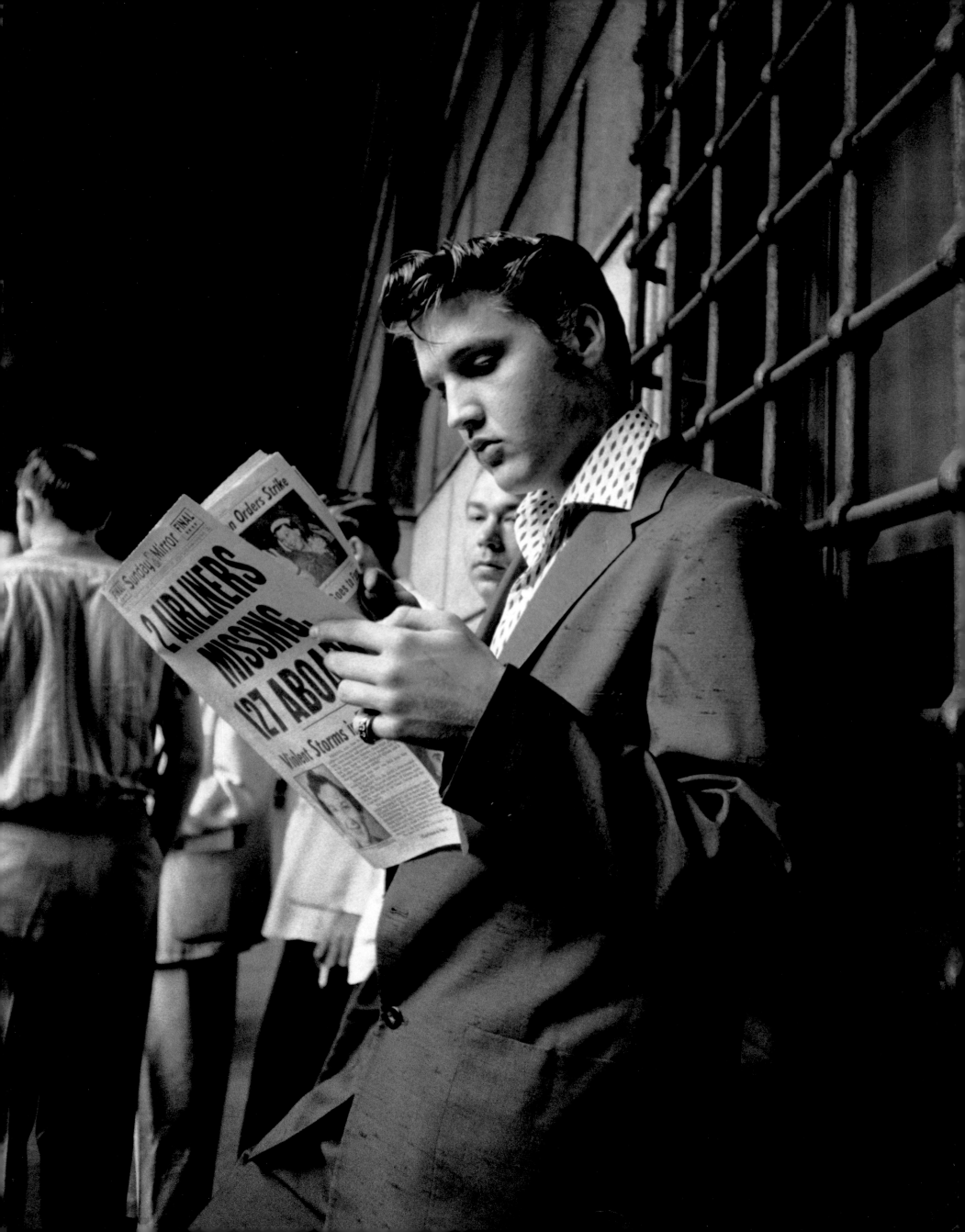

ELVIS AT 21 NEW YORK TO MEMPHIS

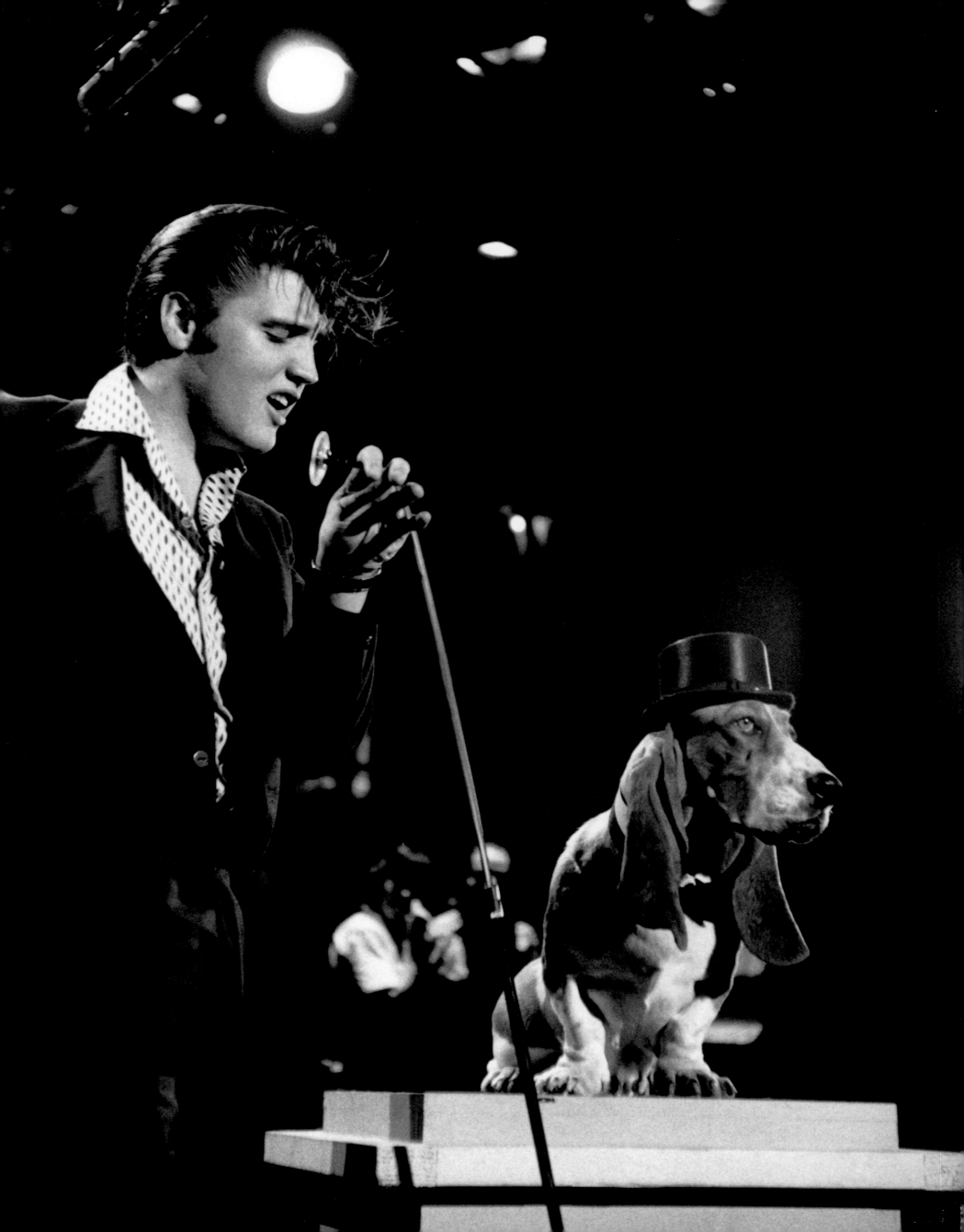

ELVIS AT 21 NEW YORK TO MEMPHIS

TEXT AND PHOTOGRAPHY BY

ALFRED WERTHEIMER

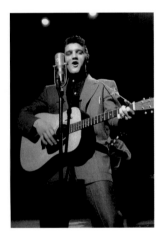

FOREWORD BY PETER GURALNICK

INTRODUCTION BY CHRIS MURRAY

INSIGHT EDITIONS

San Rafael, California

CONTENTS

11

FOREWORD BY PETER GURALNICK

13

INTRODUCTION BY CHRIS MURRAY

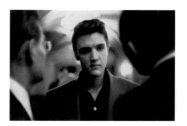

16

STAGE SHOW: STUDIO 50

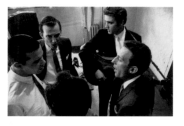

52

THE STEVE ALLEN SHOW REHEARSAL

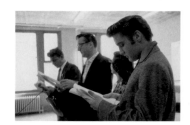

66

MOSQUE THEATER, RICHMOND, VIRGINIA

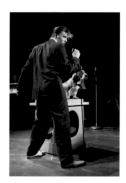

112

HUDSON THEATER, NEW YORK CITY

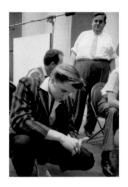

132

Recording Session, Studio One

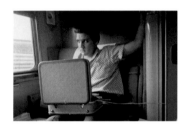

152

From New York to Memphis

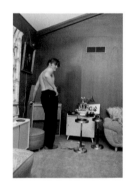

192

Home Sweet Home

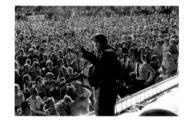

238

Russwood Park, Memphis

253

Acknowledgments

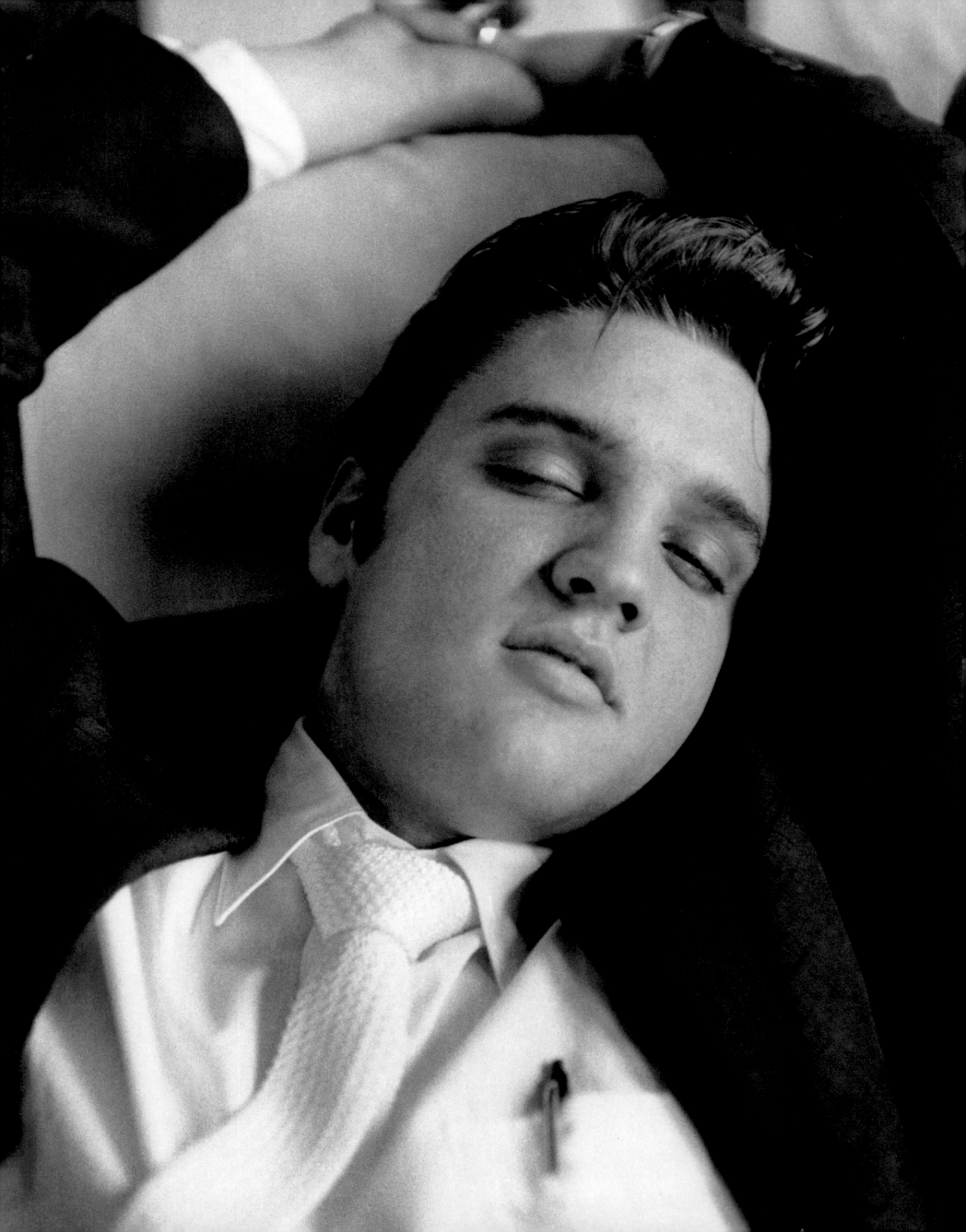

ART IS ABOUT CHOICES. The same scene presents itself to all of us. We are each given the same subject. It is in the selection of detail, what is included and what is left out, the angle of perception from which the scene is observed, that the true artist finds his or her own unique form of expression.

What is so remarkable about Al Wertheimer's documentary portrait of Elvis Presley, very much like the music of the artist it chronicles, is how fresh and contemporary the picture still seems, how utterly unlike any other portrait of this endlessly scrutinized figure. It is, clearly, not just a matter of access, for Wertheimer was with his subject for no more than a week all told on two separate occasions in 1956. Nor is it as if the photographer was being invited to record some momentous historic event. He was just there to photograph a couple of television appearances, on Jimmy and Tommy Dorsey's *Stage Show* on March 17 and *The Steve Allen Show* on July 2, with the rehearsals attendant on each performance. Another photographer might simply have dismissed this as a not very challenging assignment about a not particularly interesting teenage fad. Another photographer might simply have taken it as an easy payday, an opportunity to snap a few dozen performance shots and move on as quickly as possible to the next job. Wertheimer saw the possibilities of the subject not because he was a fan (he had never even heard of Elvis when he was called by the record company two days before the first shoot), but because he was a keen student of human nature, because he was curious, because, like Elvis, he could be swept up by the purity of experience, by the unscripted eloquence of the moment.

Wertheimer's photography scrupulously reflected the William Carlos Williams dictum, "No ideas but in things" (Williams was the poet who famously wrote, "So much depends upon a red wheel barrow"). When Wertheimer discovered Elvis alone at the piano in the corner of a blank high-ceilinged room, with sunlight hitting a disconsolate group of empty chairs, he saw it not as a symbol, not as the mythic logo for a generation, but as *itself*, as a powerful picture that could suggest multiple layers of moods and meanings. That there was actually someone else in the room at the time has no bearing on a striking aesthetic vision that demands attention strictly on its own terms. In the same way Wertheimer took the recording session on the day after *The Steve Allen Show* not as the occasion for a pictorial news account of a mundane event (as it happened, Elvis recorded both "Hound Dog" and "Don't Be Cruel" on that day) but as an opportunity to explore, through a series of sharply evocative images rendered in exquisite detail, the unrelenting concentration, joy, pain, and release of the creative act. And, following the session, he jumped on a train to Memphis with Elvis and his manager, Colonel Parker, not because he knew what was going to happen on the journey—but because he didn't.

"Mind if I tag along?" was his only security badge, Elvis's shrug all the validation he needed. When Elvis goes into the bathroom to shave, the moment is recorded with the subject's permission. The precise choreography of flirtation, the purchase of a ring from a worn-out-looking jewelry salesman, a transcendent instant on stage, grabbing a catnap on the train, an unrehearsed family reunion, all are captured, in true verité fashion, without the slightest hint of irony or visual comment. We are scarcely aware of the photographer, though he is always present. He never flinches. *He never turns away.*

Al Wertheimer continued, of course, to take photographs; he went on to a distinguished career as a documentary filmmaker and cinematographer, but would never again, he has sometimes said, capture the moment in quite the same way—any more than his subject would. If he had been given the assignment two or three years later, he suggests wryly, he might have screwed it up by trying to improve on reality. But whether because, as he suggests, he simply didn't know any better, or because, as his photographs show, he had a profound eye for the unmanipulated image, in this case he was content to simply leave matters alone. "I learned that when somebody is doing something that is more important in his or her life than having their photograph taken, you're going to get good pictures." He understates his achievement. He got *great* pictures. Like Elvis, by embracing spontaneity, by prizing feeling over mere technique, he found something new in familiar forms, and the result is work that can stand gloriously on its own, unaffected by the eddying tides of fashion or the shifting sands of time.

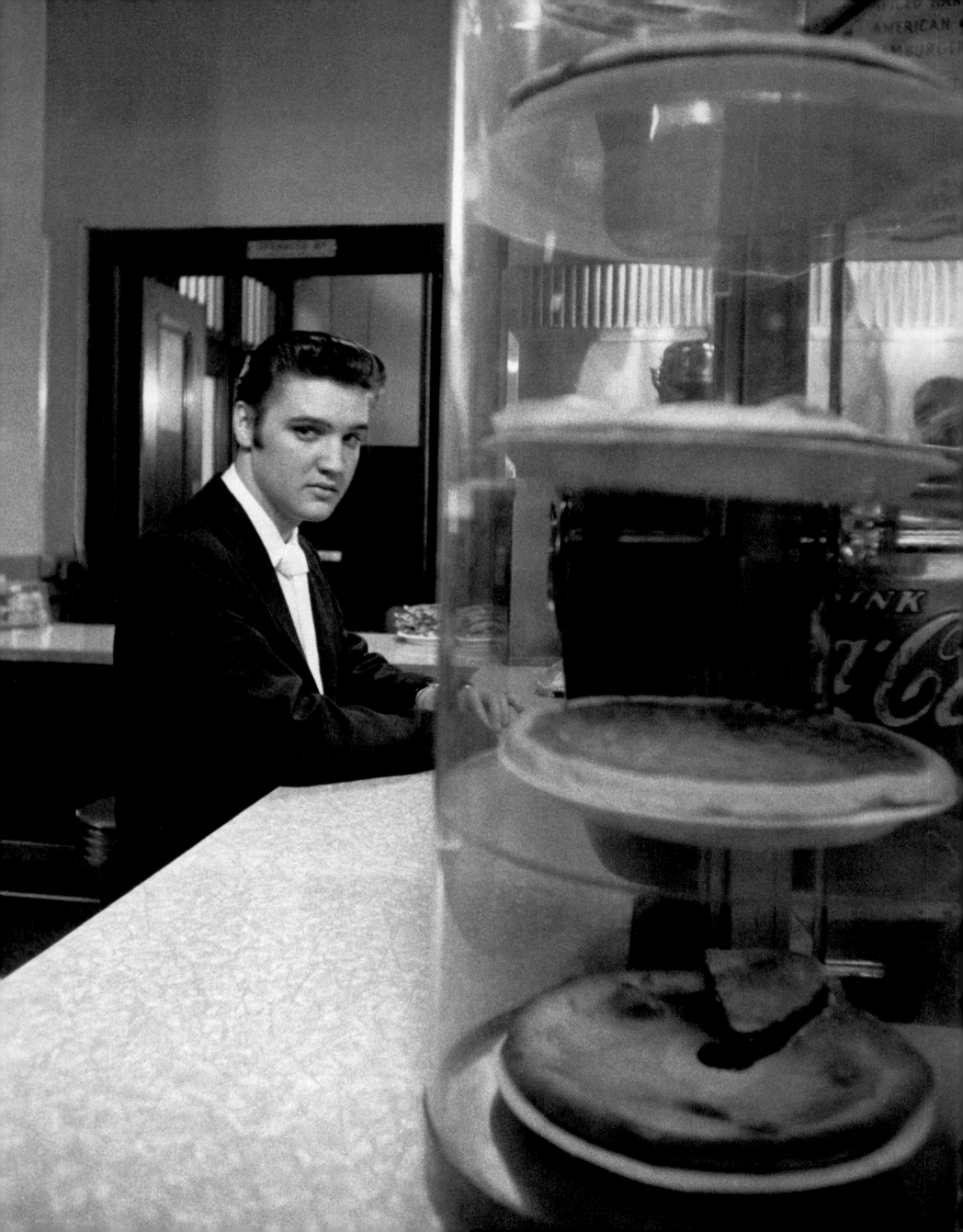

*B*EFORE ELVIS, there was nothing.

—JOHN LENNON

A LFRED WERTHEIMER'S PHOTOGRAPHS OF ELVIS PRESLEY are a national treasure. They are a unique visual record of the most exciting and influential performer of our time. Taken in 1956, Wertheimer's photographs document Elvis Presley at the quintessential moment of his explosive appearance onto the cultural landscape. After the photos in this book were taken, no photographer ever again had the access to Elvis that Wertheimer enjoyed. Wertheimer has described his photographs as "the first and last look at the day-to-day life of Elvis Presley." Apart from Elvis's own recordings from this period, Wertheimer's photographs are the most compelling vintage document of Elvis in 1956, a very special year for the young man from Memphis who was about to shake up the world. *Elvis at 21: New York to Memphis* is an extraordinary record of how these two storytellers' lives came together, of a twenty-one-year-old singer on the verge of fame and fortune crossing paths with a twenty-six-year-old photographer about to document a legend.

Only six years old, Alfred Wertheimer left Hitler's Germany with his father Julius, his mother Katy, and his brother Henry in 1936. Julius was a delicatessen butcher with a little shop in Coburg, Germany. After leaving their home behind, young Alfred and his family came to New York City and after several moves rented an apartment at 842 Nostrand Avenue in Brooklyn. Julius got a job at Carmel Kosher Provision, and the Wertheimer family settled into their new life in America.

Al looked up to his older brother Henry and, following in his footsteps, attended Haaren High School in Manhattan. It was during this time that Al got his first camera, a gift from Henry. It was a folding camera called a Prontor S. Al was overjoyed. He loved the idea that he could record events. At the age of nineteen, Henry was drafted into the Army and was shipped out to Italy with the 10th Mountain Infantry. Haaren High School taught an aviation class, so Al decided that he wanted to join the military as well and become a pilot after high school. Henry, however, convinced his younger brother to learn something more practical and told him to study drafting. Taking his brother's advice, Al started studying mechanical drawing, which he enjoyed and was very good at. He learned about perspective and many other techniques that later served him well as a photographer and filmmaker.

After graduating from high school in 1947, he spent a year at City College and studied drawing before being accepted at Cooper Union's school of art in Manhattan in 1948. Cooper Union was tuition-free, which Al very much appreciated since he could not afford to pay for college. He describes himself as "one of the lucky ninety," as only ninety students were admitted that year. At Cooper Union, he photographed his first events with the camera Henry had given him. Using available light, Al photographed his classes, including his drawing class and teacher, the artist Robert Gwathmey. Al was delighted to see his photos published in the Cooper Union newspaper.

In 1951, he graduated with a major in advertising design. The following year, he was drafted into the Army. Al now had both a Leica and a Contax camera and he set about documenting the sixteen-week basic training experience at Fort Dix, New Jersey. He compiled a photo essay of the training into an album, which he presented to the commanding officer of his company. The captain liked the photos very much and had Al make a second album for the base commander of Fort Dix. Though Al's original Military Occupation Specialty was as a mortar base plate carrier, he was reassigned as a photographer. Stationed near Heidelberg, Germany, he used a military-issued Speed Graphic camera and took photographs for the local Army newspaper.

After finishing his service in 1954, Al returned to New York City where he found a job with fashion photographer Tom Palumbo. Palumbo worked on assignment for *Harper's Bazaar* magazine under the legendary art director Alexey Brodovitch, who also became a mentor to photographers Richard Avedon and Irving Penn, among many others. Palumbo's studio was in the Sherwood Building at 57th Street and 6th Avenue, where many photographers had studios. Al worked hard for Palumbo, developing film, printing photographs, setting up and cleaning the studio, keeping track of his negatives, assisting at shoots, and going to the color lab for processing. Al also organized Palumbo's vast music library of 78rpm recordings and developed an appreciation for classical music.

After working for Palumbo for about a year, Al started his own business as a freelance photographer in the middle of 1955. Though he worked independently, he shared studio space with a group of photographers at Dave Linton's Studio at 3rd Avenue and 74th Street. Al's good friend Paul Schutzer, a talented photojournalist, worked there along with Jerry Yulesman and Roland Mitchell, who did a lot of darkroom work for Al. During this time, Paul introduced Wertheimer to a woman named Ann Fulchino, the publicist at RCA for the Pop Record Division. Ann hired photographers to take pictures of the RCA talent for publicity and promotional use. On assignment for RCA, Al photographed Julius LaRosa, Perry Como, Arthur Rubinstein, Lena Horn, Nelson Eddy, Jeannette McDonald, Sir Thomas Beecham, and many others. One day, Ann asked Al to take photos of RCA's latest acquisition, a young singer named Elvis Presley. Al had never heard of this new singer when Ann called him that day in March 1956. But in just a few months, the whole world would know the name Elvis Presley.

My own journey with Elvis began at home in New York City in 1955 at the age of eight. My older brother Matthew loved rock and roll music and constantly played Elvis's original Sun Records 45rpm recordings for me, much to my mother's chagrin. Listening to those classic Sun recordings changed my consciousness. In Elvis's music, I heard something utterly mysterious yet startlingly familiar. By the time he entered our home live on national television and had recorded "Don't Be Cruel" and "Hound Dog," I was ready to go wherever Elvis took me. It seemed the entire country was listening to and talking about Elvis Presley. It is hard to describe the magnitude of his impact at that time, but whatever it was and however you measured it, Elvis and his music were wonderful. As Sun Records proprietor Sam Phillips said of the kind of music Elvis was making, "This is where the soul of man never dies." I was growing up on rock and roll, and Elvis was an electrifying start.

While browsing through a bookstore almost forty years later, I came across a book called *Last Train to Memphis* by Peter Guralnick. The cover featured a photograph of Elvis sitting alone playing the piano. The moment I saw that image, all of the feelings and memories evoked by Elvis's extraordinary music in 1956 resonated within me again in 1994. That photograph seemed to capture the essence of everything I felt about Elvis.

I bought *Last Train to Memphis* and read it with an enthusiasm I had not experienced in a book for a long time. Guralnick's biography of the rise of Elvis Presley is a masterpiece. Moreover, I noted that the photo credit for the cover that so mesmerized me was for a gentleman named Alfred Wertheimer. As director of Govinda Gallery in Washington, D.C., I had organized a number of groundbreaking exhibitions featuring significant photographs and art relating to contemporary musicians and performers, including John Lennon's *Bag One* series (1981), the first exhibitions of Annie Leibovitz's photographs (1984 and 1987), Michael Cooper's *Sgt. Pepper* photographs (1989), Peter Blake's drawings of Eric Clapton and his band (1992), and Linda McCartney's photographs of the sixties (1993). By the time I came across *Last Train to Memphis*, I had just mounted an exhibition of photographs by Henry Diltz and Baron Wolman, among others, in celebration of the twenty-fifth anniversary of Woodstock. Coincidentally, Wertheimer was the one of the principal cameramen on the documentary film *Woodstock*. Both as a fan of Elvis's music and as a curator, I was determined to seek out Wertheimer and his photographs. In the spring of 1995, I found him alive and well, living in New York City. Meeting him began a treasured friendship that led to several exhibitions and the publication of this book. *Elvis at 21: New York to Memphis* is the realization of my decade-long dream to work with Wertheimer and his brilliant photographs.

Both Elvis Presley and Al Wertheimer are storytellers. Elvis's stories are in his songs, while Al's are in his pictures. About his experience revealing Elvis's environment and how he lived in it, Al has remarked that "I was a reporter whose pen was a camera." His photographs of the rehearsals and performances on *Stage Show* and *The Steve Allen Show* chronicle the mutual development of two cultural phenomena, television and Elvis Presley. Wertheimer's pictures of Elvis sitting at the lunch counter of the Jefferson Hotel coffee shop in Richmond, Virginia are a slice of 1950s Americana. Later that day at Richmond's Mosque Theater, Elvis greets fans, prepares for the shows in his dressing room, and then puts on two powerful performances that leave the audiences in a frenzy. Those photographs taken on a hot summer day in Virginia produced a masterpiece image called "The Kiss," a dramatic illustration of Al's self-described "fly-on-the-wall" approach to photography.

Elvis's 45rpm recording of "Hound Dog" and "Don't Be Cruel" is the best rock and roll single ever produced. Al was there at Studio One in New York City on July 2, 1956, documenting that legendary session with his camera. The photos of that RCA session are true rarities and an important legacy of a monumental moment in contemporary American music. His pictures of Elvis's train ride from New York to Memphis bring us along on Elvis's journey home. We see his parents, Gladys and Vernon, his cousins, girlfriends, and neighbors. We see him on his motorcycle, horsing around in his swimming pool, and relaxing at home after taking a shower. When Elvis takes the stage at Russwood Park in Memphis on the evening of July 4th, he tells the audience of 14,000 people, "I'm gonna show you what the real Elvis is like tonight." Wertheimer, with his camera, is our witness to the hero's return.

Al Wertheimer has said, "My photographs speak for themselves." That they resonate so splendidly is a result of his awareness and sensitivity as a skilled photographer, qualities that complemented his charismatic subject. Elvis Presley invented the rock and roll persona as we know it. Both on stage and off, he defined the very notion of "rock style." Everyone in rock and roll still owes a debt to Elvis, especially from that magical time in 1956 depicted in Al's photographs. From the Beatles to the Rolling Stones, Bob Dylan to Jimi Hendrix, Bruce Springsteen to Patti Smith, Joe Strummer to Bono…it all goes back to Elvis in 1956. Elvis was beautiful, his voice was amazing, and his music, an electrifying synthesis of rhythm and blues, gospel, and country, was rock and roll at its very finest.

These photographs of Elvis Presley are without a doubt the most important and compelling images ever taken of the greatest rock and roll icon of all time. No other photographer has ever come closer to catching Elvis Presley's magic than Alfred Wertheimer.

—Chris Murray

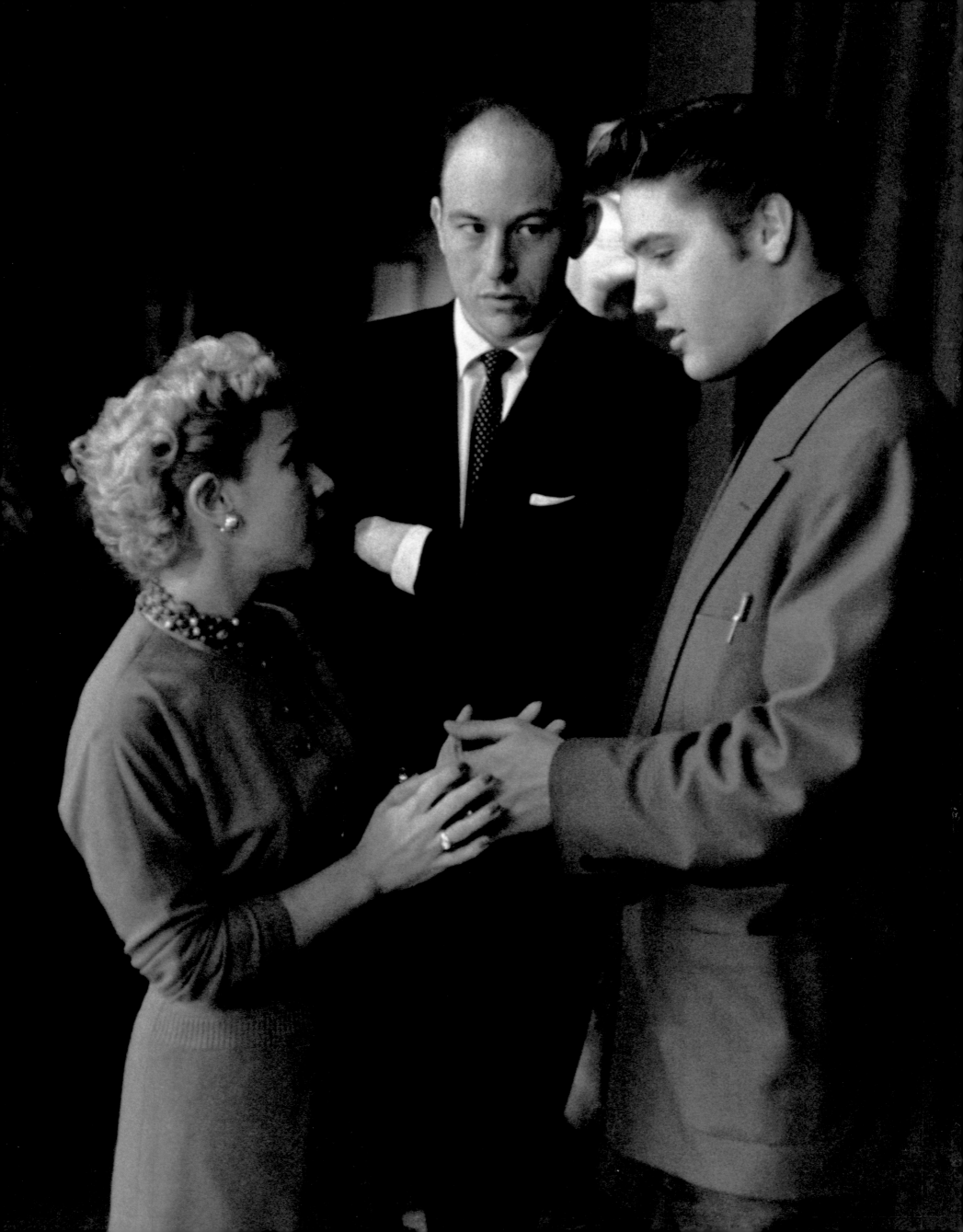

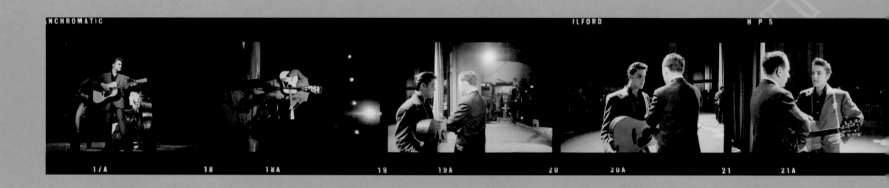

CHAPTER I

STAGE SHOW

STUDIO 50

STAGE
SHOW
STUDIO 50

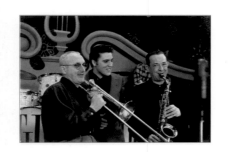

THE PUBLICIST AT RCA's POP RECORD DIVISION, Ann Fulchino (p. 16), called me one day in 1956 and said, "Al, what are you doing on Saturday, March 17th?"

"Why? What's up?"

"I'd like you to go down to Studio 50 to photograph Tommy and Jimmy Dorsey's *Stage Show*." Once used for taping radio programs, the CBS studio on Broadway was converted for television broadcasts in 1950 and would be known later as the Ed Sullivan Theater. In those days it was called Studio 50 where, from 1954 to 1956, *Stage Show* was broadcast.

"Wonderful. Tommy Dorsey is one of my heroes, like Benny Goodman, Glenn Miller, and the whole Big Band era."

"No, I'm not concerned with Tommy Dorsey. I want you to photograph Elvis Presley."

After a long silence, I said, "Elvis who?"

"Elvis Presley."

"I've never heard of him. What does he do?"

"He's a singer."

"When did you guys sign him up?"

"In November of 1955. I'd like you to cover him on the 17th and help me build my photo file on him."

"Fine, Ann. I'll be glad to do it."

I got myself ready on that Saturday and went down to Studio 50 with my camera bag and a tiny little Braun strobe unit. After introducing myself to the doorman, I went looking for Ann, who was backstage somewhere in one of the dressing rooms.

"Hello, Ann. How are you?" We gave each other a hug and I asked, "Where is Elvis?"

She dragged me down the hall to another dressing room. We went in, and reflected in the mirror, was Elvis with his feet up on the table and his argyle socks showing. To Elvis's right was a man in his mid-forties handing Elvis a ring. Apparently a jewelry salesman had talked the singer into buying that ring and was delivering it to him. Interrupting the transaction, Ann introduced me. "Elvis, this is Al Wertheimer. He's going to be taking some pictures of you for us." Uninterested in any photographs, Elvis grunted, "Okay, fine."

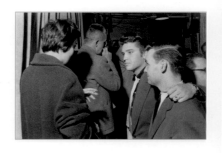

I pulled out my camera and started to shoot him inspecting the diamond-studded horseshoe ring adorned with a horse's head. Holding it and looking at it from a distance, Elvis seemed content with his new piece of jewelry while the salesman unsuccessfully tried to interest him in some more. Once they both left the room, Elvis began wandering around backstage greeting a few people and checking out the buffet table. Tagging along like a little dog, I just kept snapping.

Eventually, he got tired of being backstage with all the smoke-filled confusion and the June Taylor dancers rehearsing for that evening's show. His rehearsal wasn't going to begin for another twenty minutes so he decided to refresh himself. Stepping outside of the stage door into a very cold March day, Elvis was greeted by a group of people wearing heavy coats and shawls over their heads.

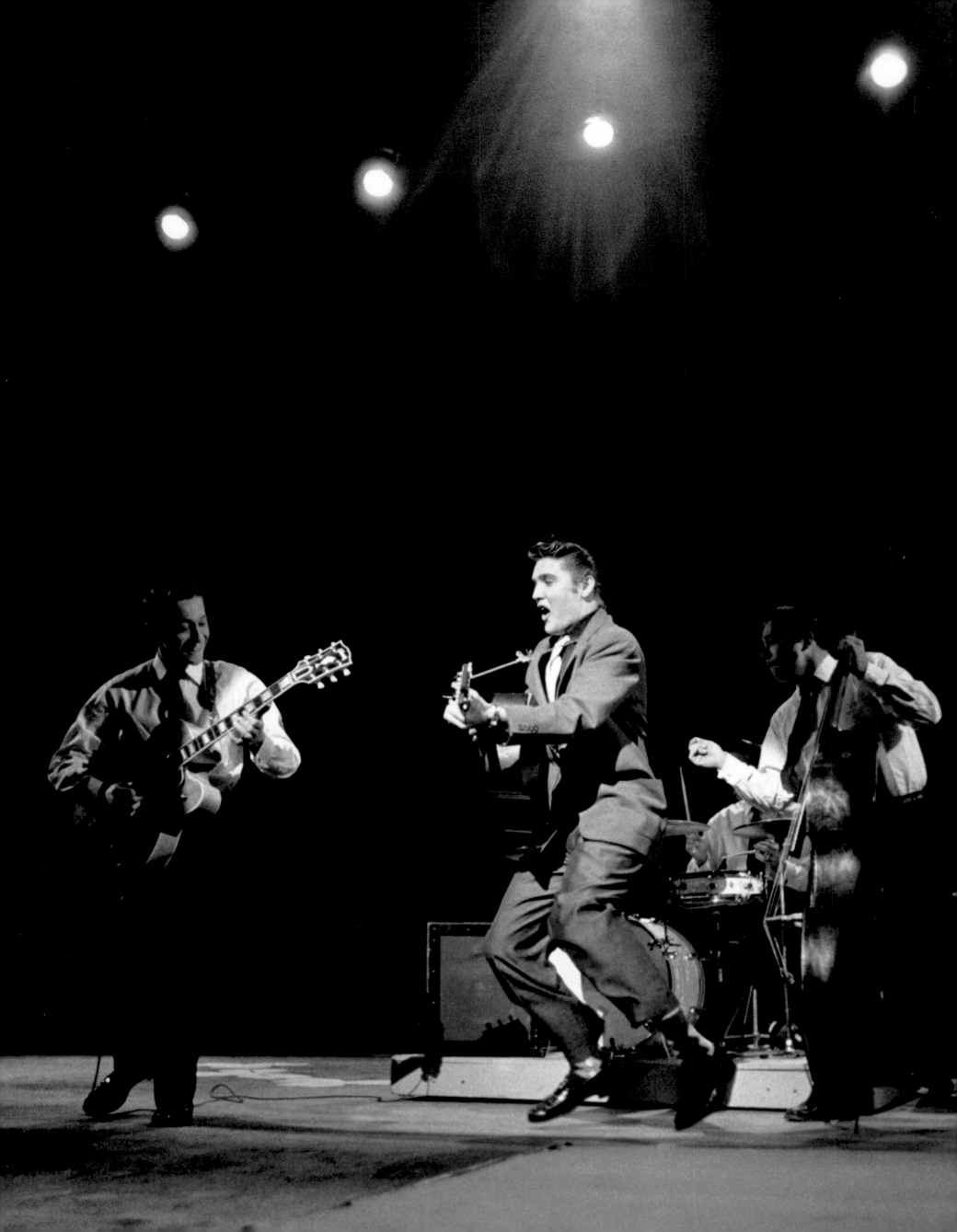

Even in the freezing temperature, there were five or six girls out there very happy to see him. They just wanted to talk to Elvis, and he liked being around women. He certainly was more comfortable with them than in that scene backstage.

After signing some autographs, he went back inside and was called to the telephone. His finger in his ear, Elvis answered with a "Yeah, hello," followed by a short conversation. As soon as he hung up the phone, someone from the television crew came up to him and said, "Mr. Presley, you're wanted for group rehearsal." Elvis rounded up the guys who were working with him at the time—Scotty Moore, Bill Black, and DJ Fontana. They rehearsed two songs, "Heartbreak Hotel" (which would become his first gold record) and "Blue Suede Shoes," from about noon until five P.M.

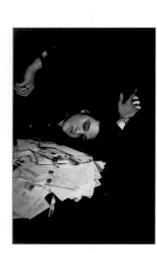

The show was broadcast live at eight P.M. so they could take a break until around seven P.M. when they had to be back at the studio. Back then, tape hadn't been invented yet so the show couldn't be recorded at one time and broadcast later. However, a live broadcast at eight P.M. in New York meant that the show aired at five P.M. in California, which was not a good hour to be getting audiences to watch East Coast programs like *Stage Show*. Until November 1956, when a company called Ampex invented two-inch tape that allowed studios to rebroadcast shows, the only way to preserve a live television event was through kinescopes. Set up in front of the television tube, these 16-millimeter cameras with large film loads shot directly off the screen at thirty frames per second. Of course, they looked very washed out and you could see the little lines of the television scanning process. But these films or "kines" (many of which later were lost or destroyed) and still photographs are the only record left of these important early years of television.

After the rehearsal, Elvis decided to return to his suite at the Warwick Hotel on 56th Street off of 6th Avenue. By now, I had become his shadow. It was March, so it was already pretty dark as we walked through Broadway. On the way, we stopped off at the Supreme Men's Shop because he wanted to buy a shirt, which at the time cost around three dollars, while tuxedos cost thirty. Holding up different shirts, he would ask me, "Al, what do you think of this one? Think it will it look good on me?"

He was asking me? "Elvis, I'm just not a fashion guy," I replied. "You can't ask me to make decisions about fashion."

Elvis wandered around the store a bit before stopping in front of a door with about ten glossies of local celebrities on it. I thought that one of these days, he would be on the Supreme Men's door like these guys. Then he walked out of the store without buying anything.

By the time we got back to the hotel, I was really tired. It had been a long day and Elvis was pretty tired as well. A box full of fan mail was left for him on the couch, so he flopped down and threw his feet up. Taking a fistful of letters, he began opening and seriously reading them. Some of them were six or seven pages long. Looking at him on the couch, I thought, "What do I photograph now?" This was a normal part of his life. This was his reality, not a fashion shoot where you tried to capture fantasy on film. Once Elvis finished reading, he tore each letter up into little shreds and put them on the coffee table.

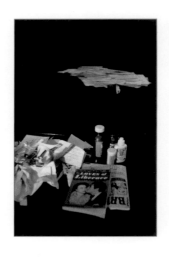

"Why are you doing that, Elvis?"

"I'm not going to carry them with me. I've read them and seen what's in them. It's nobody else's business."

"Well, that's not so dumb," I thought. "He's his own paper shredder." I started to look around. On the table were these scraps of fan mail, a couple of pill bottles (probably cold or sinus medication), a newspaper and a single paperback book, *The Loves of Liberace*. It had a picture of Liberace on the cover and had just come out that year. When I glanced back at Elvis, I saw that he was finally dozing off so I decided to do the same. I had to conserve my energy for that evening.

I fell asleep in a chair across the room for maybe half an hour when suddenly I noticed this buzzing sound, like a bee. The couch was empty and Elvis was nowhere in the room. Had he left already? What was going on? There were sounds of movement coming from the bathroom and then I realized that he was in there with a Norelco electric shaver buzzing away. "Well," I said to myself, "let me try some chutzpah here."

"Elvis, do you mind if I come in the bathroom and photograph you?"

I guess he felt that somebody should be photographing him because one of these days he was going to be famous. People often asked me later on, "What was so different about Elvis?" I didn't know it at the time, but I would soon understand that first of all, he made the girls cry and second, he permitted closeness.

I was using two black Nikon split-rangefinder 35-millimeter cameras that were extremely quiet. The tendency of a young photographer just starting out might be to back way off and shoot from halfway across the room with a 105- or 135-millimeter lens, but the walls in the background and the faces would be compressed. With a little more courage, you would move in with a 50- or 55-millimeter. Then, feeling really strong and full of yourself, you would take your 35- and 28-millimeter lenses, but you would have to get in close or the subject would look too small.

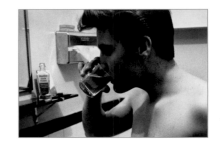

So I got right in the bathroom. A pair of slacks and a towel over his shoulder were all that Elvis was wearing. You could see the pimples on his back but he didn't seem to care. He used Vaseline Hair Tonic, not "bear grease," on his head. Elvis had a complicated hairstyle. He needed a small compact mirror in order to see the back of his head in the large mirror. I call those shots my prelude to the decisive moment images. Henri Cartier-Bresson was known for his decisive moments, that one instant when everything falls into place. But I wanted to be known for the moment before or after the decisive moment—Elvis loading his toothbrush full of toothpaste just before sticking it in his mouth, or taking one more look after he's combed his hair and is about to go out.

Elvis went through his whole routine in the bathroom with me just photographing him. He carried on as if nobody were there. I kept thinking, "Is this what normal subjects do, or is he unusual?" I didn't have enough experience to compare him to other people, but I knew that this was certainly giving me good photographs. I was right in there, not with a telephoto lens, but with a 35-millimeter one. Up close, not only could I fill up the frame with my subject and get everything from foreground to background pretty sharp, but I was also making myself vulnerable. I have always been aware of the fact that the subject reacts to the photographer and vice versa. In close quarters, if that person likes you, he'll like you more, and if that person hates you, he'll hate you more. Fortunately, things got off on the right foot in my first few hours with Elvis.

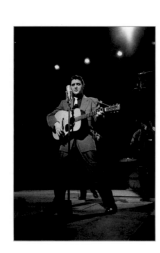

Once this ablution of sorts was complete, we left the Warwick and wound up back at the theater, where *Stage Show* was about to go on. Along with the musicians, dancers, juggling acts, and all kinds of other entertainment featured in this variety show, Elvis got six minutes to perform two songs. This was a nationally televised program, and photographing him on stage was a different matter compared to the time I had spent with him so far. After all, the still photographer was a very small fly on the back of a large elephant.

Since Studio 50 was a theater converted for television, a platform was built out from the stage for the technicians and cameras to roll back and shoot the performers. That area took up about a third of the audience space, leaving enough room for maybe a couple hundred people, so there wasn't as much audience participation. It also meant that I had to use a longer lens, or a wide-angle one, in order to shoot the scene. During the actual show, I had to get off the stage and shoot from down in the pit, right at stage level. The best I could do was just to get as close to the edge of the stage as possible. Fortunately, I was using a Nikon with a much quieter shutter than something like a single-lens reflex that would go "clunk" every time you took a picture. They didn't mind my shooting during the performance as long as I waited for the loud part of the music. There was so much screaming anyway, you couldn't even hear the song.

When Elvis finished "Heartbreak Hotel" and "Blue Suede Shoes," my job was to stick with him. As a photographer, I knew that I had to anticipate a situation visually and how it would unfold before my subject entered it. Otherwise, I would always be too late. If I were right, I would get good

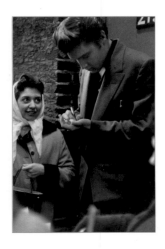

pictures. If I were wrong, I'd end up with nothing. There's a certain instinct that you build up after a while. At the end of his performance, I left the studio quickly to get out the stage door before him. A mass of people had gathered already. Because I was down at crowd level, I had to figure out how I was going to see Elvis's face. A couple of trashcans did the job. I turned them upside down and stood on them, which gave me a nice view to shoot down at the scene. For me, photography was like sketching; instead of pencil and paper, I had my camera and available light. This alley, however, was pitch black. I had to pull out my Braun strobe unit or I wouldn't have seen anything.

When he went through the stage door again and out into the alleyway, there must have been over a hundred girls and a few guys, all wanting his autograph and pressing him up against the door. Someone came out to throw a coat over Elvis's shoulders so that he wouldn't catch pneumonia. Seeing the light flashing, a girl ran up to me yelling, "Are you anybody?" I said, "Yeah, I'm somebody. I'm the photographer photographing Elvis." In the midst of all this madness, she wasn't sure if it was worth getting my autograph. Eventually, Elvis went back inside the studio and waited for the crowd to dissipate before returning to the hotel. I went home to get some much-needed sleep.

That first day I shot about twenty rolls. The next evening I went into the studio to process the film. Dave Linton's Studio was busy during the day with Dave and his wife setting up, four or five other photographers milling about, and messengers coming and going. There was too much confusion, so I usually waited until seven or eight in the evening when everyone was gone except maybe my friend Roland Mitchell, who often helped me with my processing. At that hour, I could have the whole place to myself. Then we would spread out and use the developing and print rooms in peace. I processed the twenty rolls in three shifts, about six rolls at a time, and hung them in a drying cabinet with a 50-watt light bulb for heat. The cabinet also kept dust from getting on the negatives. Once they were dry, I cut them up in strips of six frames each and printed contact sheets. One set I kept and the other I sent to Ann by messenger. Meanwhile, I went ahead and printed some good shots I thought she would want. Of course, I knew she wasn't going to use the images that interested me, like the ones of Elvis lying asleep on his fan mail, walking down Broadway at night, or trying to buy a new shirt. Those weren't publicity shots in those days. I knew Ann would prefer ones of him at the microphone or with the Jordanaires or talking to Steve Sholes (p.16), RCA's A&R man and head of the Pop Records Division. Along with my bill, I sent her a selection of about six such prints by another messenger and probably got paid a month later.

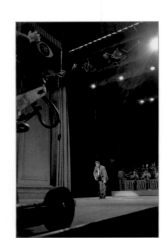

It was good to have so many shots of Elvis, though. I remember Roland Mitchell didn't think he was such a big deal. At this point, Elvis didn't have a gold record and was just another singer. He was also a rebel who caused a lot of confusion and the older folks didn't like that. On the other hand, fan magazines always had Hollywood personalities on the cover and loved a rebel, especially since the biggest audience for these magazines consisted of teenage girls. I began getting some phone calls for Elvis photographs, which was fine with me because in those days, photo magazines were buying prints for $5 apiece. Two main personalities—James Dean and Elizabeth Taylor—seemed to be on the cover practically every week. Then James Dean and his Porsche were demolished on a road in California. All of a sudden, the magazines had lost their rebel.

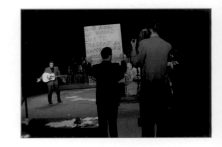

Along came Elvis, a new James Dean. Although he was in the record business, his movie debut made him a Hollywood figure by the end of the year. I sensed from my first day with Elvis that this guy could cause a big fuss. He was a maverick who certainly got the attention of the young girls. When the William Morris agents who booked *Stage Show* (p. 28) were huddled in the corner telling him, "Elvis, you gotta stay cool. Don't move around too much," he would dutifully listen to every bit of advice or criticism they had. They tried to be gentle yet firm. He wouldn't object because he knew he needed people and didn't want to offend anyone. But once Elvis got on stage, he always did it his way. He *really* did it his way.

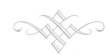

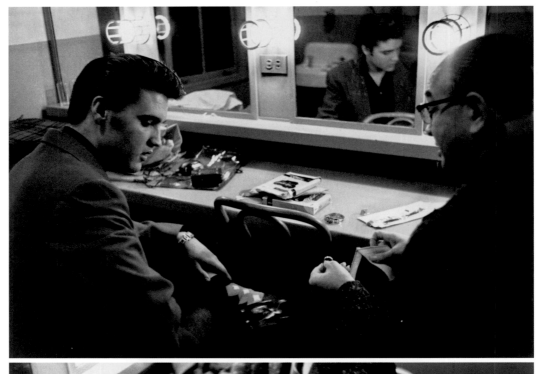

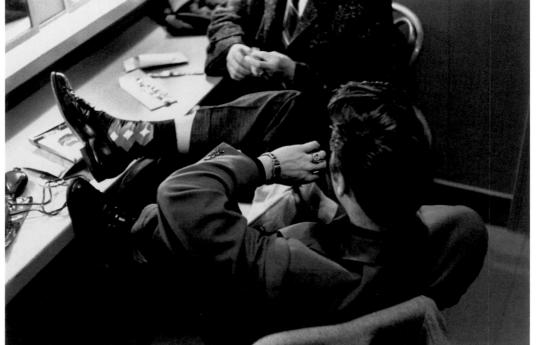

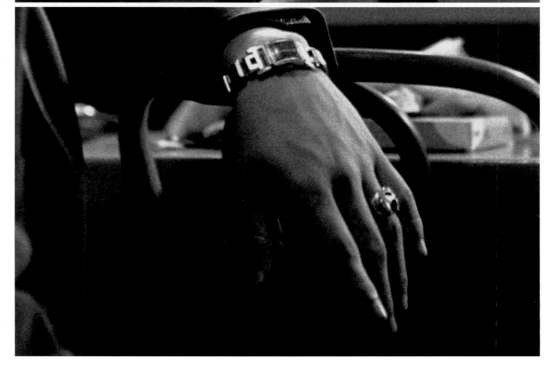

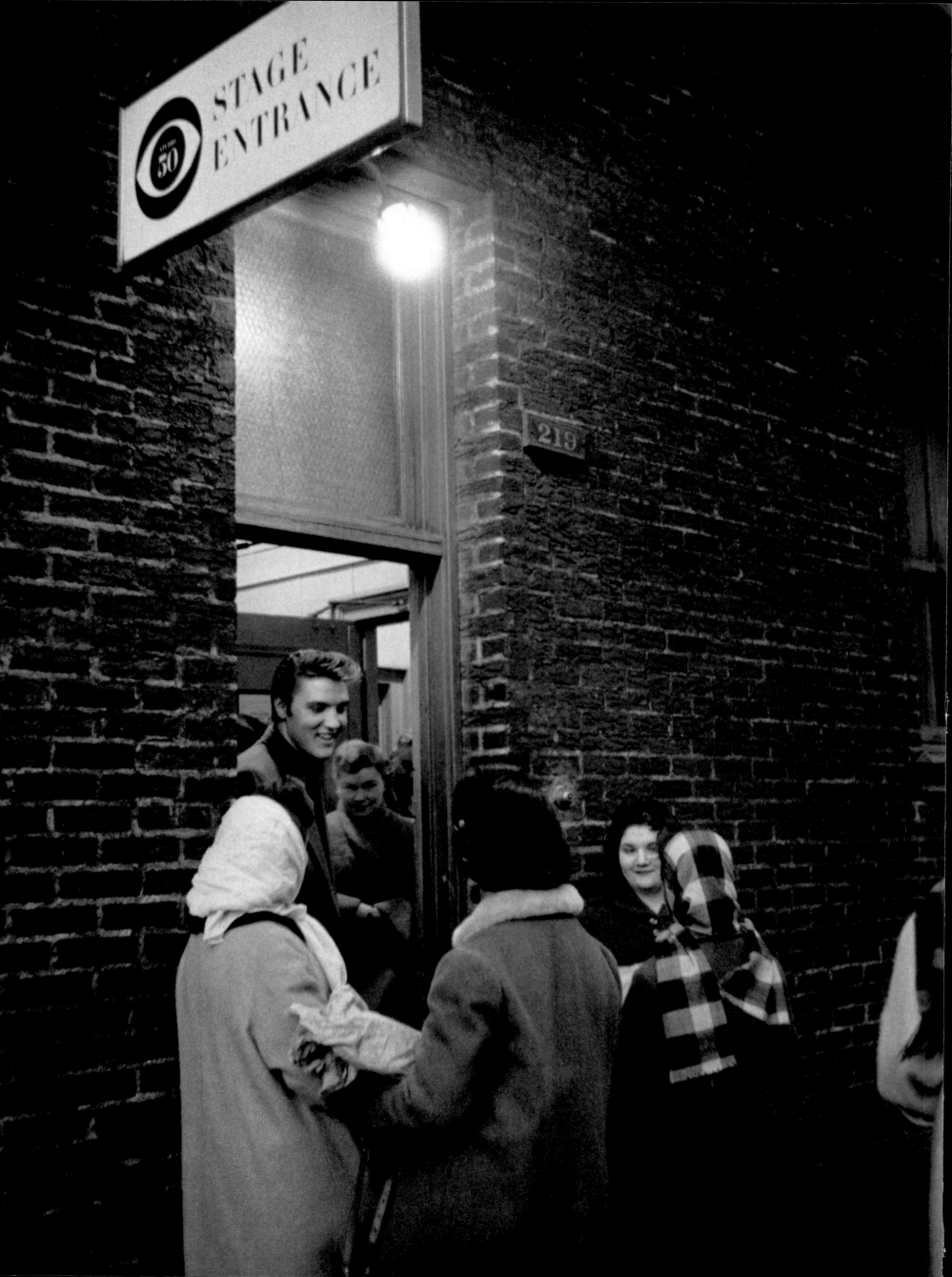

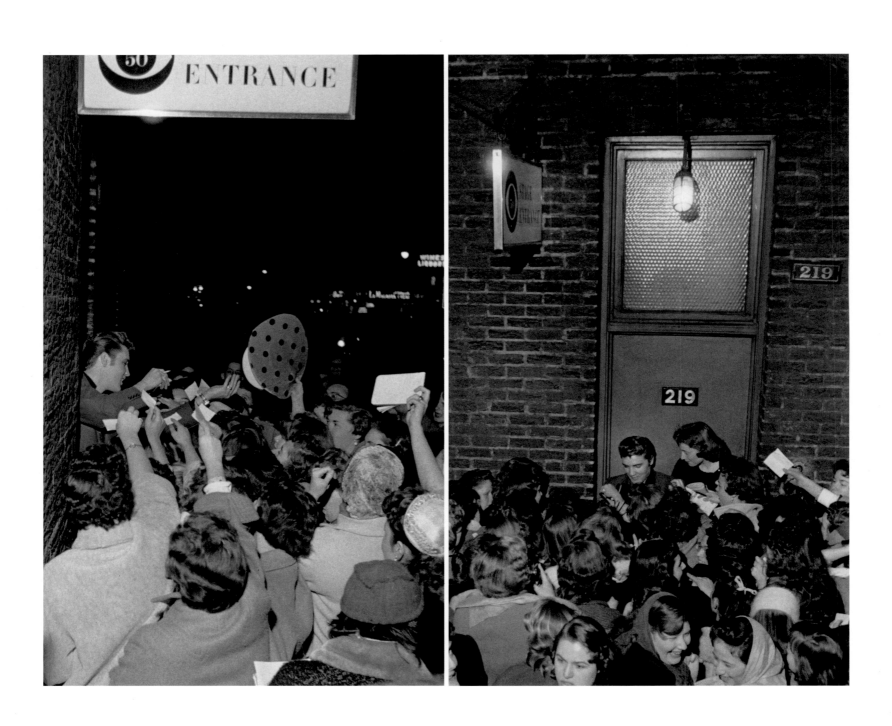

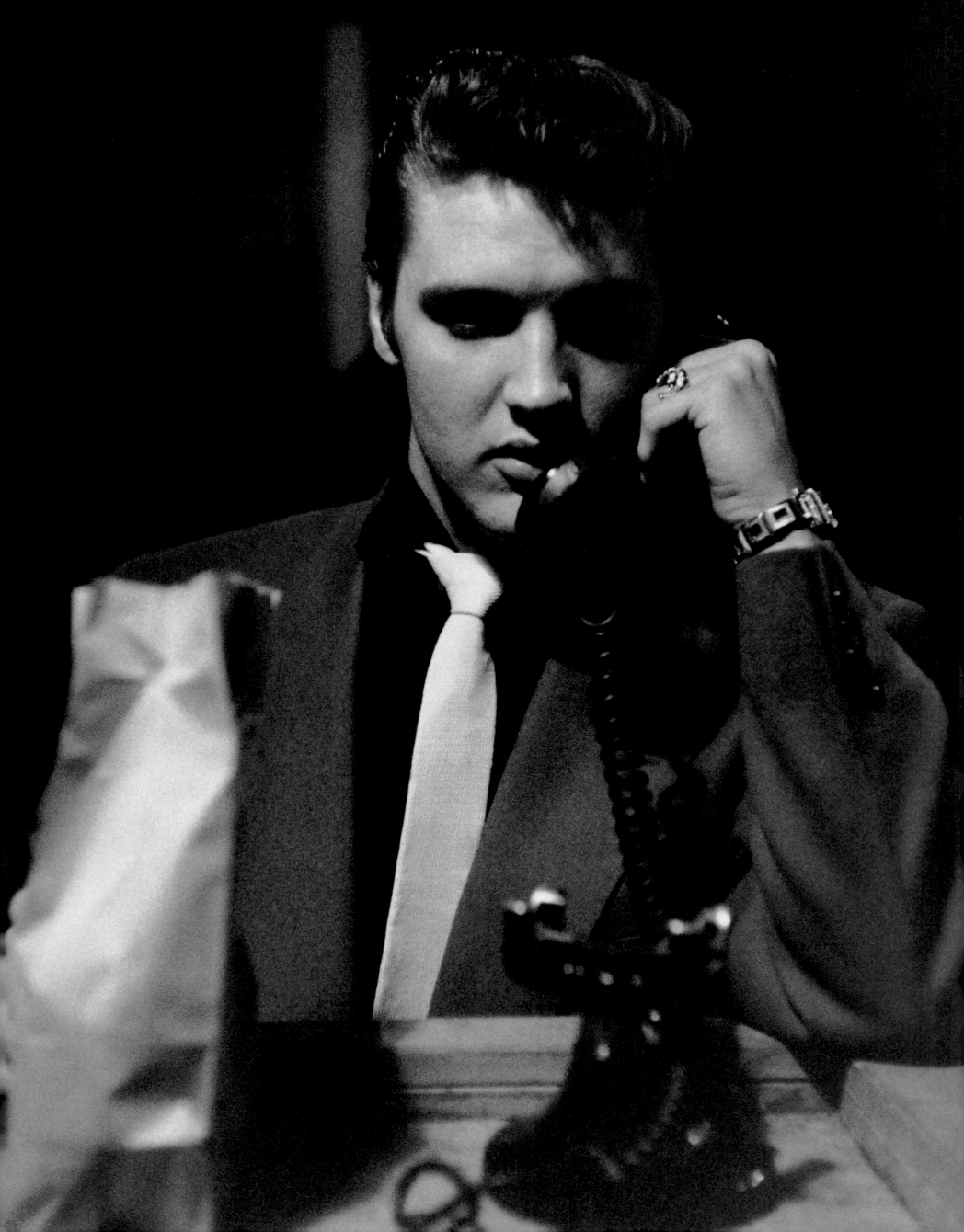

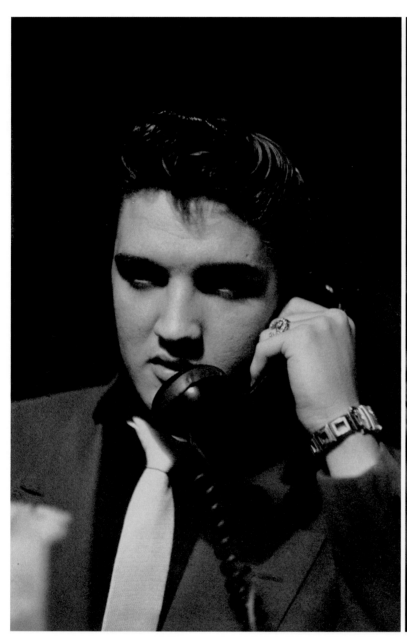
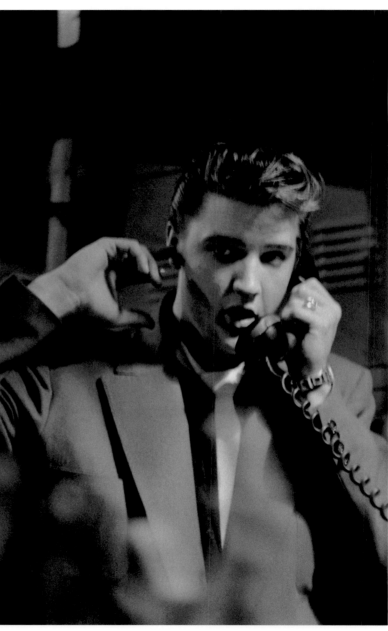

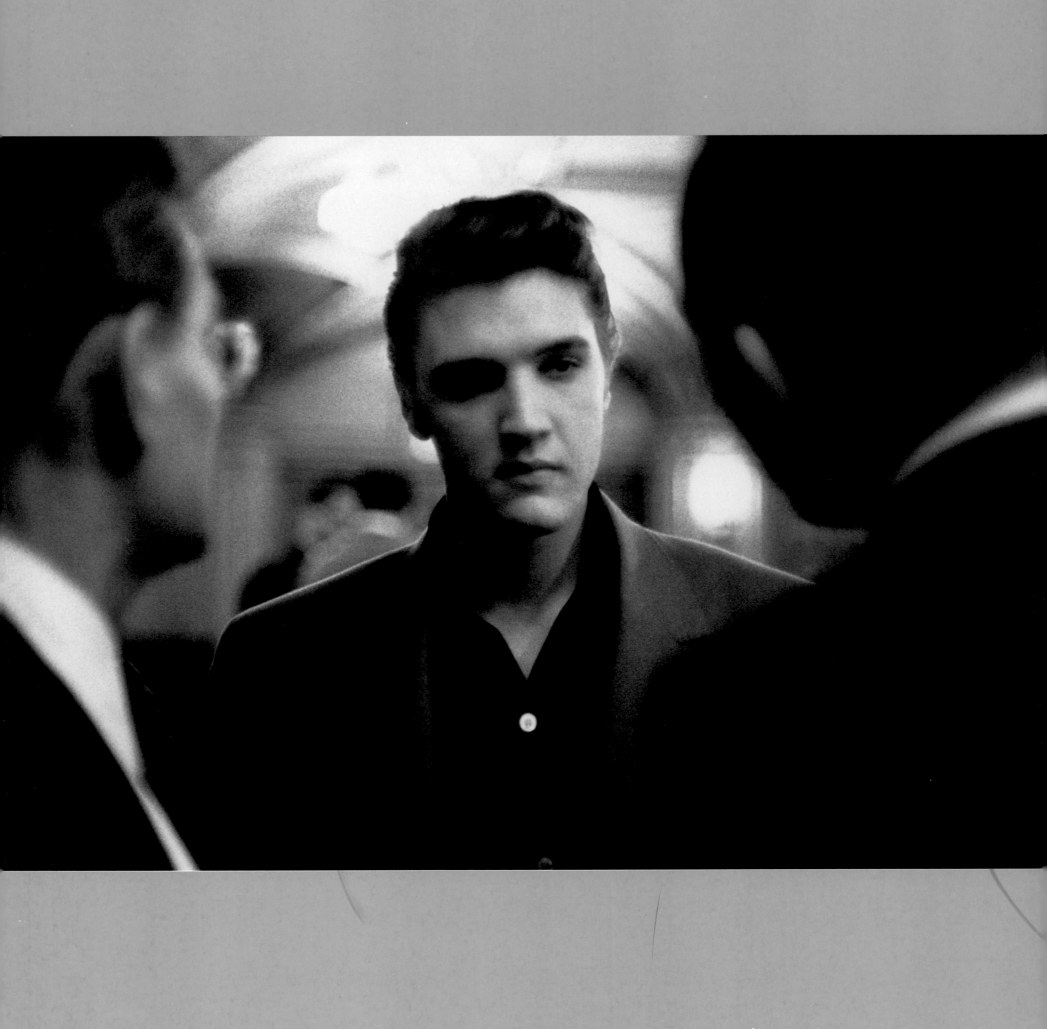

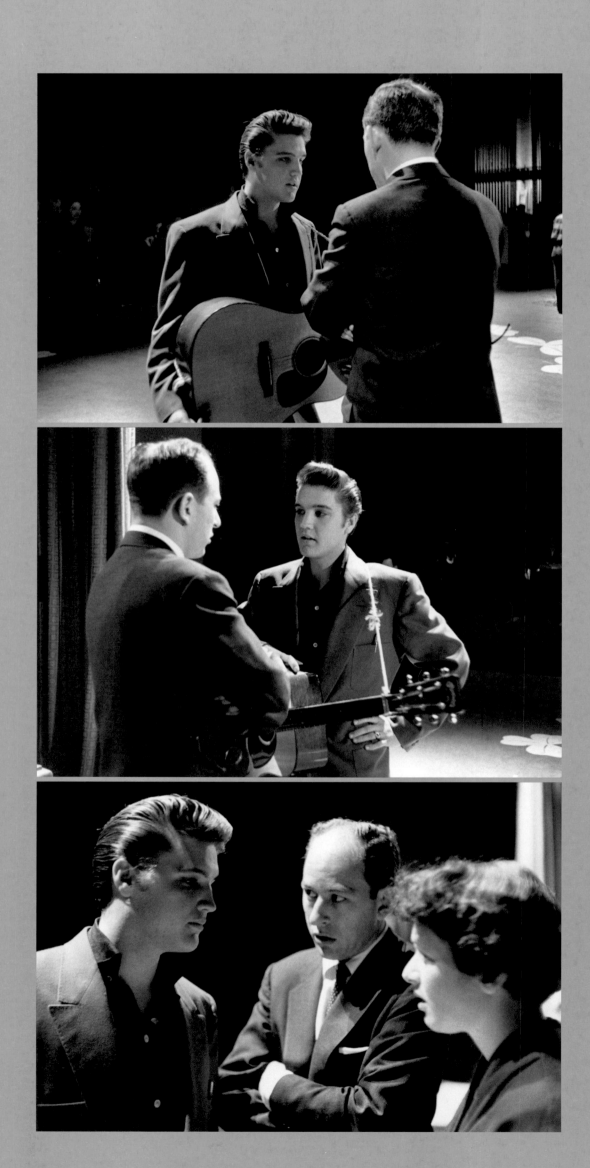

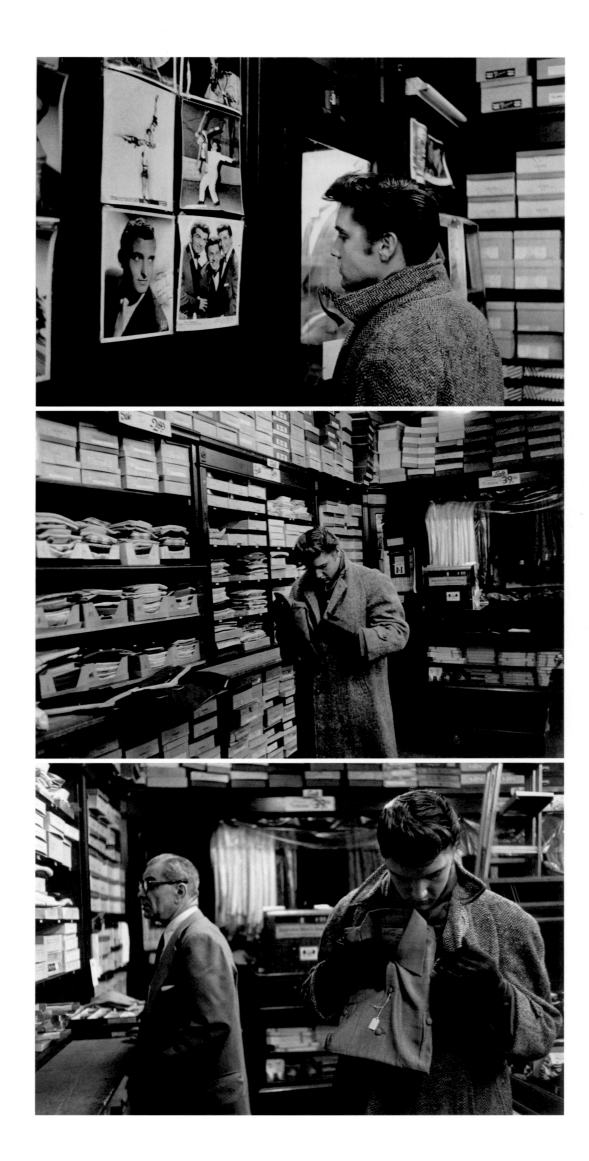

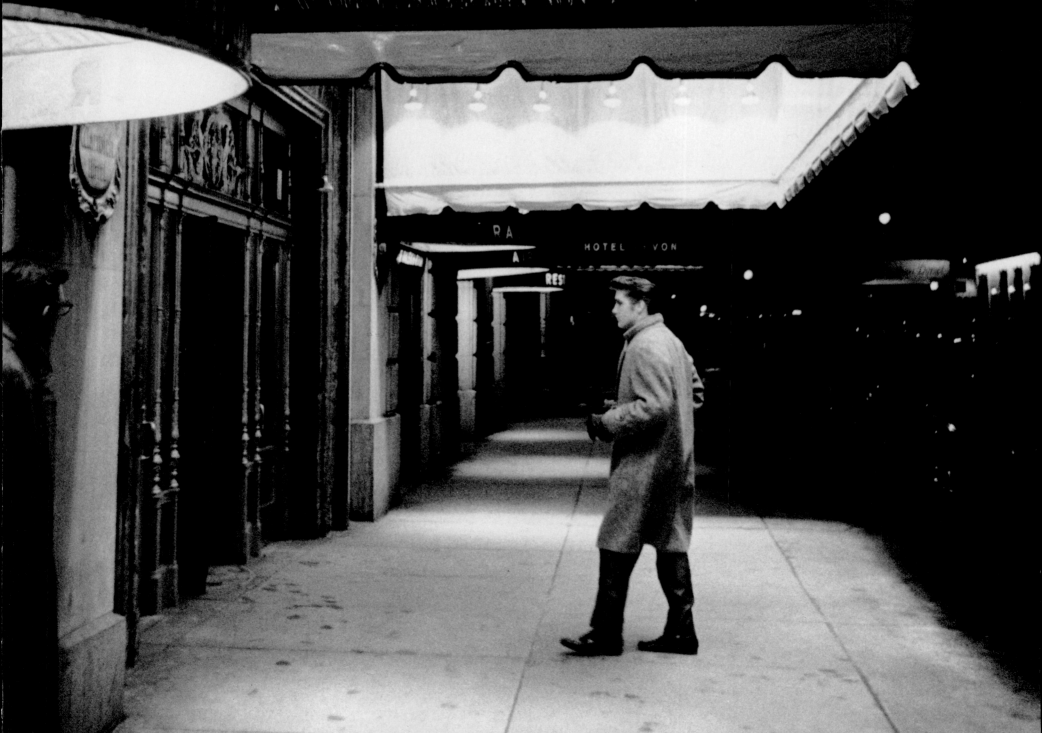

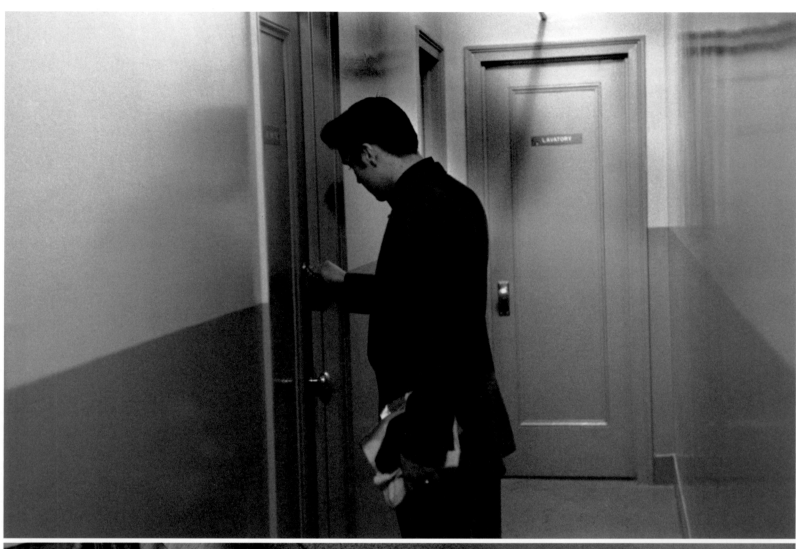

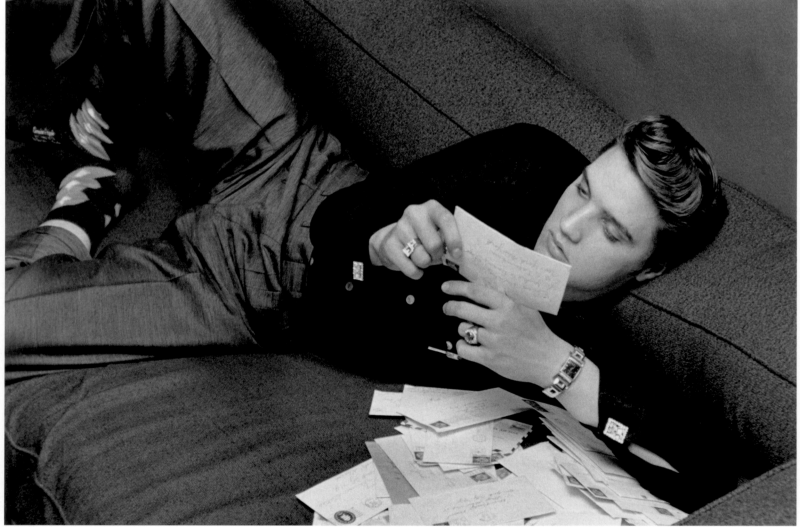

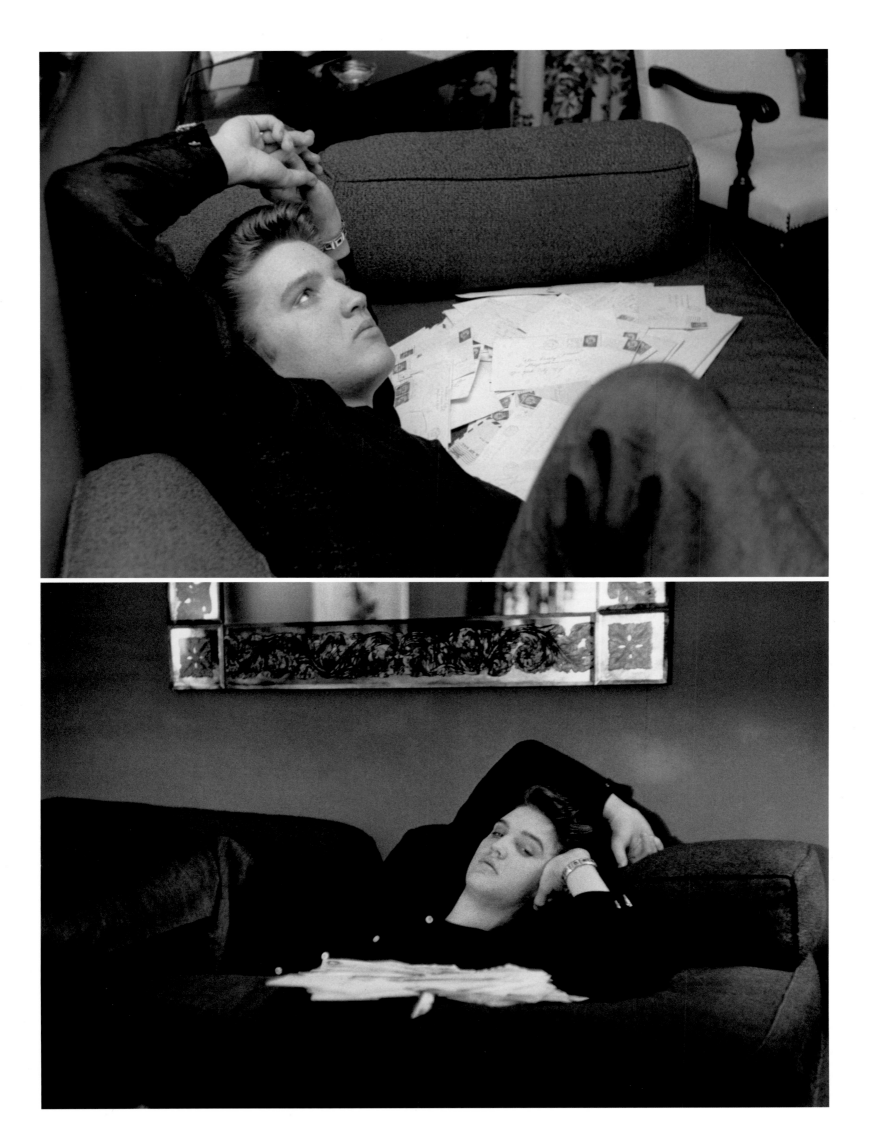

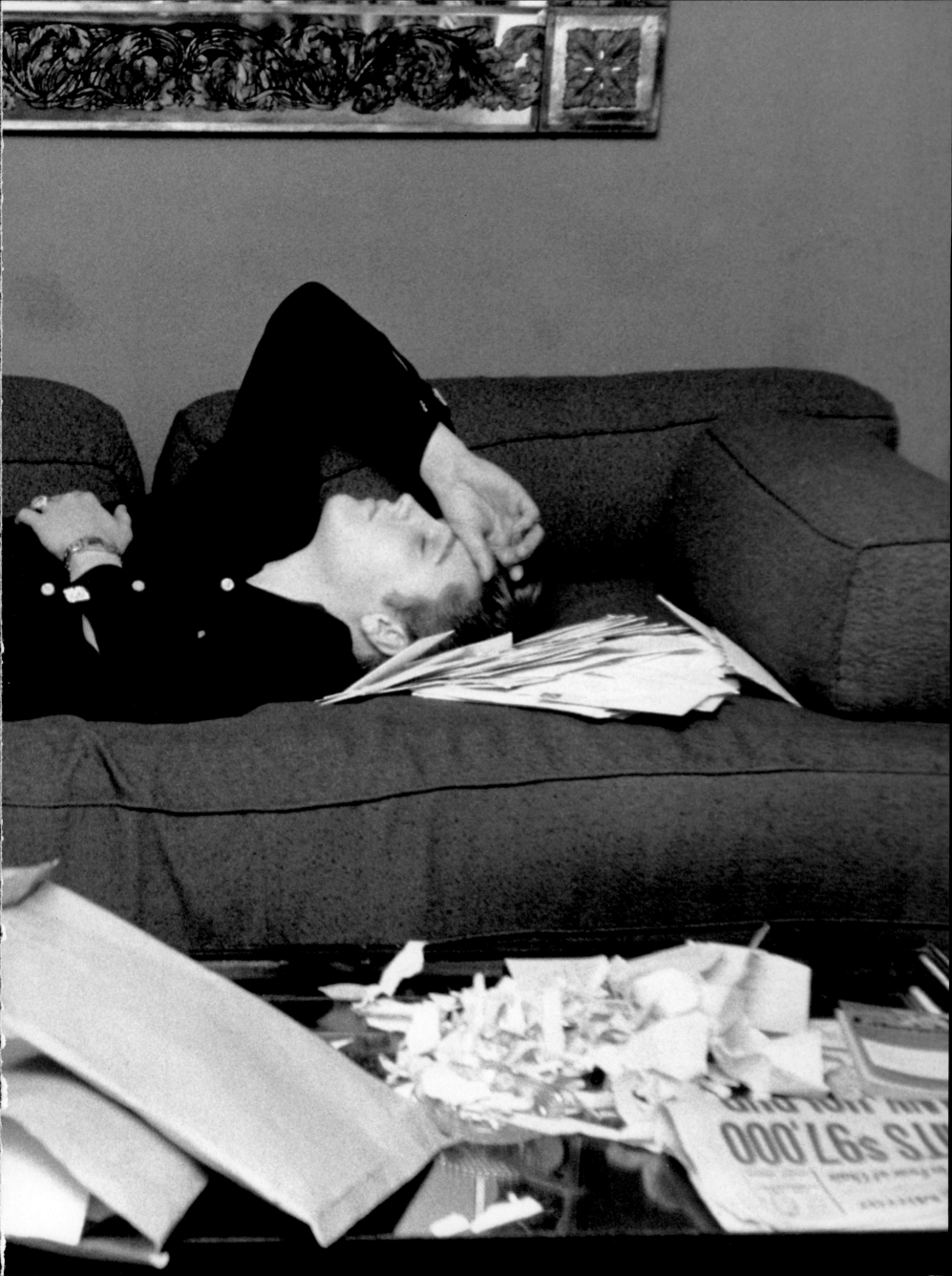

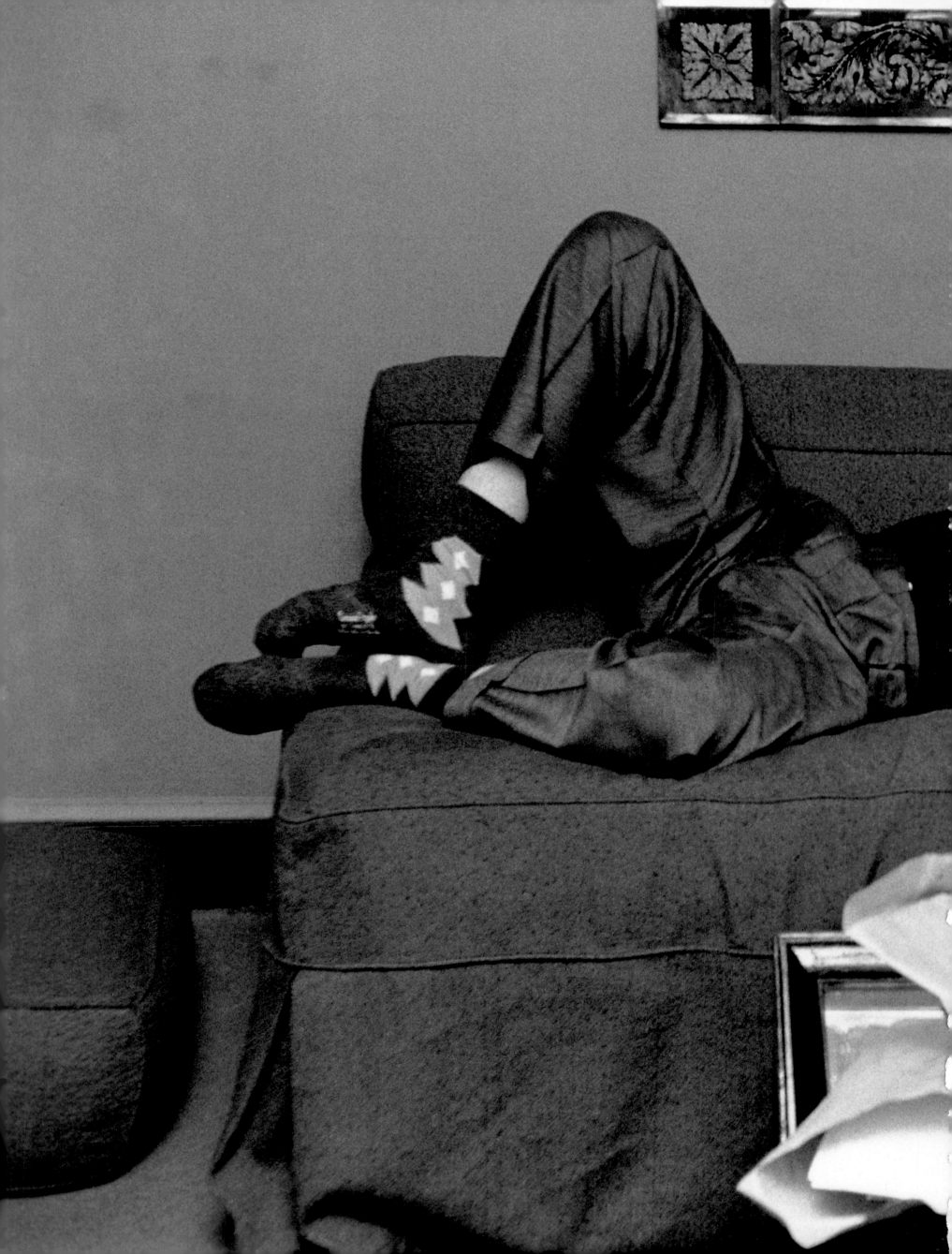

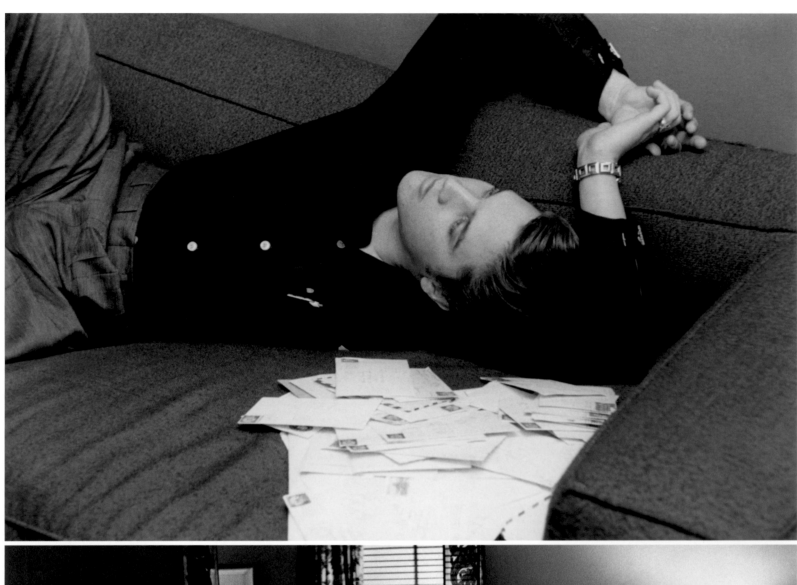

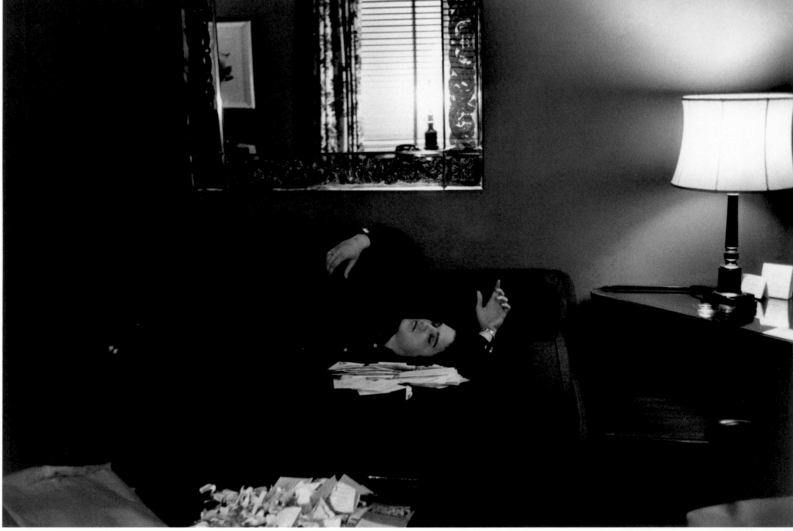

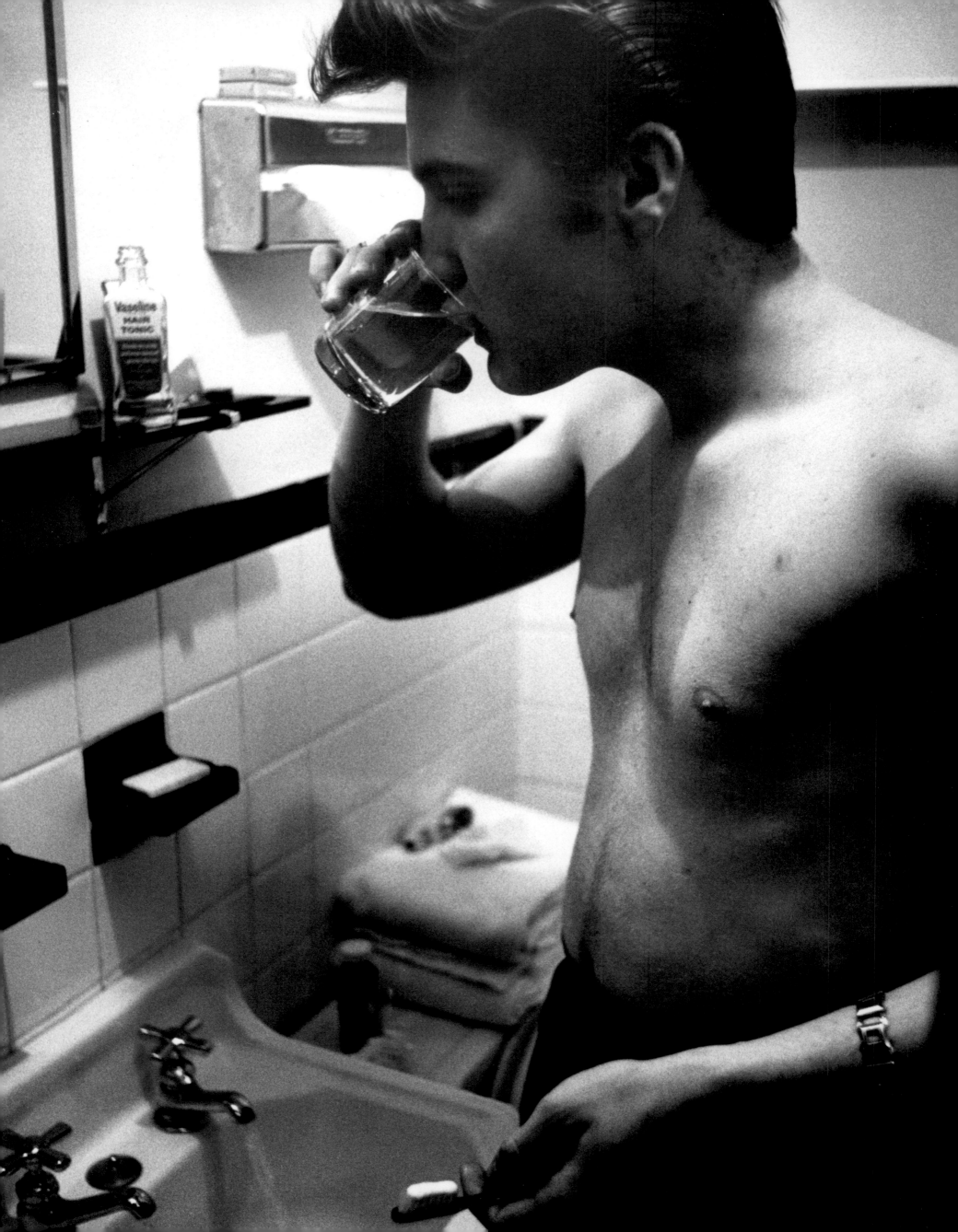

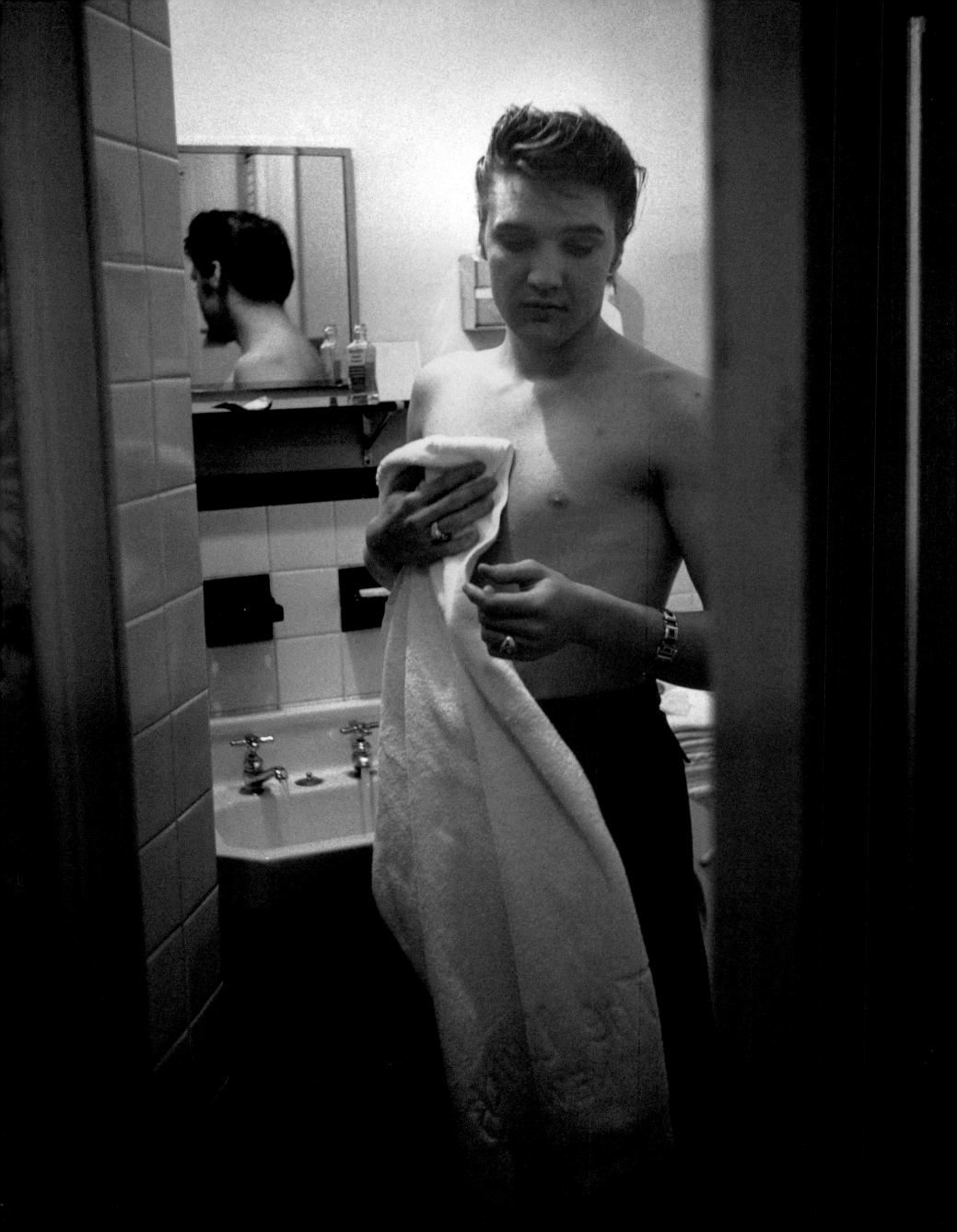

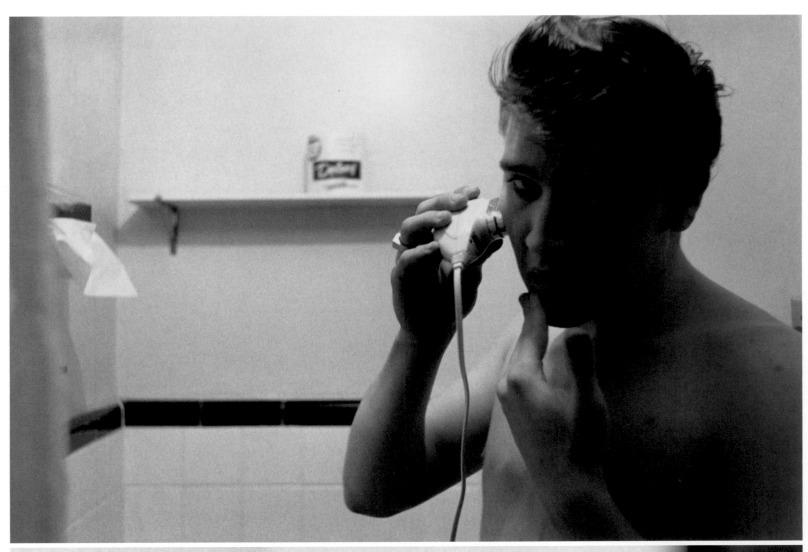

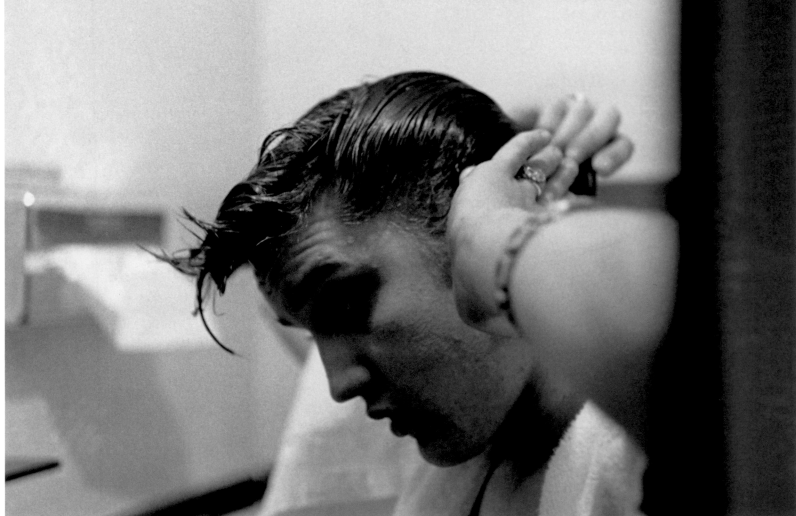

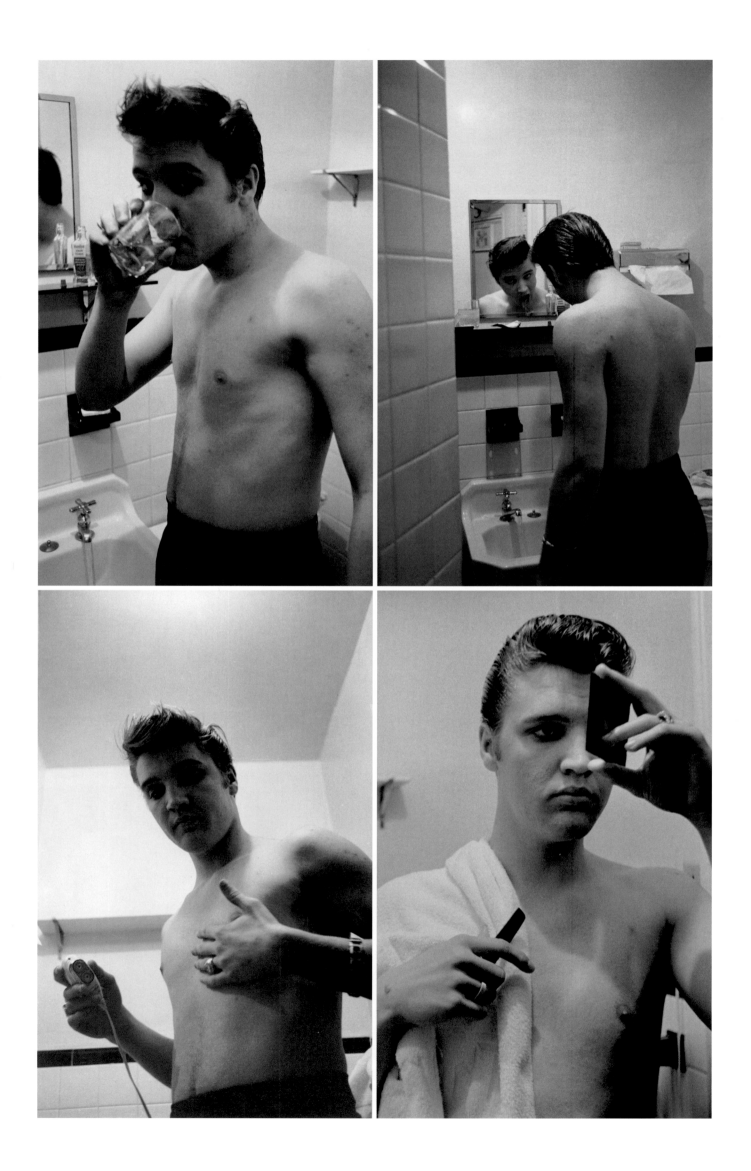

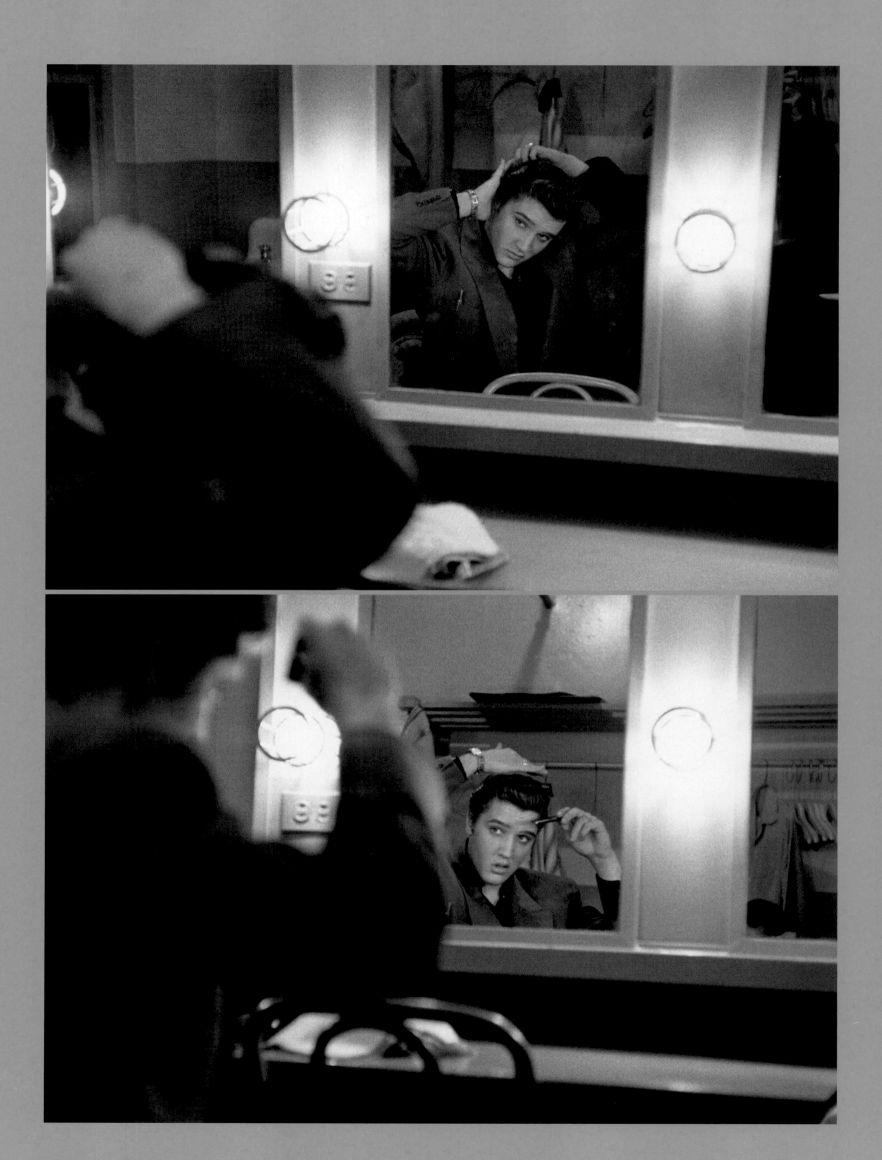

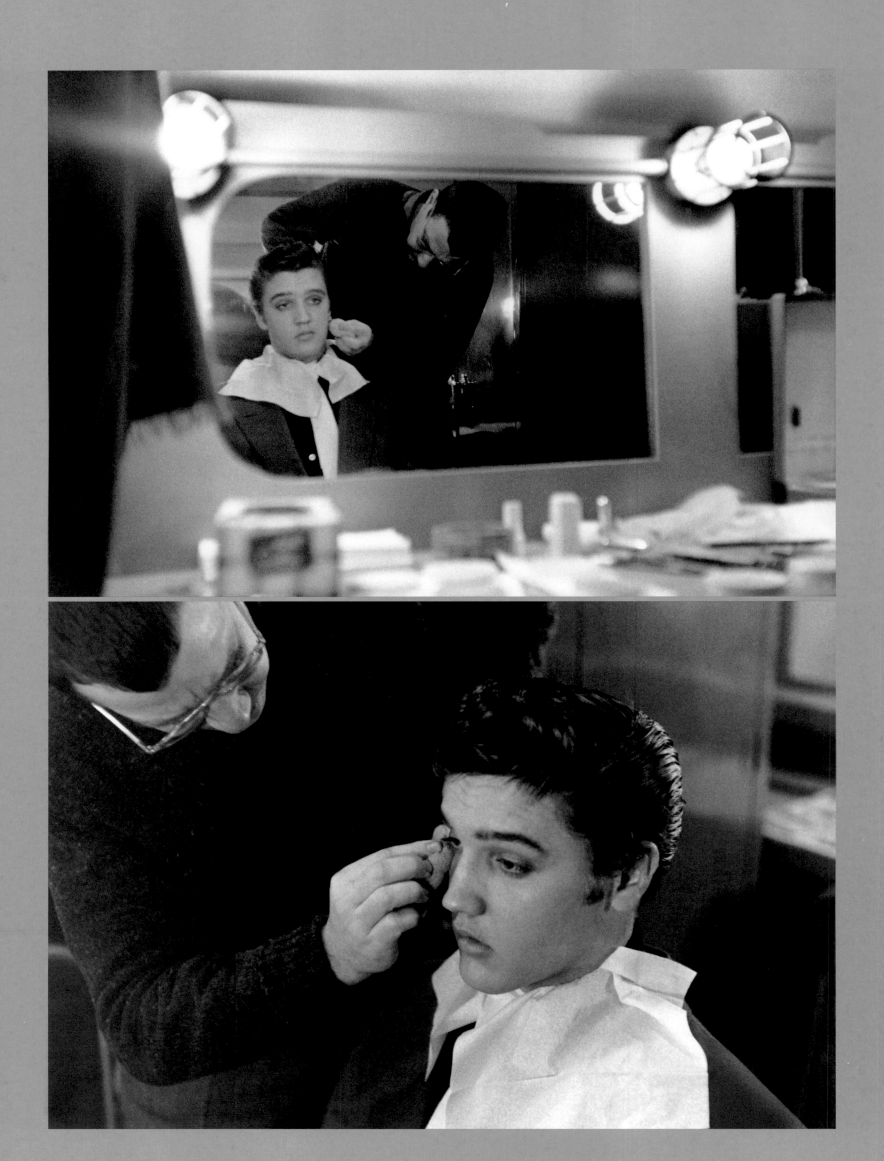

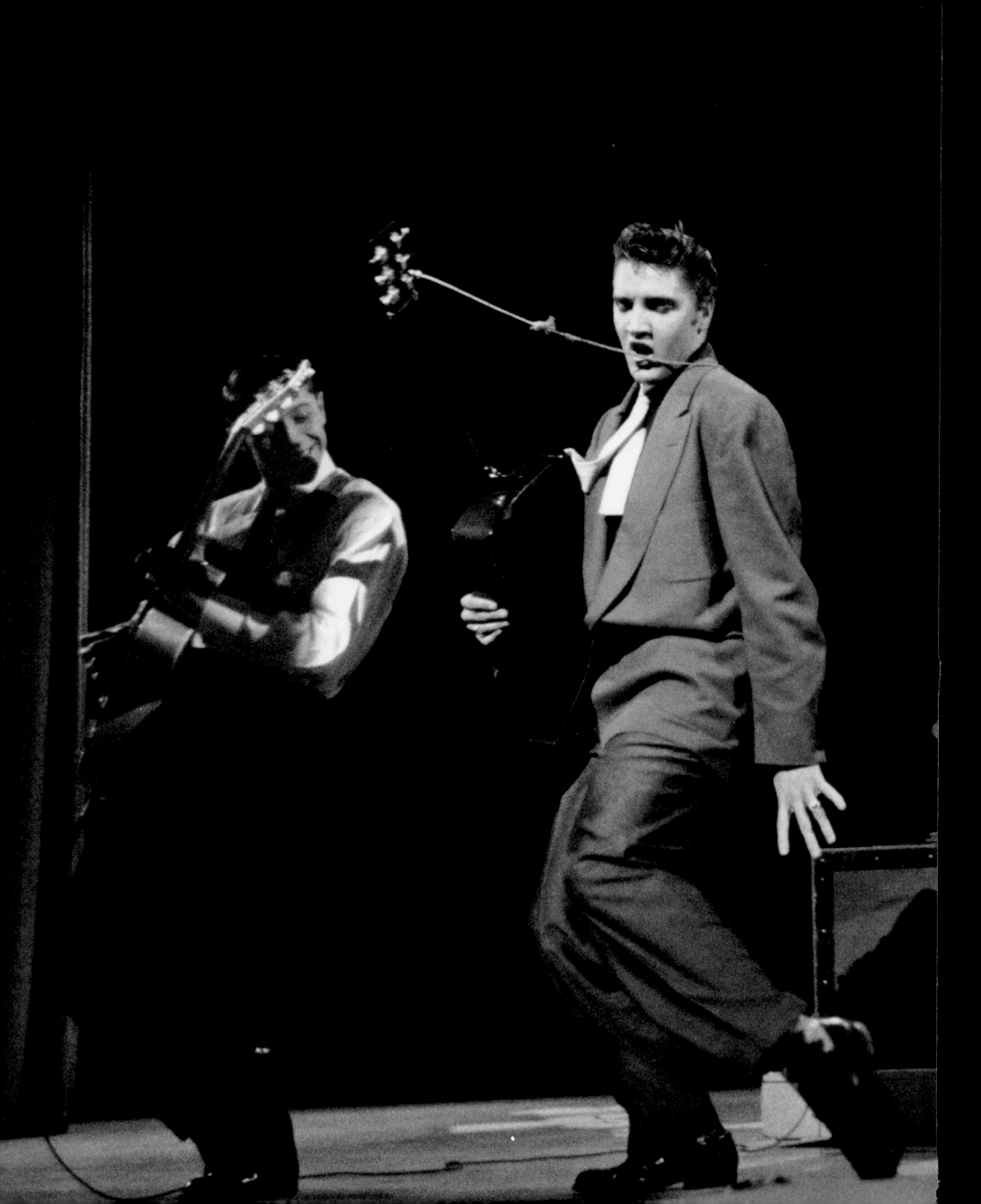

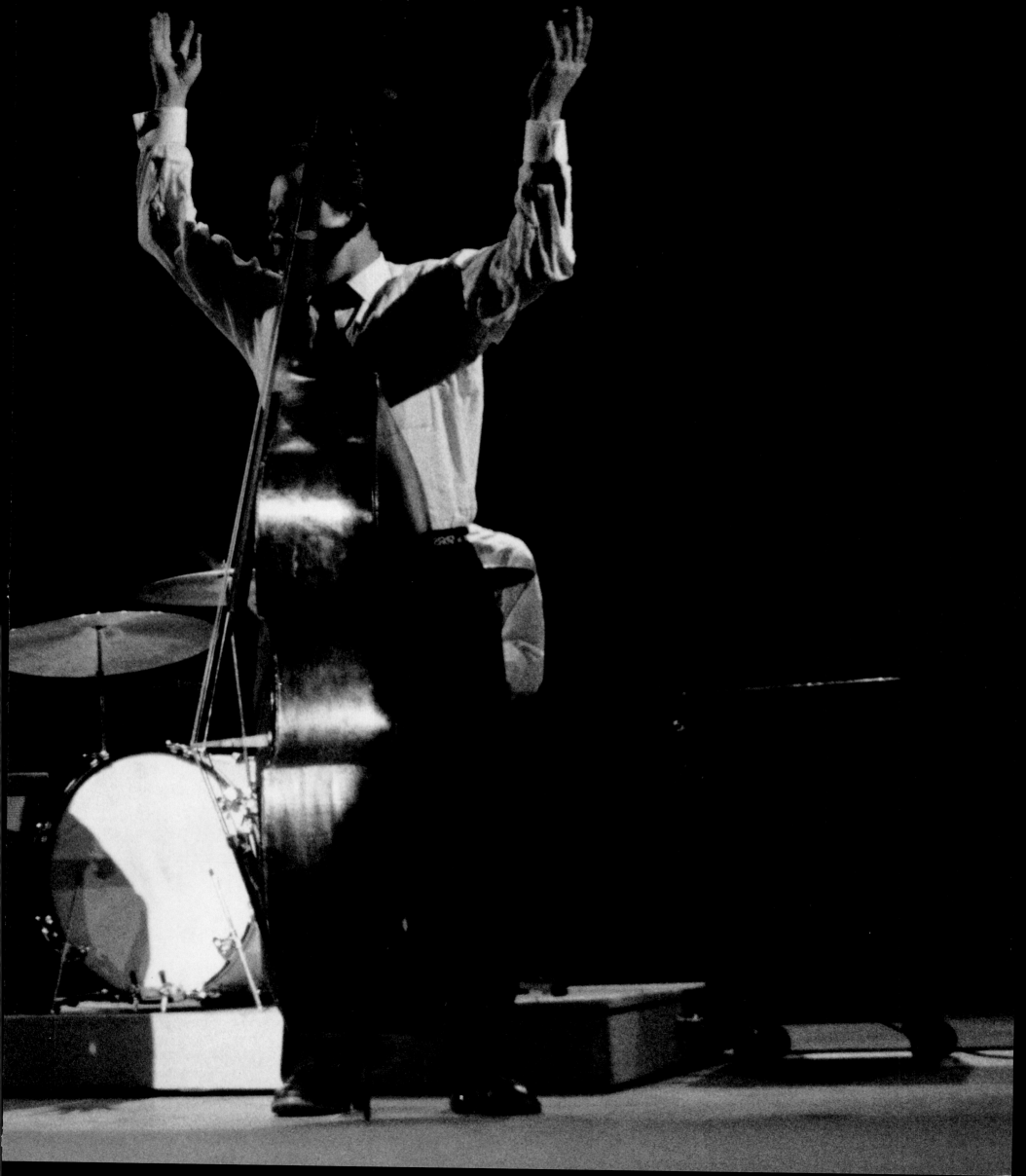

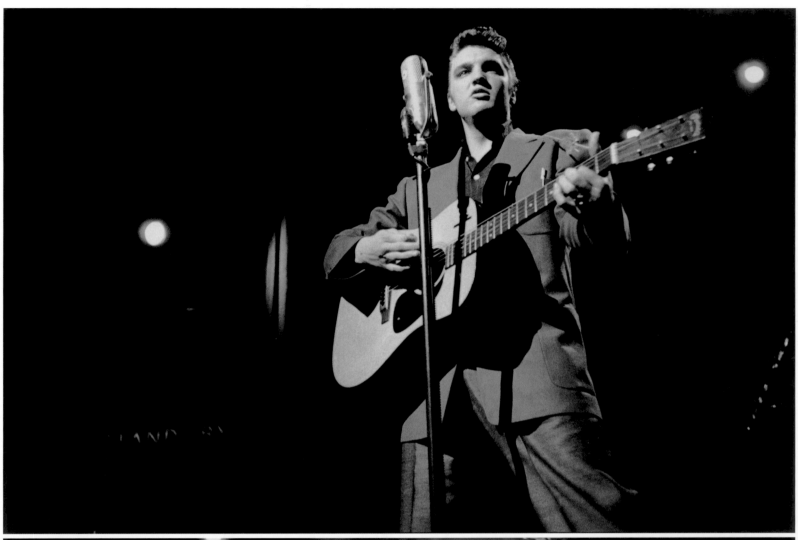
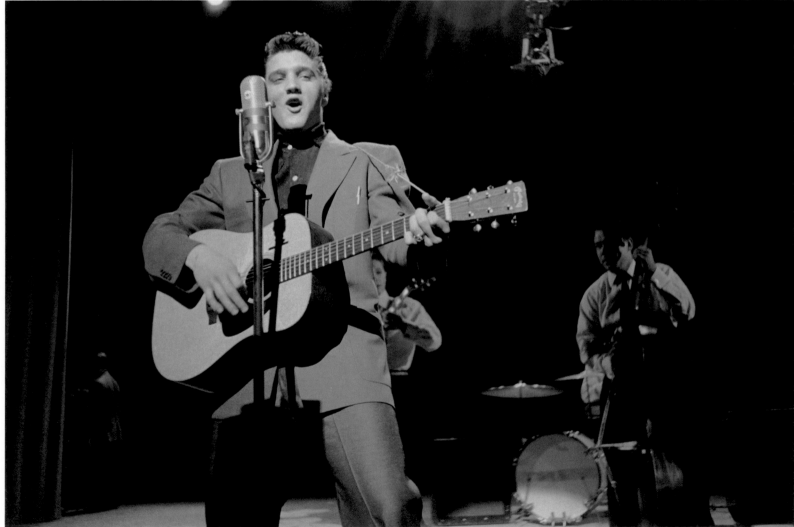

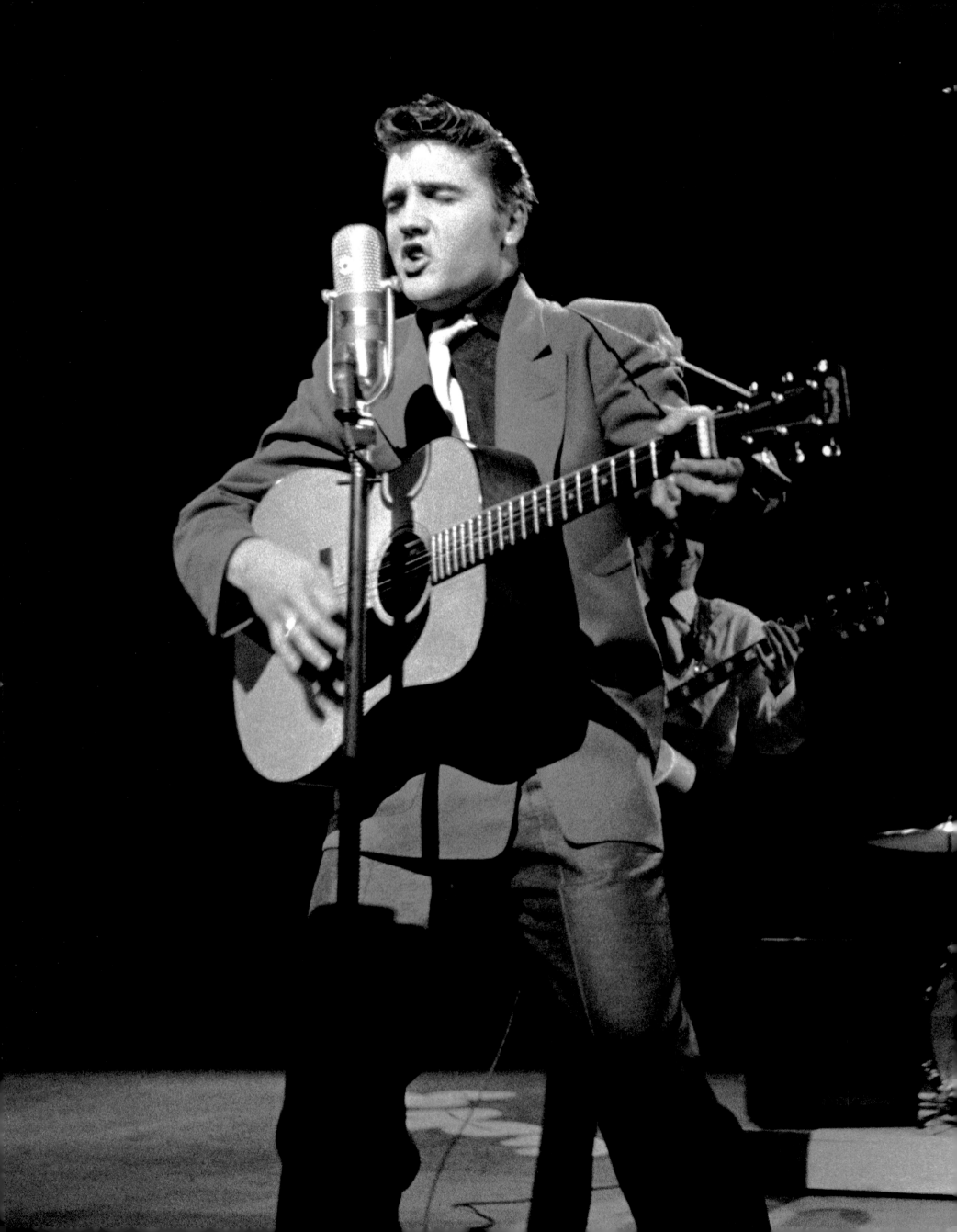

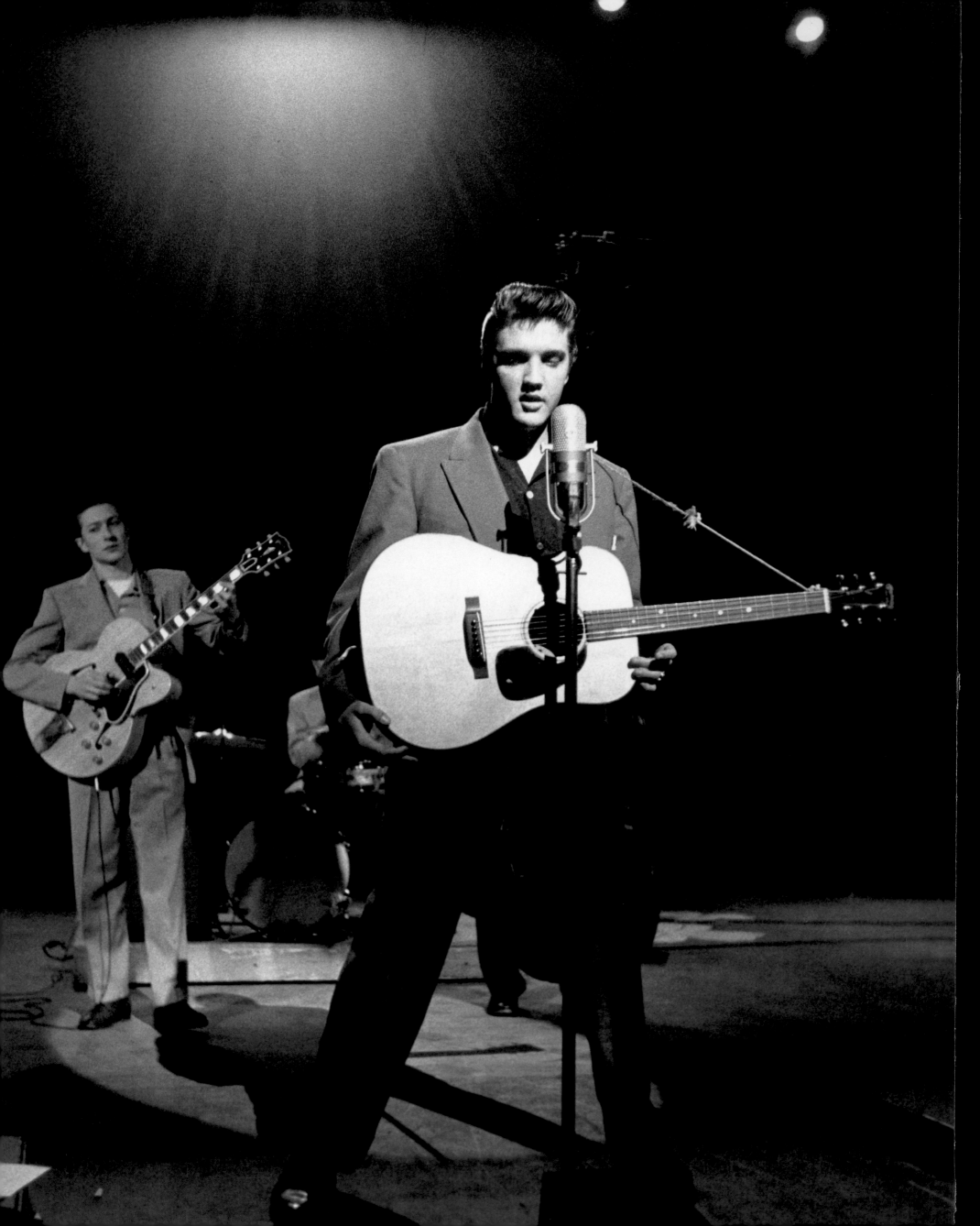

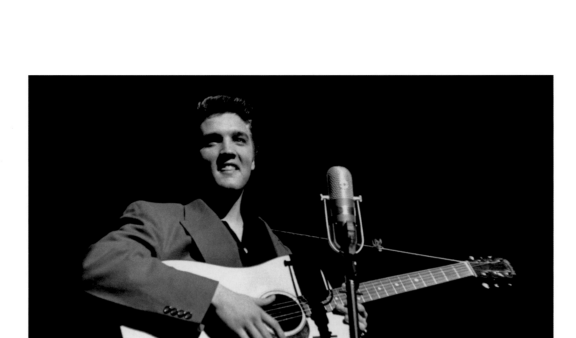

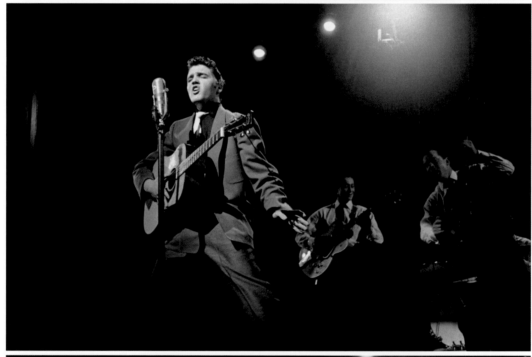

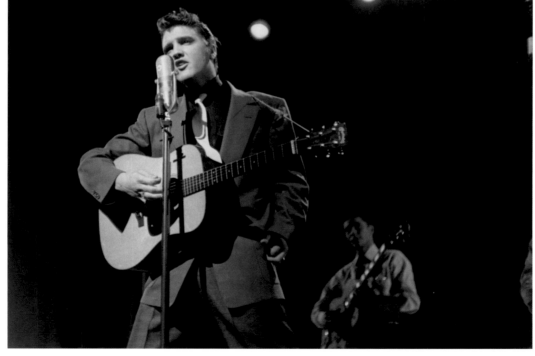

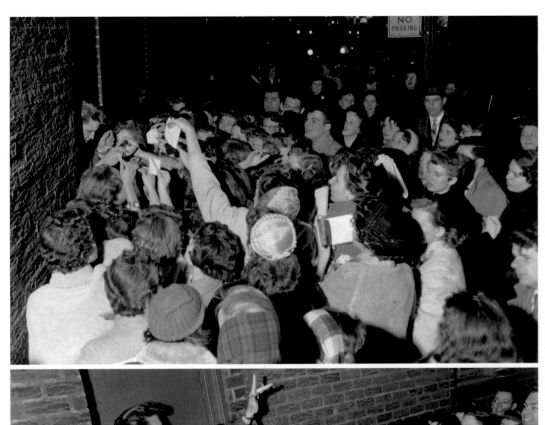

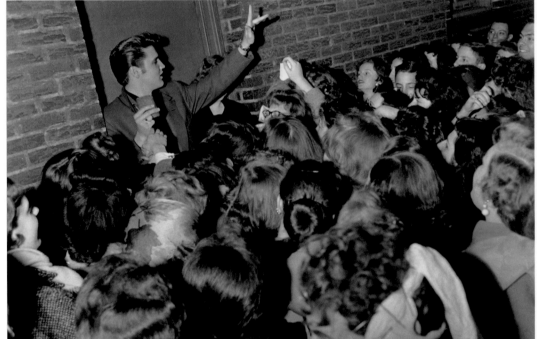

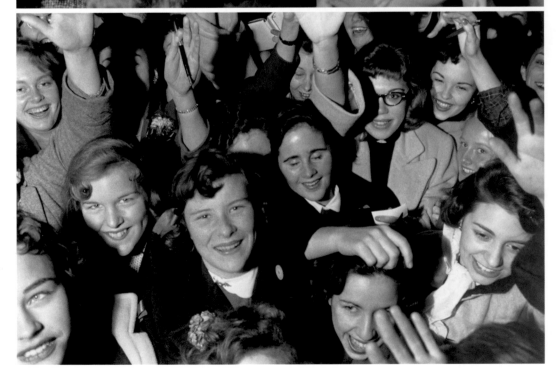

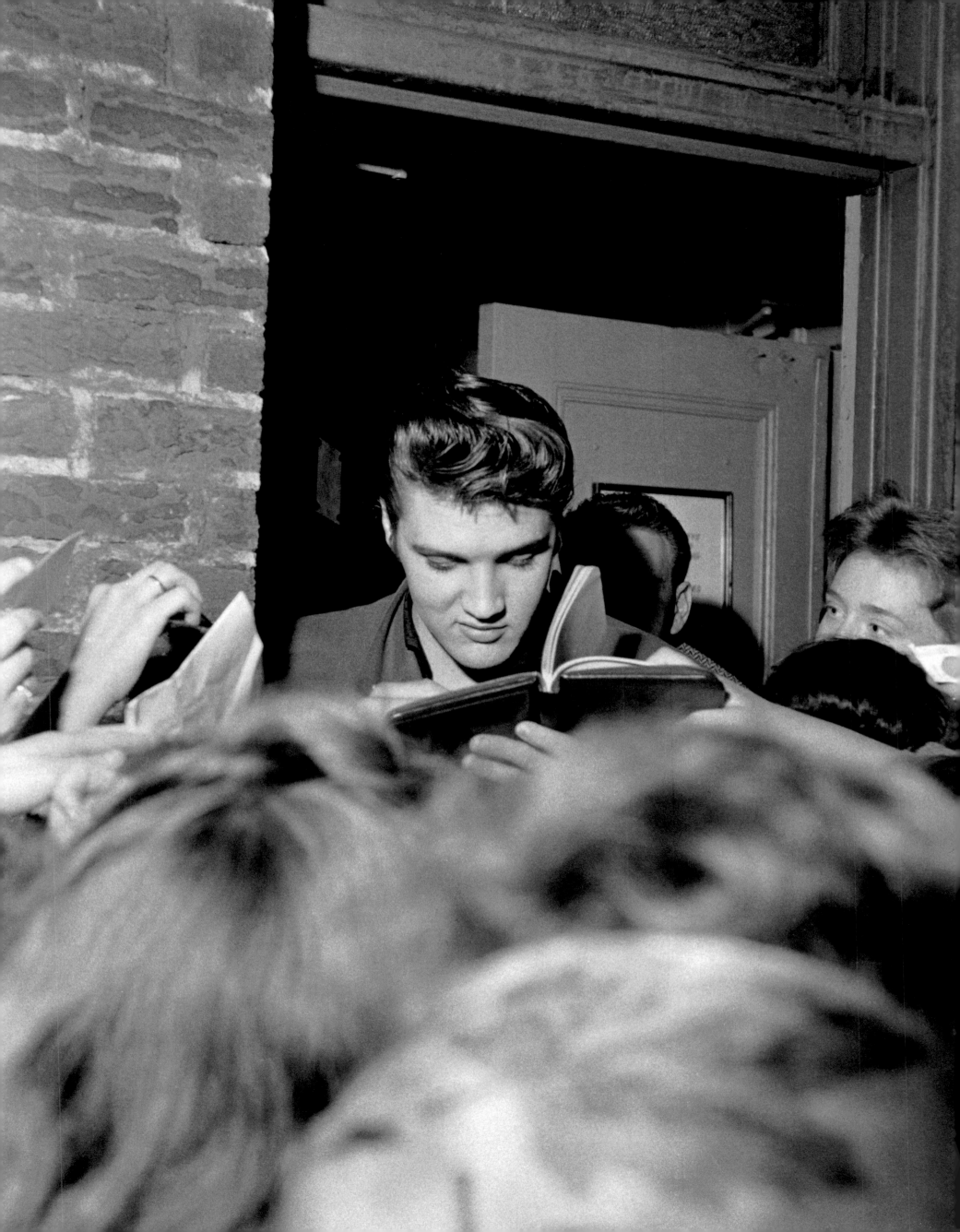

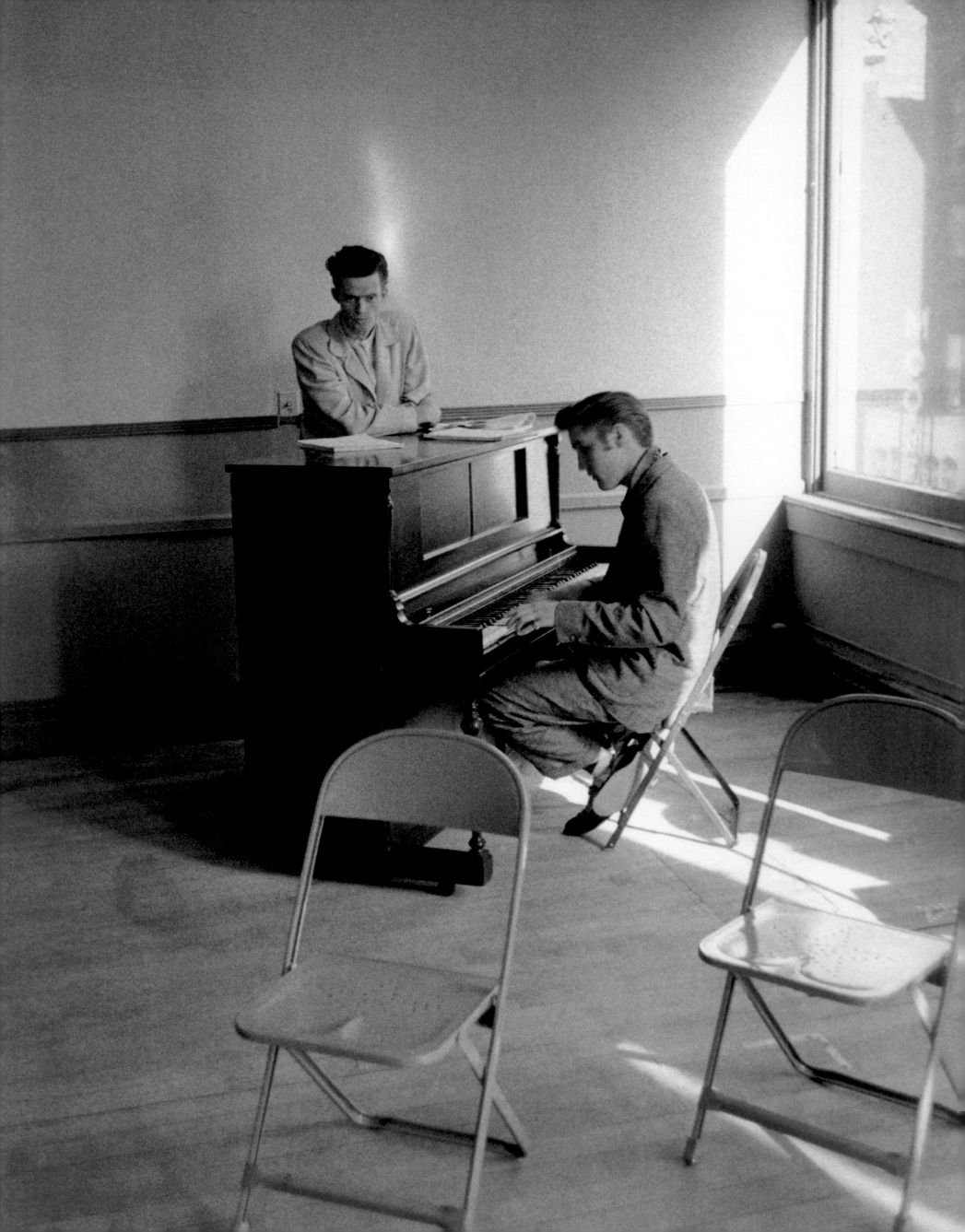

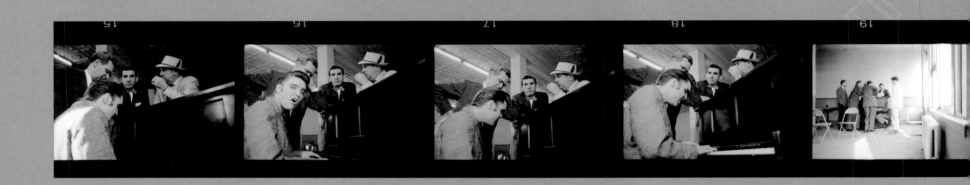

CHAPTER II

STEVE ALLEN SHOW

REHEARSAL

THE STEVE ALLEN SHOW
Rehearsal

The next time I met Elvis was on June 29th, when he arrived in New York for the rehearsal of *The Steve Allen Show*. Instead of tying up an expensive studio and dealing with the unions, actors were called up to loft spaces to go through their lines and block out scenes. Rehearsal for the next show was called for that afternoon in a building in mid-Manhattan. Getting there a little early, I entered this large informal space to find Elvis over in the corner. He was playing the piano by himself. I call that shot "First Arrival."

A guy with an intense face was just hanging around while Elvis played some gospel music. Elvis's go-fer (and cousin), Junior Smith, had a mean look that told me this ex-GI probably had seen a lot of combat during his time in Korea. Although he looked like the kind of guy you wouldn't want to meet in a dark alley at night, Junior was very devoted to Elvis and Elvis was devoted to Junior. Elvis always kept him around, as someone from back home that he trusted. When they traveled, it was Junior that sat next to him, not a musician. When Elvis wanted a Coke, Junior would go get it. If something had to be paid, Junior would pay for it since Elvis never carried any money. Elvis was busy being Elvis.

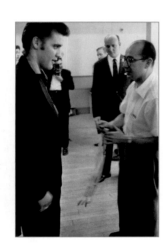

Next, the William Morris people wandered in, followed by the Colonel wearing his hat with the feather. Since the rehearsal couldn't begin until Steve Allen got there, everyone gathered around the piano. Elvis just continued to play and sing some gospel music. He always needed an excuse to get away from the conversation. Whether it was an accordion, guitar, or piano, he would pick up whatever musical instrument happened to be there. It was his way of calming himself down and letting people know that he was absorbed in his music. The agents and others that started arriving were impressed by the fact that Elvis could even sing gospel. Everyone always thought of him as a rock and roll singer.

Eventually, Steve Allen, his wife Audrey, and Skitch Henderson, the musical director, walked in. Next came the director of the show, followed by Imogene Coca and Andy Griffith. Once all were present, each person was handed a script and asked to do a run through. Elvis stood up from the piano, but before he could get his script, the tailor asked him to go into a closet and change into a tuxedo for a fitting. Steve had arranged for Elvis to wear a blue shirt with a blue tie and a tuxedo to make him look more respectable. As soon as Elvis stepped out of the closet, the tailor was bending down, rolling up the cuffs and measuring the inseam while the Colonel adjusted the jacket, Junior stood by, and I took pictures. Once the fitting was out of the way, they asked him to go back into the closet and change into his regular clothes. Then it was time for rehearsal.

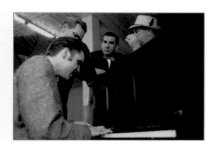

The *Steve Allen Show* aired opposite *Ed Sullivan* on NBC. With Elvis in the program, Steve wanted to make sure that his show was going to be without any controversy. Elvis was criticized for his earlier television performance on the *Milton Berle Show*. Steve wrote three different scenes for Elvis's appearance that night and the director began blocking them out. For the first performance, Elvis would sing a ballad onstage with his musicians silhouetted against some Greek columns set up in

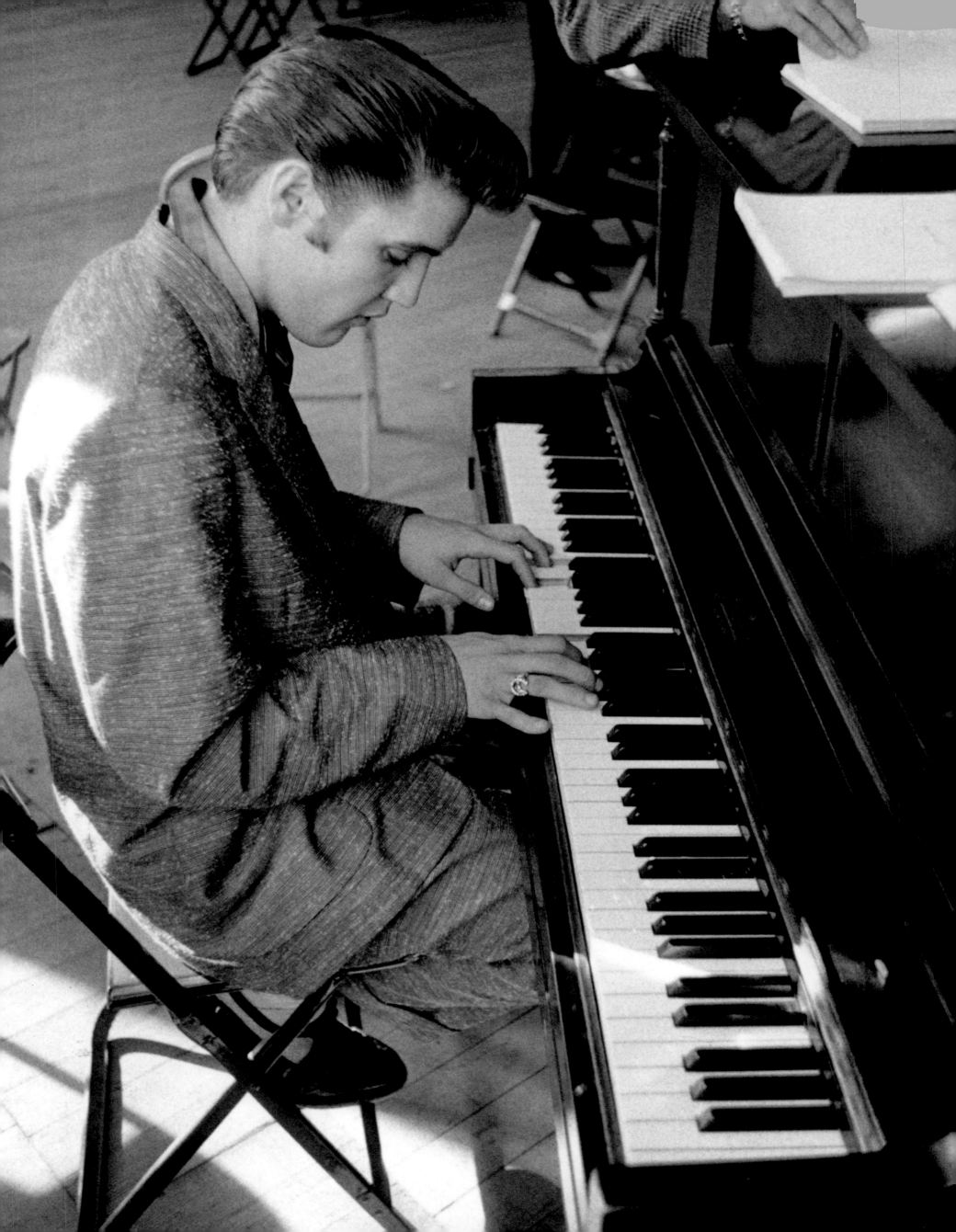

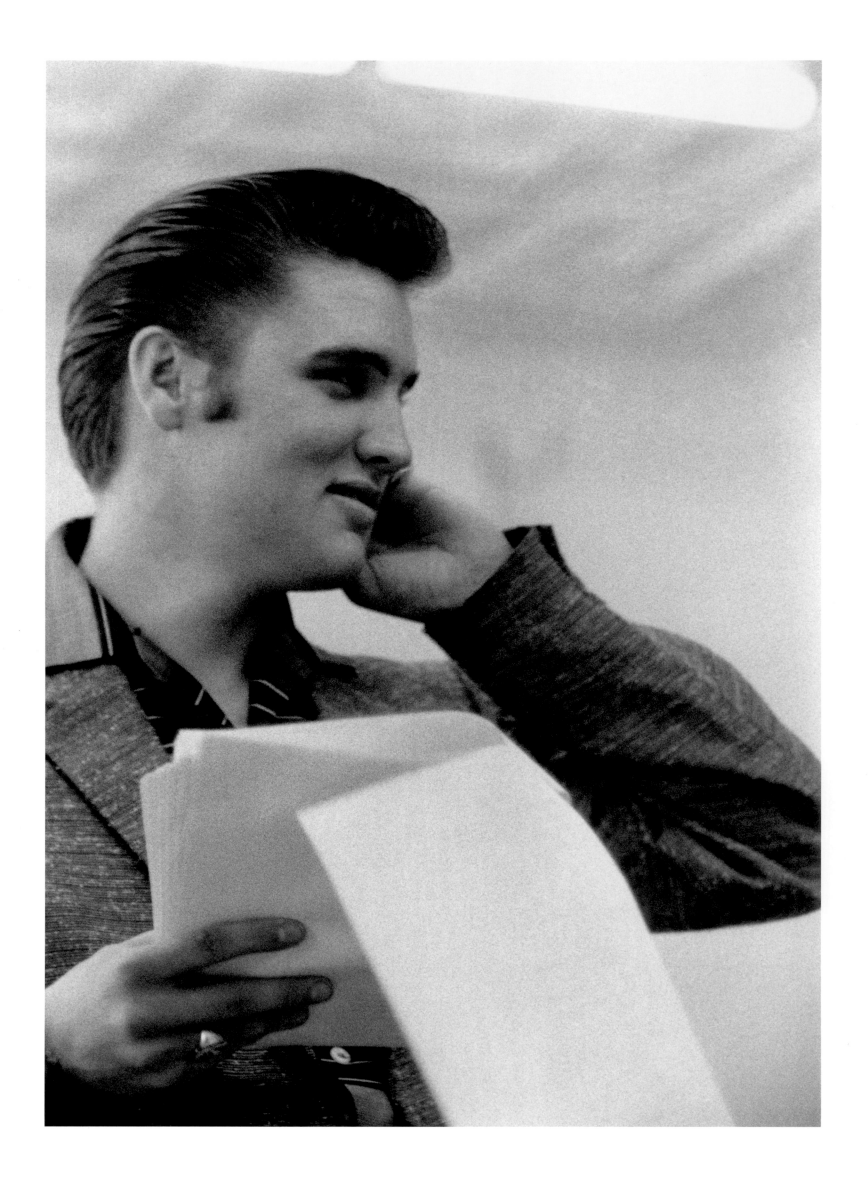

the background. The ballad would eliminate most of the gyrations and the columns would give the whole scene a classical look.

For Elvis's second act, he would play a part in a skit called "Range Roundup," with Imogene Coca, Andy Griffith, and Steve Allen. During rehearsal, Elvis followed the script and Steve threw the lines. Of course, Steve had most of the good ones, while Elvis didn't say much more than "yup," "yup," "no," "yup," "no," "yup." The scene closed with Elvis taking a six-shooter from his hip, aiming and shooting at a Tonto bar being pulled across the stage with a nylon thread while he mimicked galloping at full speed. "Tumbleweed Presley," Elvis's first performance as an actor, was born.

In the final performance, Elvis would sing to a hound dog wearing a little black top hat and sitting on a pedestal. If Elvis jumped around too much, the dog would jump off the pedestal, and you couldn't have that. Not only was Elvis being put in a tux, but Steve had devised ways to contain him and keep the show clean. Elvis didn't like the idea of singing to a hound dog but had enough good humor to go along with it since he was a guest on Steve Allen's show. Moreover, Elvis was a twenty-one-year-old singer being introduced to the American public. He didn't have much weight to throw around…yet.

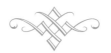

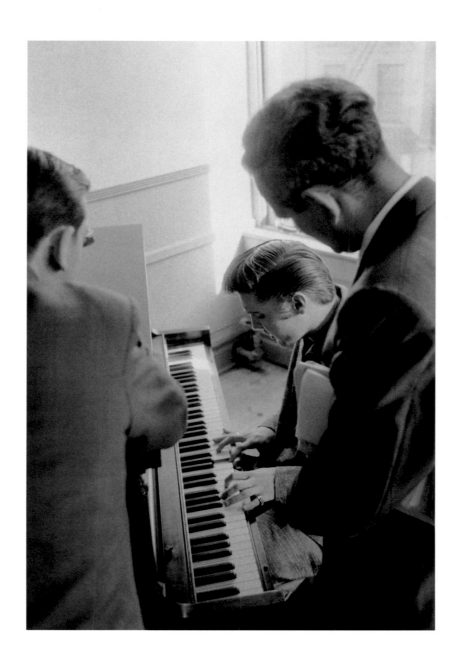

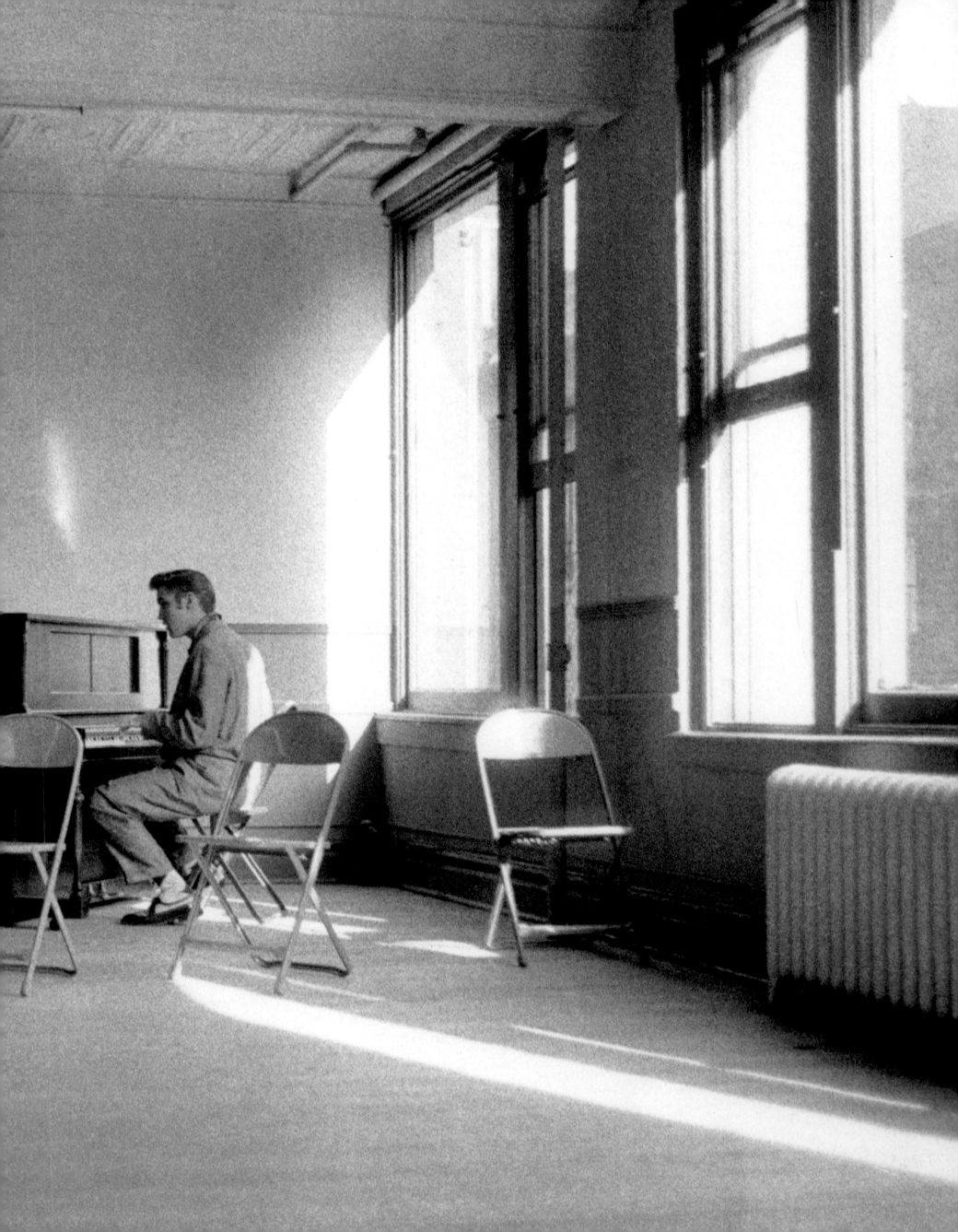

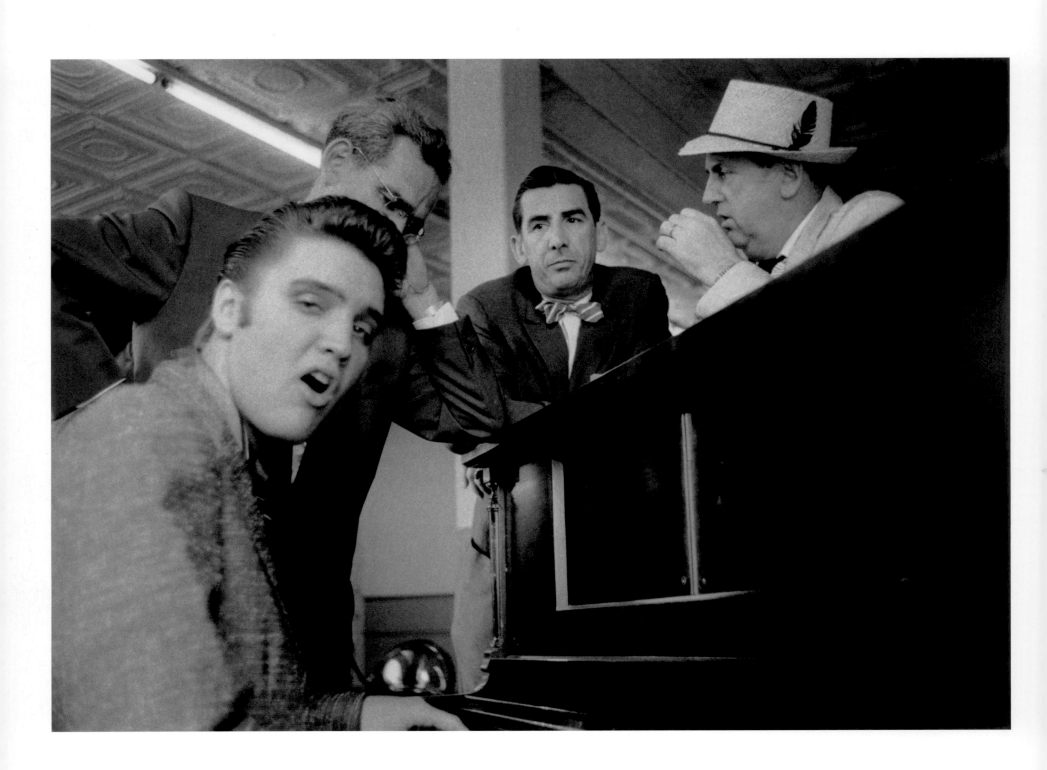

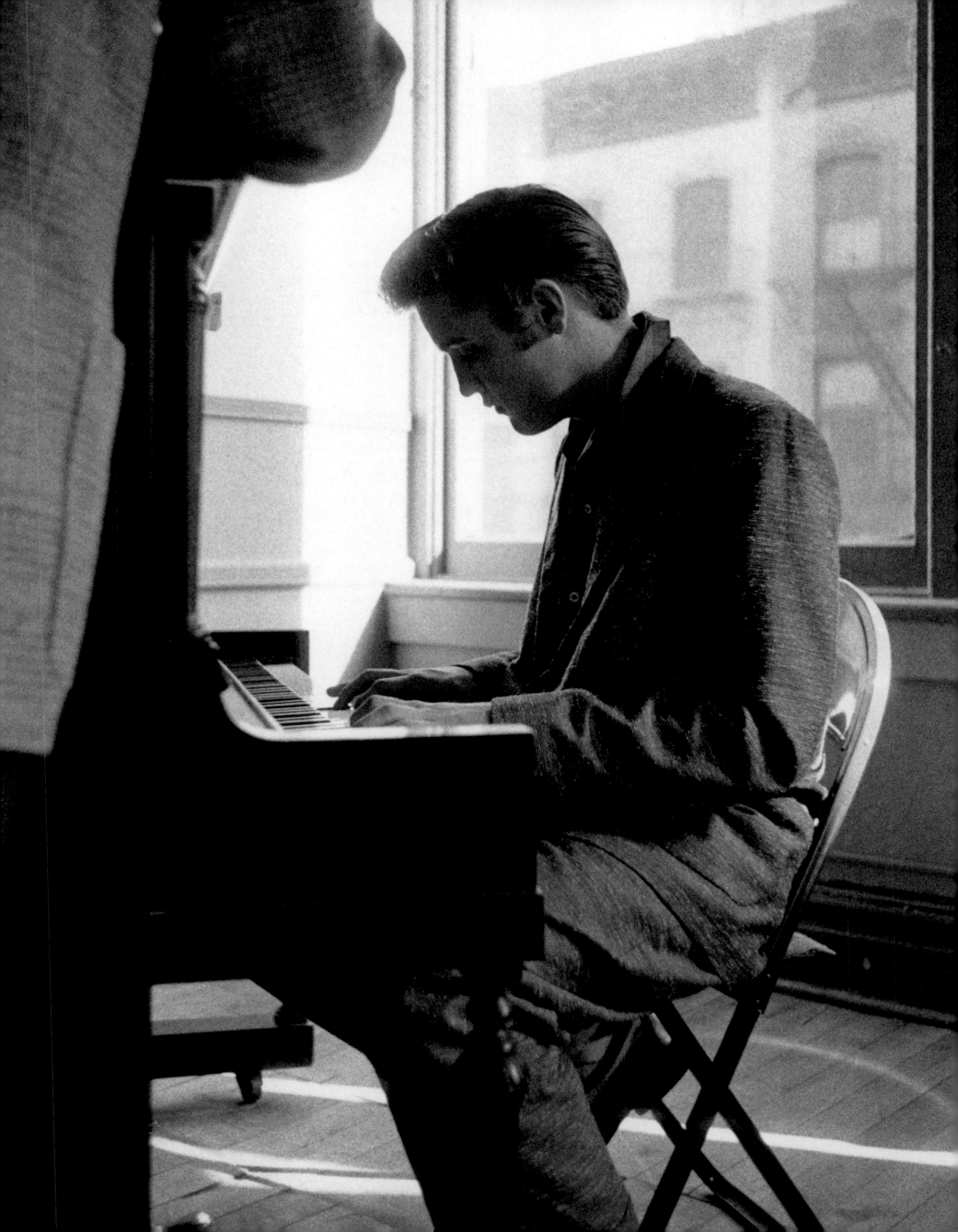

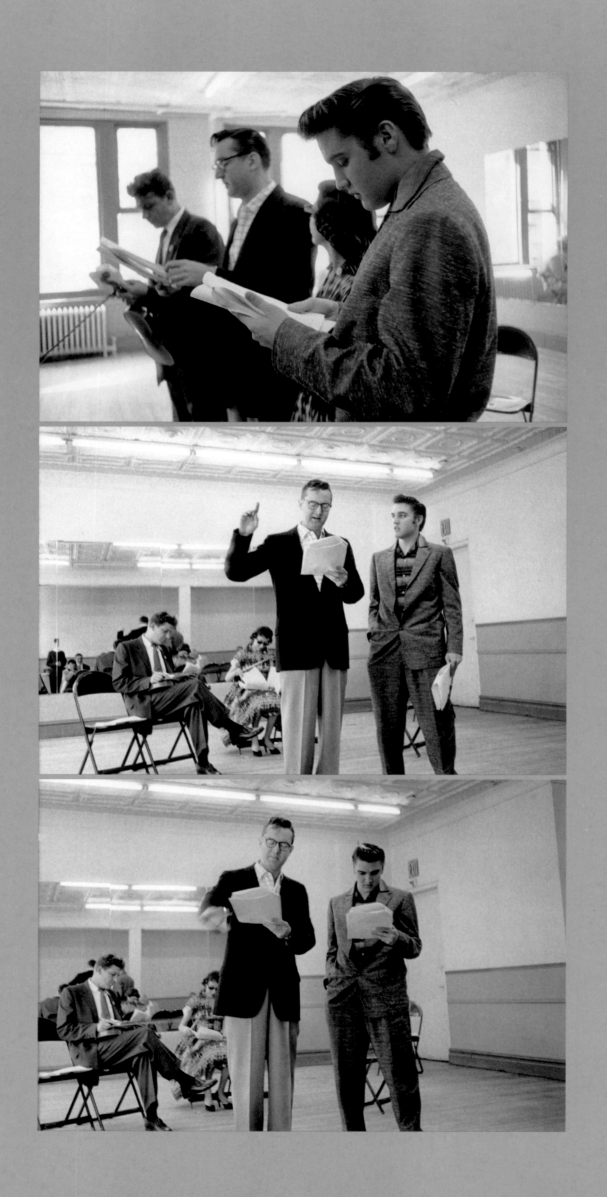

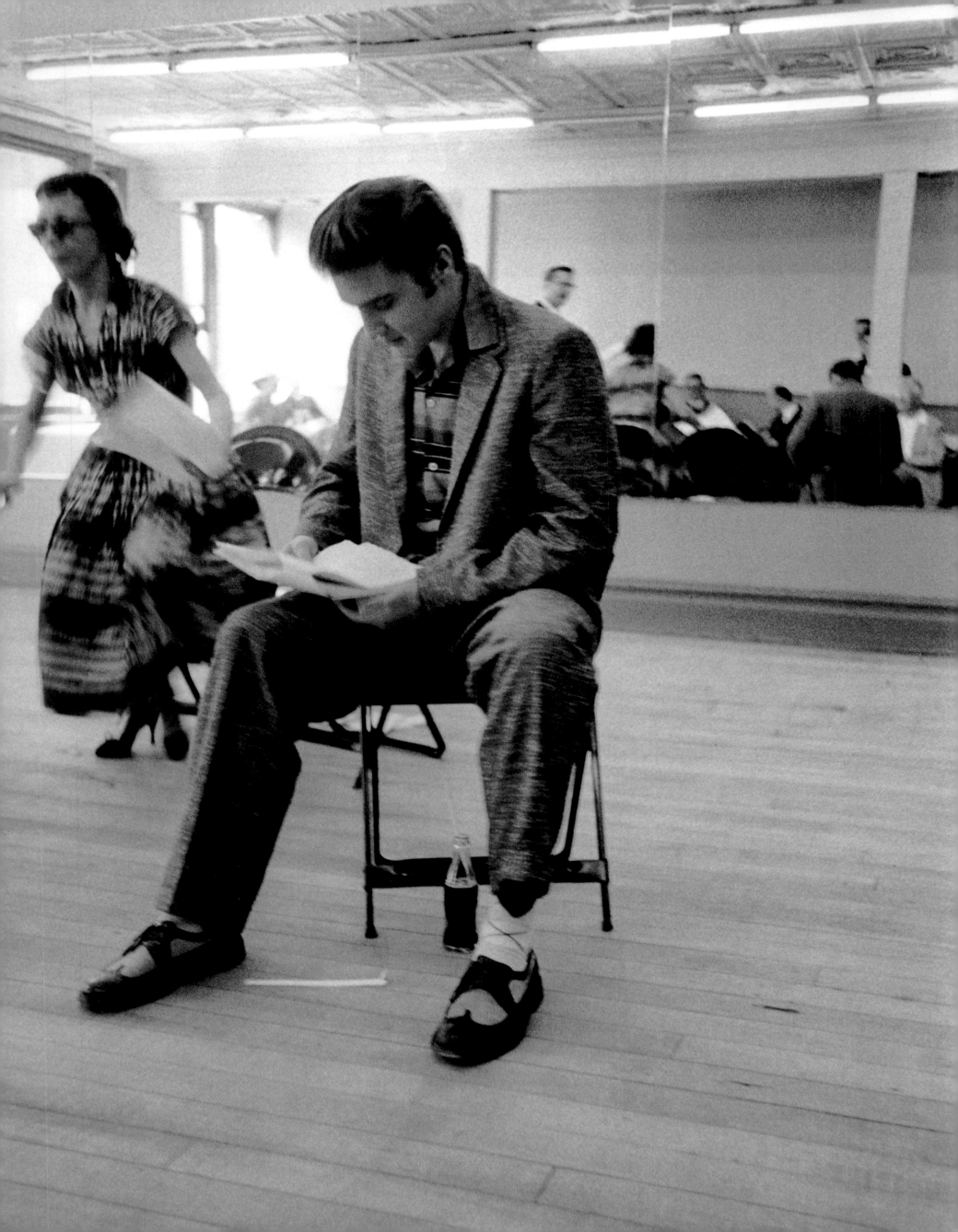

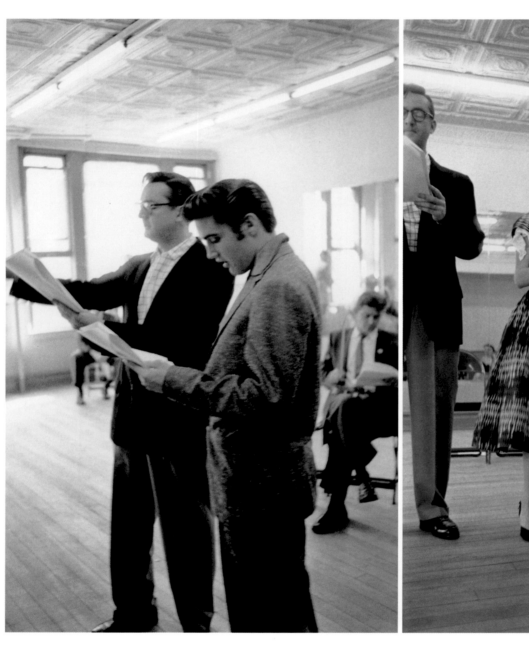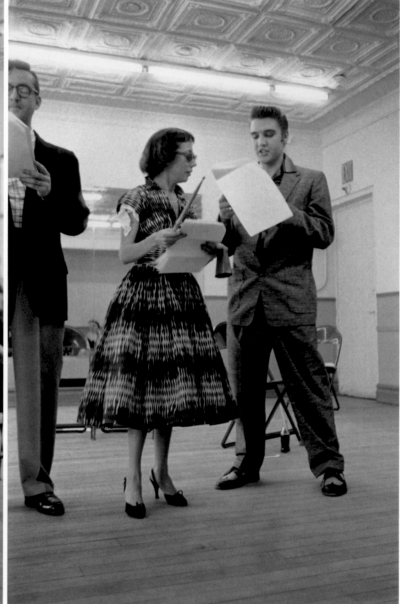

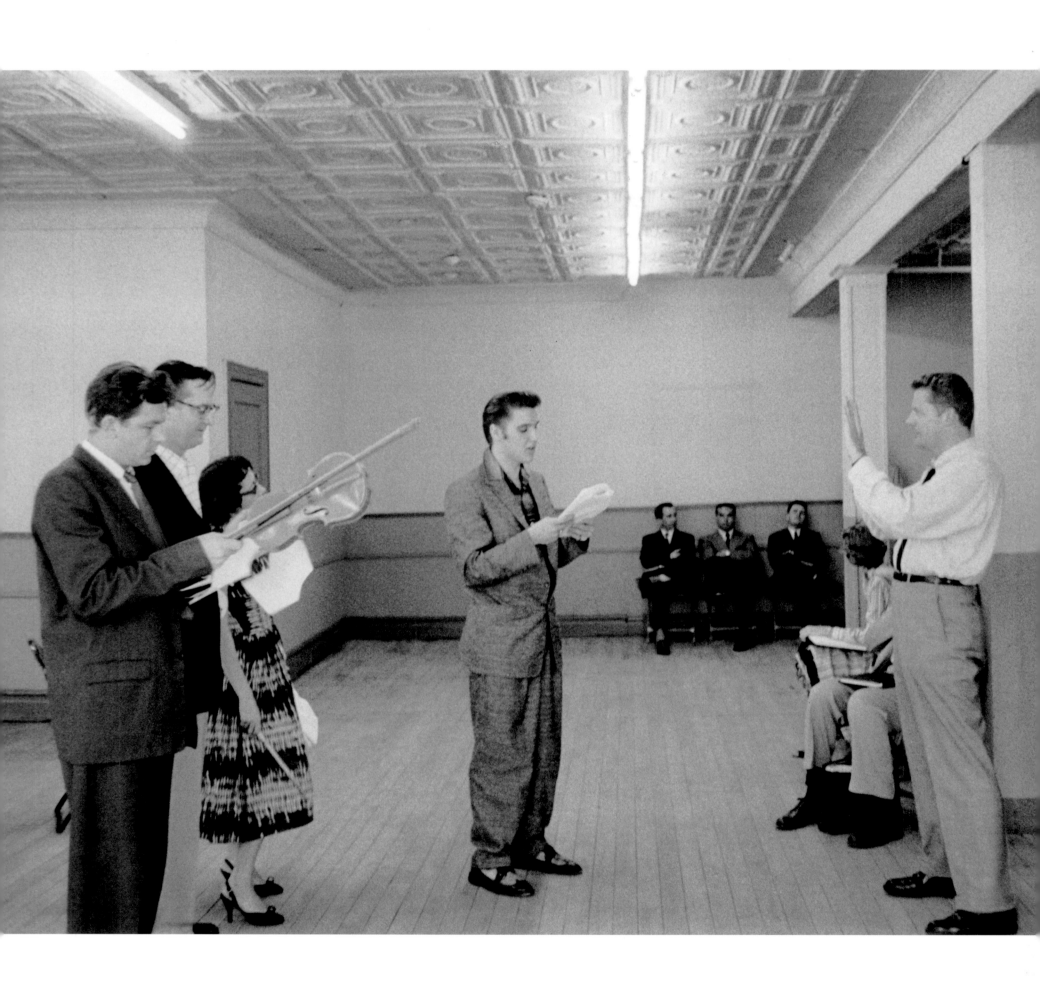

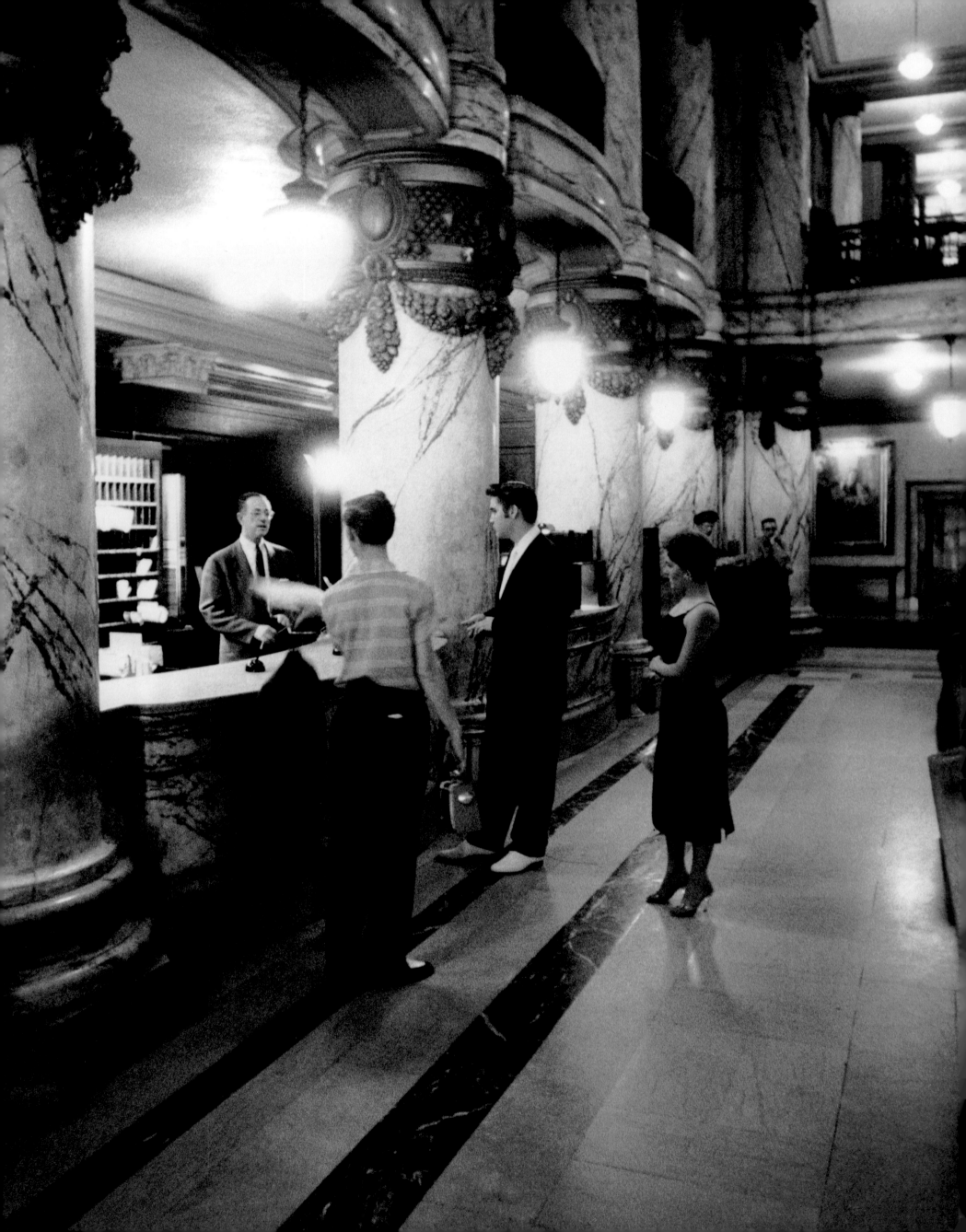

CHAPTER III

MOSQUE THEATER
RICHMOND, VIRGINIA

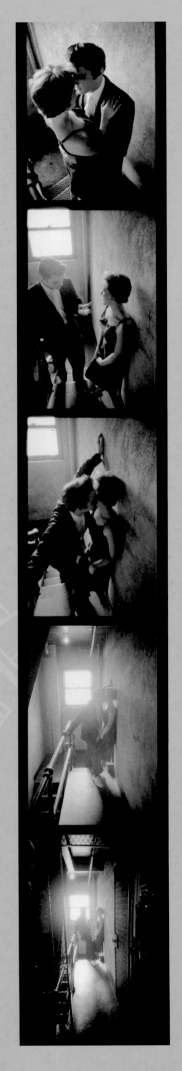

MOSQUE THEATER
RICHMOND, VIRGINIA

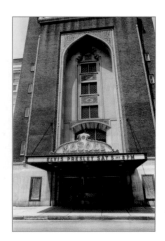

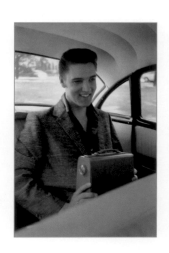

AFTER HIS FIRST ACTING GIG ON TELEVISION, Elvis headed to Richmond for two shows at the Mosque Theater. Very early on the morning of June 30th, I arrived at the train station in Richmond and grabbed a cab to the Jefferson Hotel. Ann Fulchino didn't ask me to go down that day, but having a foot in the door, I took advantage of this opportunity to shoot him again in Richmond. This was a chance for me to observe him down south, outside the bustle of New York and closer to his home environment.

Since RCA was his record label, Elvis just assumed that I was doing something for them. Whether he was expecting me or not, I wasn't sure. Elvis was a bit of a fatalist; whatever was, that was how it would be. Questions and explanations were unnecessary. His job was to be down there for a one-night stand of two shows and, well, I must have had a good reason for going through all the trouble of going down there too. Besides, there were no other photographers around. Now, at least, someone was there to record this day in the life of an up-and-coming star.

After checking in at the hotel, I returned to the train station to wait for Elvis. A short while later, the train pulled in. I could see the conductor (whom I called Chicken Neck). Junior Smith was walking off the train with Elvis. Elvis took a look around, smiled and turned on his little radio. It wasn't one of those huge boom boxes that you'd see thirty years later, but an RCA Transistor 7 portable radio that had been given to him as a present by Steve Sholes's recording department. The next thing I saw was Elvis exiting the train station with his radio blaring. I took a picture of him from the rear, which in retrospect, really captures Elvis's pelvis.

Junior was already putting Elvis's wardrobe bag into a cab. Those two got in the backseat while I hopped into the front next to the driver. I asked the cabbie to stop and let me out at the corner just before the Jefferson Hotel, so that when the cab pulled up to the entrance I would be ready. I wanted to get a shot of Elvis entering the hotel and wasn't about to tell him to do it again and again until I got it right. If I didn't get there quickly, it would be over before I knew it. I had just enough time to position myself, frame the large hotel sign, and take a picture. As soon as Elvis got out with his portable radio and Junior followed, I shot Elvis walking under the marquee into the hotel.

Elvis had the radio blaring when he walked into the rather conservative lobby of the Jefferson. There were a couple of little old ladies there, so he kept that thing blasting. He liked to stir things up a bit and pretend to ignore the reaction. He went up to the front desk and told the clerk that he was Elvis Presley and he had a reservation. The man replied, "Yes, Mr. Presley, we have your room." and handed him the key. In the elevator, there was a young lady who was trying not to pay any attention to us. Naturally, Elvis stood right in front of her and looked her straight in the face until she giggled.

After he cleaned up a bit, the three of us came downstairs for breakfast. We went into the dining room. This was no luncheonette. This was the type of place where families normally ate and the tables had tablecloths. Elvis and Junior sat down and the waitress brought menus over. I recognized that perplexed look on Elvis's face as he thought seriously about what this next meal was going to be. We've all gone through this at restaurants, staring at the menu and really concentrating while the

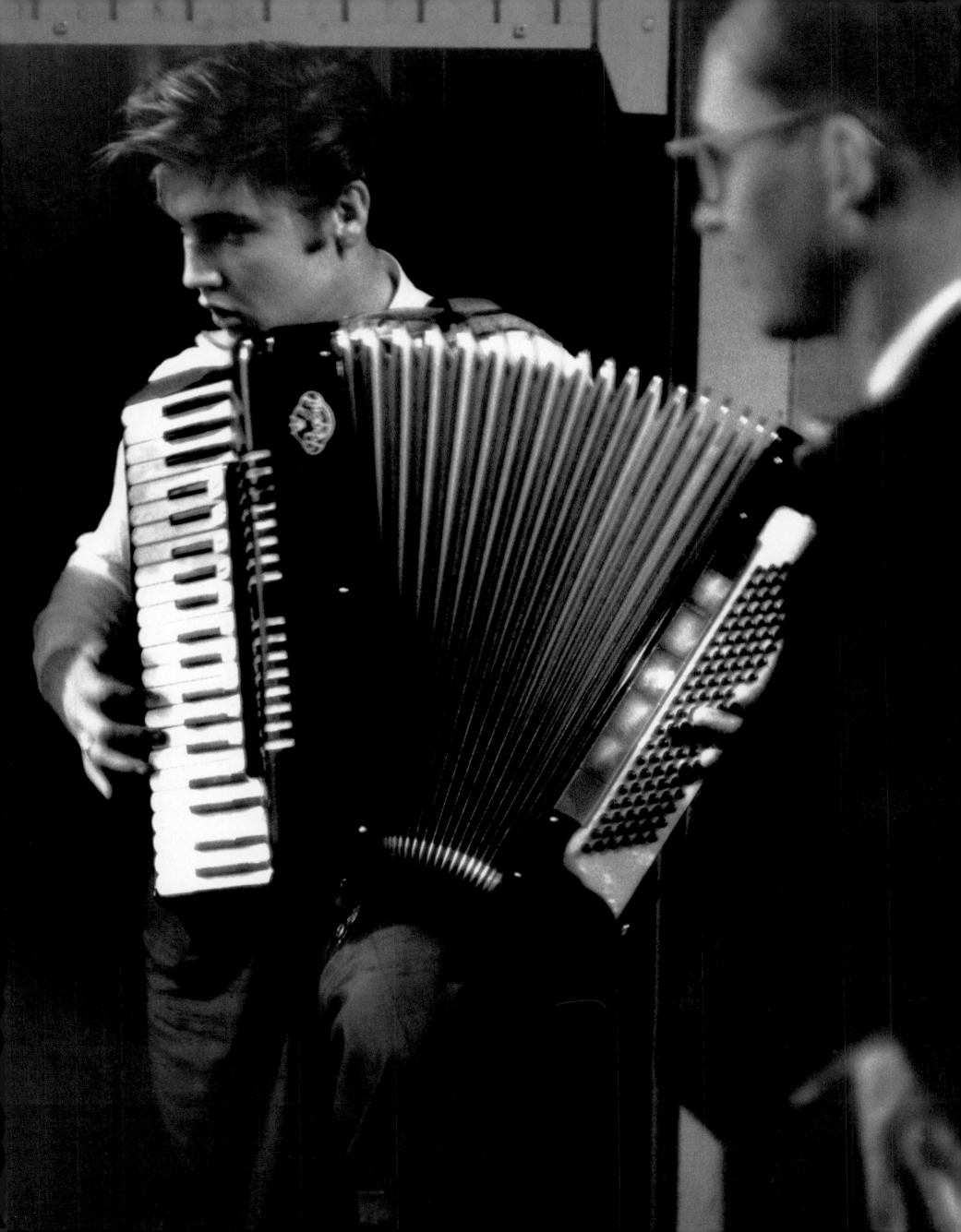

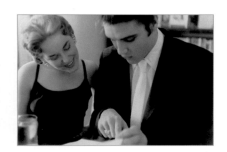

waitress waits patiently. Bacon, eggs, and home fries with a glass of milk. Cantaloupe with ice cream for dessert. With that taken care of, he could turn to other things. Within fifteen minutes of their first encounter, Elvis had his arm around the waitress's waist. While Junior was scrunching his forehead in that typically ominous way, Elvis just naturally knew how to get to the ladies. How often have you put your arm around a woman you never knew existed just twenty minutes earlier? He was charming and she loved it.

Adjacent to the dining room was a luncheonette with a magazine rack. Elvis wandered in to pick up a magazine that had a picture of Jerry Lewis on the cover. Once he finished that story, he flipped through the other magazines. Another gentleman was doing the same, but they weren't paying any attention to each other. This older man and Elvis stood quietly together, each looking for some kind of heroic action in the magazines. About an hour later, Elvis went up to his room to rest and I had a chance to check out the Mosque Theater and think through my strategy for the evening.

By the time I got back to the hotel, I found Elvis sitting at the counter inside the luncheonette with some soup and crackers, a cup of coffee, and (of course) a young woman next to him. Junior was at one end of the counter and Bobby Smith, another cousin, was at the other end. These two were his bodyguards, the beginning of the Memphis Mafia. Elvis gave work to everybody in the family. He trusted them and they protected him. He had with him the script for *The Steve Allen Show* featuring Tumbleweed Presley. Flipping through some of the pages, he was trying to impress this young lady whose name I forgot to get. But she remained cool, not wanting to look too impressed. Elvis continued to try and loosen her up with conversation. At one point, he came in close, within three inches of her face, and just shouted, "Ahhh!"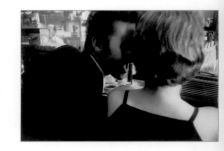

Meanwhile, I kept shooting pictures, one of which I call "Grilled Cheese 20 Cents," (p. 86-87) because there were signs up behind the counter announcing the menu—"Grilled Cheese and Tomato," "Tuna Fish," etc. It was getting late, so Junior finally got up and told Elvis it was time to go. The first show at the Mosque Theater was to begin at five P.M.

E lvis, Junior, and I piled into a cab. It was just like that morning from the train station, only now with the girl from the luncheonette sitting in the middle doing silly things like pointing to the light fixtures or making little comments. Elvis continued to be at turns debonair and playful, or stern and wrapping both his hands around her neck in a mock ceremony of choking her, trying to get her to loosen up. He had style, you had to admit that. Junior, on the other hand, was scowling in the backseat and paying no attention to the two lovebirds. As we arrived at the theater, some people were waiting outside. No rebellious sort of dress here. The guys had slacks on and the girls were dressed to kill in high heels and dresses, like their mothers taught them. They were all waiting to have their pictures taken with Elvis up against one of the walls at the back of the Mosque Theater. I remember one girl who leaned out of the second floor window and shouted with a mild southern accent, "Elvis, I'll be right down." So that would make fifteen girls down there, not just fourteen. Each girl took the other one's camera and photographed each other with Elvis, while DJ Fontana (to the right) kept stroking his hair.

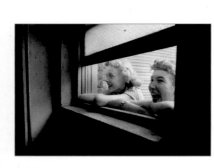

After this impromptu fan session, we found ourselves in the green room at the Mosque. A lot of activity was taking place onstage because there were eight or ten other acts scheduled that night as well. Elvis Presley had the last twenty minutes to close the show. In the din of all this screaming going on outside the building, Elvis and the Jordanaires, his back-up group, were trying to rehearse some of the songs they were going to sing that evening. While he was trying to harmonize with the Jordanaires, some of the girls discovered that if they could climb up on a ledge, they could stick their face in an open window and call out to him. Unfortunately, the camera couldn't capture the full ambience of all the chaos and noise, but that was what was going on. Elvis actually had to go to the window and say, "Look, we're trying to rehearse in here. We're doing it so that you'll get a good performance, so could you tone it down?" He was good natured about it. All he had to do was tell them to be quiet and they

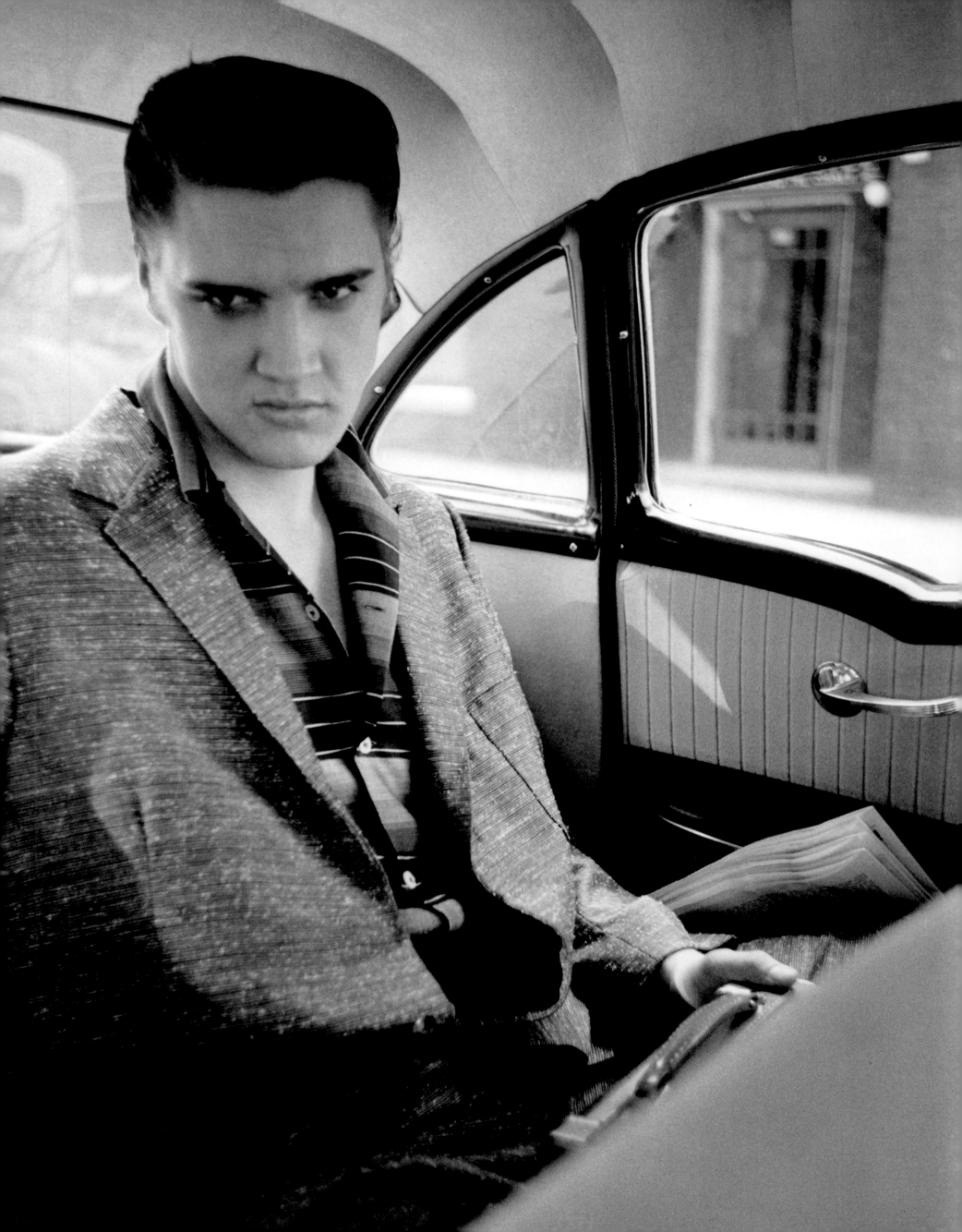

did. Meanwhile, DJ Fontana had some girl with her arms around him and Scotty tended to his guitar. Bill Black, the bass player, was nowhere to be seen until he showed up onstage.

Once the songs and sequence had been selected, the next step was to find a place to change clothes, which turned out to be a bathroom one flight up from the stage level. Inside the bathroom, Elvis was busy combing his hair in the mirror while the Jordanaires were changing their clothes. Junior stood by to give him encouragement.

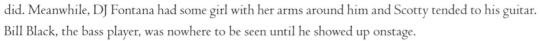

Suddenly I noticed that Elvis was gone. He had disappeared when I turned to take a few more pictures. A photojournalist was supposed to stay near his subject and keep track of his movements. Otherwise, how were you going to get a complete document? I quickly went on a hunt, which took me down these fire stairs enclosed by some sort of wire mesh. It was rather dark as I descended. Coming around the corner, I spotted two people at the end of a long, narrow passageway. I found Elvis with his girl for the day, the one from the hotel luncheonette. There was a very intimate feeling about the situation, as if they were about to kiss each other.

How could I get in close without offending him? There was still much more of the day left and I didn't want him to get angry and say, "Beat it!" I was a voyeur in a very dimly lit scene of two lovers almost in silhouette. In order to capture it on film, I had to bring the exposures down to one-half, maybe one-fifth of a second and click a few shots with both my wide-angle lens and my medium tele-photo lens from about twenty feet away. I had to get in a bit closer. After all, I was here to do a story and this was a part of it, not just the stage stuff. I edged in to within five feet. I considered getting up on a railing to the upper left and shooting down, but I was still worried about how Elvis was going to react to the invasion of his privacy. He couldn't have cared less; his focus was entirely on giving this girl a kiss. I took my shots from the left, but I felt I needed another angle. With my maintenance man voice, I grumbled, "Excuse me, please—coming through." Squeezing past them, I positioned myself on the other side with the window behind me at a slightly lower landing. At last, I had a much better view and front lighting. They were so involved with each other that they didn't even notice all this movement.

"I'll bet you can't kiss me, Elvis," she said and stuck out her tongue mocking him. Finally, she was letting her guard (and her pocketbook) down.

"I'll bet ya I can," he said and stuck out his tongue. On his first try, he overshot the mark and bent her nose.

Always remaining cool, Elvis backed up slightly and the tips of their tongues just touched.

I got it, the whole sequence, all the way through to the kiss, I thought to myself. "Excuse me, coming through." The maintenance man left them alone.

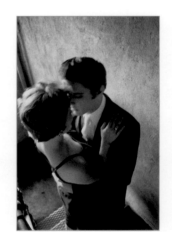

When I returned to the stage area, the commotion in the audience had already begun. "We want Elvis, we want Elvis." Thousands of girls were getting tired of these small acts and the chant started going up. Five minutes later, Elvis came out from the back, combed his hair one more time, grabbed his guitar, and jumped onstage in front of 3,000 screaming fans.

As usual, during the performance three or four policemen stood around making sure there were no riots. Some young men had their arms crossed, trying to figure out who was stealing their girls from them. They didn't know what to make of it, but 90 percent of the audience was female and they knew very well what was going on. The girls were loving every minute of it. Elvis was working up a sweat, being very intimate and letting the girls see him fall apart on stage. That got them excited. They started to cry, clutching each other while mascara ran down their cheeks. They were having such a good time falling apart with him and he loved it. It was like a catharsis, a spiritual experience for the girls. There was such a feverish pitch that the police kept watch with their squinty eyes to make sure nothing was going wrong. But everyone had her clothes on.

Once the performance was over, the Colonel had the auditorium cleared for the next crowd. There were two shows, an early one and a late one, with at least an hour-and-a-half in between. The Colonel would book them, rent the theaters and fill them up with the help of his right hand man, Tom Diskin. Tom would remain in the box office selling the tickets and collecting the money while the Colonel oversaw the whole affair. Tom also would hire a couple of high school kids to hand out leaflets publicizing the event and to be ushers during the performance. Posters were made at the local printer. It was a bare-bones operation at the time.

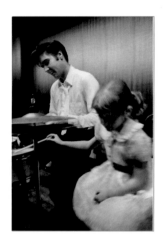

Meanwhile, Elvis relaxed at DJ's drum set, casually drumming away. All of a sudden, this cute little blonde eight-year-old, a daughter of one of the other performers, sat down next to him and picked up a drumstick. She started tapping on one of the drum heads, trying to play in rhythm with him. The brunette from the kiss stood over at the far wall watching the scene. A reporter from the local newspaper was also there with his notepad. Tapping away at the drums, Elvis answered all kinds of questions, like: "What are you going to do next?" and "Are you going to be on *The Steve Allen Show?*" and "How do you feel about all the bad publicity you got recently about *The Milton Berle Show?*" and "What do you think of the people breaking your records, saying you're a bad influence on children and the public?"

Elvis maintained that he was just a happy performer, that people were taking things too seriously, that he wasn't such a bad person at all, and that everyone should give him a break. After he finished with the reporters, Elvis turned to the little girl and said, "How would you like to learn to play the piano?" Elvis was always looking for something to do, which was why I had decided from the beginning that I wasn't going to talk to him and get him distracted. Besides, as a young photographer, I thought it was wonderful to have a subject with such a fertile imagination providing so much visual material.

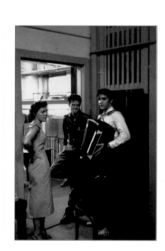

I watched him take the little girl down to a piano in the orchestra pit. A few people were milling about in the audience. Elvis sat to the left and put the little girl to his right. Then he leaned way back and raised both feet up to the keyboard. Banging away with his shoes on, he kept laughing while she played "Chopsticks" with her little fingers.

Like a racehorse cooling down, Elvis wandered about the theater. Spotting an accordion just doing nothing in the corner of the stage, he picked it up, strapped it to his body and started to play. Junior was there, chuckling away with a female companion (that was the first time I had ever seen him laugh) while Elvis played the accordion. Exhausted, he set the instrument down and found a chair backstage. Concerned, everyone gathered around him as he tried to catch his breath. Elvis settled down drinking a Coke and fifteen minutes later, we were back upstairs in the bathroom. This time, he pulled out a bright green jacket, the kind you would wear in a St. Patty's Day parade. He put that on, washed up, and combed his hair again. Elvis was ready for the next show.

❧

I had taken a lot of fairly sharp pictures of Elvis up till now. Since he was being criticized so much for his movements, I decided to do just the opposite for the second show. I sacrificed the sharpness in search of a sort of "controlled blurriness," a sense of motion without losing the clarity of the subject's face and the scene in general. After all, that was his trademark. Most singers in those days stood pretty still, using their arms or their heads but certainly not their bodies. What if I shot at a very slow shutter speed and followed his moves? Perhaps I'd get lucky and catch two or three images capturing this essential characteristic of Elvis in motion. If he moved to his right, then I would try a half-second exposure and move to my left with him.

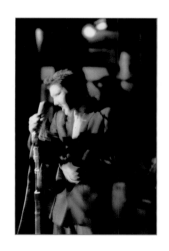

Photography allows you to do what you can't do with your naked eye. The still photograph registers things both in and out of focus at the same time while the mind only remembers the former. When I edited these images later, I realized that the center of focus, the body, ended up sharper than the peripherals, like his hands and feet, which were moving more quickly. With a bit of luck, I would get two or three good shots out of a couple dozen taken like this. That was all I needed to represent the idea. Modern cameras have got it down to one-thousandths of a second, but I discovered back then that there's a whole world of magic in photography if you just slow down the shutter speed.

At the end of the second show, Elvis was beginning to slow down a bit too. The kids screamed for more and more encores, but he was tired. A paddy wagon from the police department was sent to wait outside the theater. After one of the encore performances, Elvis rushed out the back door and into the wagon while the musicians continued to play. The crowd started chanting, "We want Elvis. We want Elvis," until someone went out on stage to make the announcement.

"Elvis has left the building." The crowd refused to believe it. Where had Elvis gone?

He was waiting in the back of the paddy wagon for the theater to empty out. Once the musicians got out, they could go straight to the station to catch the train that night. I caught up with them at the station and boarded the train. Elvis settled into his sleeper, daydreaming with his hand up to his head and staring at the ceiling. The other musicians were hanging around in his sleeper as well, but not for long. We all got out, closed the door, and Elvis went to sleep.

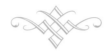

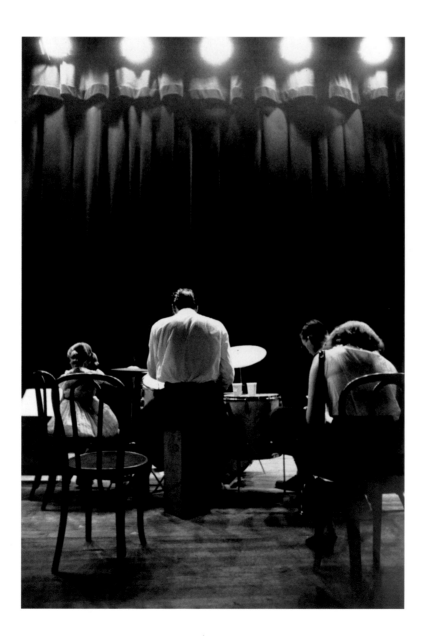

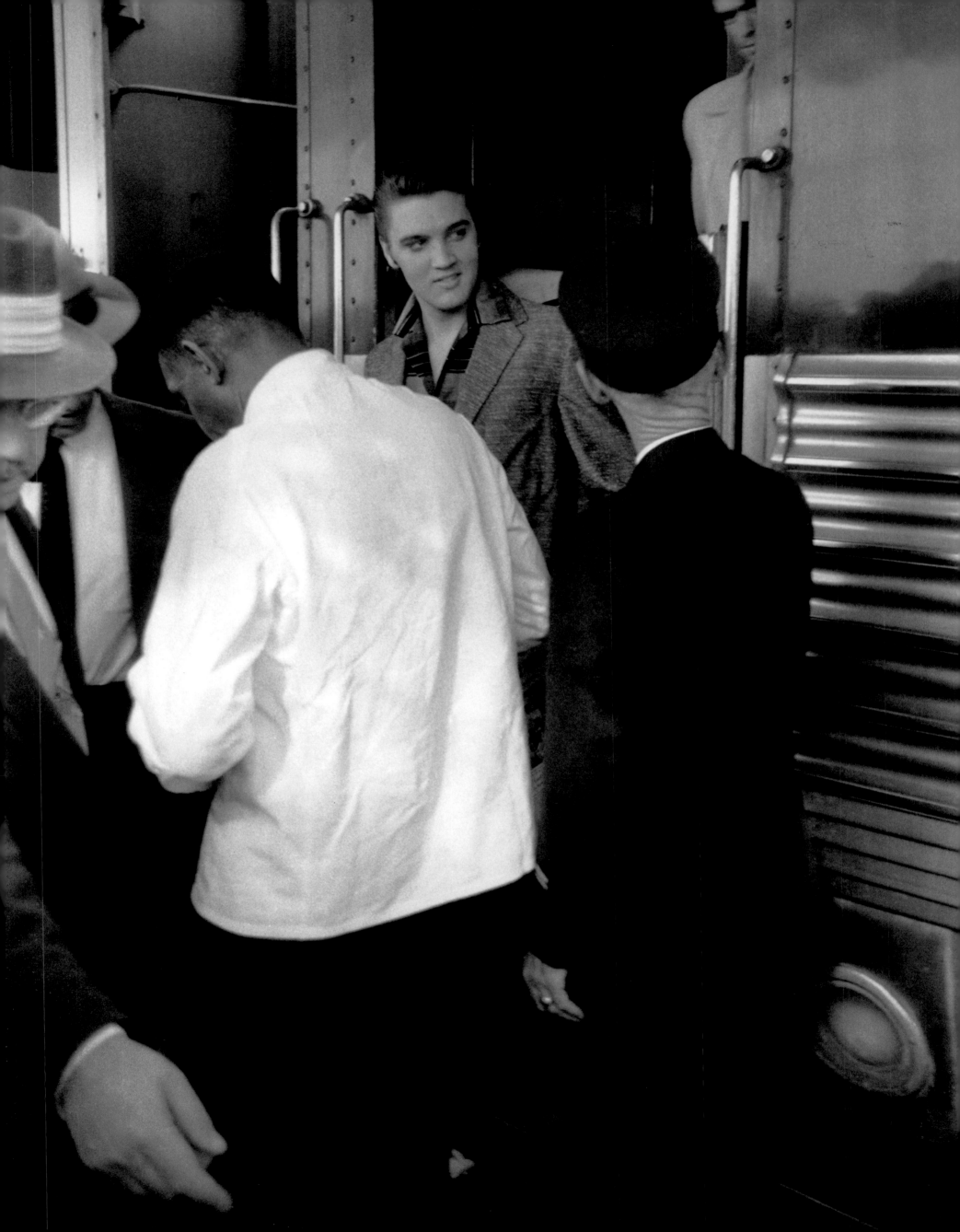

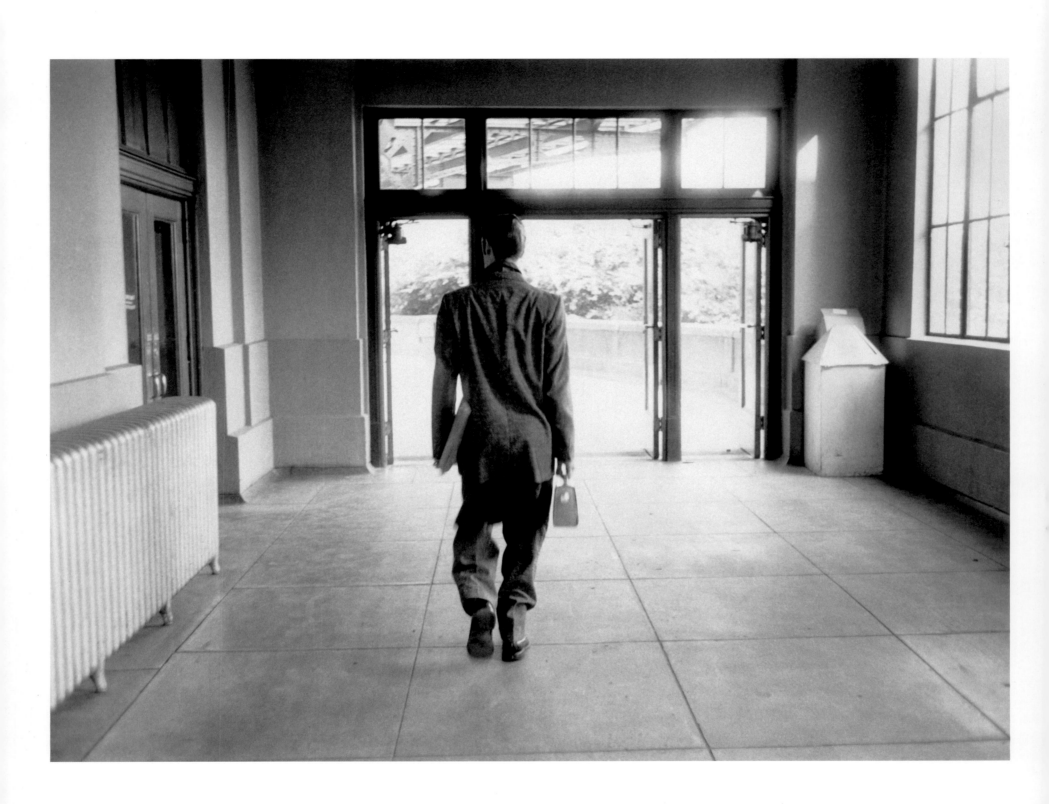

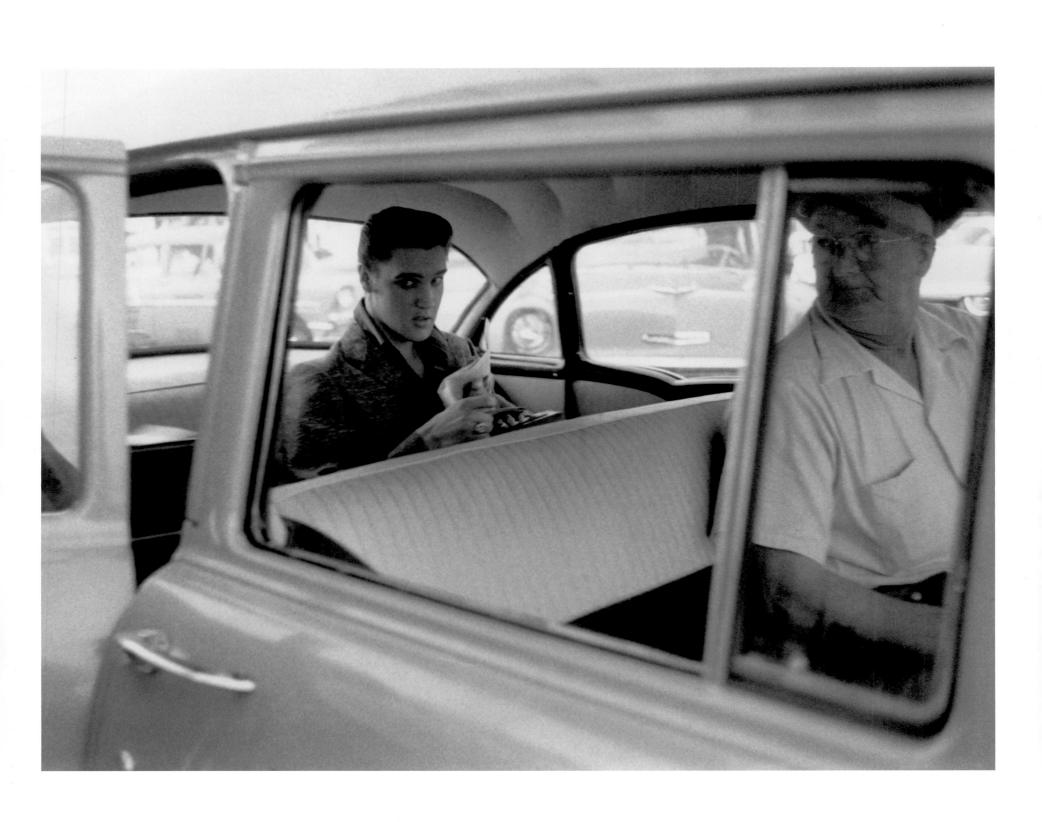

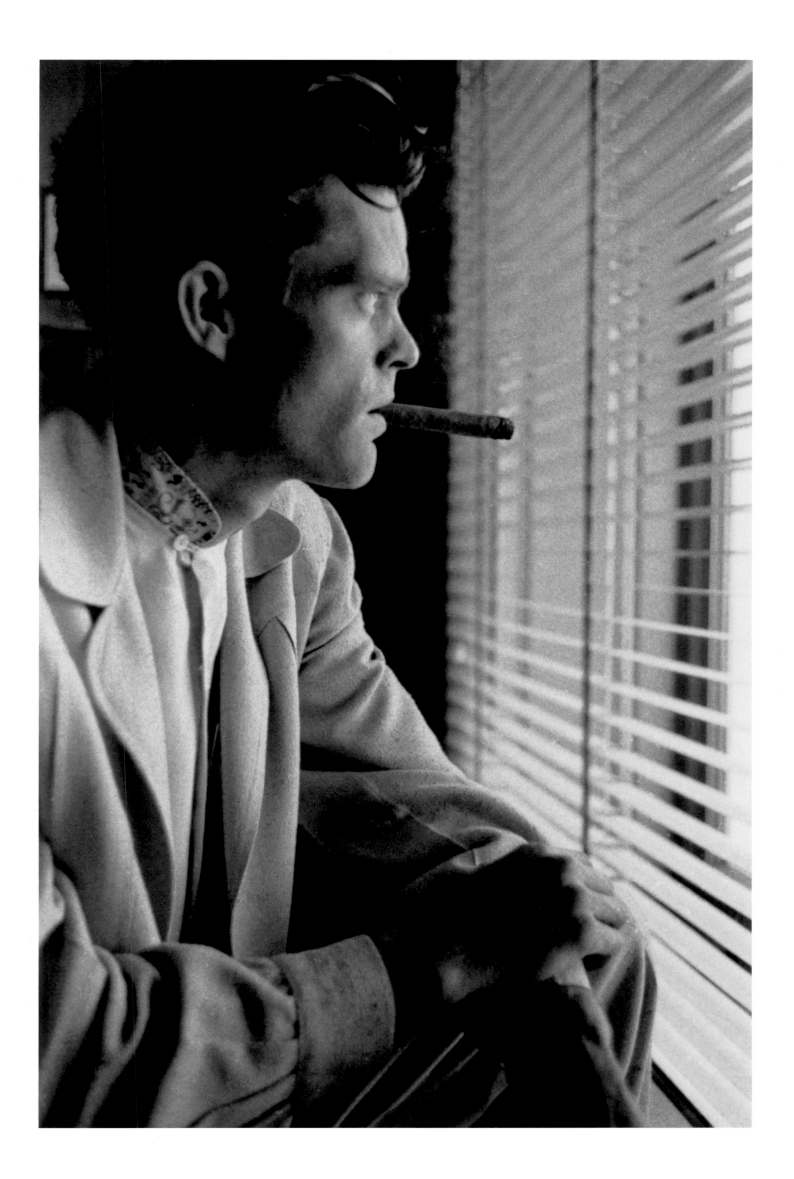

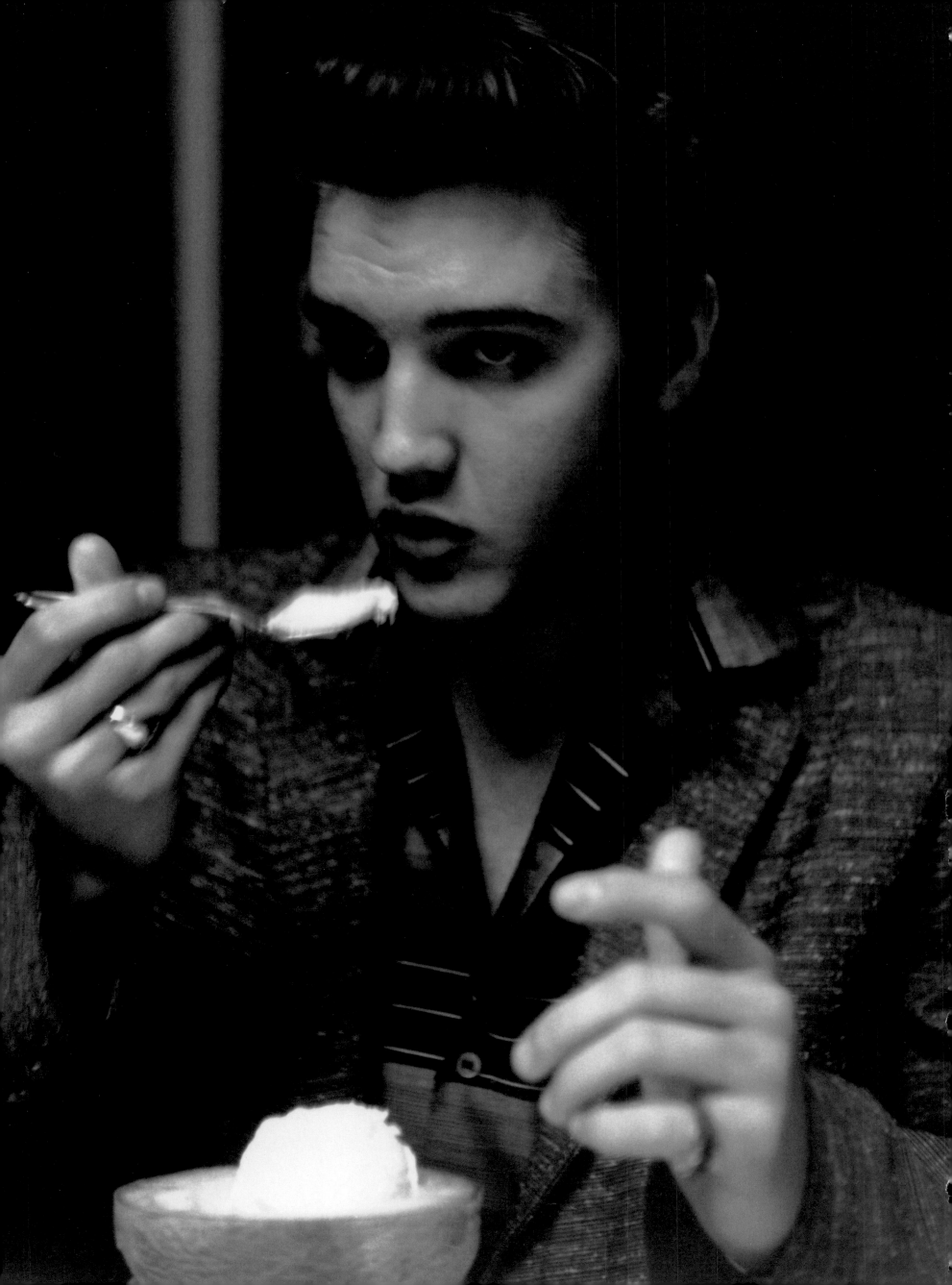

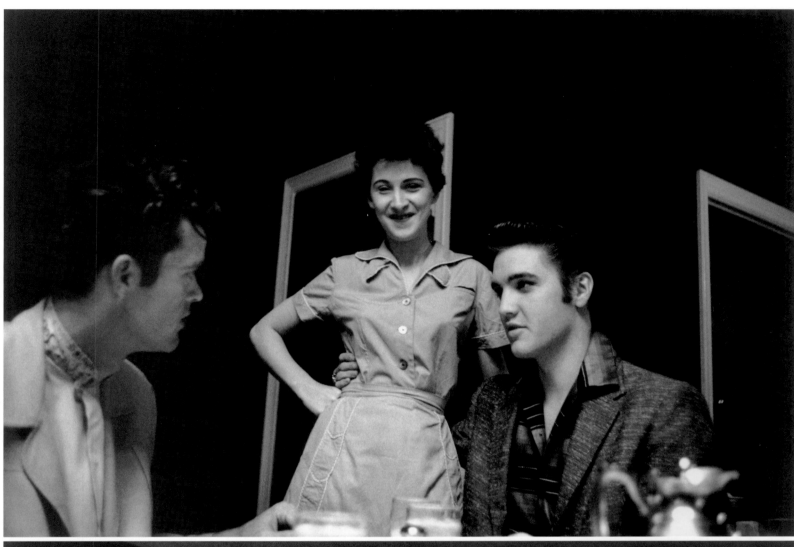
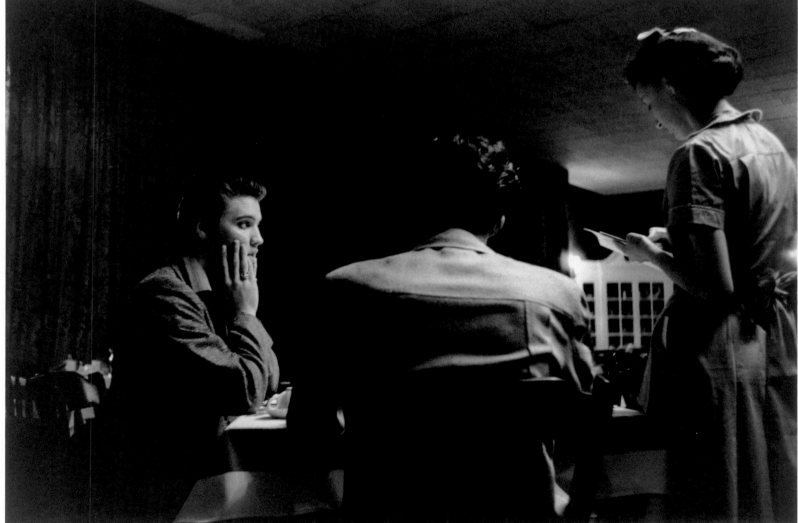

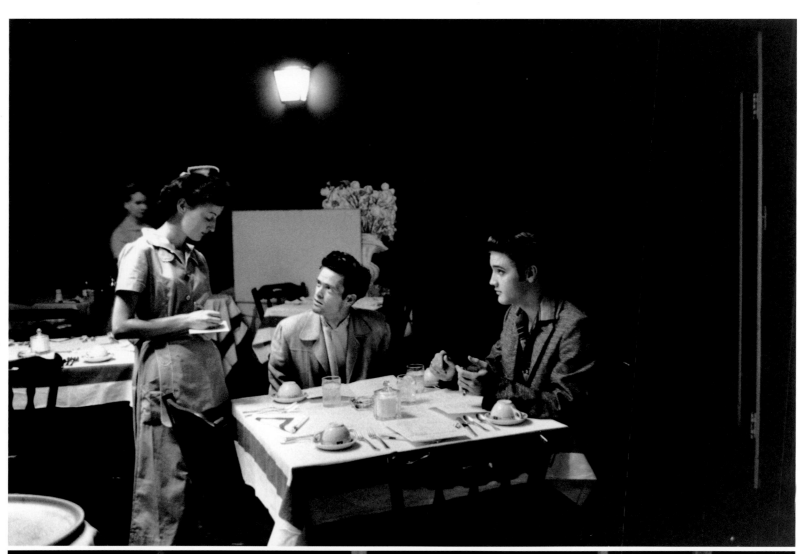

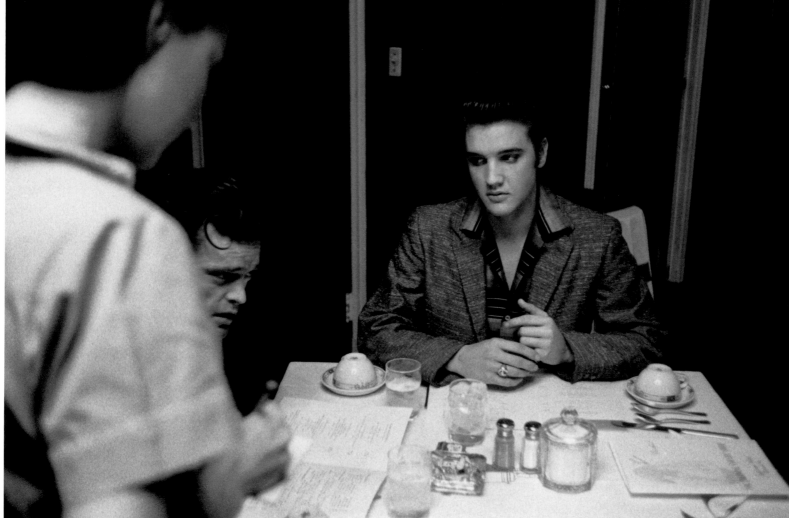

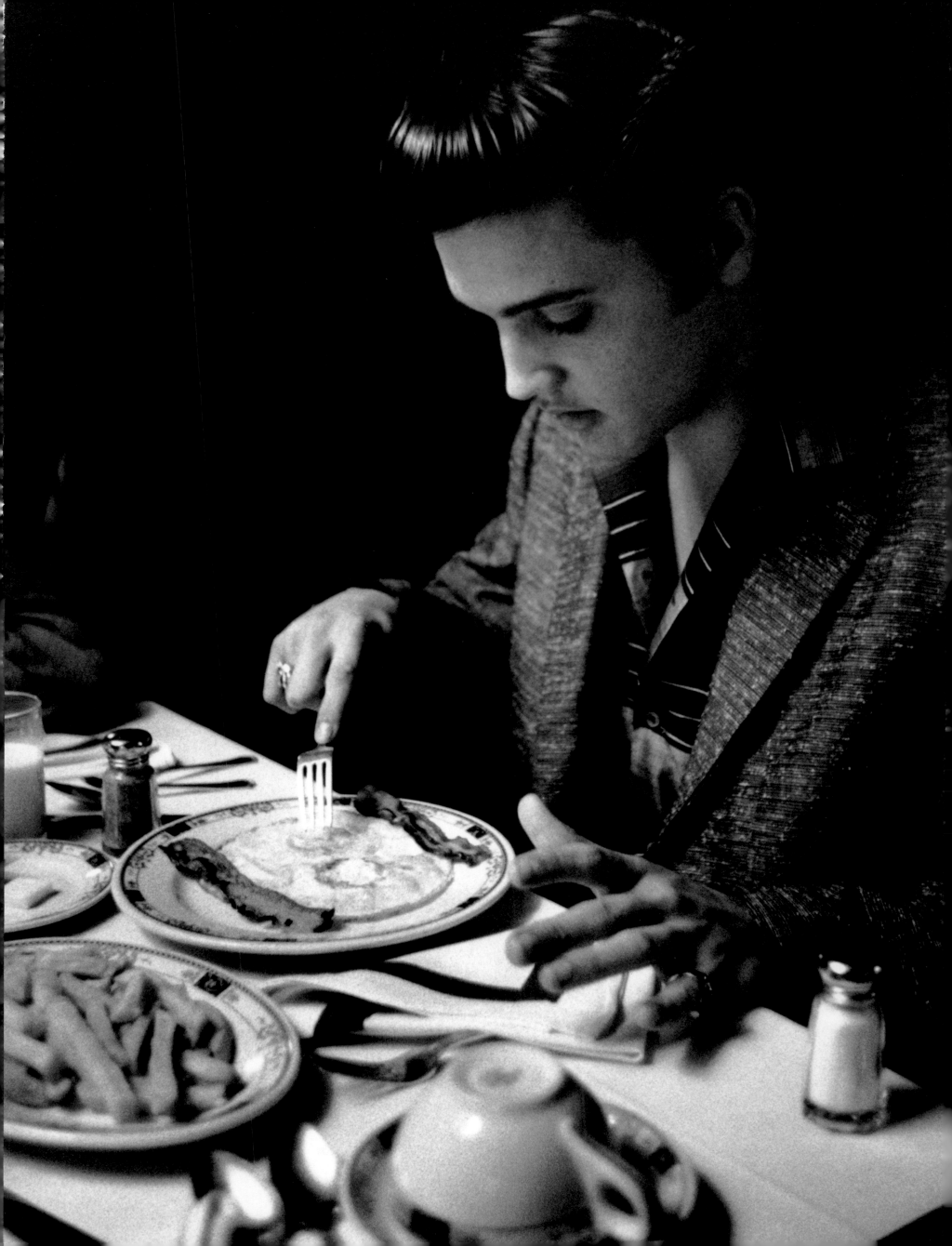

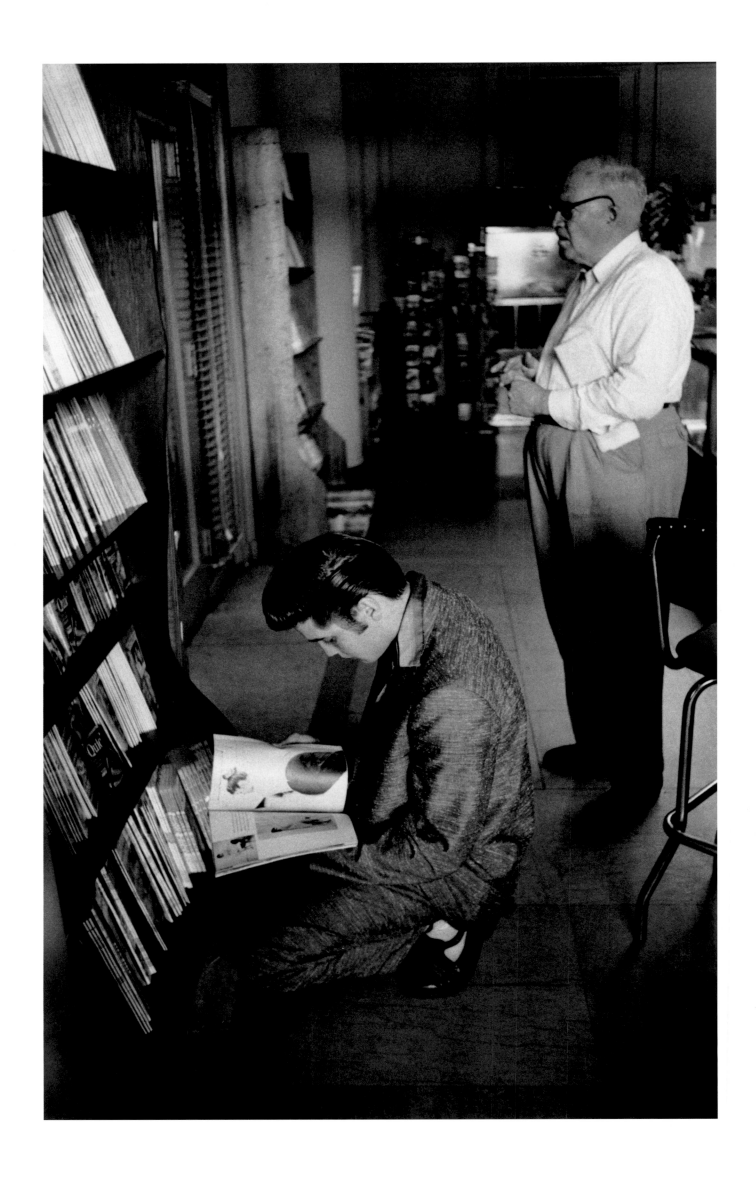

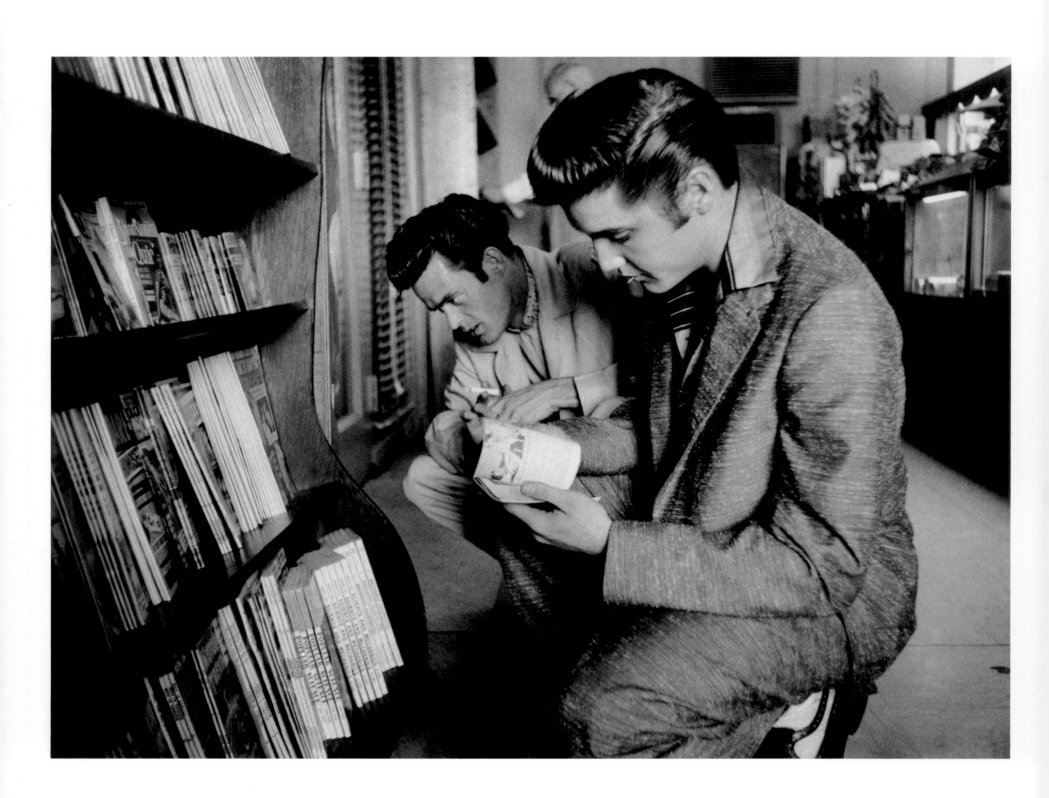

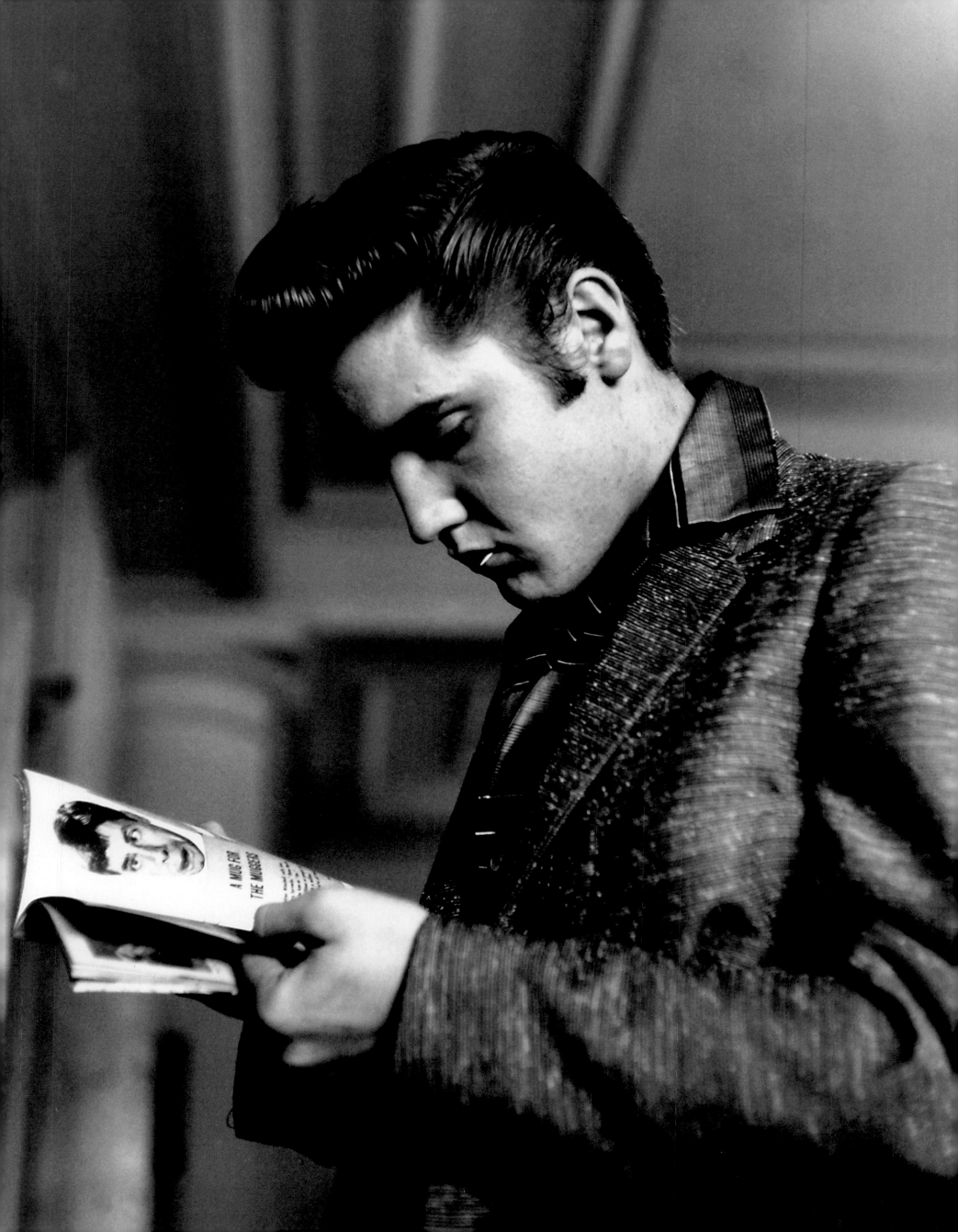

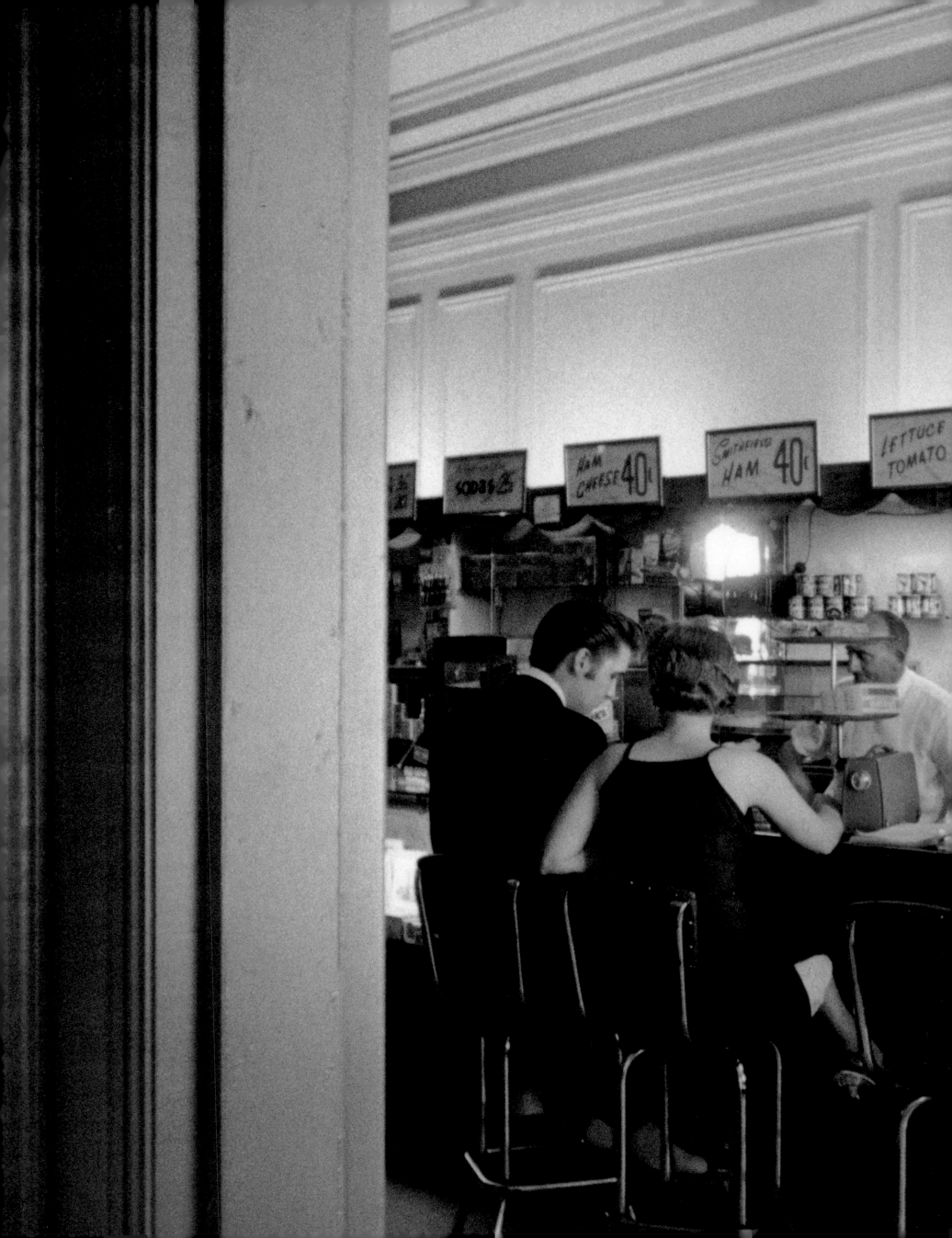

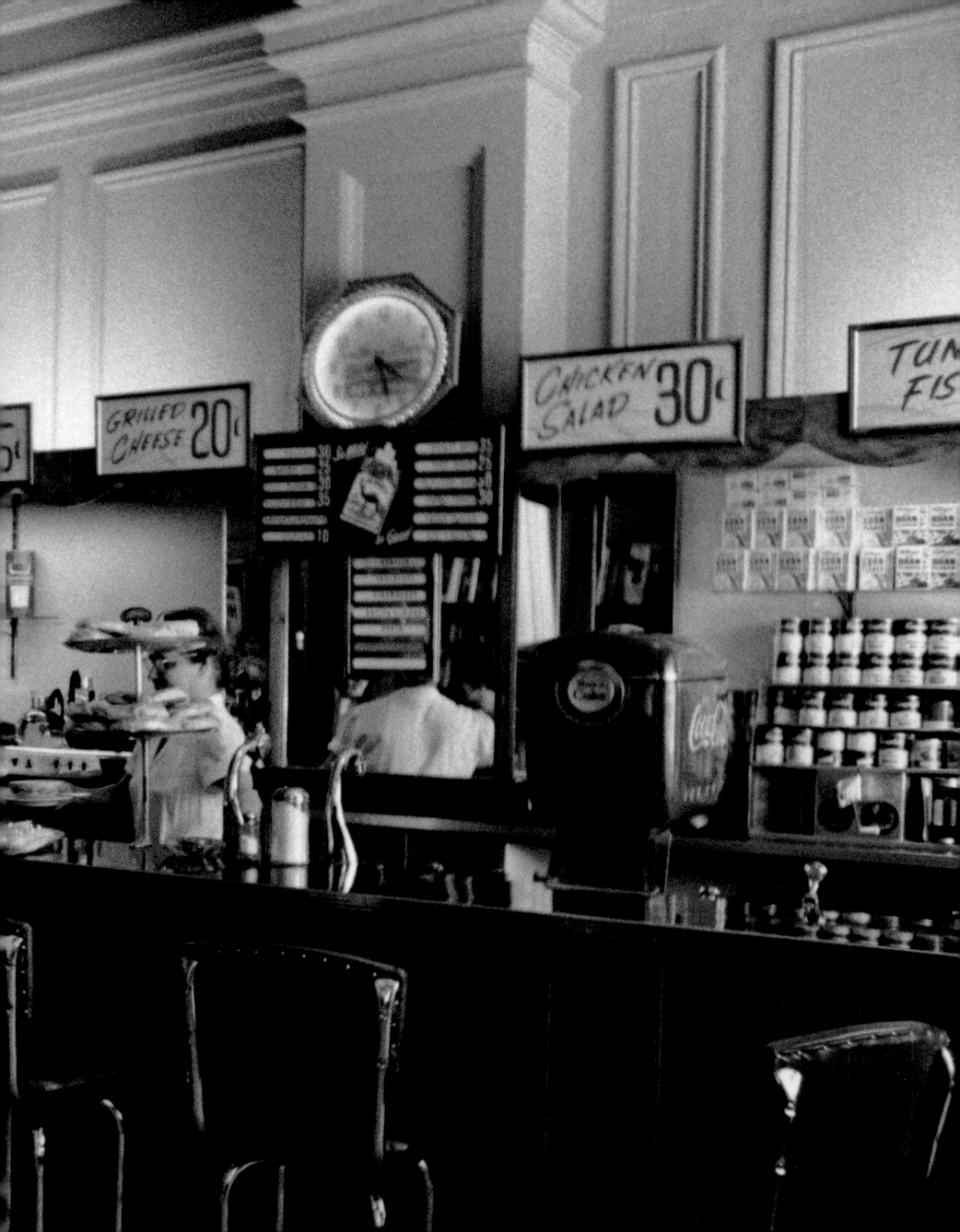

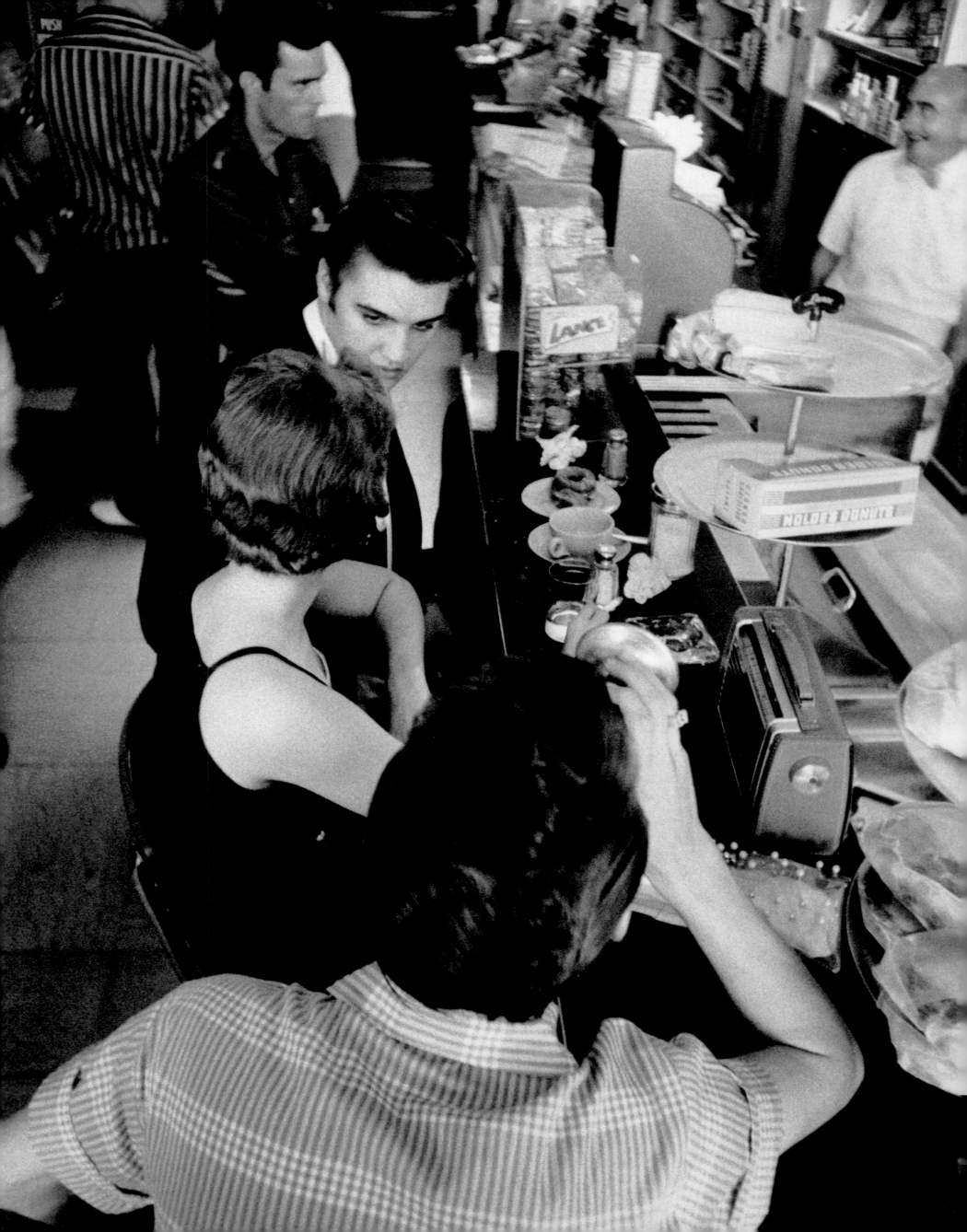

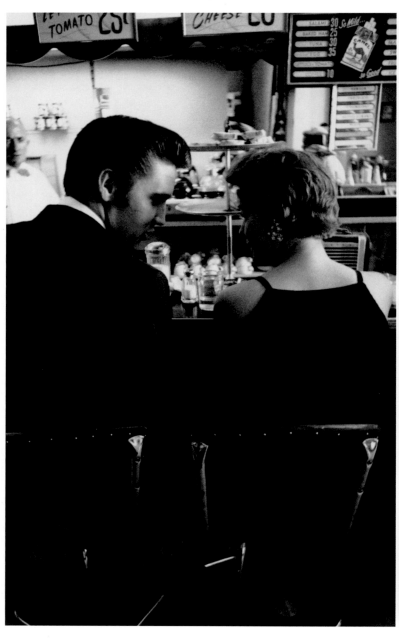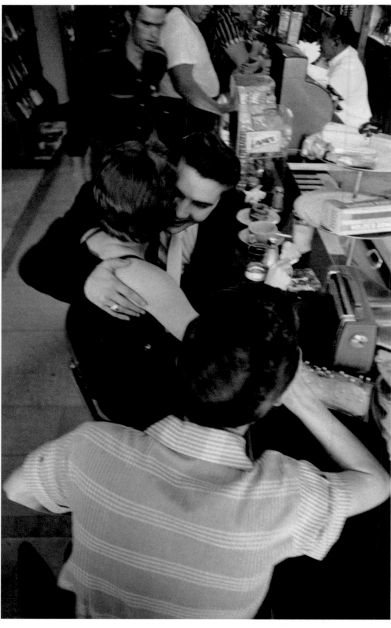

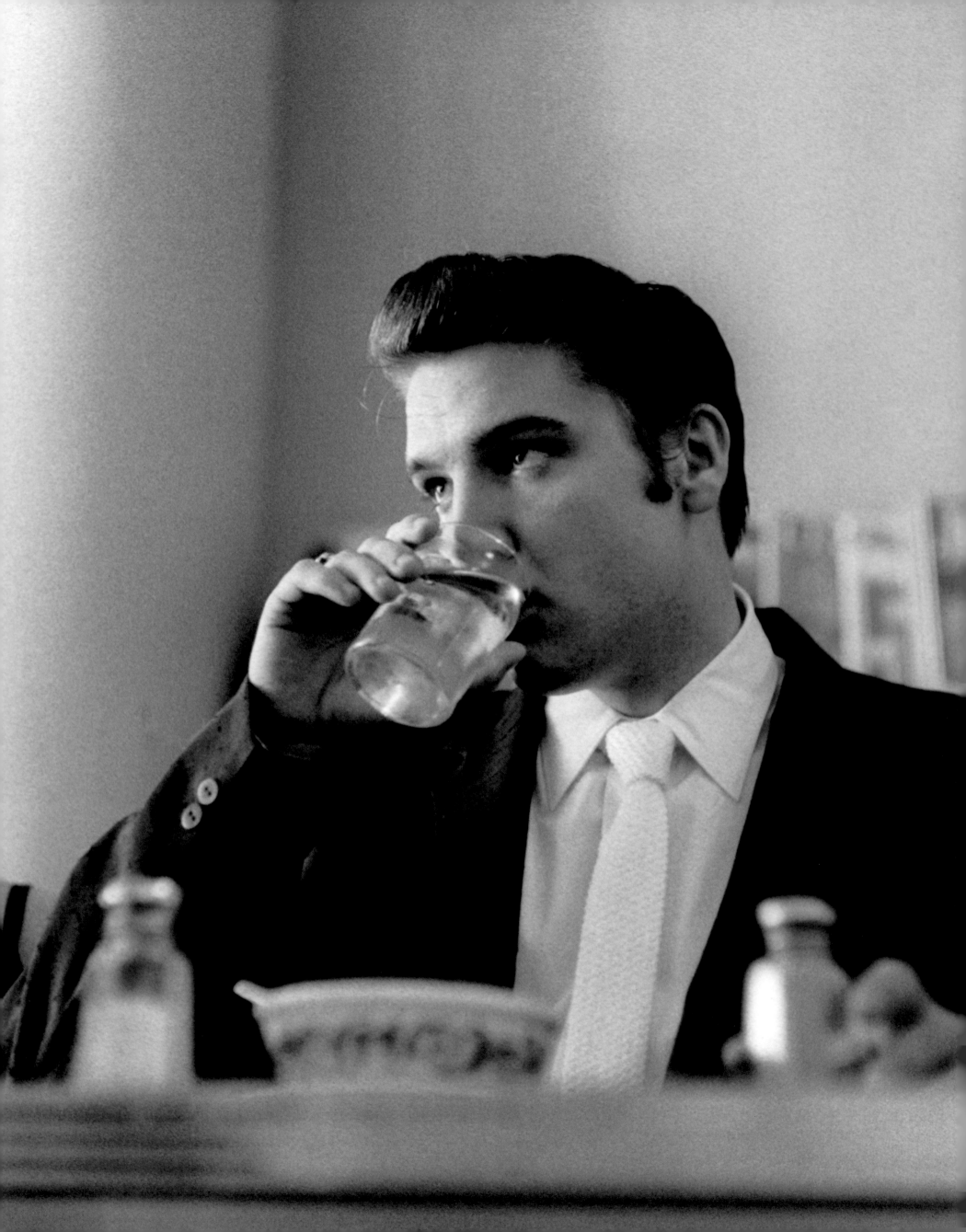

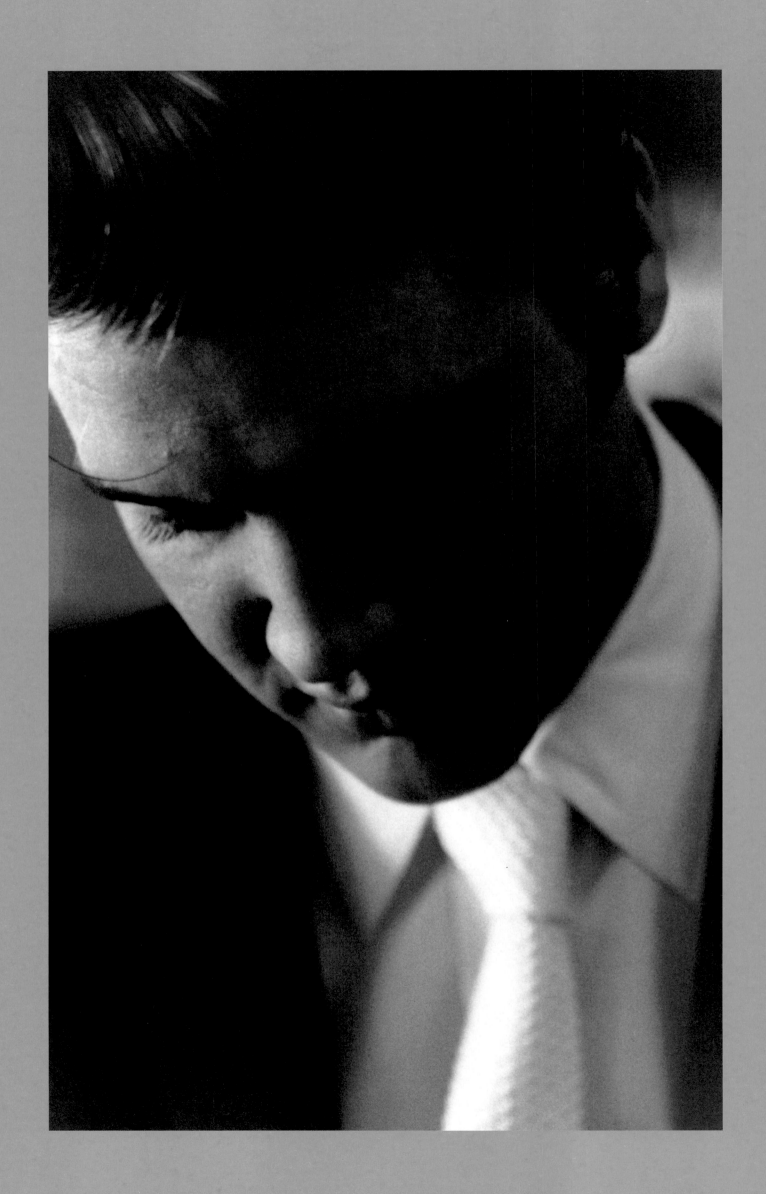

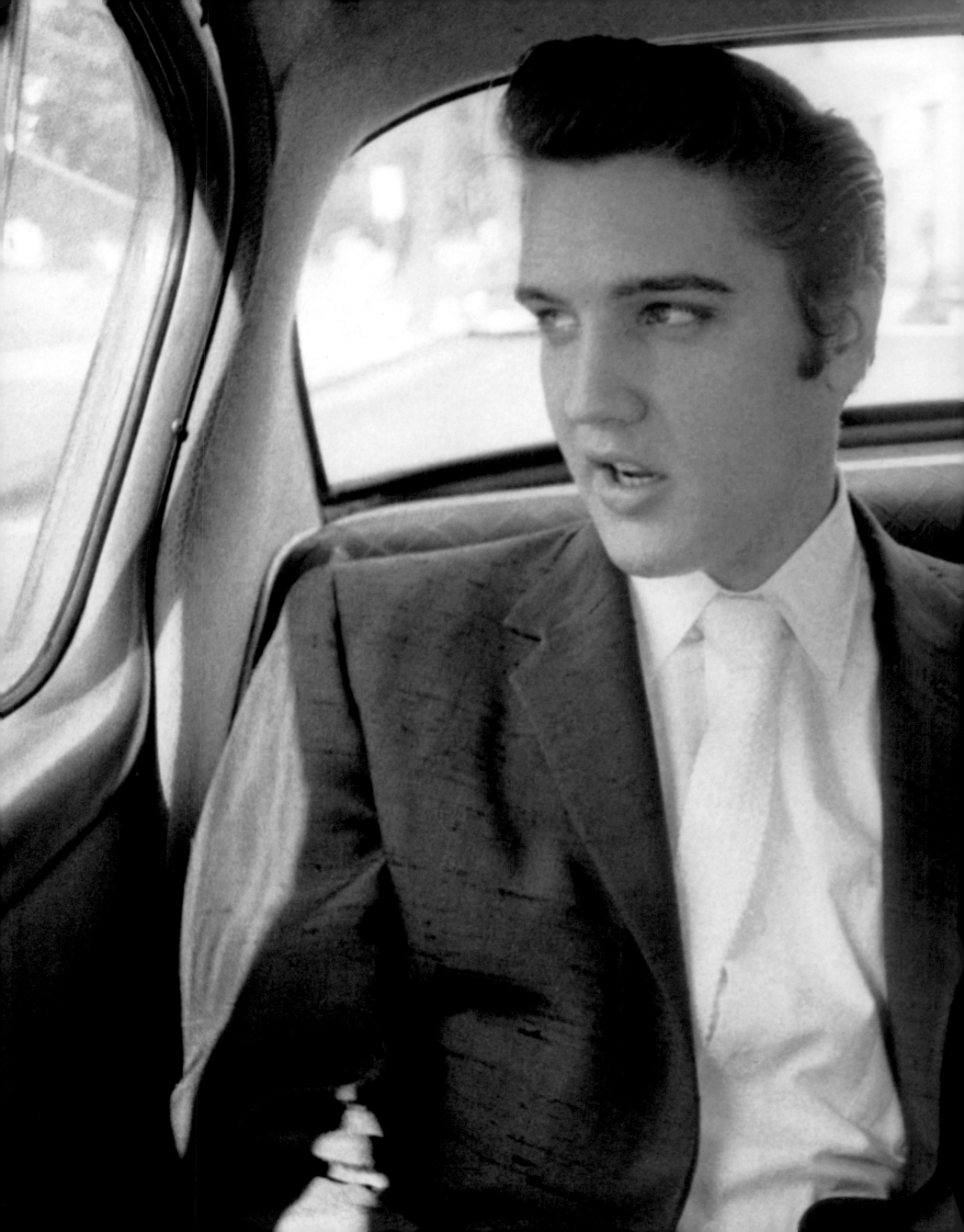

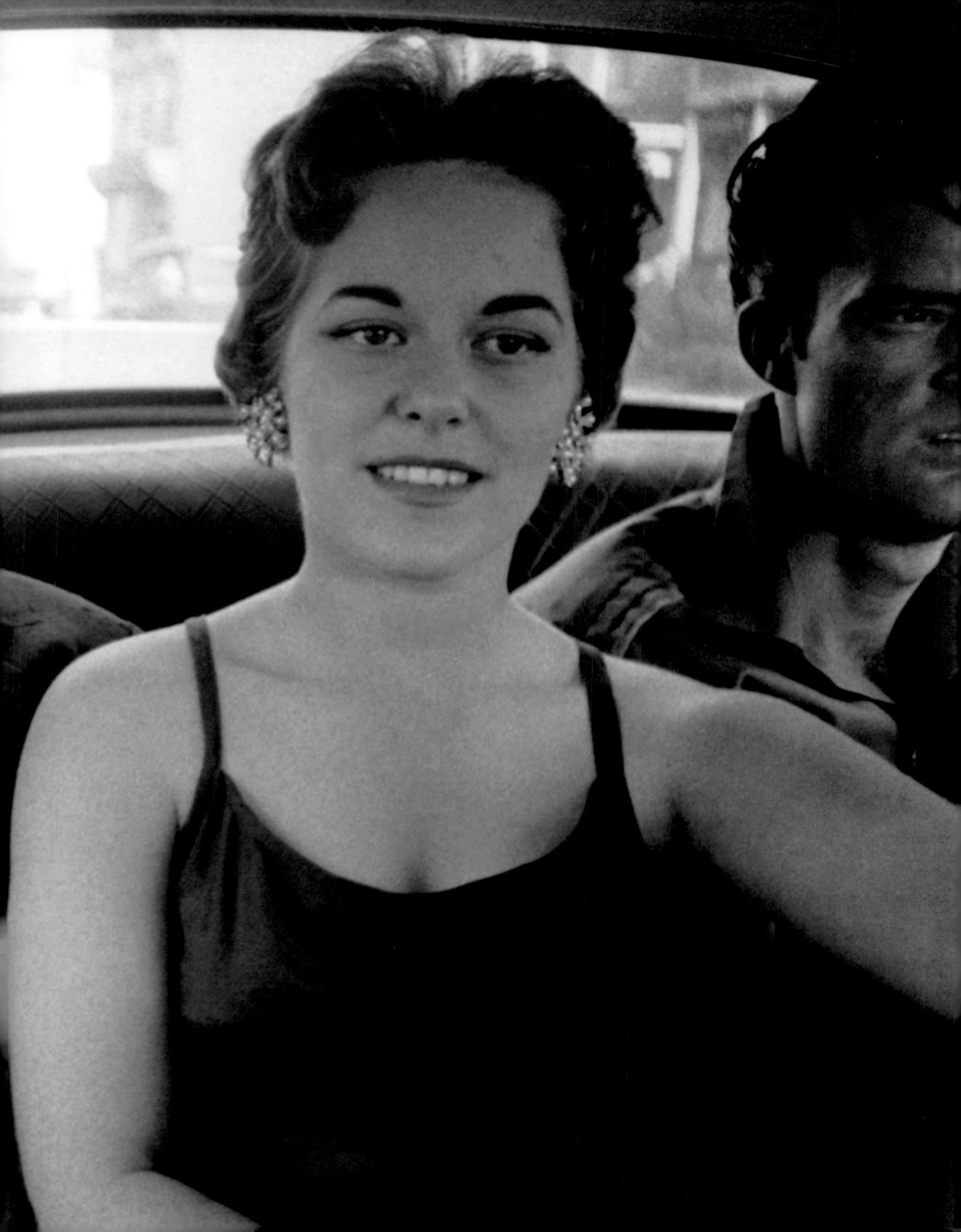

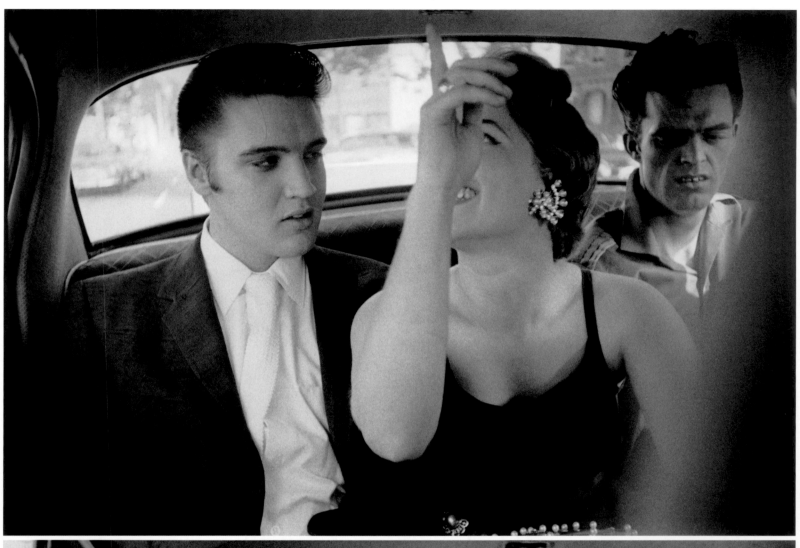

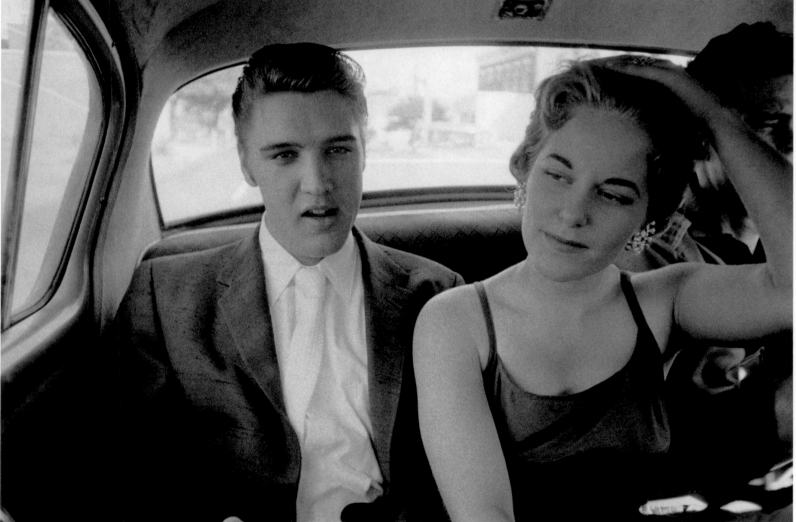

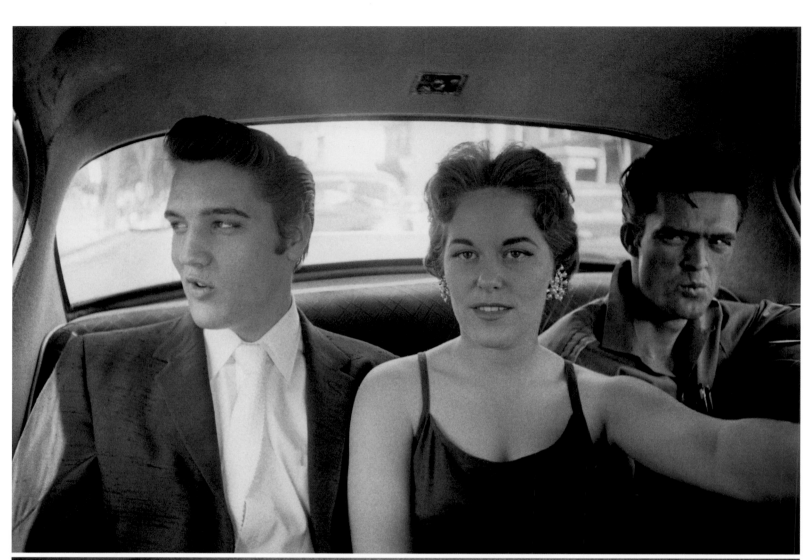

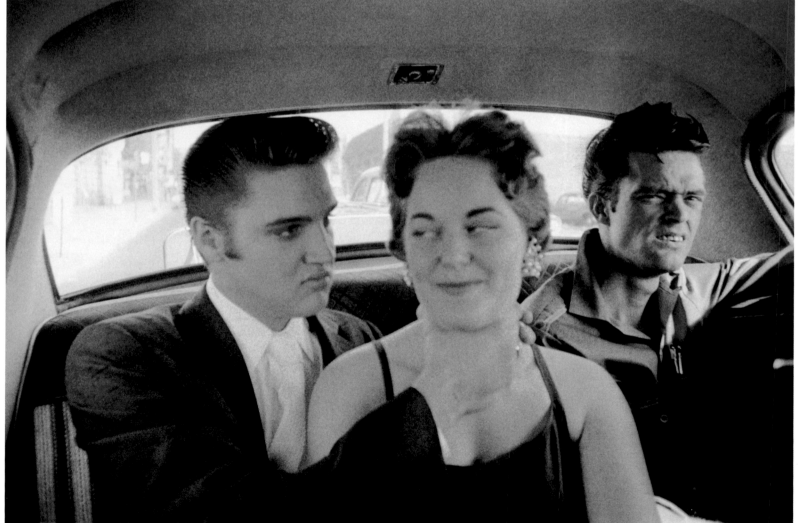

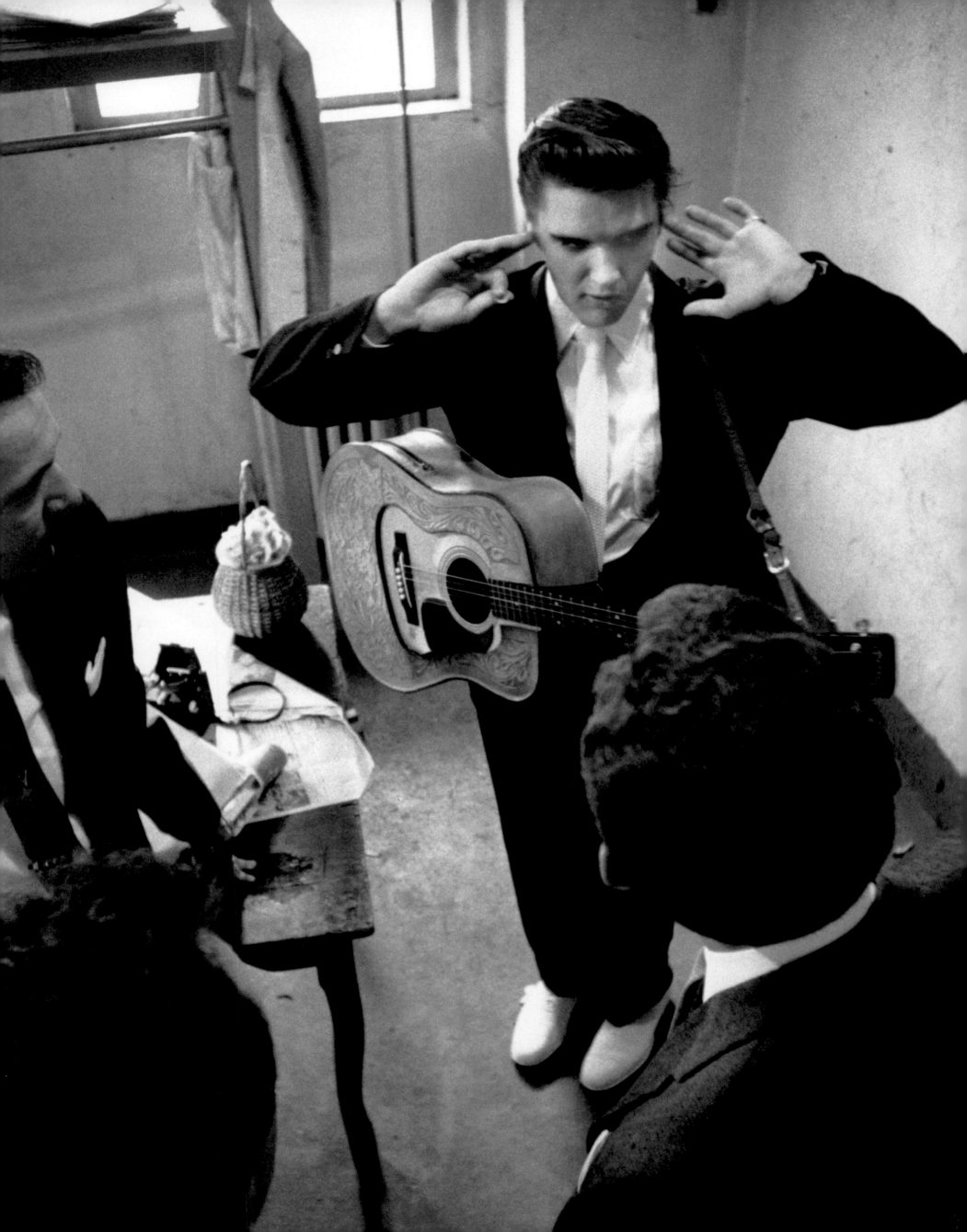

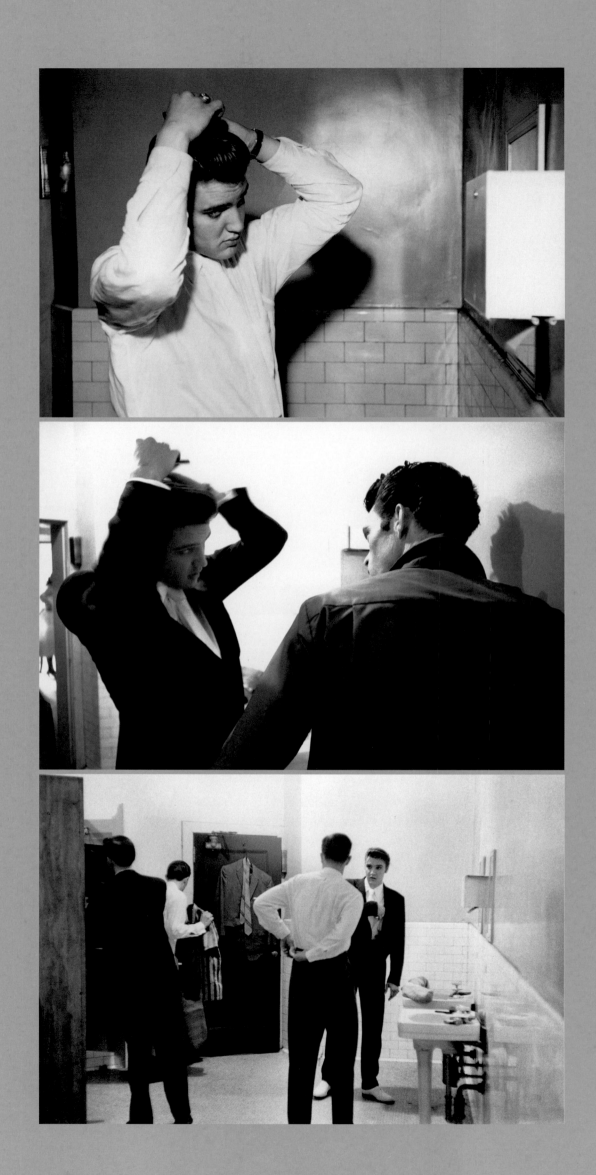

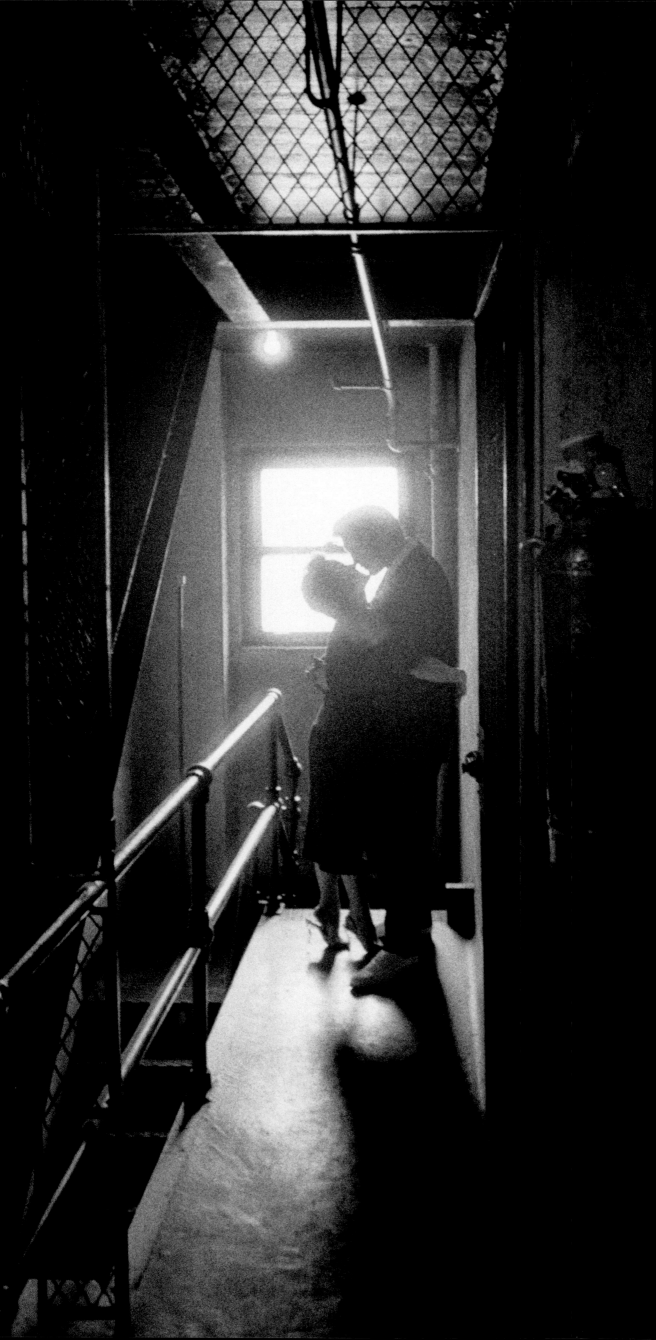

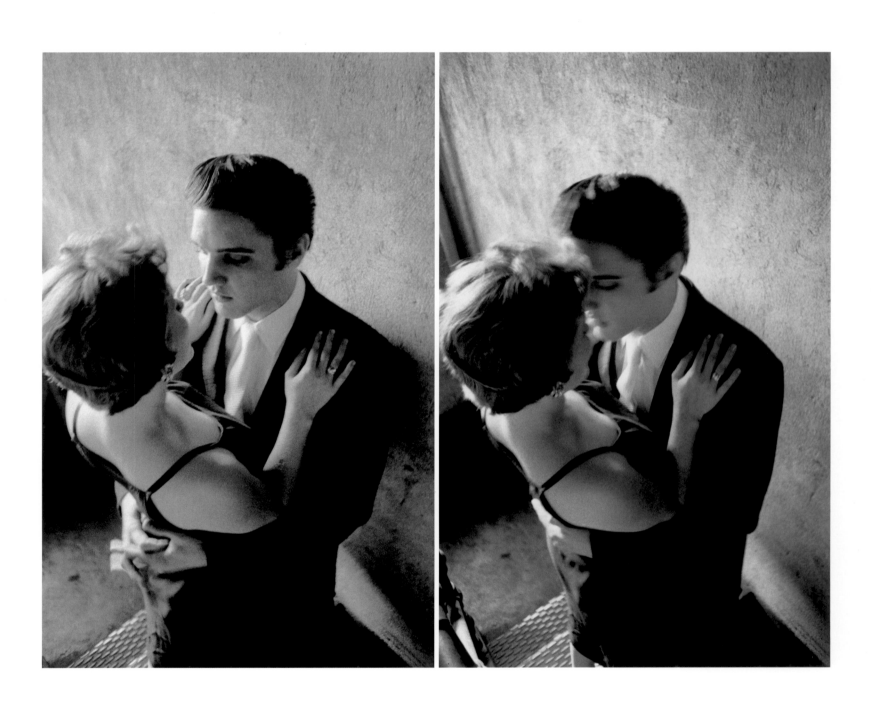

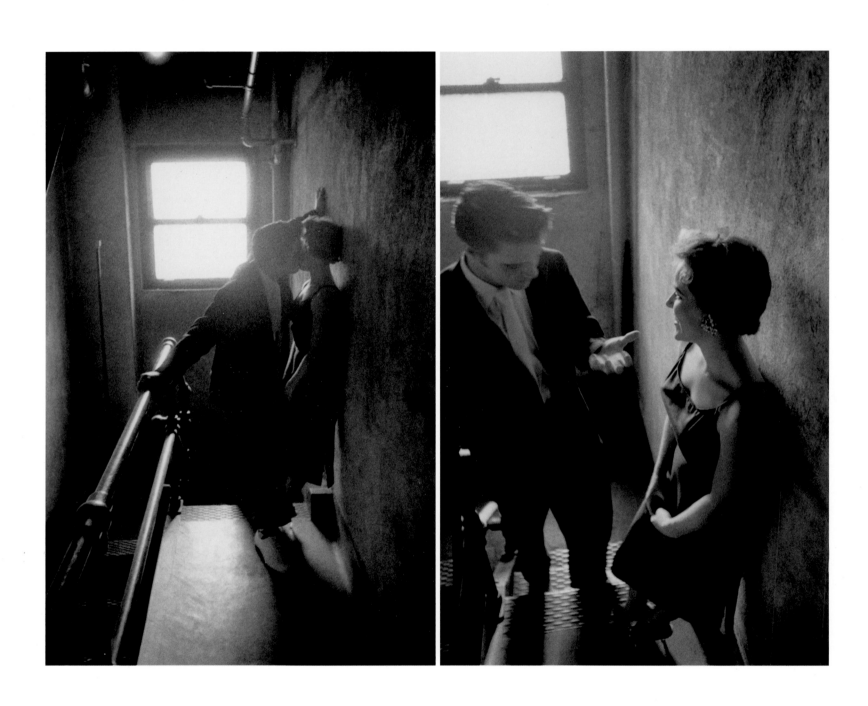

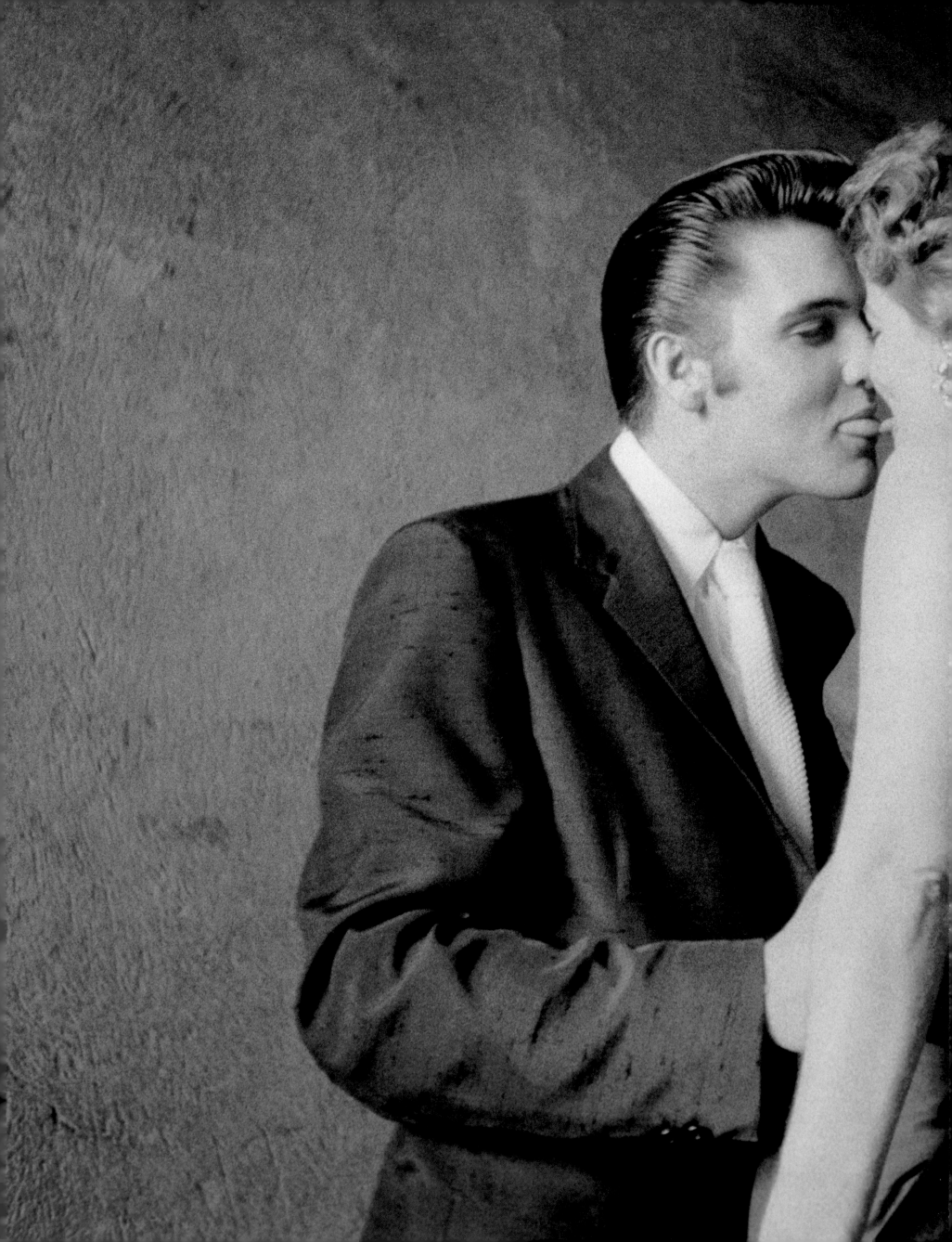

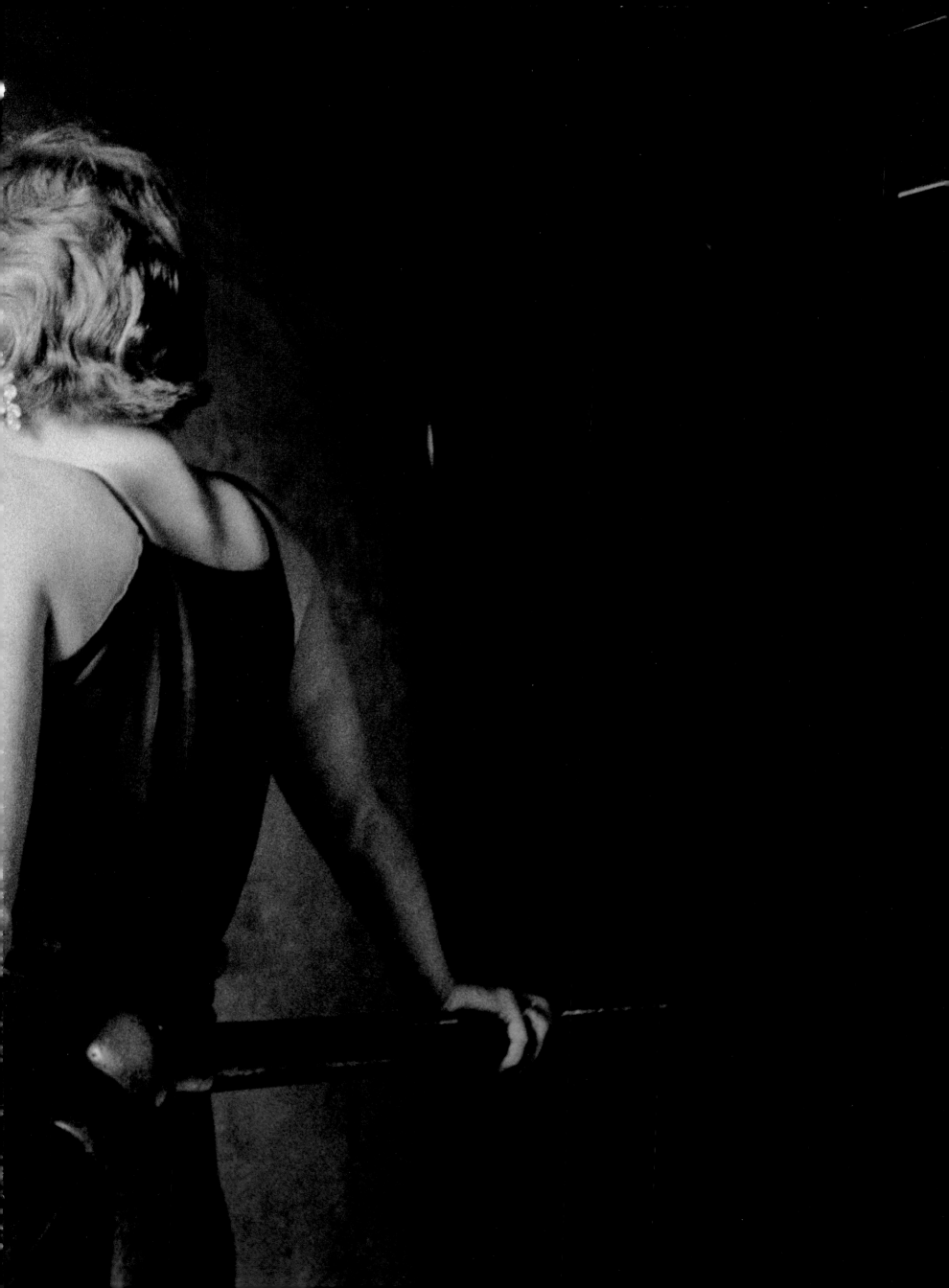

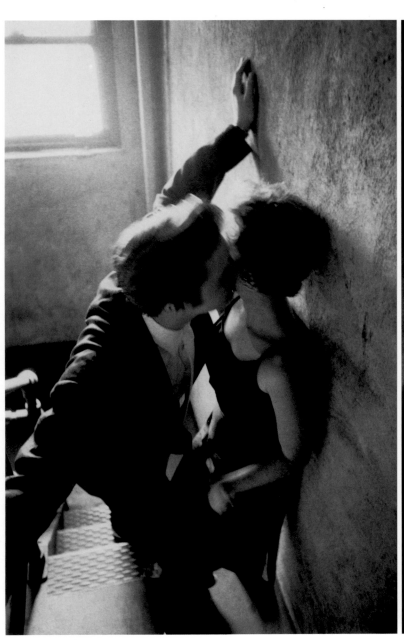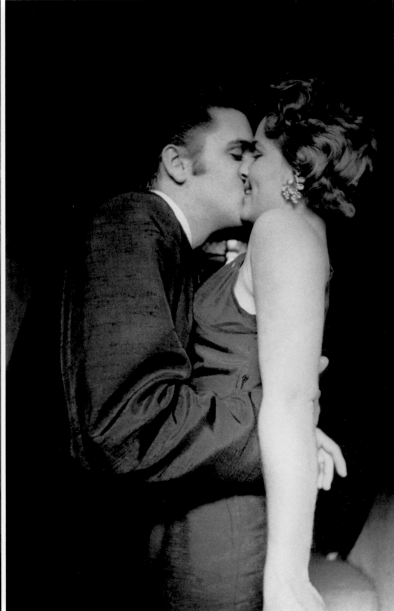

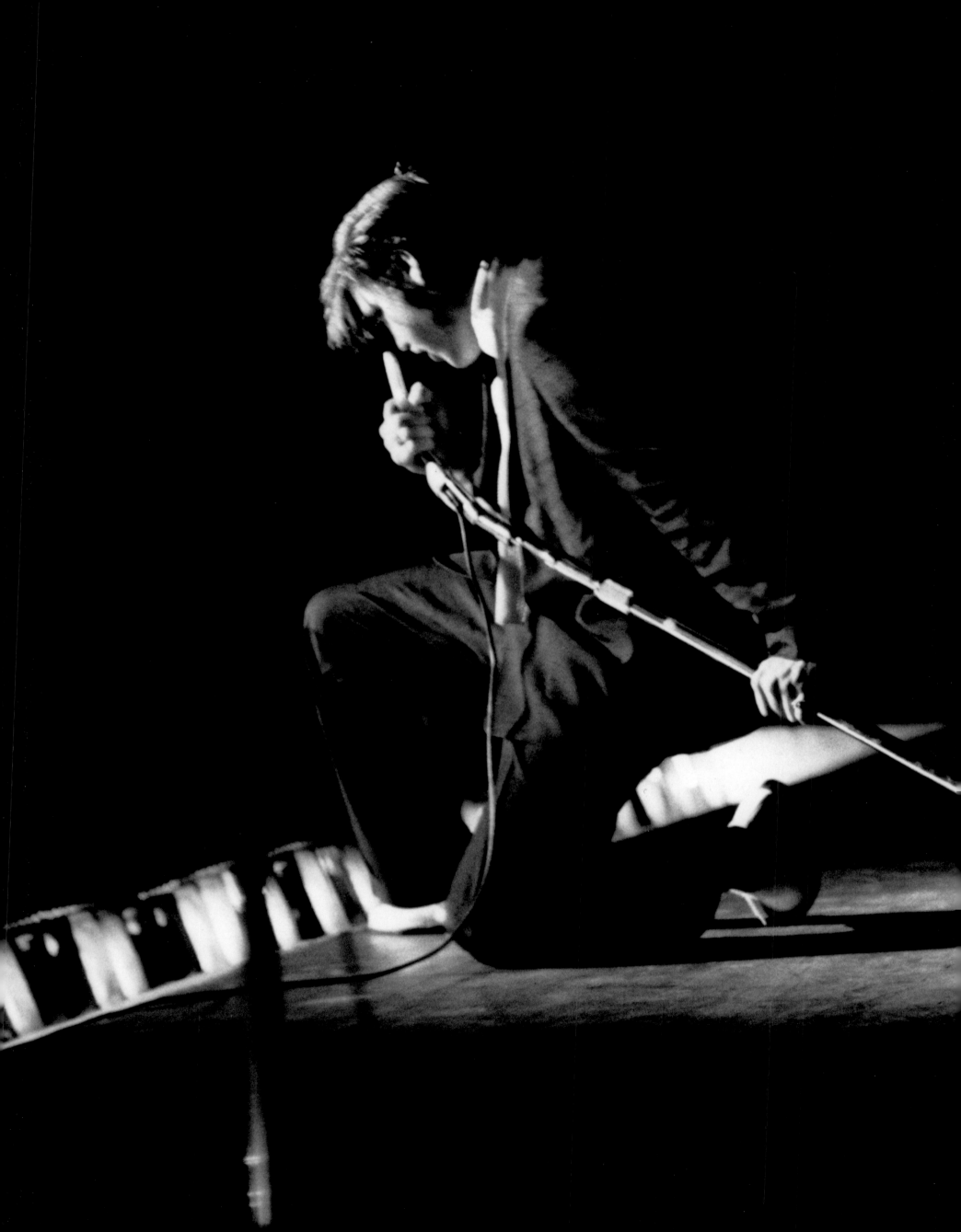

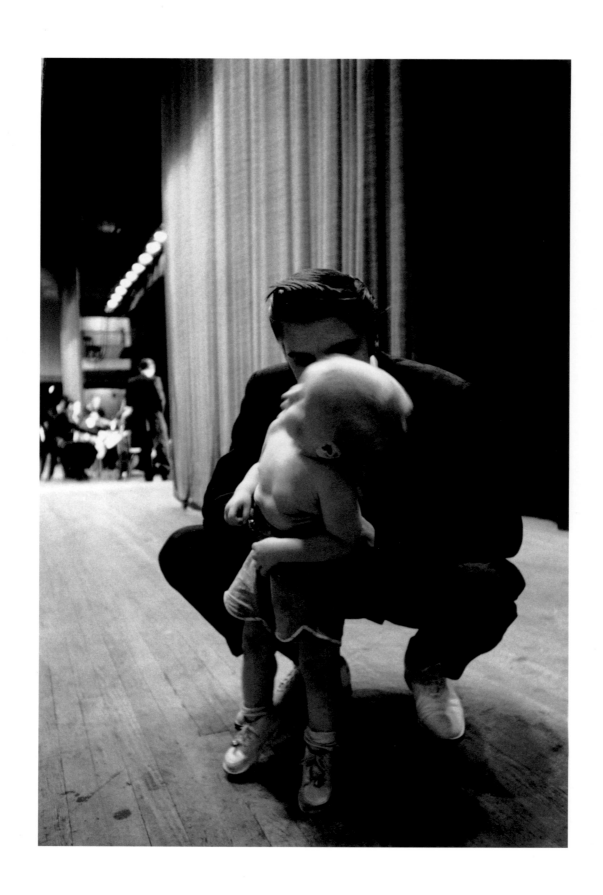

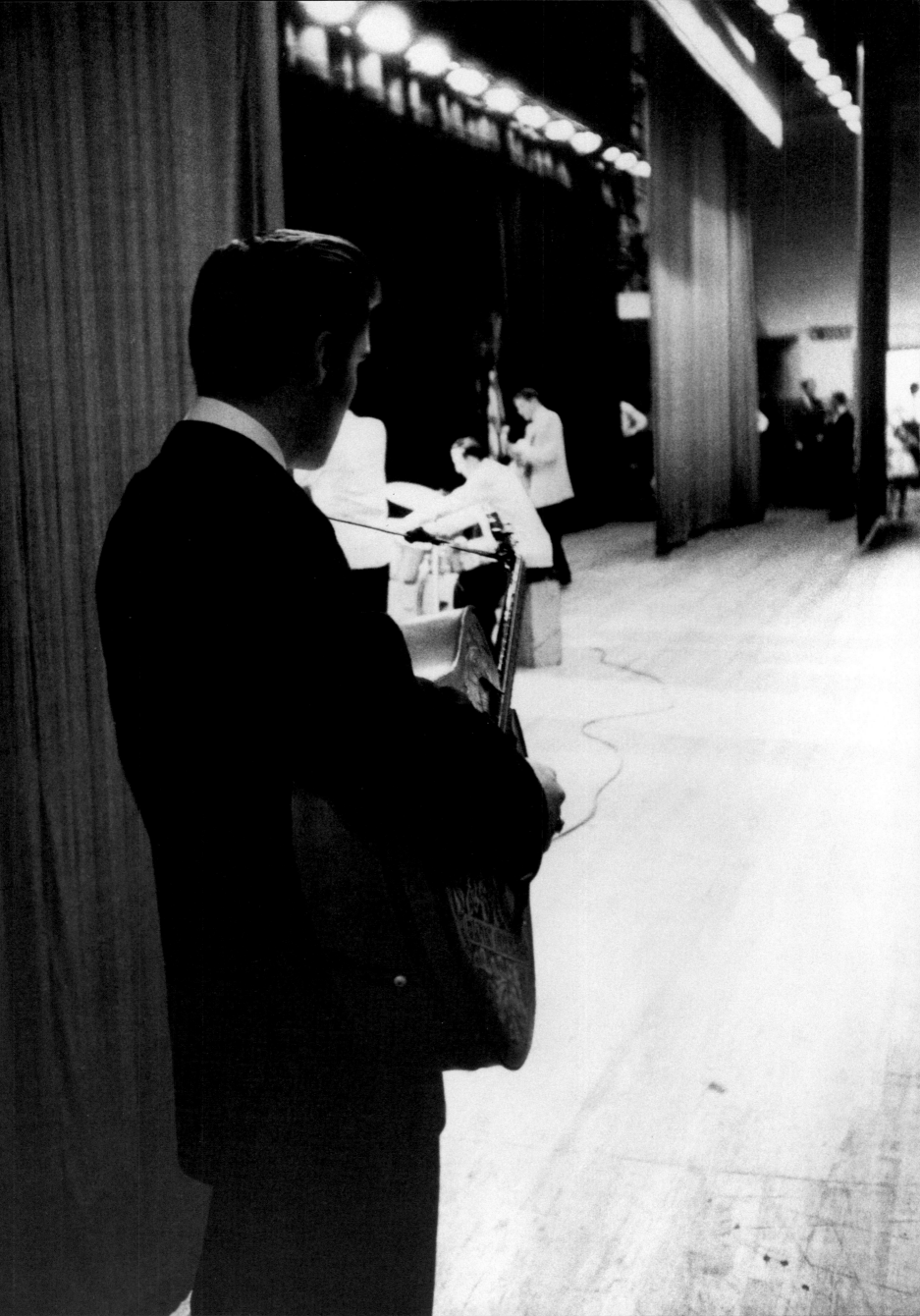

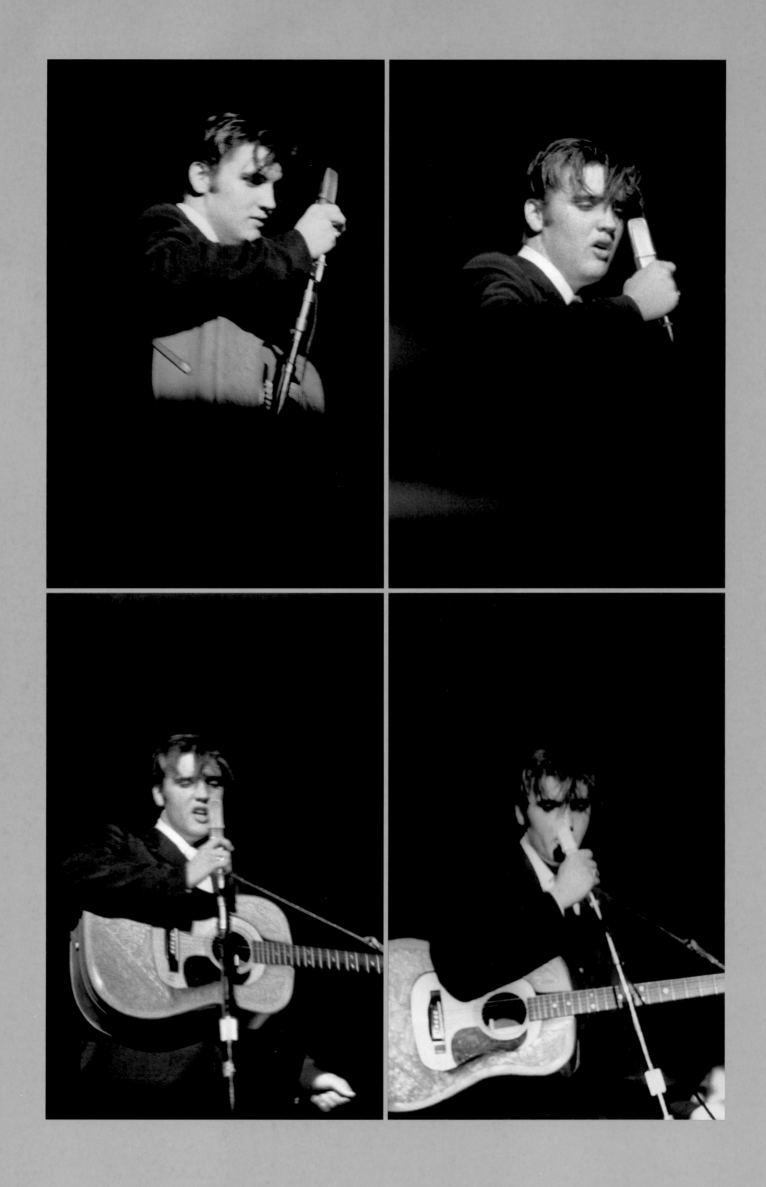

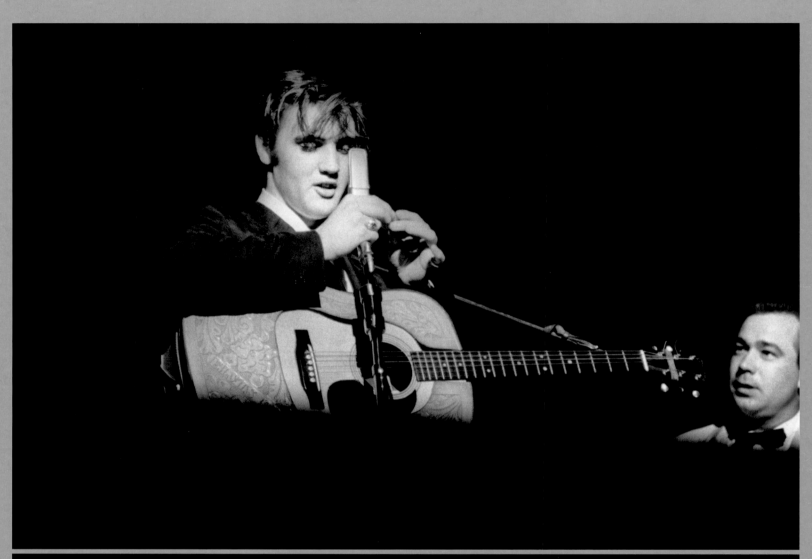

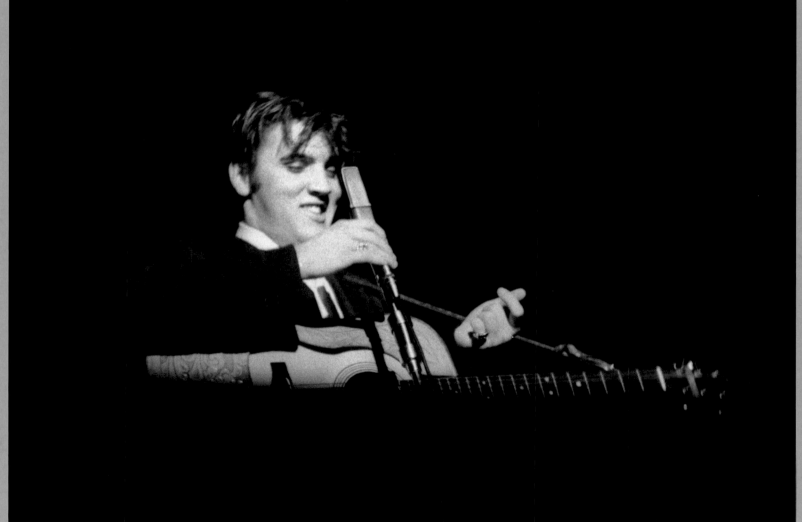

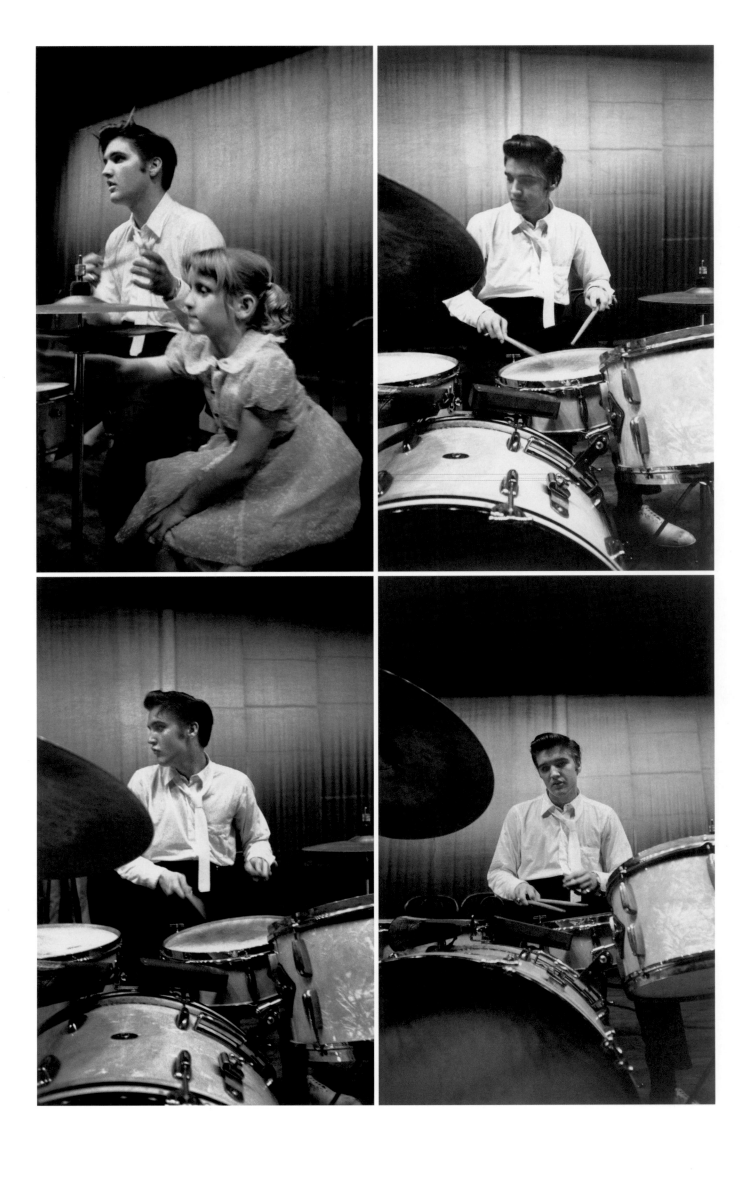

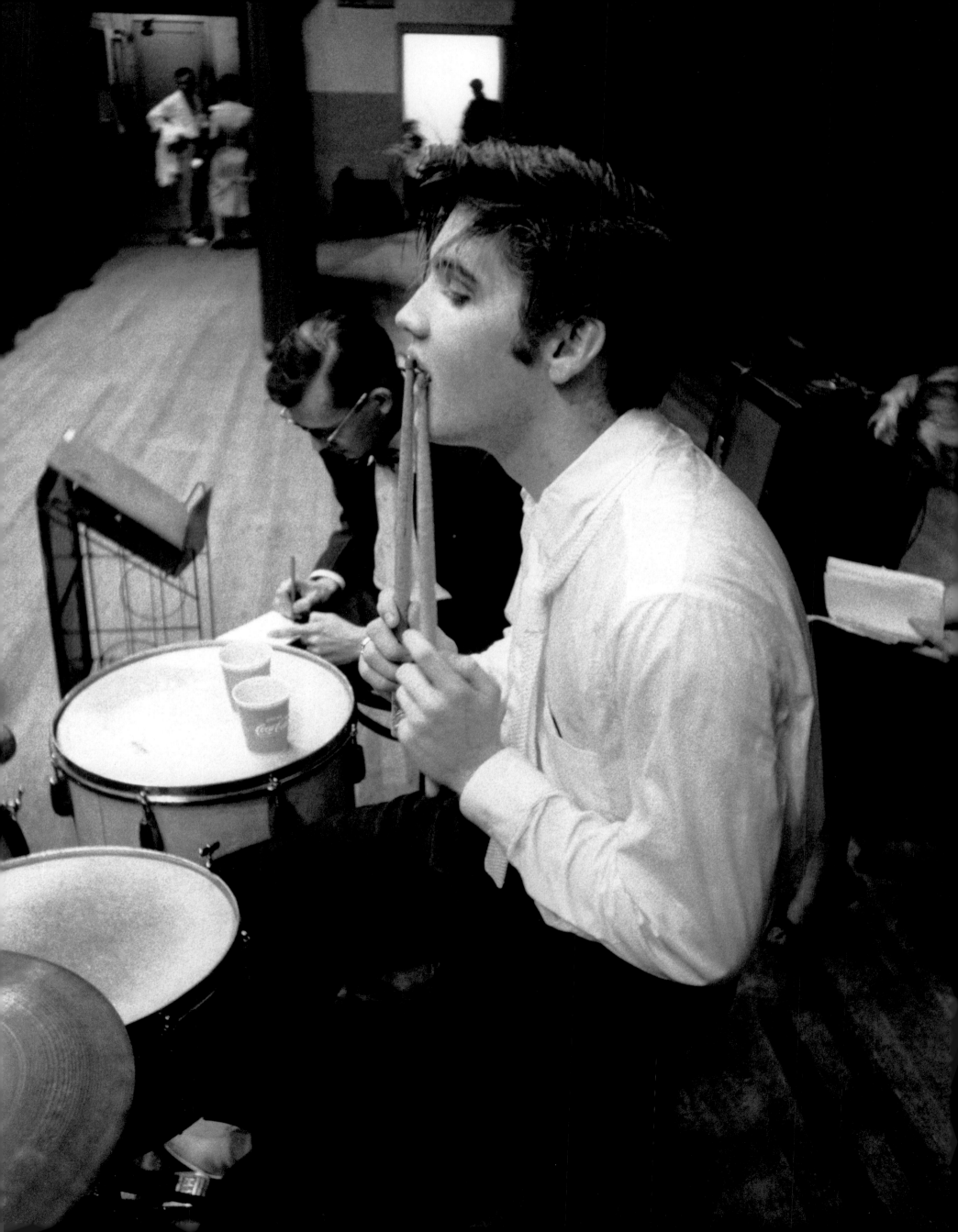

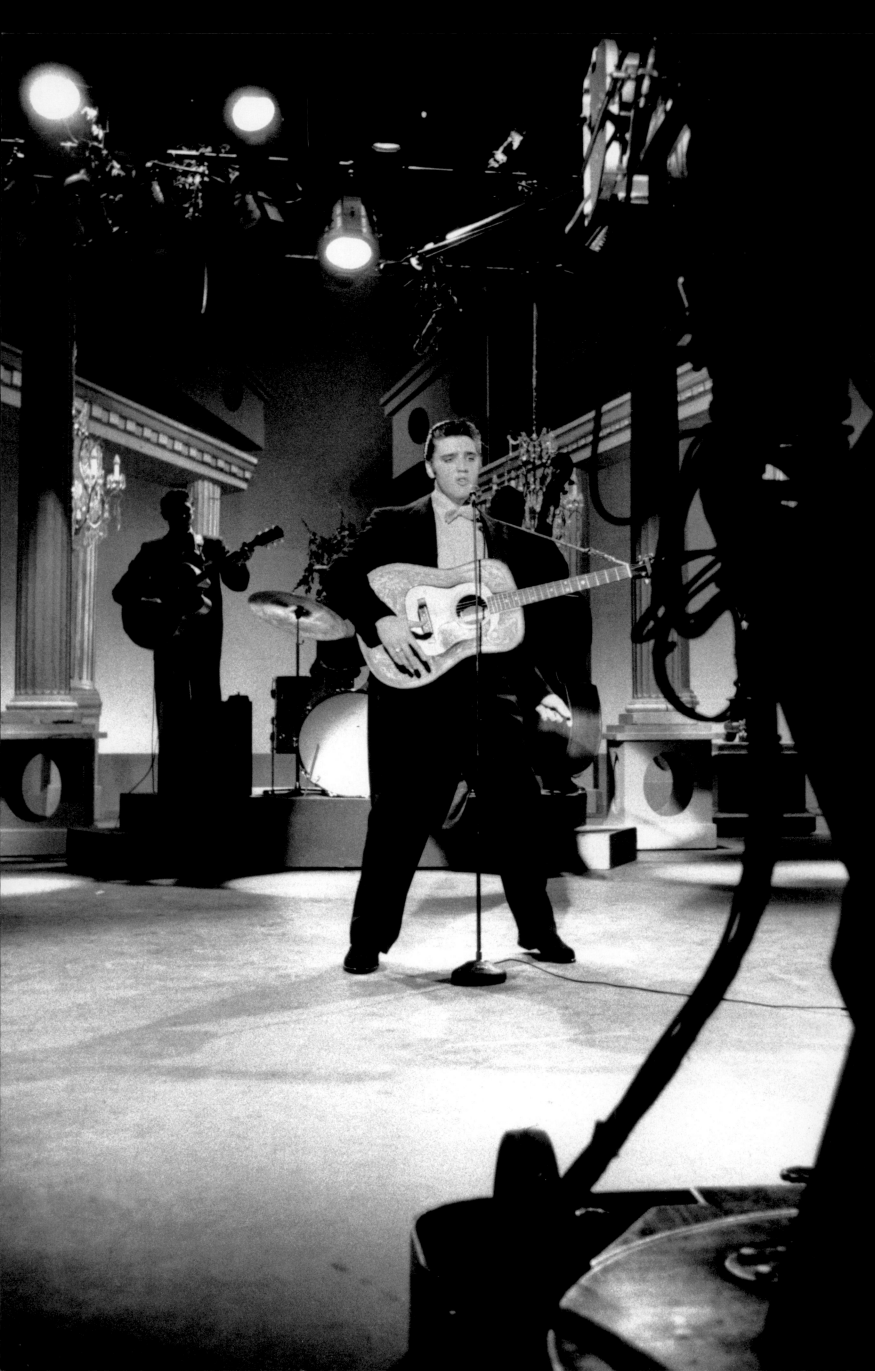

Chapter IV

HUDSON THEATER
New York City

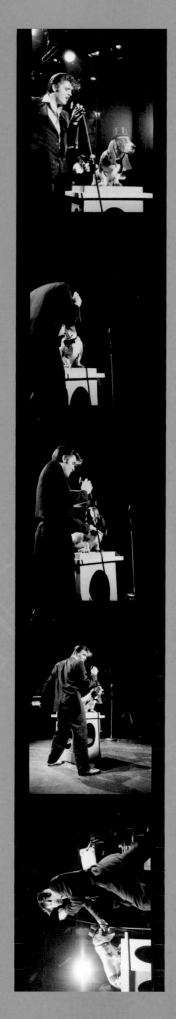

HUDSON THEATER
New York City

T HE TRAIN COMING UP NORTH WAS A SLOW ONE, but we finally arrived in New York on July 1st. Elvis, Scotty, DJ, and Bill Black, along with the Colonel, Tom Diskin, and myself, got off at Penn Station around seven-thirty in the morning. Passing a newspaper stand, Elvis saw a headline about 127 people killed in an airplane crash. Two planes had collided over the Grand Canyon in the largest air disaster ever in the United States at the time. Elvis picked up a copy of the *Sunday Mirror*, which had pictures of two of the stewardesses on the cover, and was completely preoccupied with this story. He walked through the station totally oblivious to everything else that was going on around him.

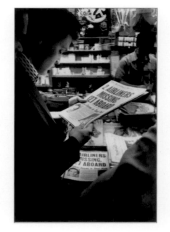

The guys followed him out, with a porter bringing all of the luggage and the musical equipment. Elvis continued reading all the way through the concourse to the taxi stand while Bill Black and DJ worried about finding cabs to the Hudson Theater. Even as we loaded up, Elvis was still reading. Junior was holding his guitar case and smoking, filling the back seat with billows of cigarette smoke. The scene brought to my mind a story Ann Fulchino told me. Apparently, Elvis had had a near-death experience in April when the plane he was in hit an air pocket and dropped about 10,000 feet before it grabbed hold again. He didn't trust planes and preferred traveling by ground until much later, when he could afford to buy his own plane and hire his own pilot.

As Elvis, Tom Diskin, Junior, and I got out of the cab in midtown Manhattan, we were greeted by a girl in a white dress and her father. Her father had brought her into the city from Long Island. A devoted Elvis fan, she was elated when he arrived. All dressed in white as if she were going to a prom or wedding, she had waited for quite some time. Elvis took her hand in his and I took some pictures. Holding her hand tightly, Elvis looked into her eyes and listened to her story. Her father stood a few feet away. Junior was busy dragging out the guitar case and collecting the now forgotten newspaper. Somebody, not Elvis of course, took care of paying the cabbie. Those 127 people moved to the back of his mind as he told her some beautiful things that she wanted to hear. Then he said, "I've got to go now. I have rehearsal," and disappeared into the Hudson Theater. Everyone else went in but I kept my camera on her. I continued shooting as she broke down and started to cry. There was no one else outside the theater. Later on, at the end of the show, about a hundred girls showed up and had to be held back by metal gates and cops. But this was just one girl having one of the most special moments of her life.

❧

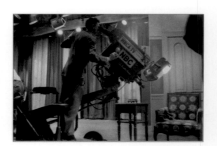

I nside this large theater, there was the normal confusion with stagehands running around. Elvis took a seat somewhere near the back with a few of his people next to him. Other personalities from *The Steve Allen Show* and the local NBC photographer with his camera were also back there. Steve Allen stood in the middle of the aisle, giving everyone a pep talk and explaining how the

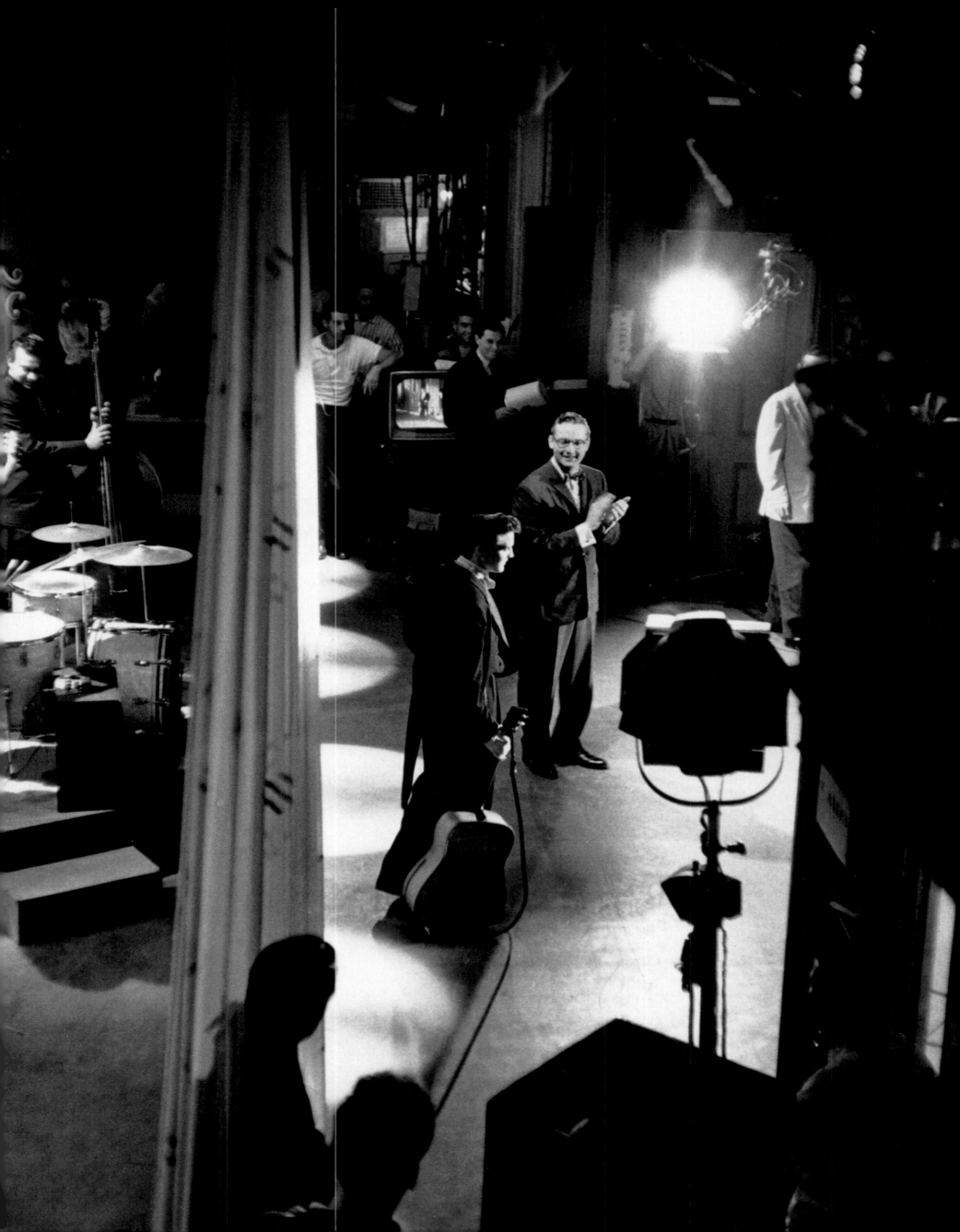

rehearsal was going to proceed. The show was broken down into six or seven different segments, each of which had to be blocked out on stage. Not everyone was in all the skits, so there were times when you had to hang around and watch until your time came.

Before the rehearsals, a press conference was called. Elvis was squeezed into an office backstage with seven or eight reporters. These were hard-bitten New York reporters with orders from their publishers to really give it to Elvis. Yet he had this way of disarming them as they stood or kneeled around him with their little pads. With his usual charm, he held court, sitting in a chair and quietly answering their questions like a gentleman with "Yes, sir" and "No, sir." By the time the press conference was finished, half of them came up asking for an autograph.

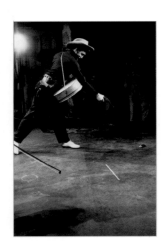

After the reporters left, Elvis was called out to go through his routines. He rehearsed the three skits that Steve Allen had written for him. First, he would open with the ballad in front of the Greek columns. Next would be his part as Tumbleweed Presley in the "Range Roundup" skit. For the last routine, he would sing, "You ain't nothing but a hound dog" to the hound dog with the top hat. Steve was a bit nervous because this was his second Sunday broadcast. He had just gotten this spot for a family show opposite Ed Sullivan, who owned Sunday night television. Running up against Sullivan was like David challenging Goliath.

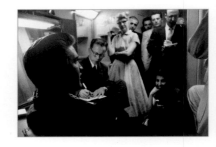

The only thing Steve had going for him was Elvis Presley, but that also came with a risk. Several weeks earlier, Milton Berle had aired that controversial performance, so Steve had to be careful and control how Elvis would be presented on Sunday night. He couldn't have Elvis running away with his show by doing anything that would cause the negative reaction that Milton's did. Steve was going to introduce America to the "new" Elvis Presley. There would be no "disciple of the devil" on *The Steve Allen Show*.

The show opened with Steve calling Elvis onto the stage. Elvis came out with a guitar in his hand and a hat in the other, wearing the light blue shirt, blue tie and tails and looking somewhat chastened. To prove that this was a new Elvis Presley fit for family audiences, Steve pulled out this scroll and, opening it up, announced that thousands of people had signed this petition to forgive Elvis, or something like that. Then Elvis walked off the stage and the program began.

I was shooting the show, but I had to be much more careful than when I shot the rehearsals. During the live broadcast, I had to be off-camera, high up on a catwalk and shooting down from about ten to fifteen feet above the stage with a medium telephoto lens. Elvis, Bill Black, DJ, and Scotty Moore watched the monitor backstage to see what the TV cameras were seeing. Elvis had his hat off and his hair fascinated me. I took some shots right above his head. With the long lens, I could see all the curls and curves of his intricate hairstyle. Many, many years later, those photos came in handy when a licensee of mine said, "Al, we're thinking of putting out an Elvis doll. Do you have any shots of his hairstyle from the top?" No one else ever documented it from this vantage point.

Above the stage, I could also watch Elvis in between acts when he rushed backstage. Another performer went out to distract the audience while two assistants helped Elvis change into his Tumbleweed Presley outfit, which basically consisted of a cowboy shirt and pants, a gun belt, and a cowboy hat. With that outfit on, he joined Imogene Coca, Andy Griffith, and Steve Allen onstage in their cowboy clothes. I think Andy had a guitar also. Bales of hay were strewn around in a takeoff of the Grand Ole Opry.

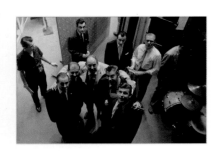

When the broadcast was over, some fans made it backstage before Elvis had a chance to get off-stage. Just as he was getting ready to pull off his shirt, girls began appearing asking for autographs. A very pretty girl started toward him, then a not-so-pretty girl showed up and, before you knew it, he was signing autographs for the second girl while glancing at the first one. In the meantime, Tom Diskin was in the background, eyeing her as well.

Once the show was over and the girls had left, Elvis began making his way through the lobby of the Hudson Theater with New York's Finest providing police protection around him. Out on

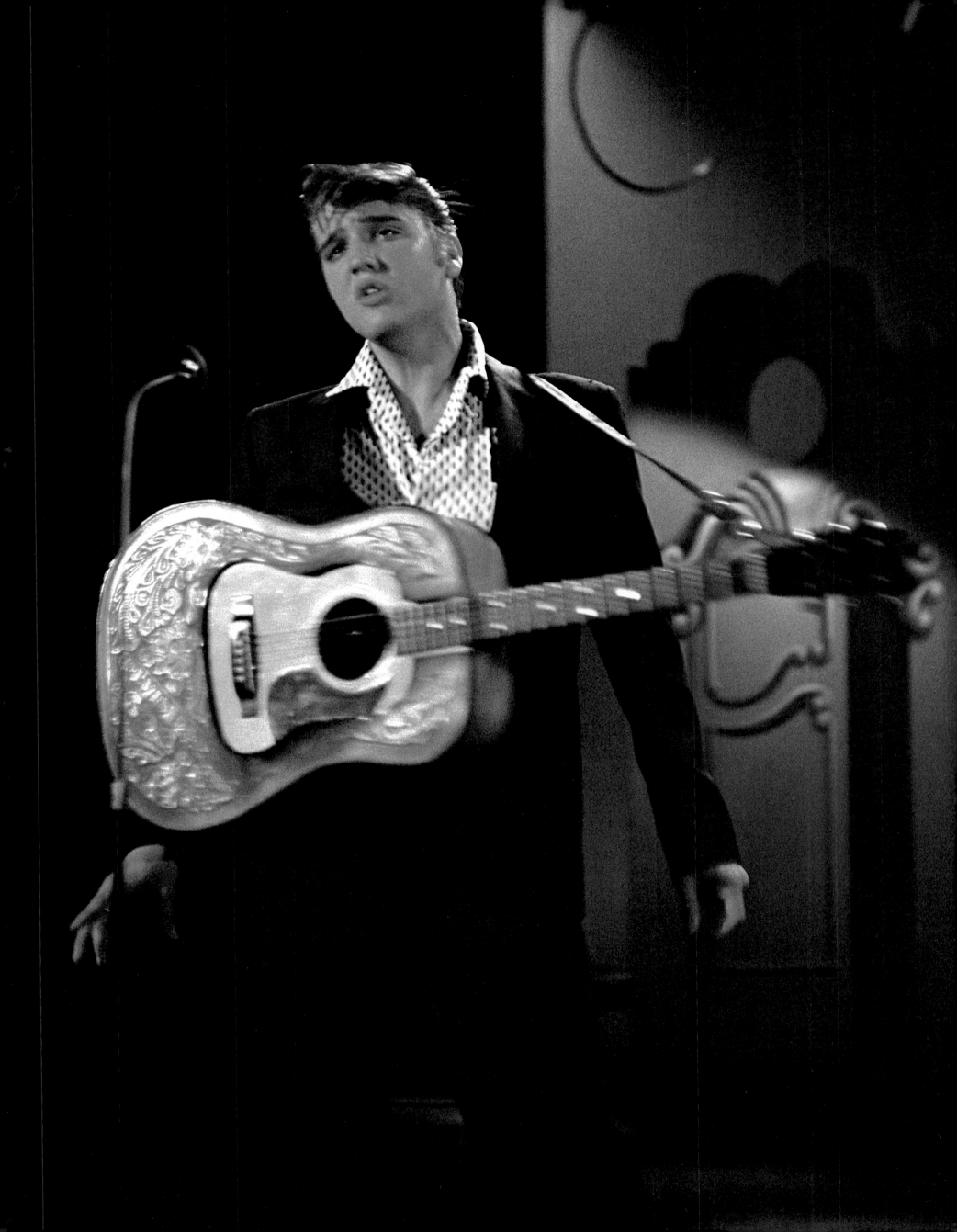

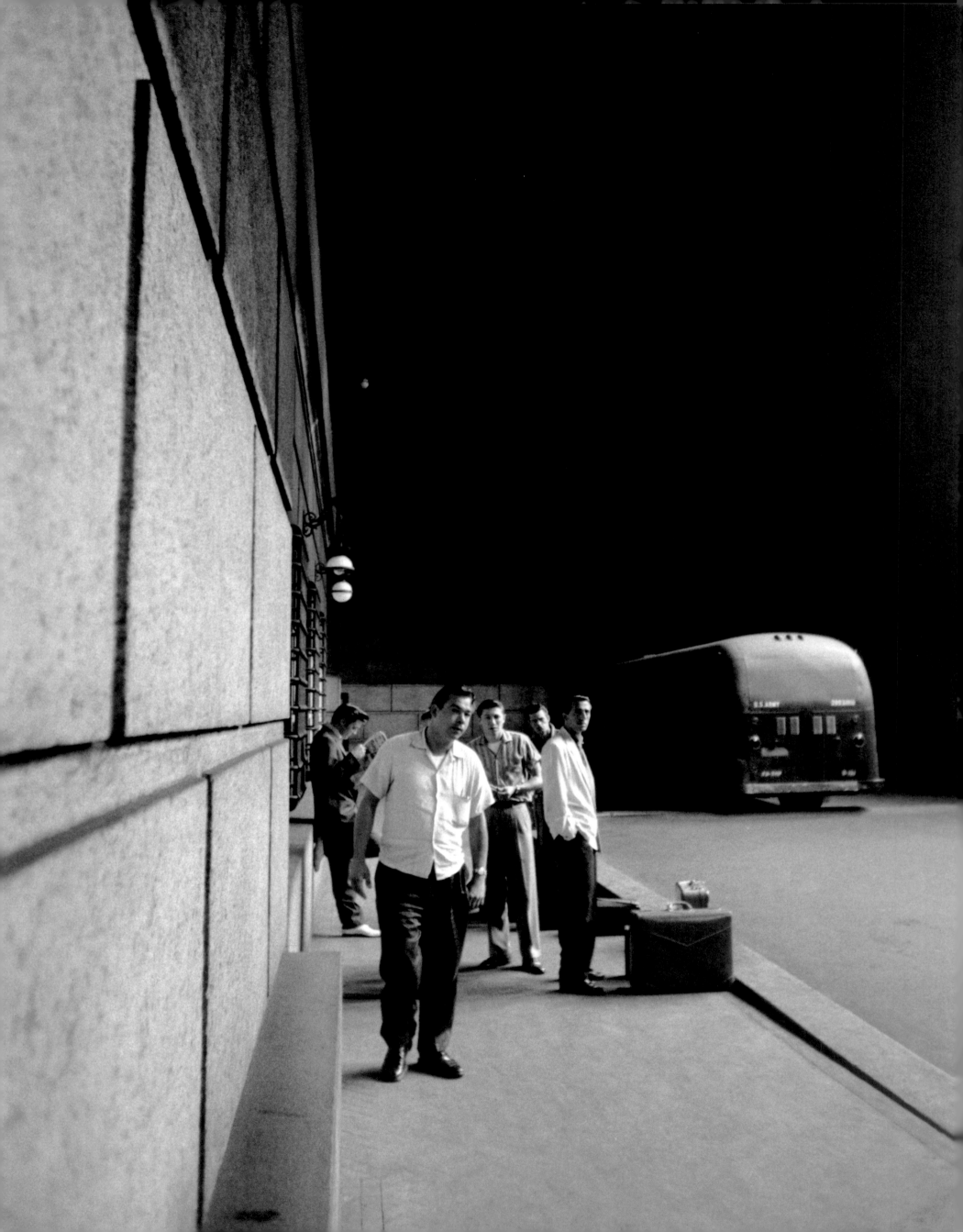

the street, a white convertible car was waiting for him, Junior and Tom Diskin. Desperate to touch him, five young black girls got to Elvis as he was settling into the backseat, while others handed him slips of paper hoping to get an autograph. At the same time, one of the cops who was supposed to be protecting Elvis was giving him a piece of paper to sign as well. Sitting up on the back of the convertible, Elvis did what he could as the driver slowly crept away. Eventually, the car pulled out of the crowd, leaving the Hudson Theater, and me, behind.

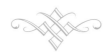

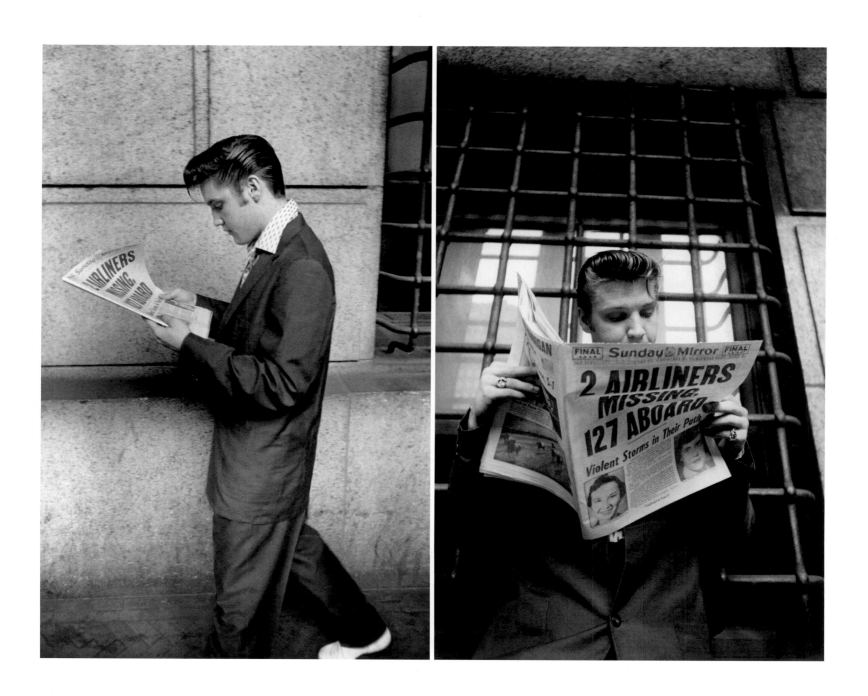

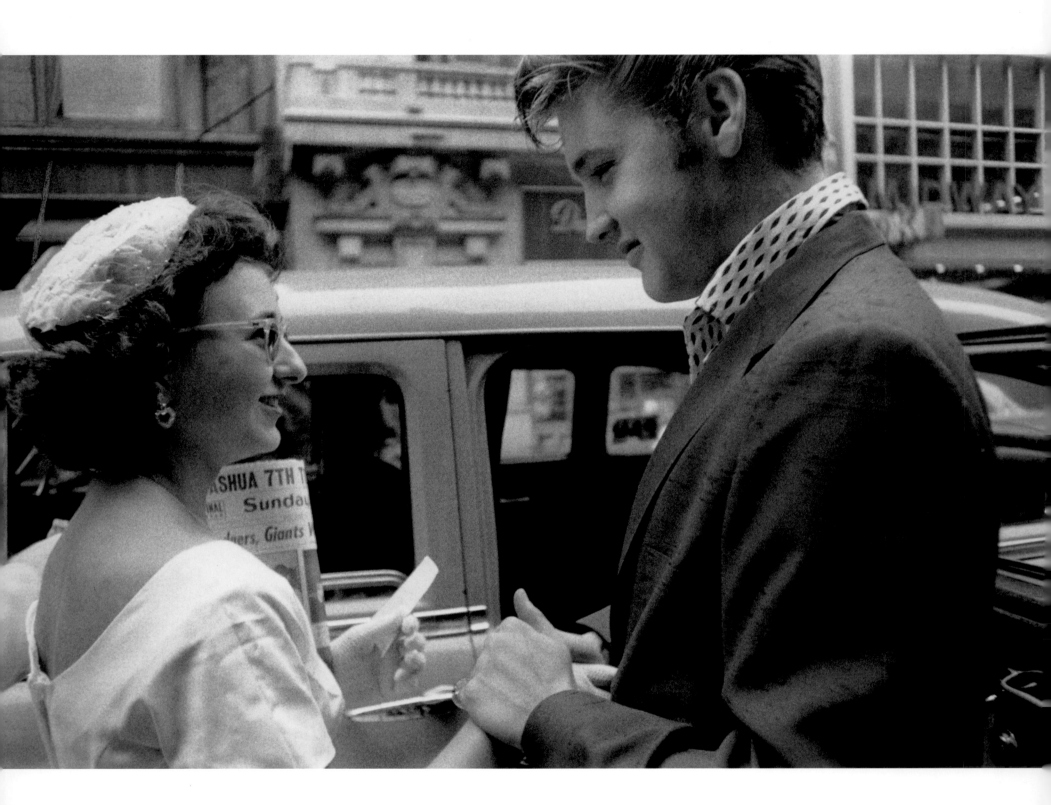

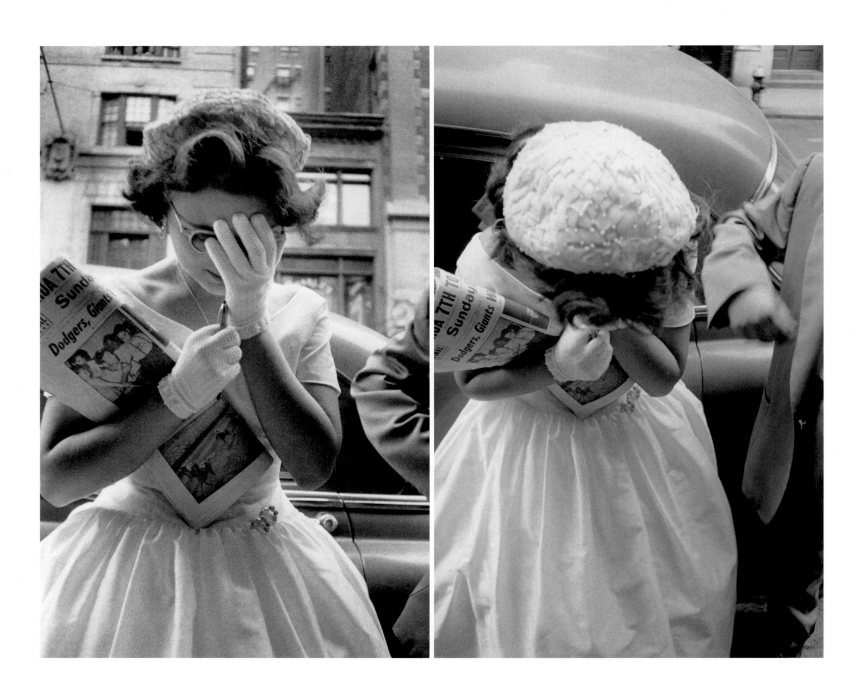

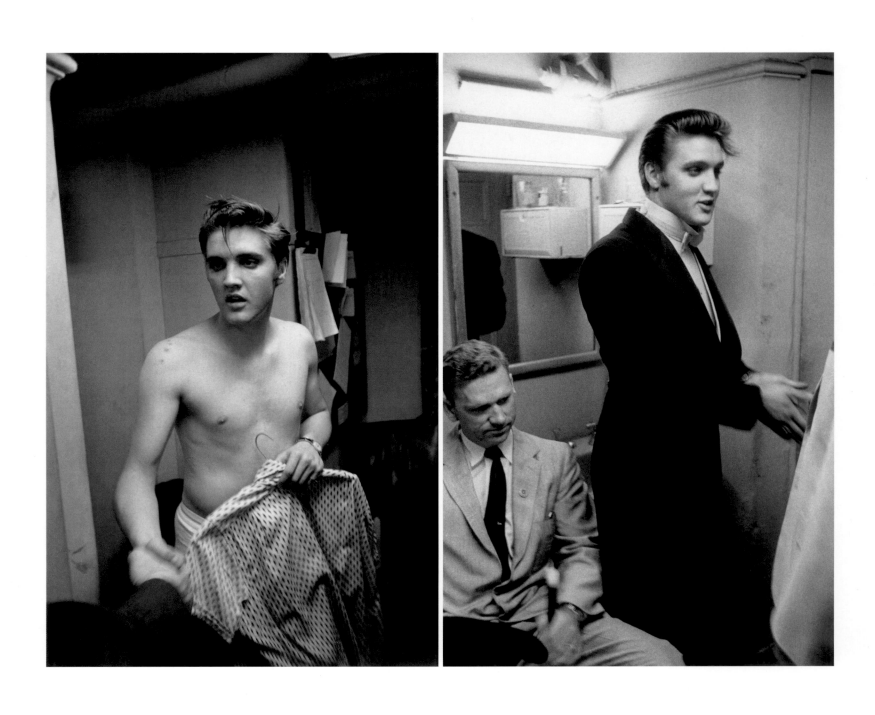

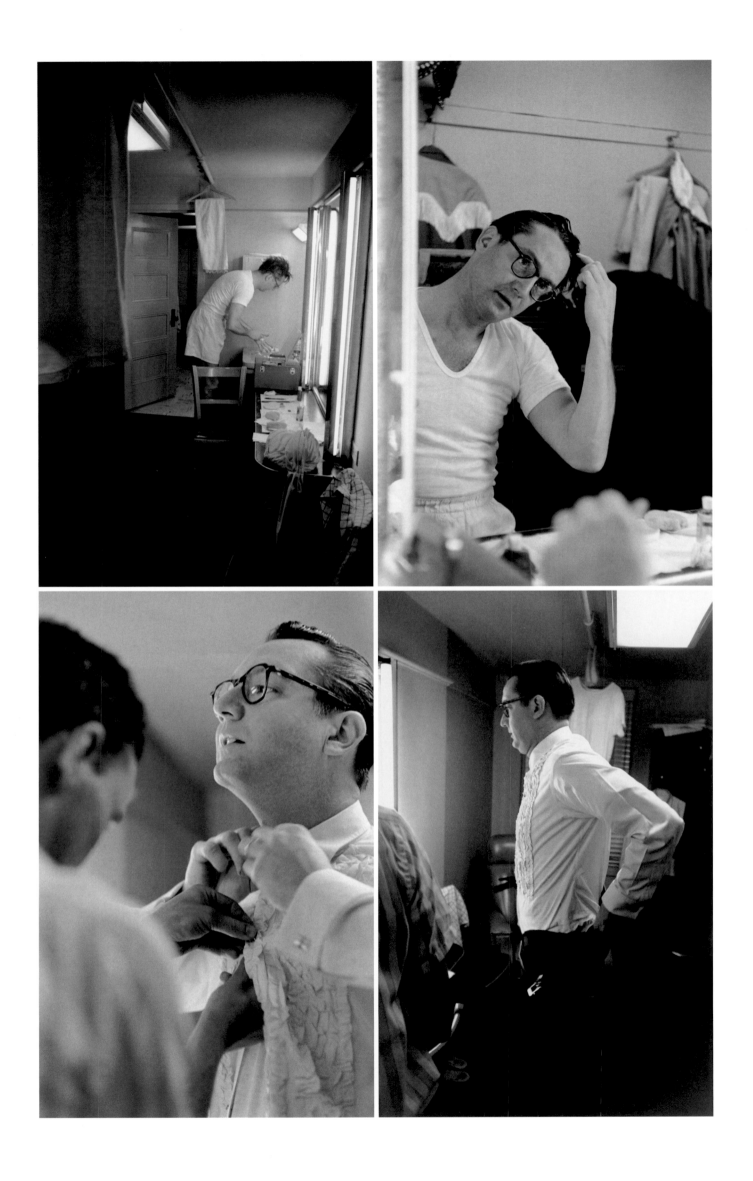

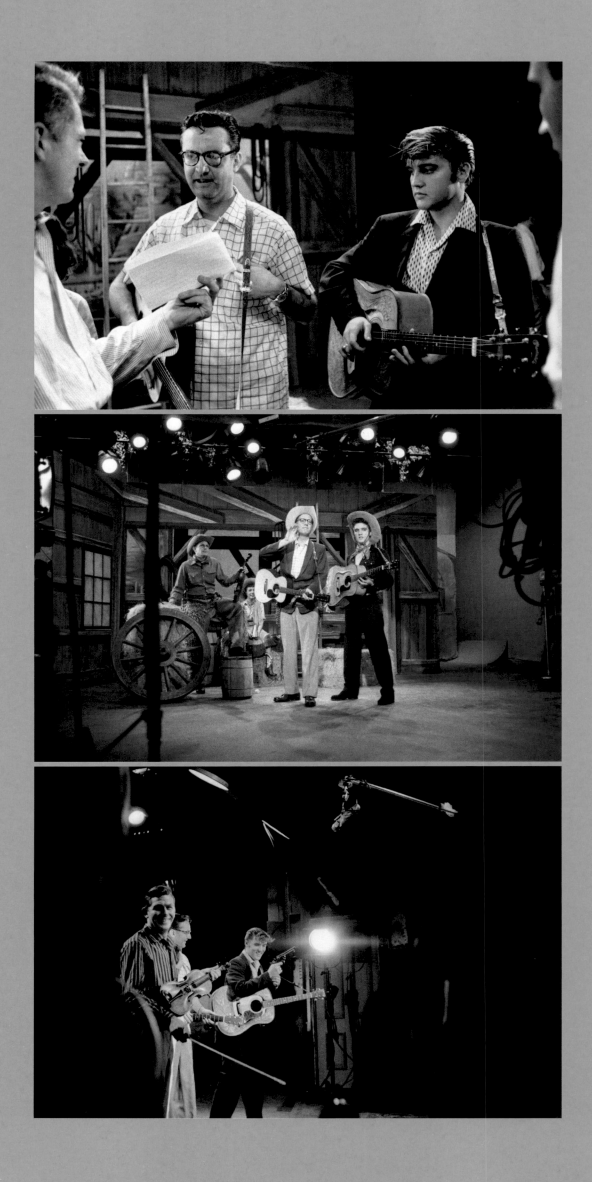

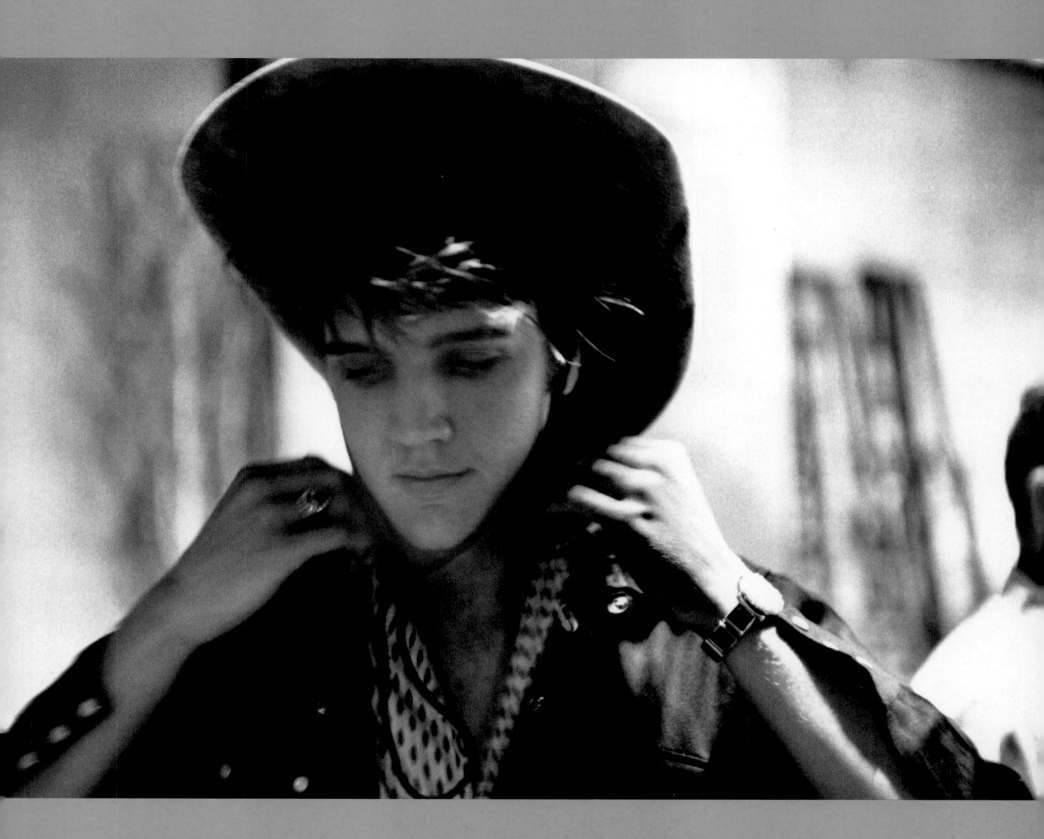

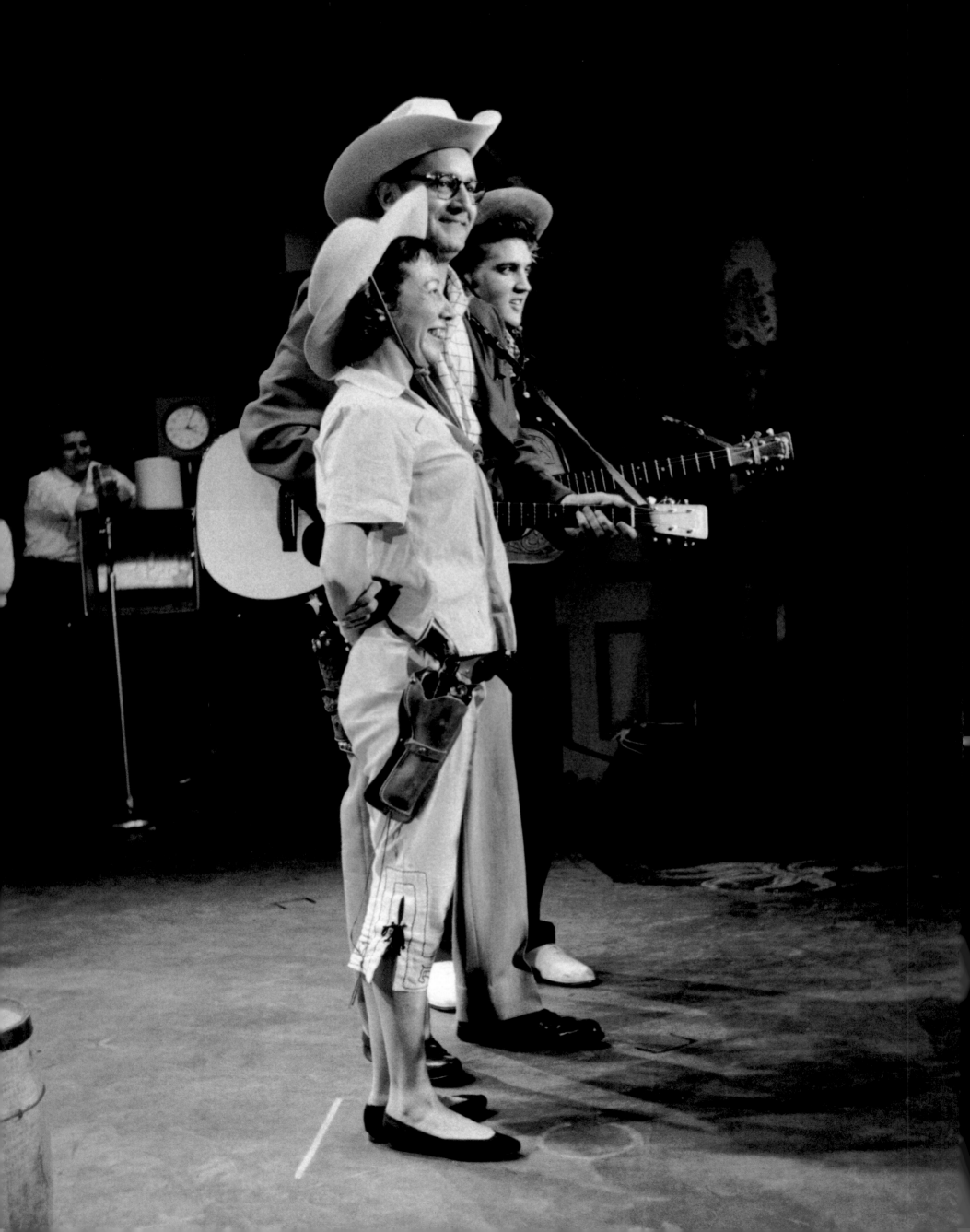

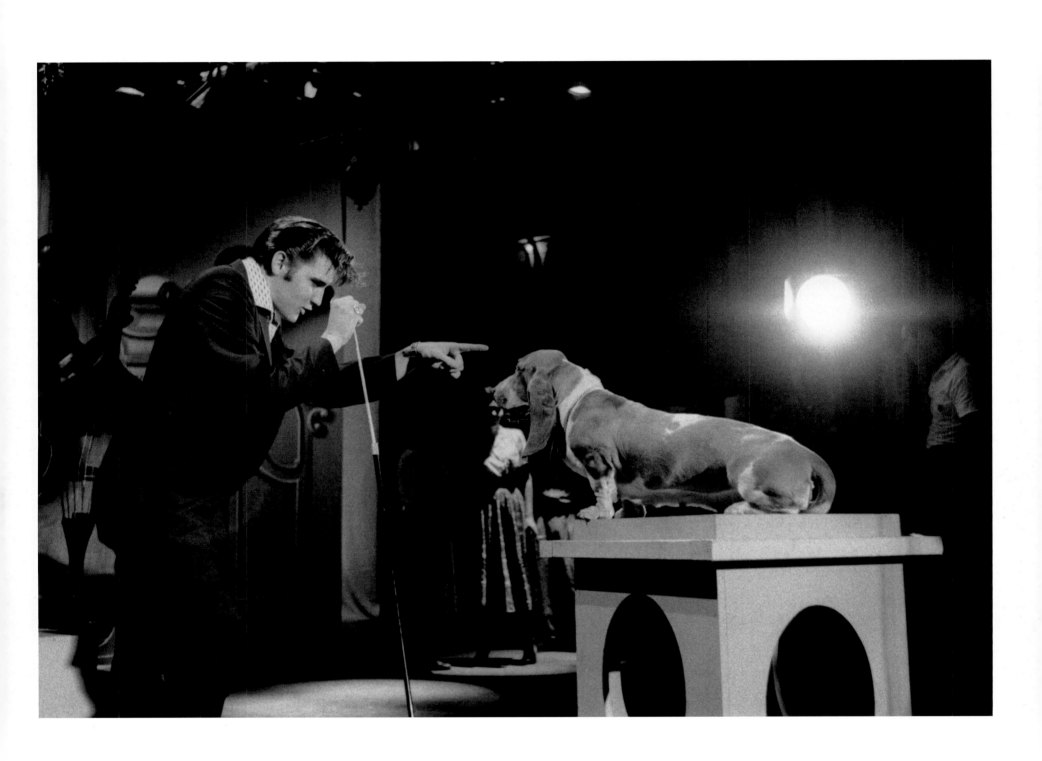

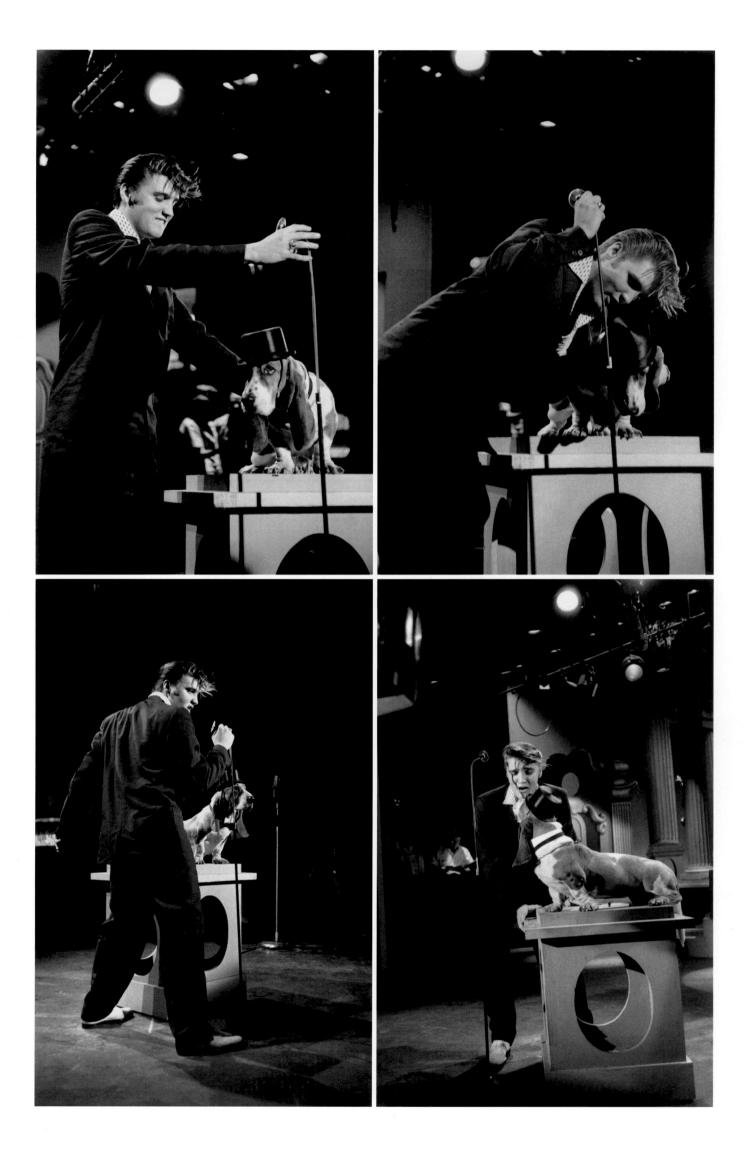

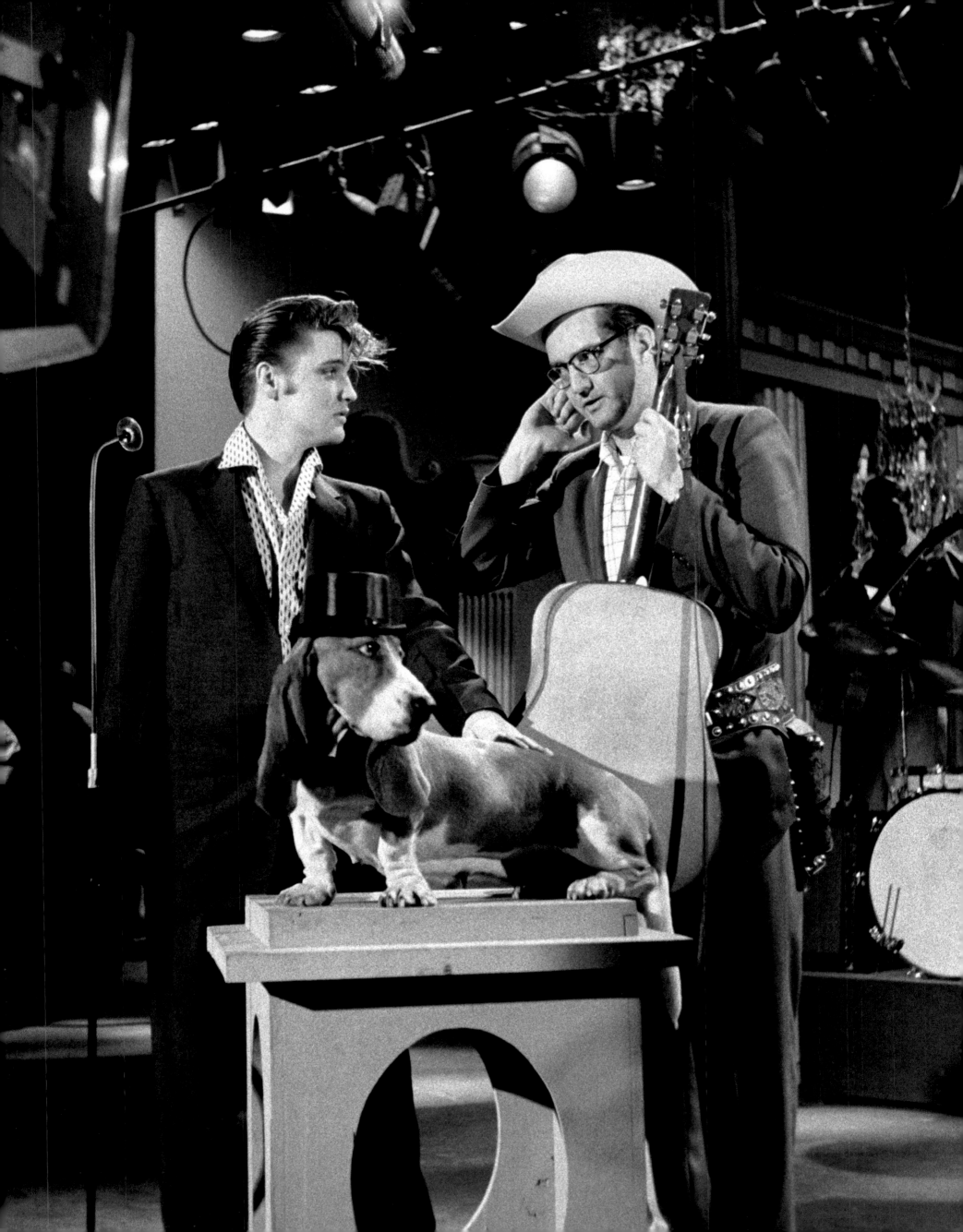

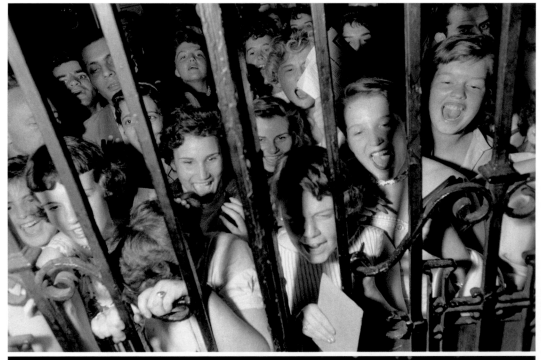
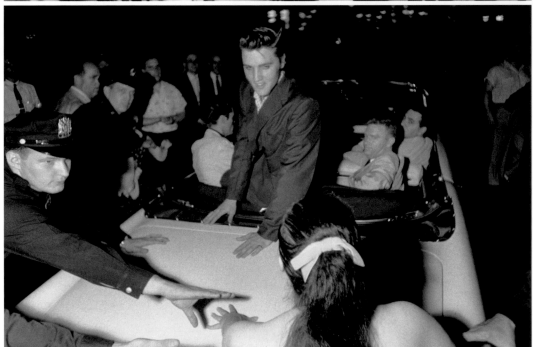
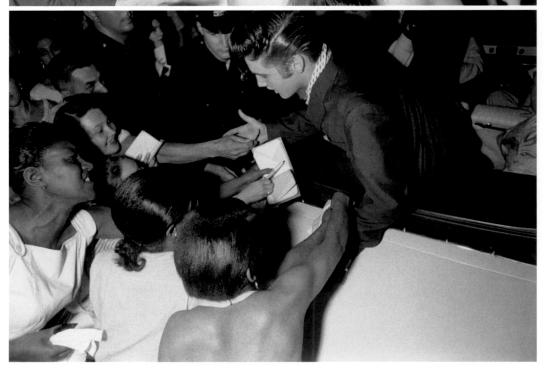

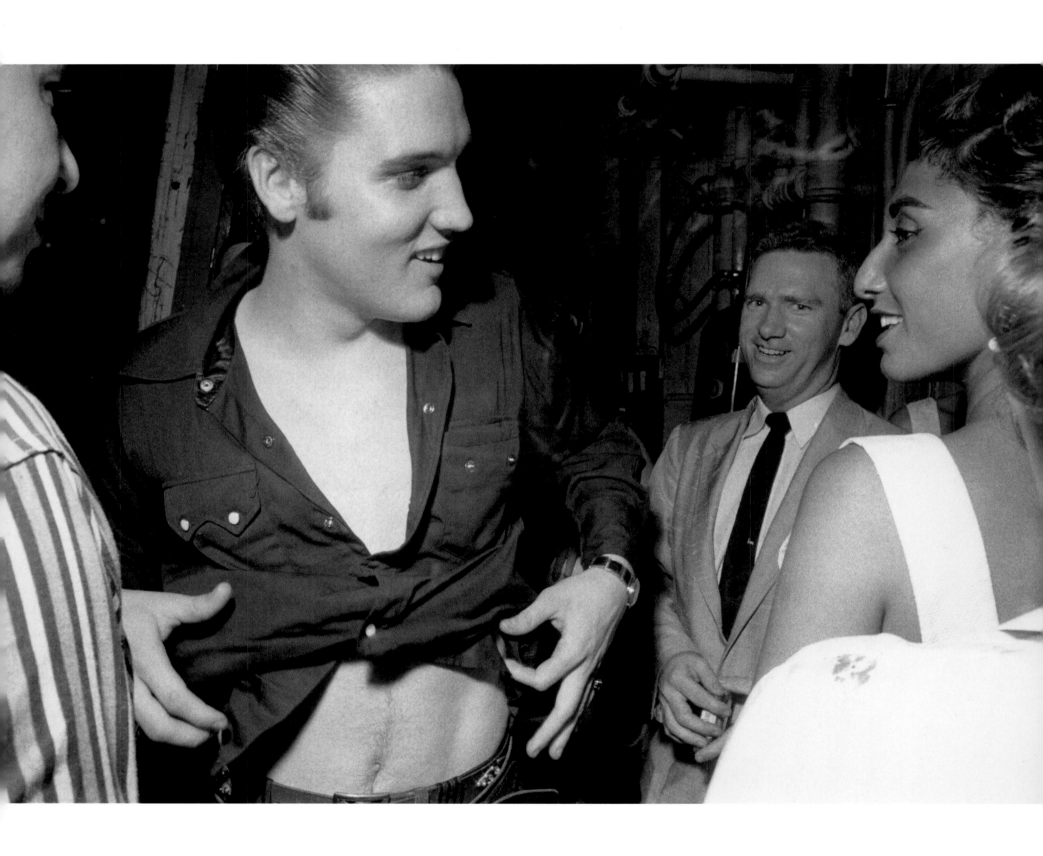

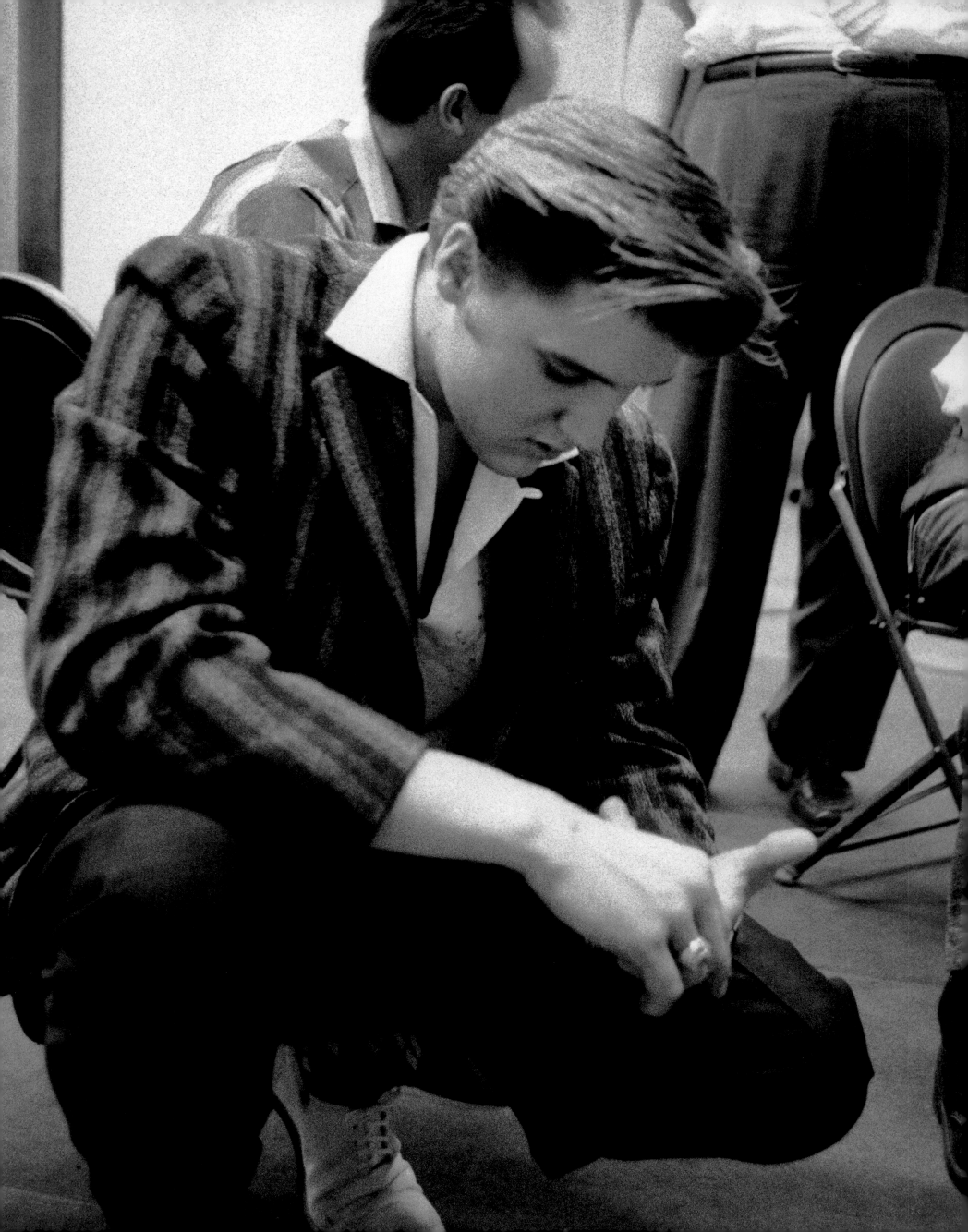

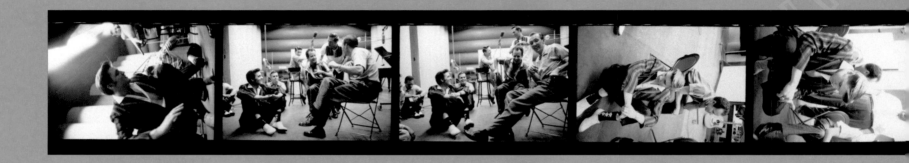

CHAPTER V

THE RECORDING SESSION

STUDIO ONE

THE RECORDING SESSION
STUDIO ONE

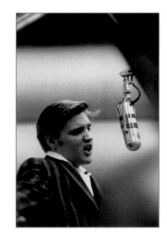

O N July 2, 1956, a defining moment in the history of rock and roll took place. Elvis recorded "Hound Dog" and "Don't Be Cruel," which were released by RCA as two sides of one single. This was the only time both sides of a single reached number one on the charts. The session at RCA Studios was also the last time Elvis would record in New York. Of course, I wasn't aware of any of this when I arrived at the building on 24th Street between Lexington and 3rd Avenues. I did sense that this recording session would provide with me a rare opportunity to observe another stage in the evolution of my subject.

Located on the ground floor, the main studio where Elvis recorded was a large room with a lot of acoustical padding covering the walls. There were two smaller adjoining rooms, one of which was reserved for the sound engineers. Instead of having to book orchestra musicians for three-hour gigs, Elvis brought his own crew—Scotty Moore on guitar, DJ Fontana on drums, Bill Black on bass, and the four Jordanaires as back-up. Shorty Long was hired as the piano player. Also present were Steve Sholes from RCA and the always necessary Junior, Elvis's go-fer. The recording session began early in the afternoon and lasted until dusk.

The studio had Neumann condenser microphones that stood about six inches high. They weren't the most modern microphones, but they gave the music a certain sound quality that Elvis liked. Baffling devices and separate microphones kept the instruments, especially the drums, from overwhelming the singer's voice. For the first song, "Hound Dog," Elvis was set up in his booth with two microphones, one for his voice and the second for his leather-covered guitar. He didn't actually play the guitar, but he slapped the back of it. The session went something like this: "You ain't nothing but a hound dog, crying all the time"—thump—"you ain't never caught a rabbit and you ain't no friend of mine"—thump. The thump was picked up by the second microphone.

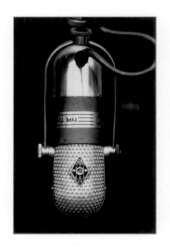

Elvis, however, still was not used to the idea of stationary microphones. He used his body when singing and preferred holding the microphone in his hand or dragging the stand wherever he was going onstage. Even in the sound booth, he had a tendency to move about, causing parts of the song to drop out of the recording. The engineers frequently would say, "Elvis, could we do it one more time? Try to stay on mike." There couldn't be any patching or splicing, so the songs had to be recorded straight through. They were using reel-to-reel Ampex tape decks, considered the Cadillac of equipment in the recording studios back then. At the end of each take, the engineers would stick a little paper tab in the reel to mark the beginning of the next take. After a while you had all these little white tabs, like butterflies, spinning around on a turntable at thirty inches per second, which was fast. Usually, he would say, "Well, let's try it again, fellas," or, "It wasn't quite right." The excitement was waiting for Elvis to declare, "Yeah, it's a take."

Then they listened to the playback. With those argyle socks peeking out above his white bucks, Elvis sat hunched down low in front of a sixteen-inch speaker. From this perspective, I could catch

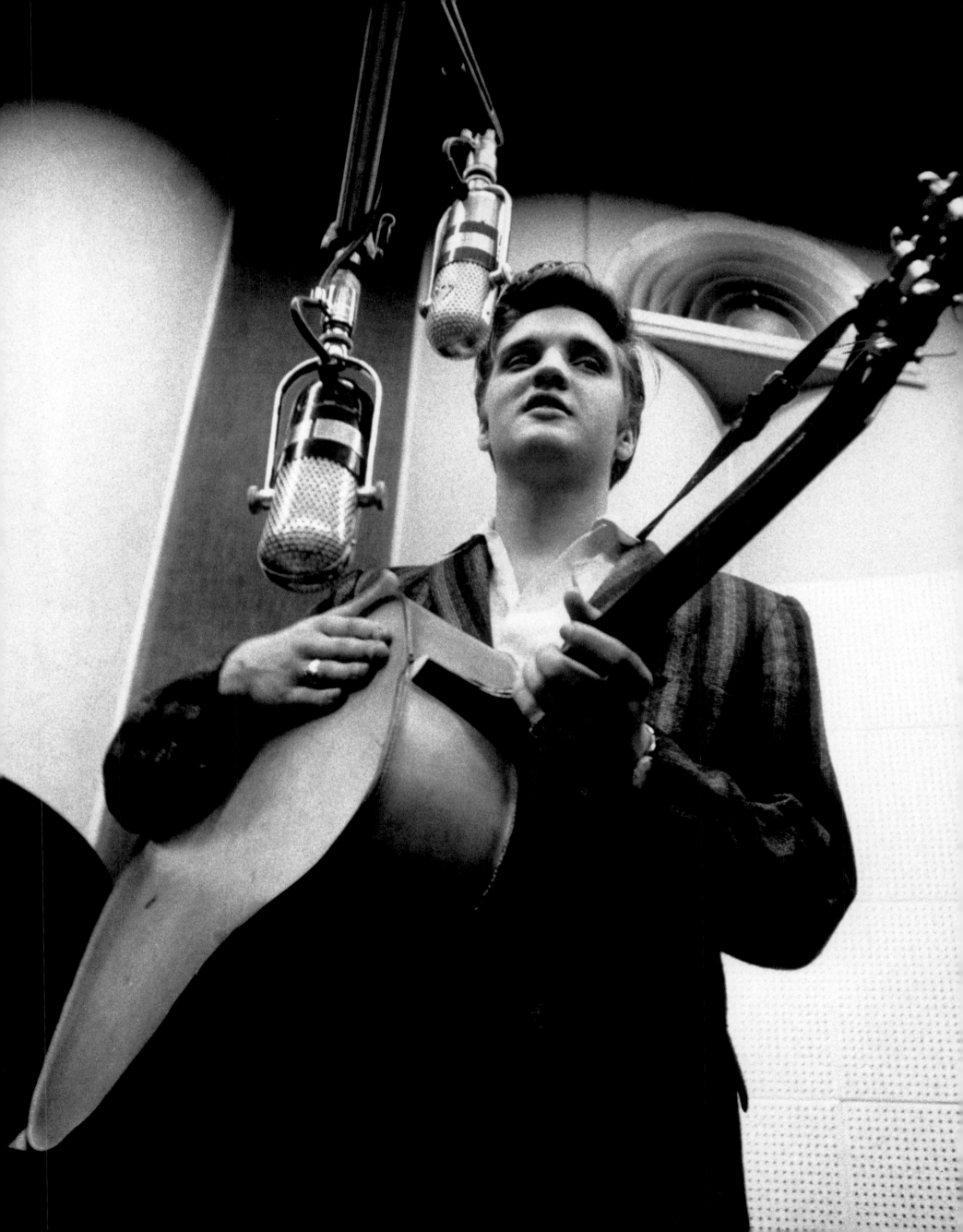

him in the foreground listening and Junior next to him, as well as the engineer's booth and the second room where visitors were allowed to watch. At the end of the playback, Steve Sholes asked, "Elvis, how do you feel about that one?"

"Steve, let's try it just one more time."

"Okay, but remember we've got two more to record."

Elvis went back into the booth and two or three takes later, he had it. That was the recording, which would be released in a few weeks. In those days, recordings weren't reworked so much by engineers as they are today. What you did in the session was pretty much what would be put out.

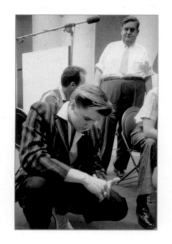

Once "Hound Dog" was taken care of, they set up the microphones for a song to put on the B-side. Meanwhile, Elvis went through a bunch of demos that had been sent down to the studio. Hoping that some big singer would record them, unknown songwriters and musicians would put these tapes together and send them to the record companies. Among these average recordings, Elvis heard "Don't Be Cruel" and decided that was the one he wanted to do next. He went over to the piano and gathered his Jordanaires around him to arrange the song on the spot. DJ Fontana was at the drum set behind the piano. When they felt as if they had something, everyone went back to their regular positions at the microphones to begin recording. "Don't be cruel"—thump—"to a heart that's true"—thump.

With two songs done, it was time to break for lunch. A little room just outside the recording studio was set with a table, a bench and a couple of chairs. Elvis went off to a corner and the others gathered around the table to have some sandwiches. Junior was there to collect the empty Pepsi bottles and sandwich wrappers and dump them in the garbage can, while everyone gravitated back to the recording studio for the next song, "Any Way You Want Me."

They got through that one pretty quickly. Years later in Memphis, Gordon Stoker, the head of the Jordanaires, came up to me and asked, "Did you notice on the last song that the piano was a little louder than on the others?"

"Why? What happened there?"

"Well, Shorty Long had to leave for a gig at five, and since I play the piano, I took over." He wanted to know if I there was a noticeable change in the piano playing.

He put me on the spot and the only thing I could do was to be honest. "I'm sorry, but I couldn't tell." That was disappointing to Stoker. He really hoped that he had made a difference.

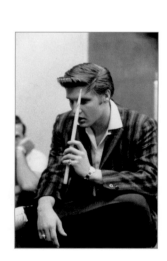

Actually, the music was the last thing on my mind at the time. I tuned out because I had to focus on what I was doing. The last guy anyone wanted in the recording studio was the photographer so I had to grab my chances to shoot during the rehearsals in between recordings. Then I could go as close as I wanted, because I wasn't using a flash. Otherwise, I was discouraged from shooting during the takes for fear of the sound of the shutter distracting the musicians and ending up on tape. I was, however, able to shoot during the "Hound Dog" takes. It was such a raucous song that the click of a camera could be drowned out. Generally though, as a fly on the wall, I had to avoid being a fly in the ointment.

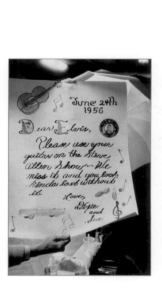

That day, three songs, "Hound Dog," "Don't Be Cruel," and "Any Way You Want Me," were recorded. The first two became Elvis's third and fourth gold records, respectively. "Hound Dog" was already very popular, so the recording was going to be released as a single with "Don't Be Cruel" on the B-side. But "Don't Be Cruel" also became a number one hit so they reissued it with "Hound Dog" as the B-side.

The sessions were a success for me as well. At that point, I felt comfortable enough to bring in a reflective white umbrella hooked up to an incandescent light. I needed that extra light so that I could shoot some color photos. I managed to get a couple of headshots of Elvis. As a working photographer, I wanted to get material for use on an album cover or in fan magazines. Back then, if you could get your photo on an album cover, you were paid $250 or $300. In contrast,

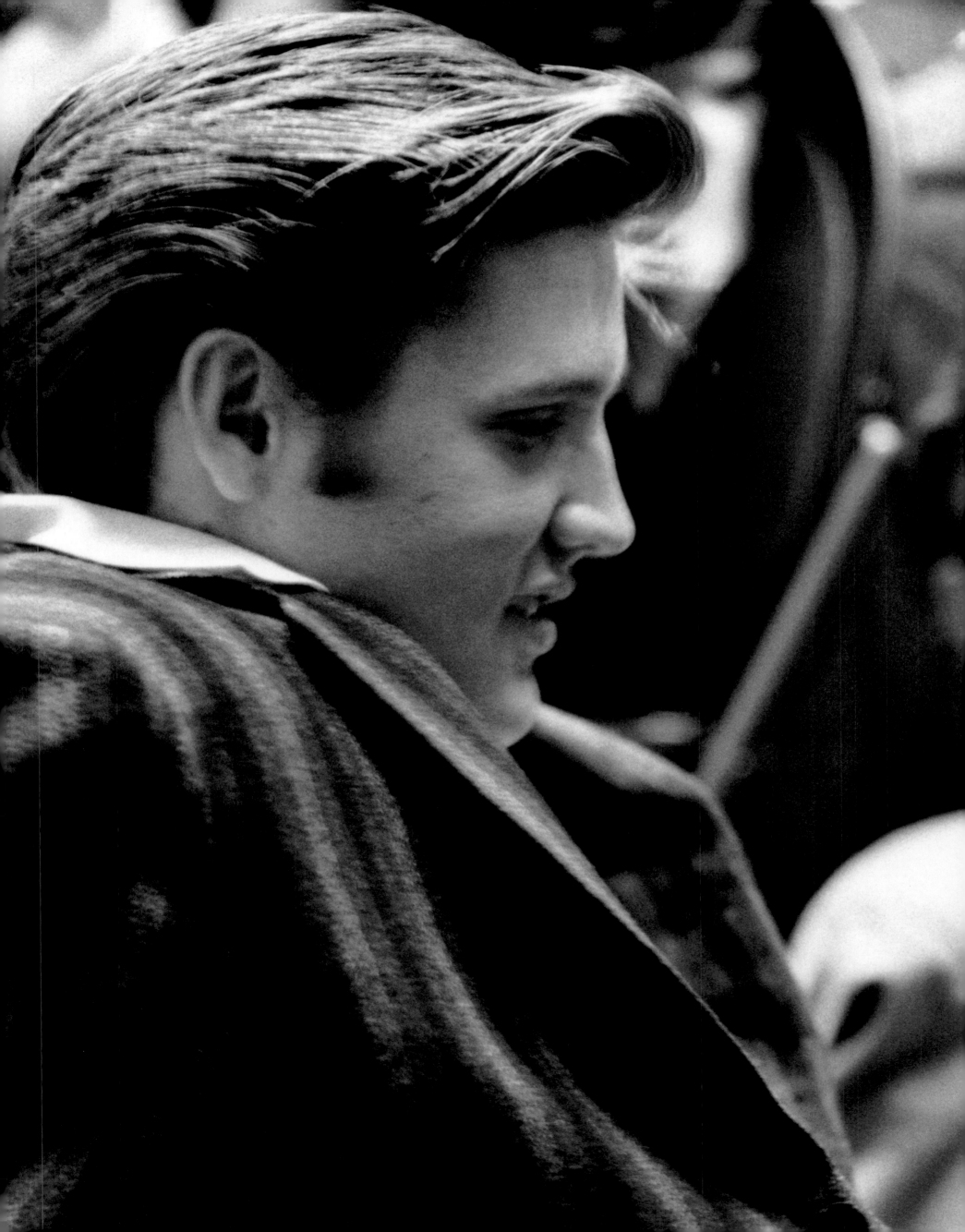

these sessions were hardly lucrative. The work I was doing for Ann's file got me just enough money to pay for the film, developing, cab fare, a set of contact sheets, and five or six prints. In the long run, doing all of this freelance work was great because I still own the negatives and none of them got lost in those music company files. The main benefit of working with RCA was getting the access to the personalities.

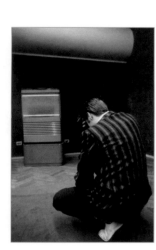

Besides, I really got a kick out of being in those sessions. I enjoyed observing the creative process of putting a record together and the sense of accomplishment and excitement that everyone felt when it was done. They'd say, "Yeah, that's going to make it. That's a winner. We know that's going up to number one." Of course, those kinds of things were said in every recording session, but sometimes they were right, and I was glad to be the one documenting this one. I knew I was getting a lot of good material in the recording session.

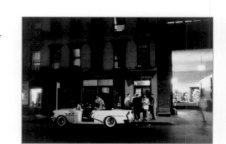

It was all over by around seven in the evening. The session was a long one and Elvis had to catch an early train to Memphis the next morning. Just before he left the studio, he was given quick acetate cuts of the day's recordings. These were wax demo discs that Elvis could take with him before the actual records were fabricated in vinyl at the factory. In two large envelopes, he would carry these all the way home to share with his family and friends.

Outside the building, a convertible was waiting and the usual bunch of kids had gathered. Across the street in front of the post office, some postal workers recognized Elvis so they came over to chat and tell him how much they liked his music. He was pleased to know that these big blue-collar guys, like the men he knew back home, were listening, not just the young girls.

Without any goodbyes, he got in his convertible and I watched them pull off into the night. I rushed back to my studio to drop off the film, go home, and pack my bags, because I had a train to catch the next morning too.

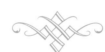

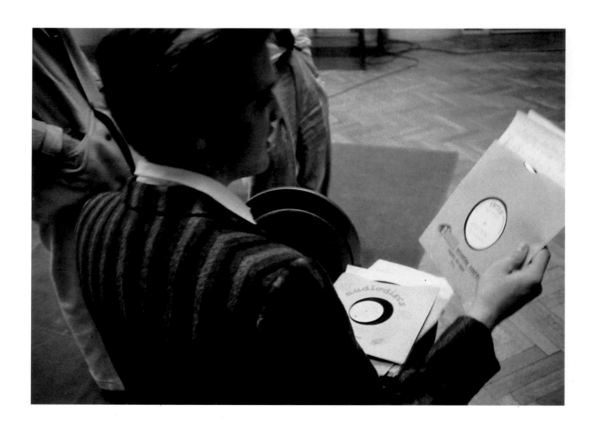

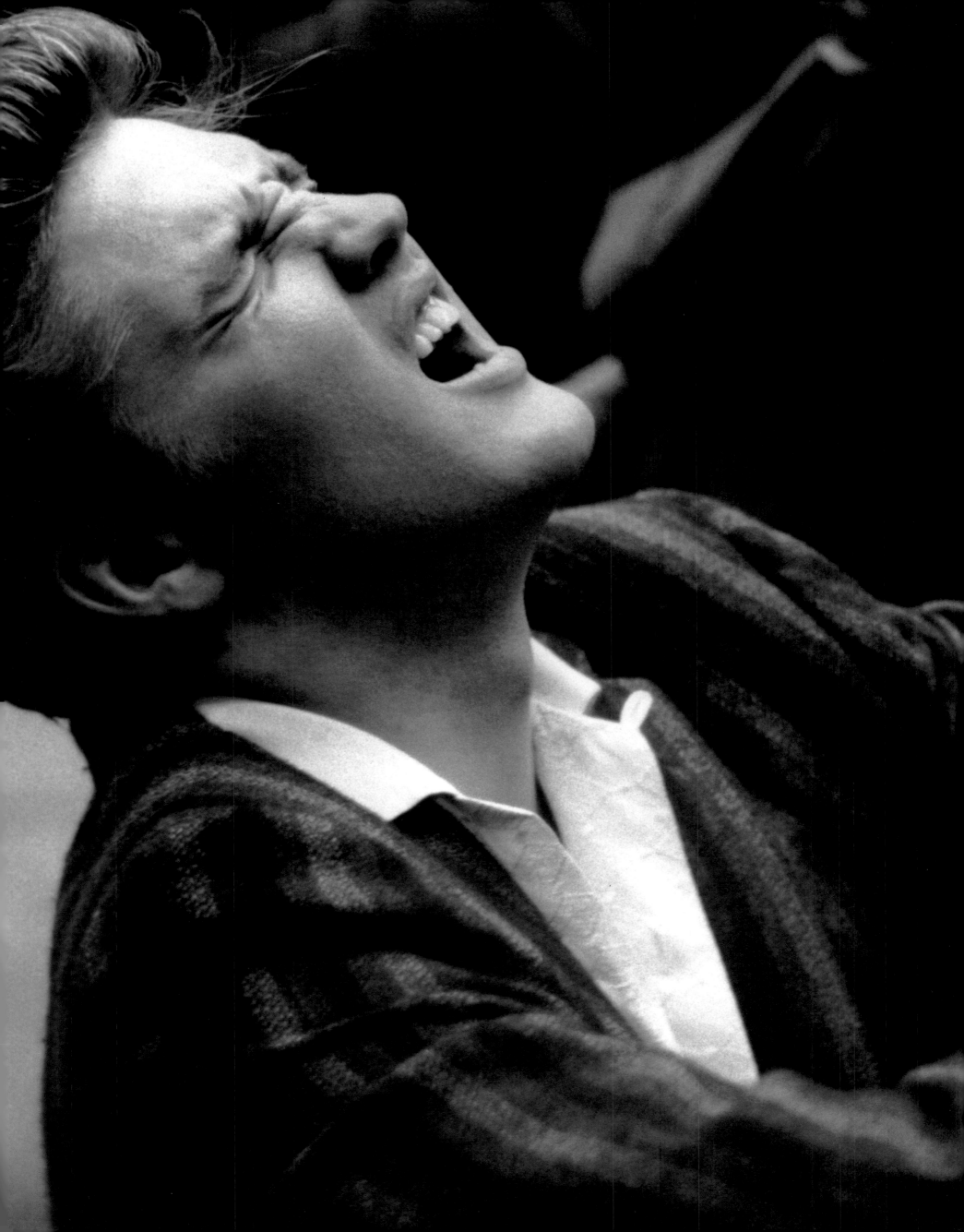

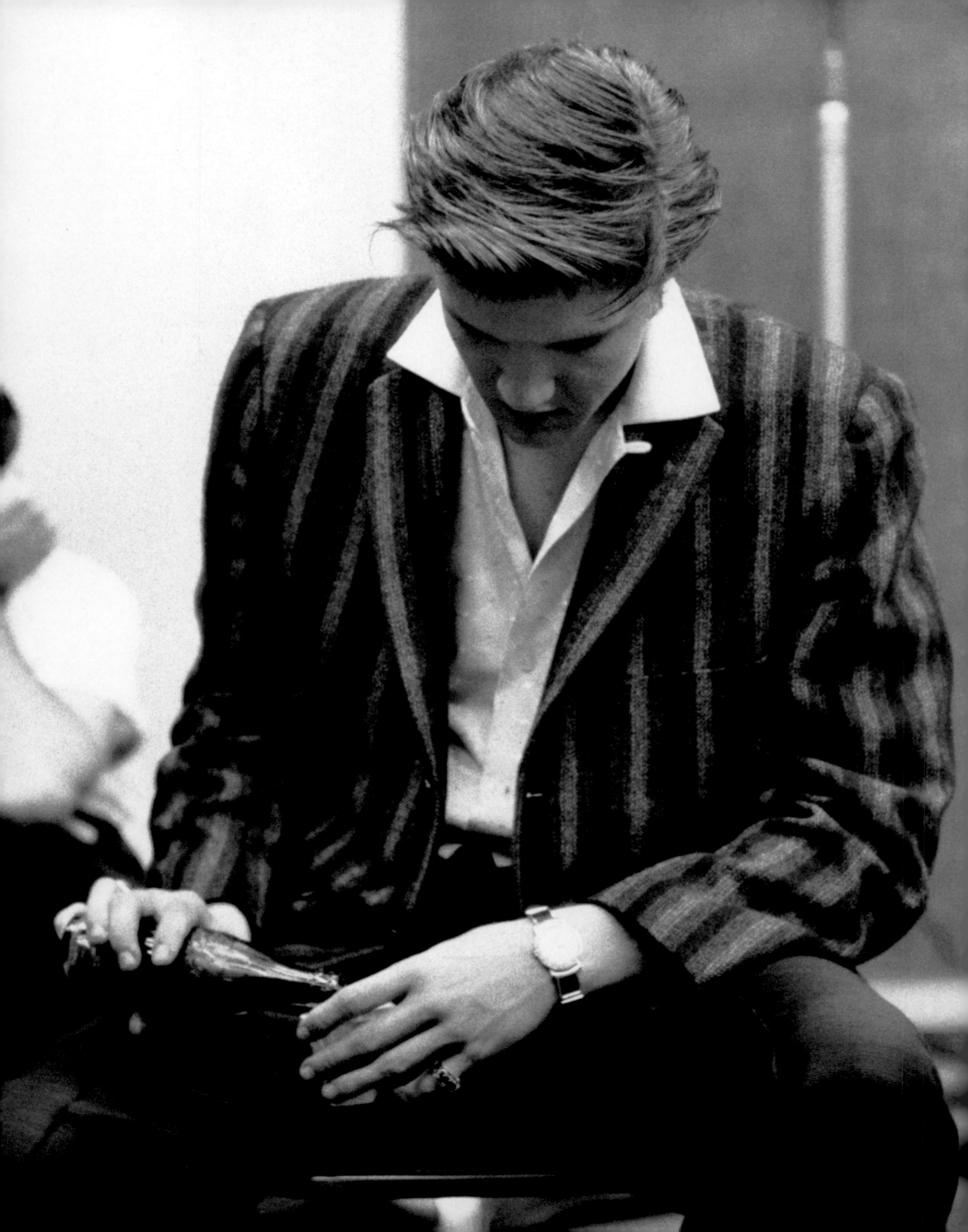

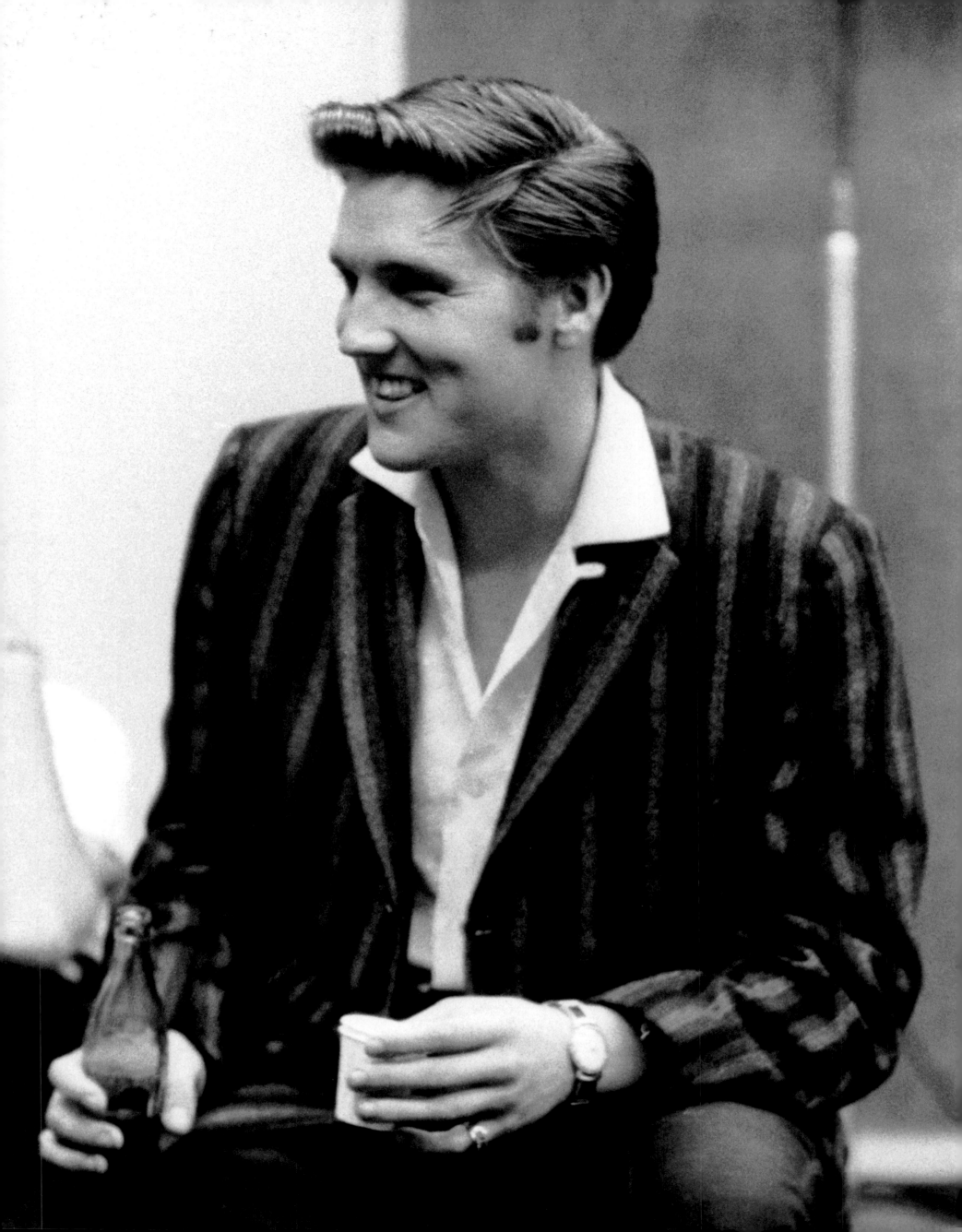

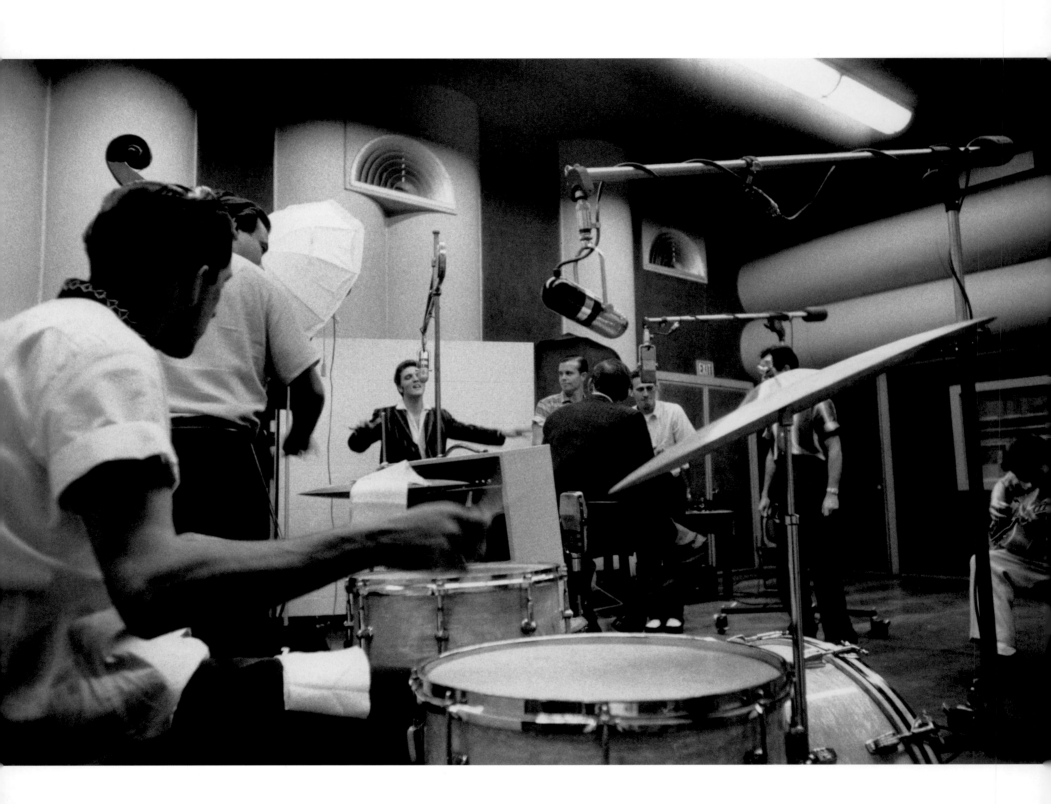

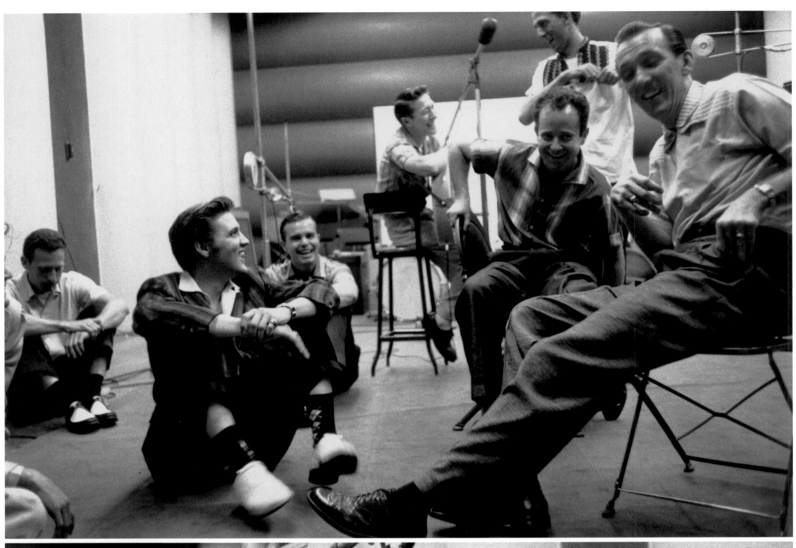

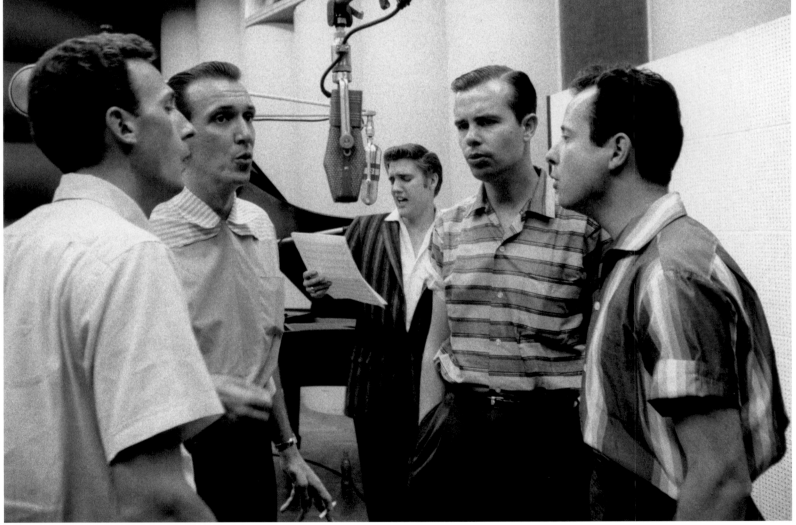

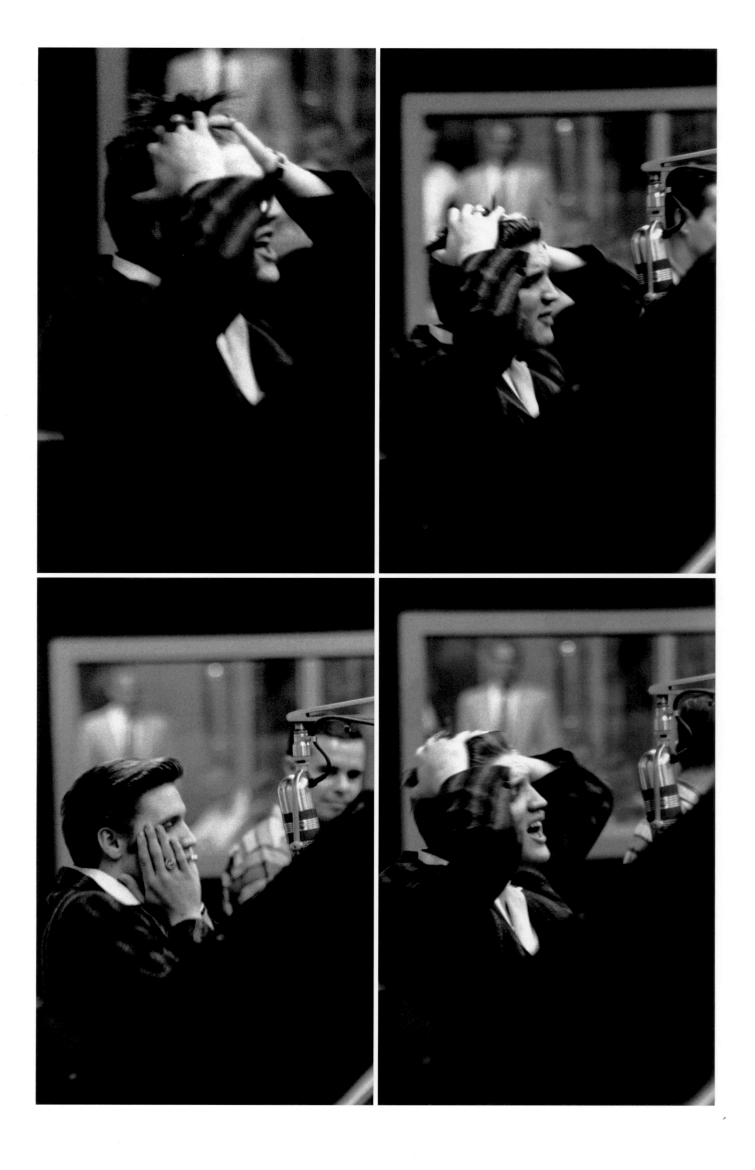

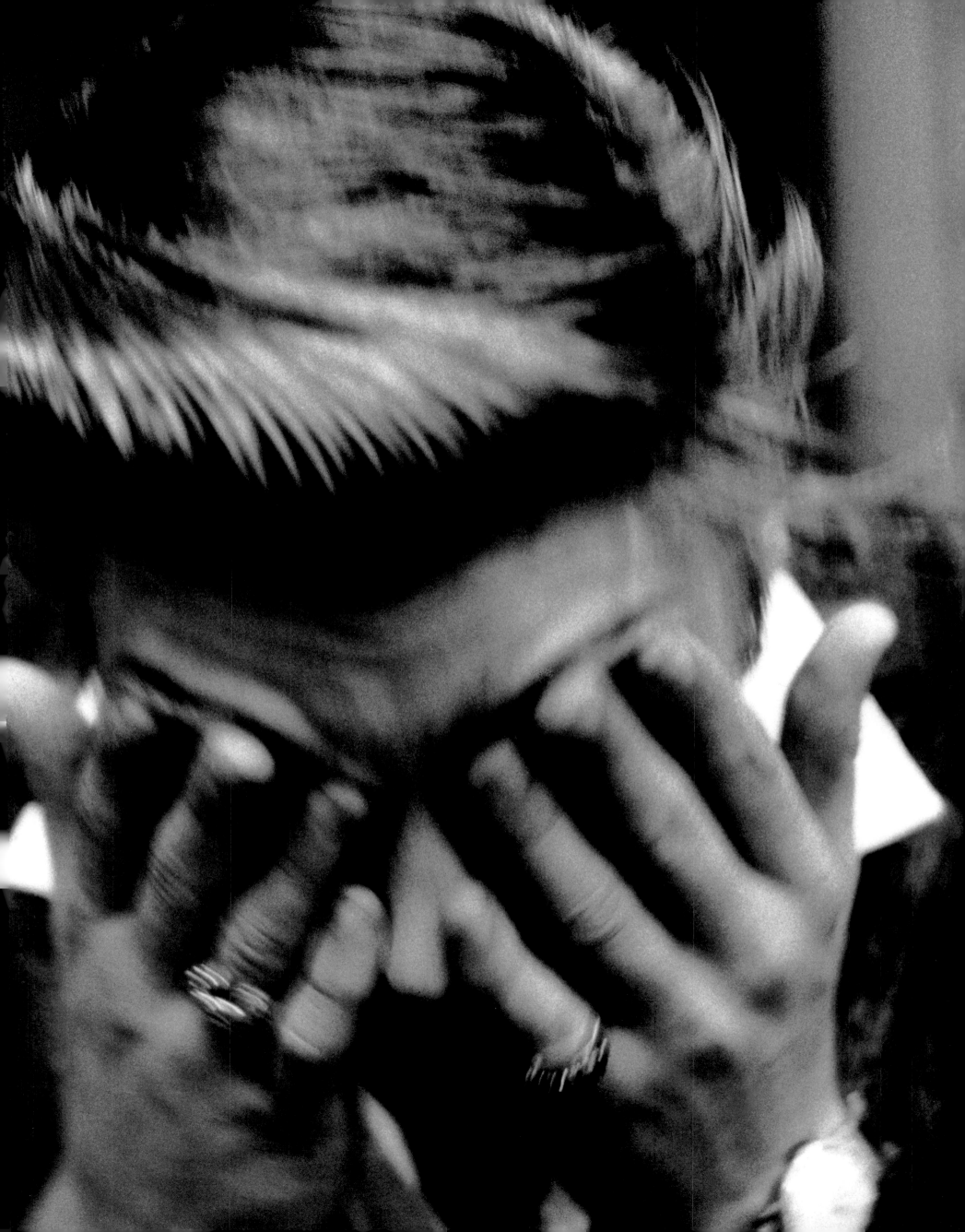

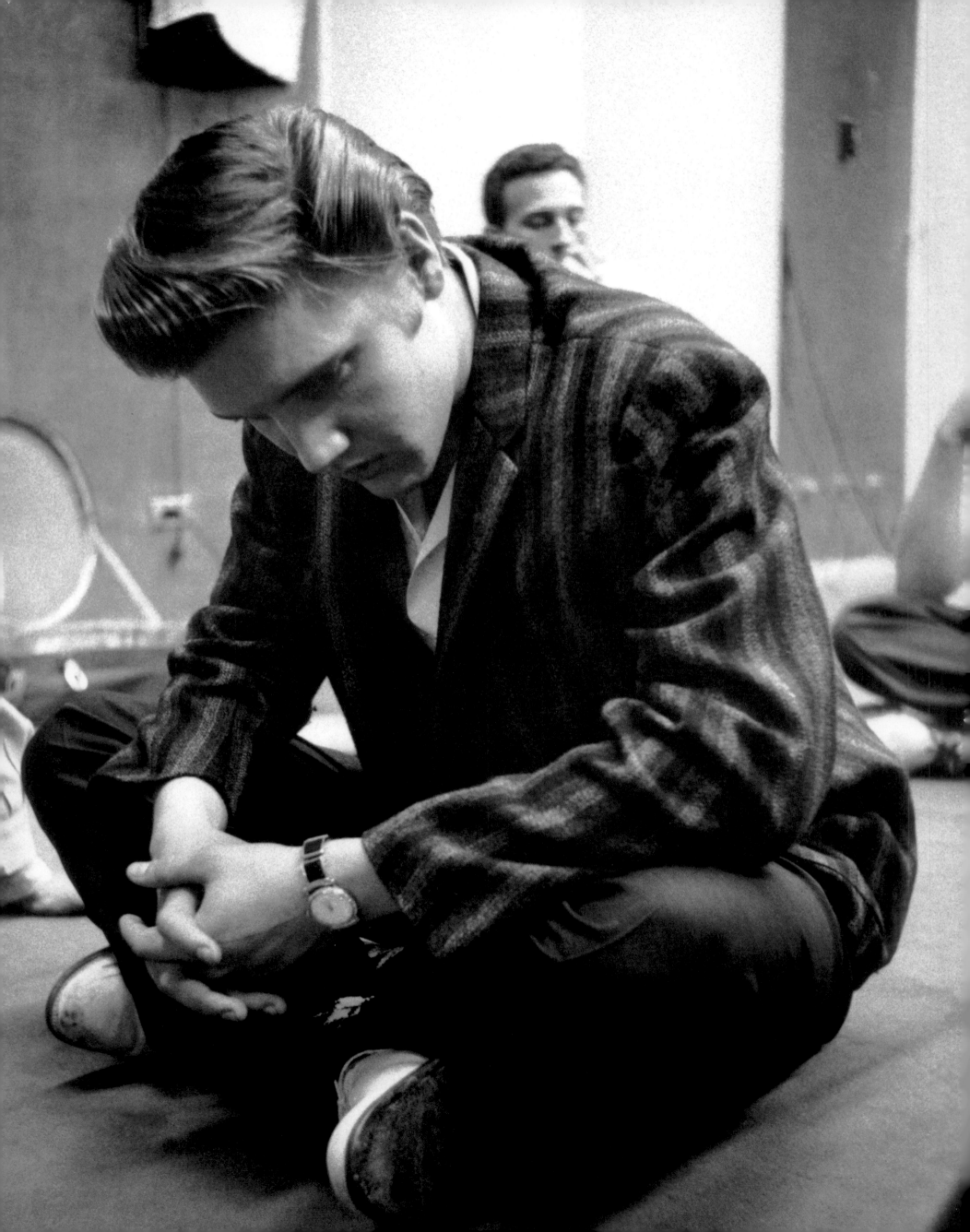

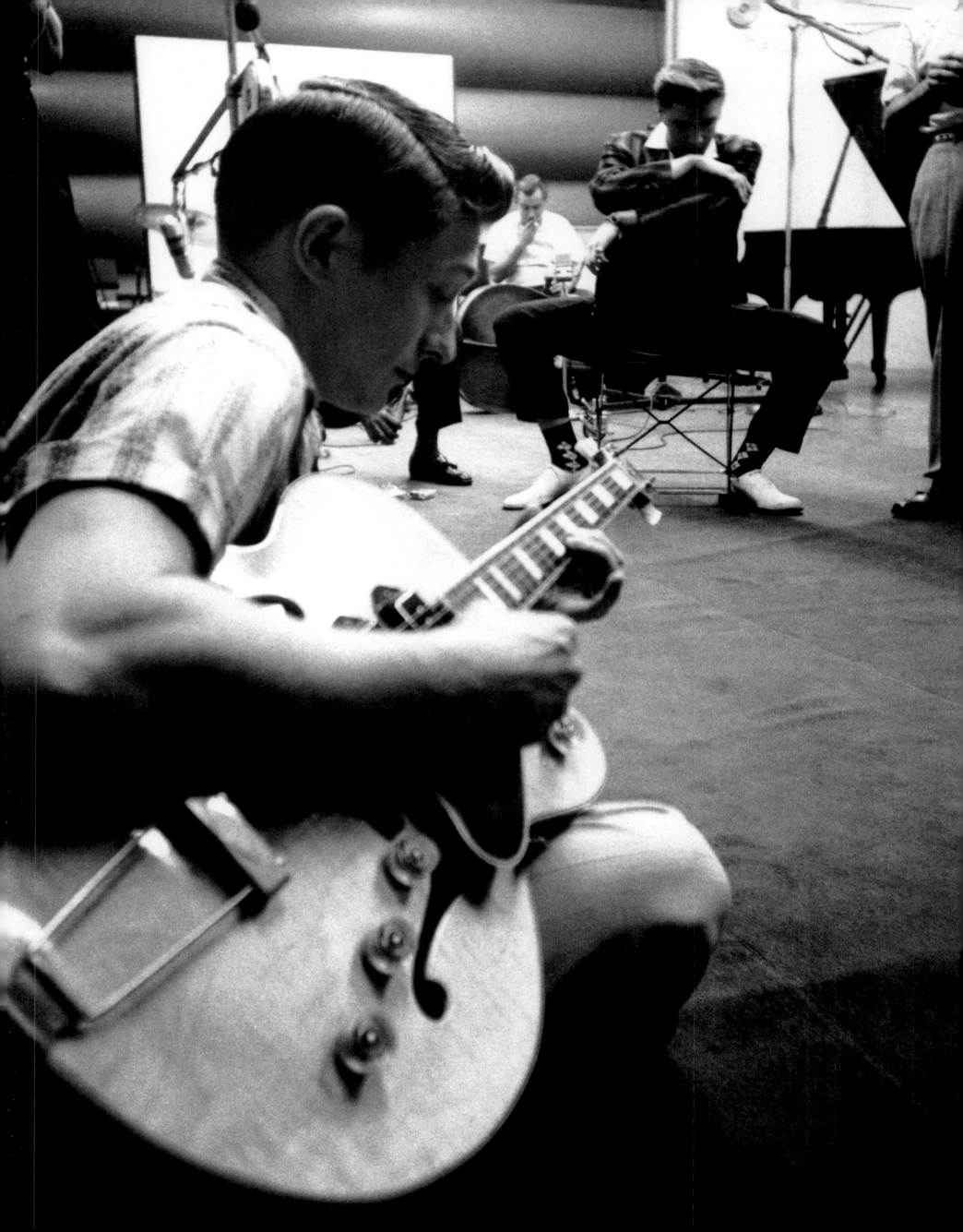

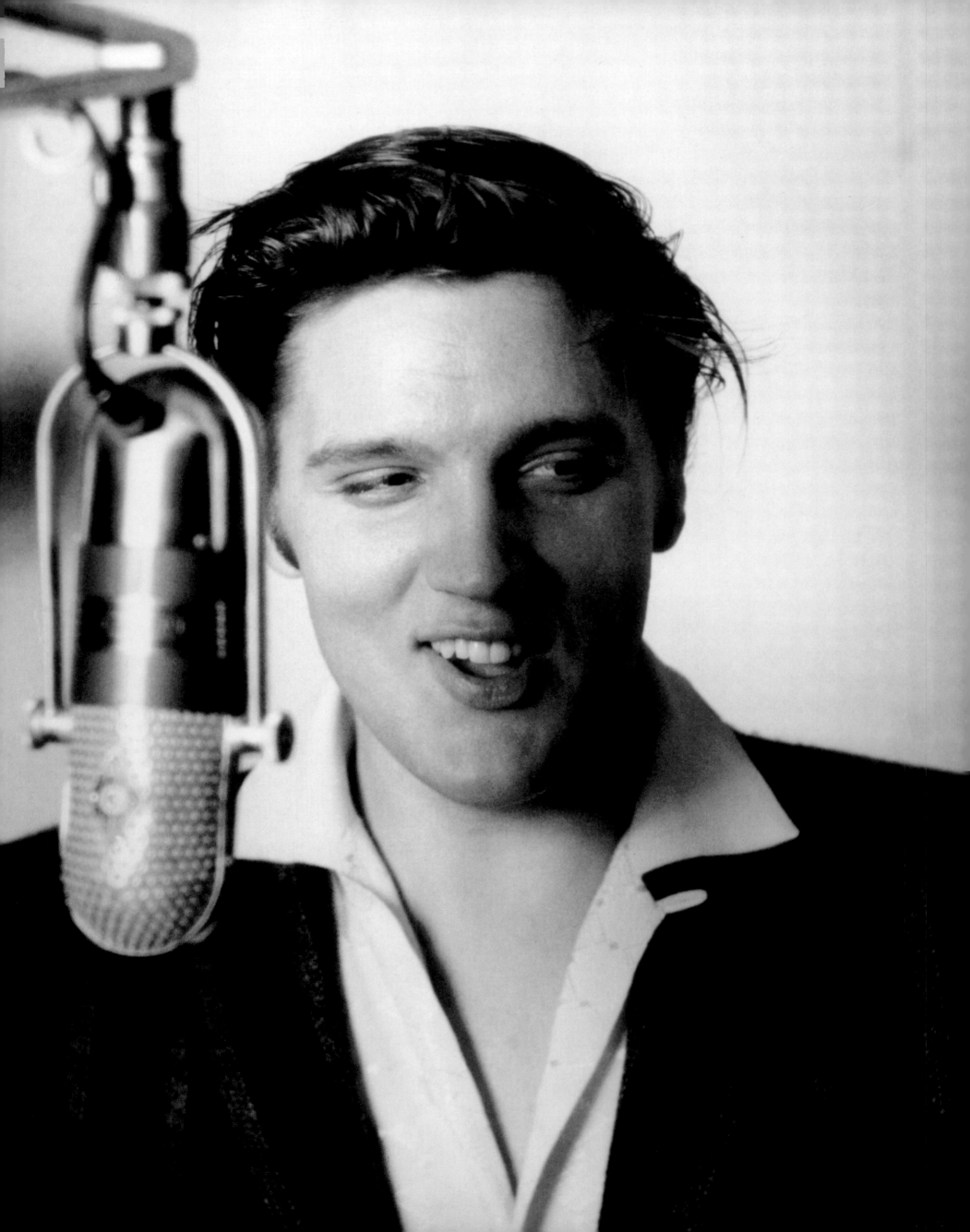

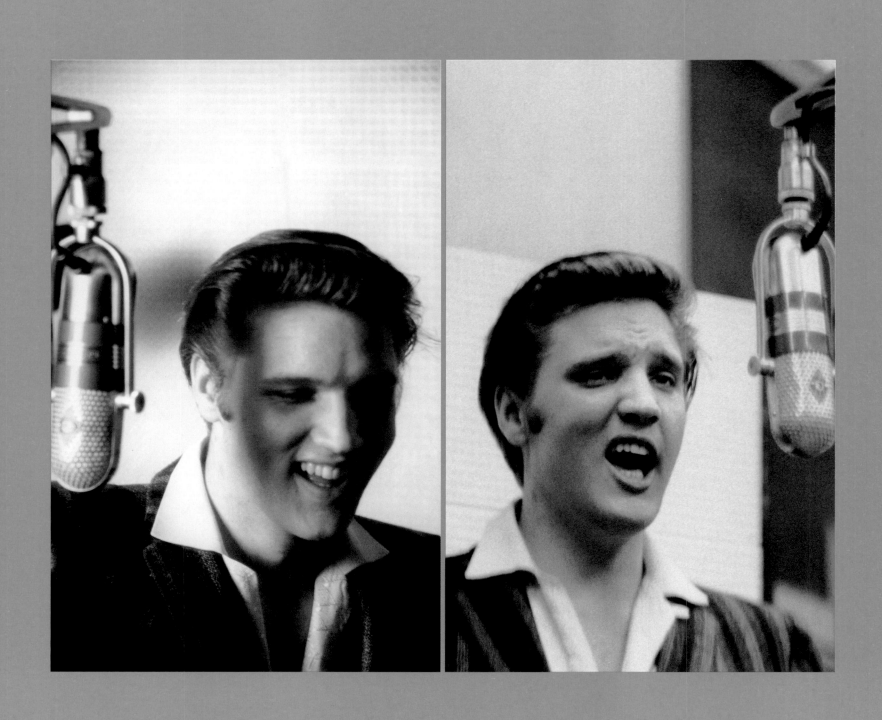

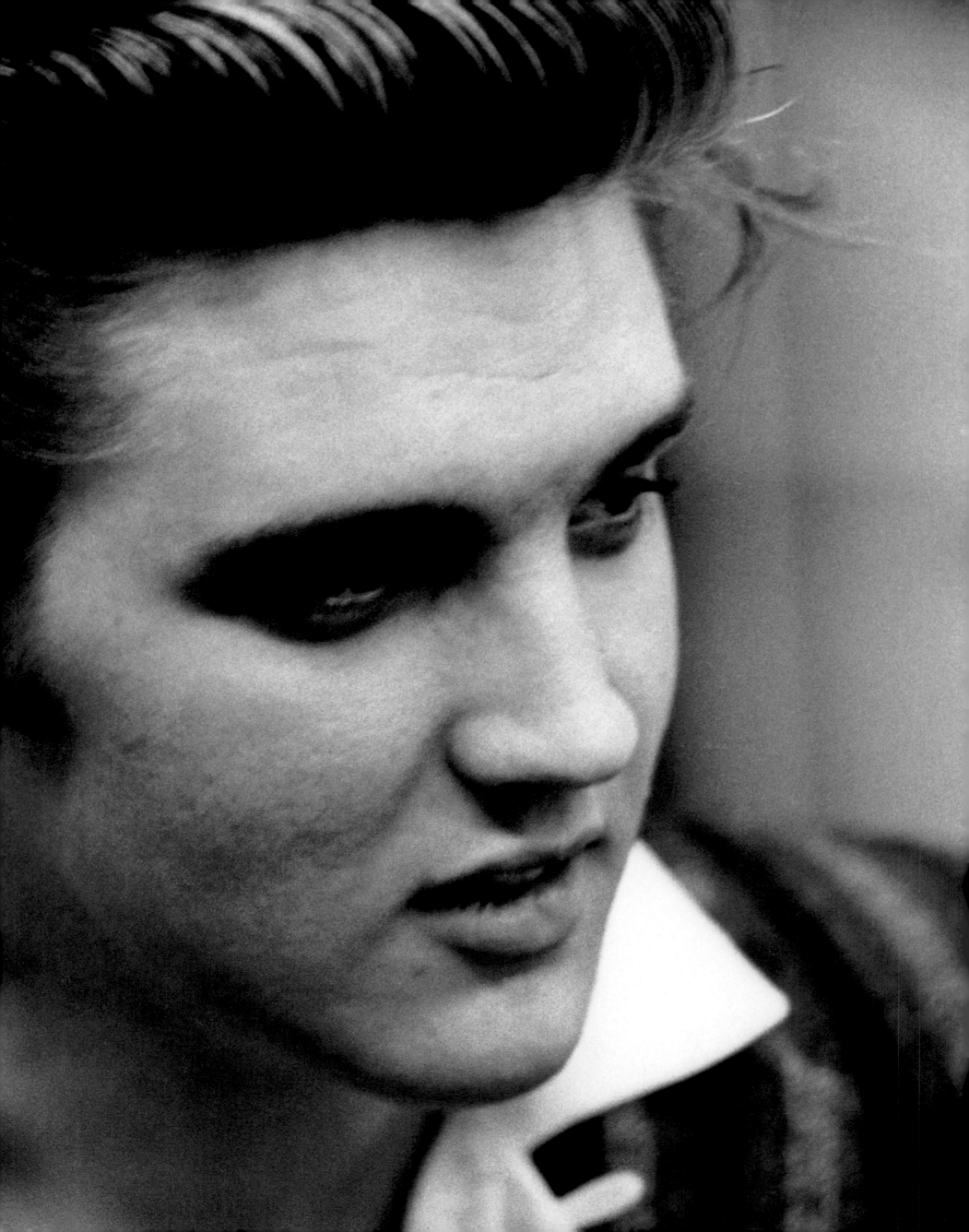

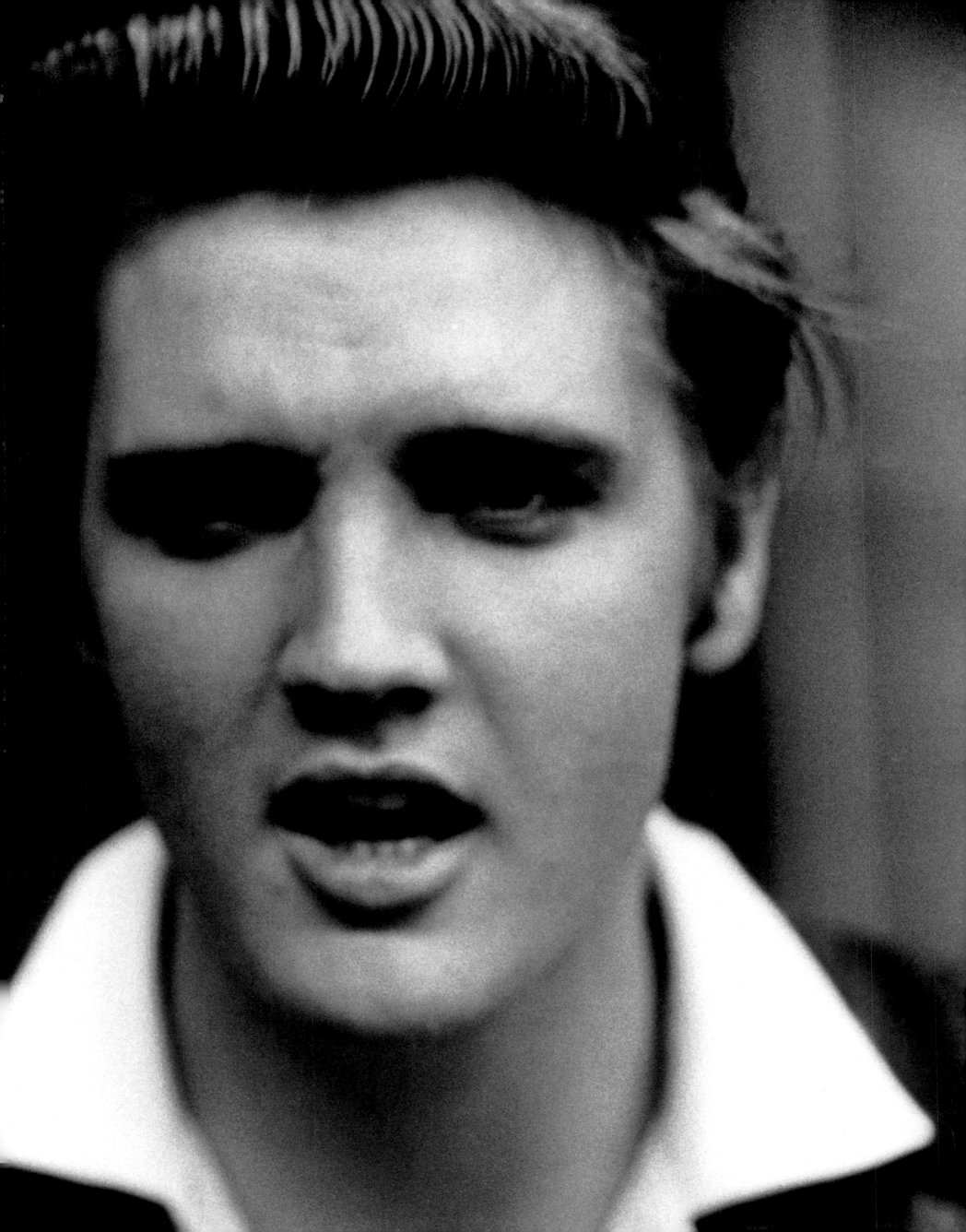

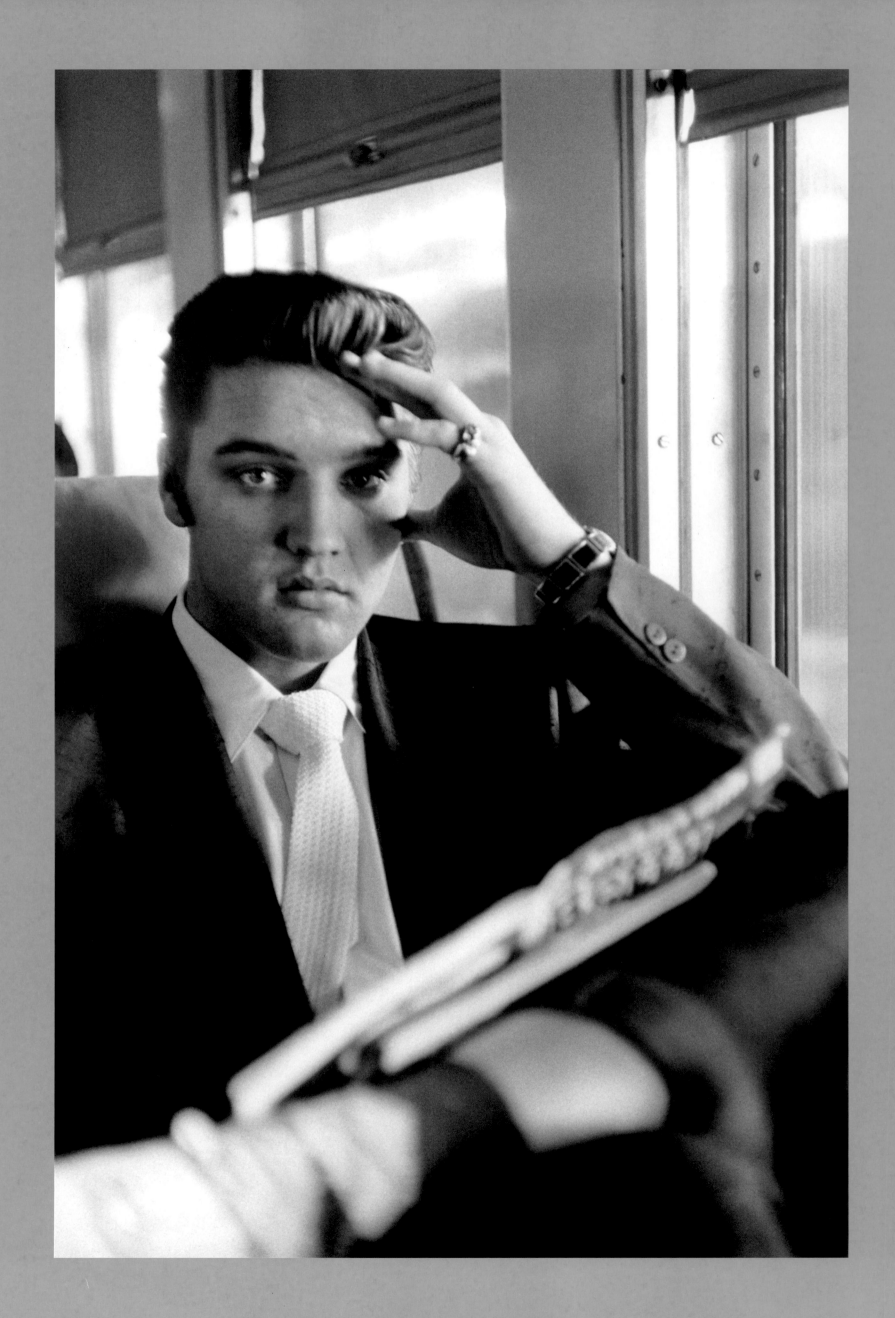

CHAPTER VI

FROM NEW YORK
TO MEMPHIS

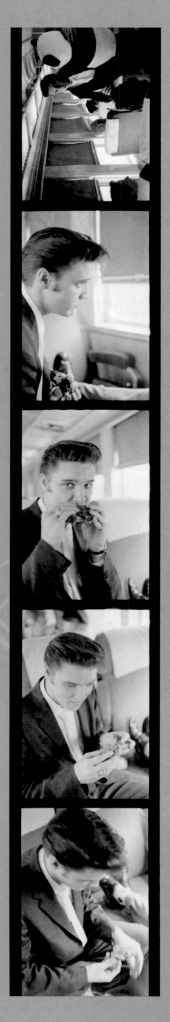

FROM NEW YORK
TO MEMPHIS

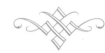

THE NEXT DAY, I caught up with Elvis and his band waiting to begin the journey south. They were standing on the concourse at Penn Station until the boarding call. With his acetates in hand and his guitar case on the floor near him, Elvis chatted with a few fans while a policeman kept an eye on the group. The next twenty-seven hours were spent mostly hanging out in and around railroad cars. From New York to Chattanooga, Elvis was preoccupied with the recording session. Finding an electric outlet in his compartment, he put a record player on his lap and repeatedly played the three tunes, "Hound Dog," "Don't Be Cruel," and "Any Way You Want Me." Every once in a while, one of the musicians would come in, get bored and then leave. Elvis kept mostly to himself for several hours, just listening intently.

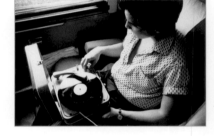

Watching him with his record player, I had to ask him, "Why do you keep playing them on this tiny little player?" It obviously wasn't very good quality, especially when just the day before we'd heard them on large speakers in a sound studio. He pointed out, "This might only be a $20 record player, but that's the way my fans would hear it." He wanted to know how he sounded to them. Despite the noise of the train and the people up and down the aisle, Elvis was completely focused on those recordings.

While he listened, I paced around, looking for images. With the medium close-up, I could get a nice shot of him from ten or twelve feet away. Since I had been thinking about getting prints to magazines, I began seeing these shots like a layout artist—what if somebody wanted to put a headline above there or drop a column of text down the right side? Elvis could be framed almost from the top of his head to the tip of his feet, sitting there by himself. How would it look on the page if I included the reflections on the metal door to the compartment and the light streaming in from the window?

The train pulled into Chattanooga station early in the morning. After a night's sleep, Elvis was in the aisle fooling around with a white knit tie. He put it around his neck, but for some reason, he just couldn't tie it. After leaving the train, he turned to someone for help on the platform. "DJ, tie my tie." Stepping behind Elvis, DJ put his arms around him and tried it as if he were tying his own tie. It looked pretty silly but it worked. Now he was ready for Chattanooga.

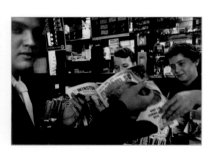

We had to wait several hours to make the connection. The Colonel passed some time telling stories that briefly seemed to have the attention of the fellows. A few moments later, Elvis wandered over to the newsstand inside the station and picked out a celebrity magazine. Flipping through it, he came across a double spread of himself.

"Al, give me a pen."

I gave him one, trying to figure out what he was up to. Elvis scrawled his name across the

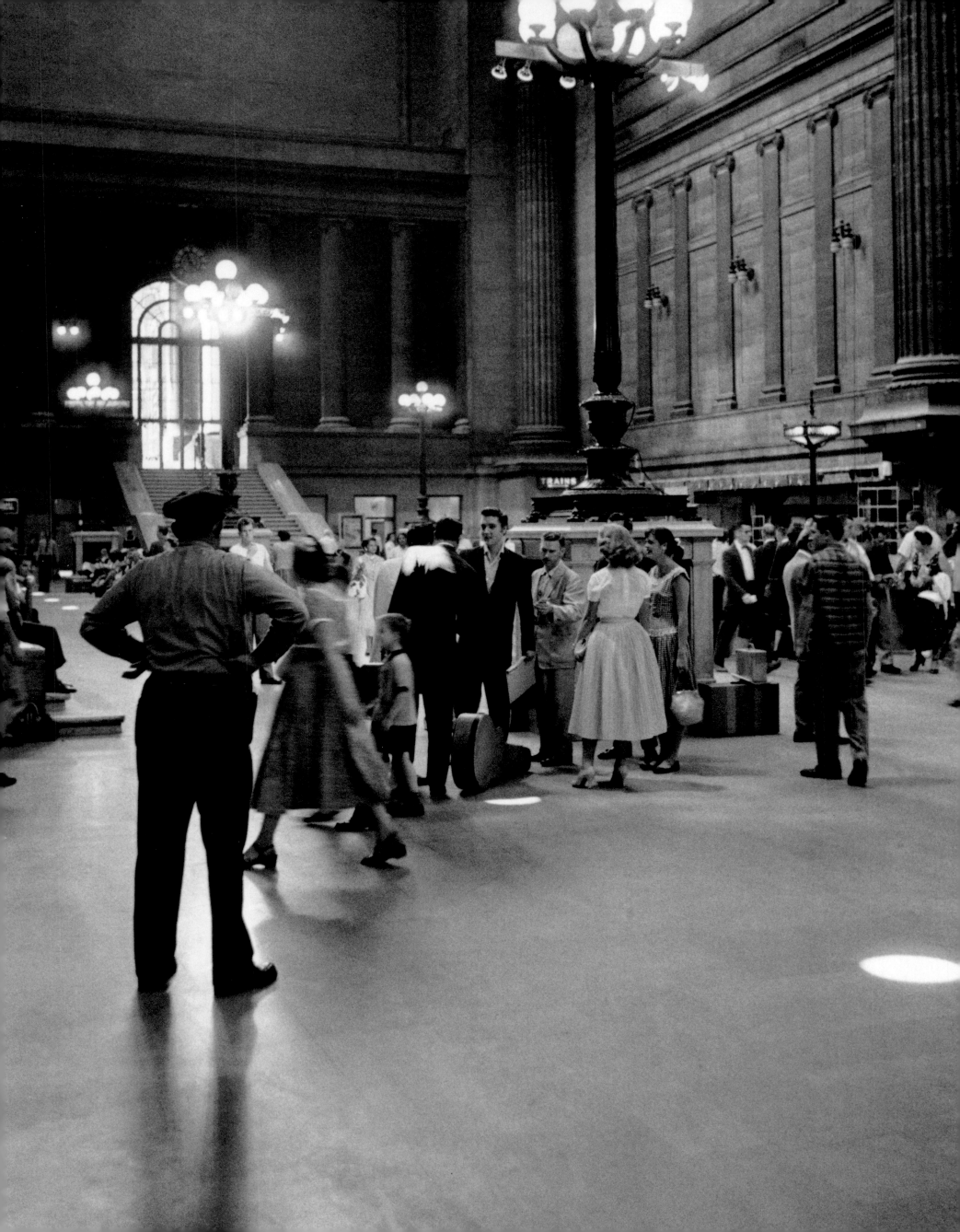

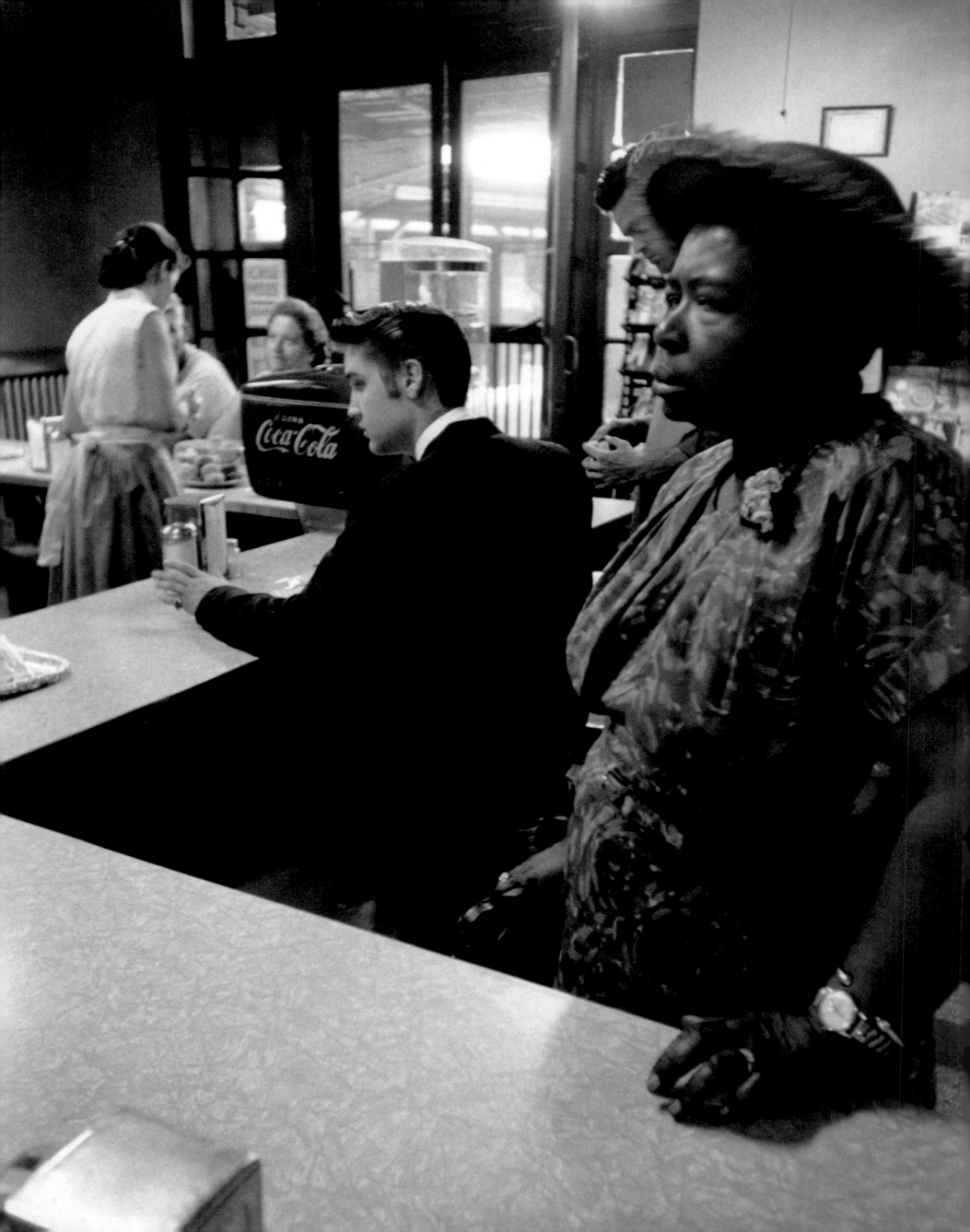

bottom of the picture in the magazine and returned my pen. He went over to the two girls at the counter and handed them the magazine with a slight grin and no explanation. The girls looked at each other, then at the picture in the magazine, and finally at him. It didn't take long to convince them. Before they could even ask for the thirty-five cents for the magazine, Elvis gave the magazine to them, even though he hadn't paid for it. Clearly, he was enjoying his early fame.

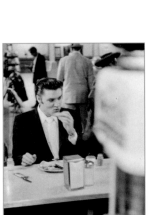

Satisfied that the girls now knew that he was Elvis Presley, he wanted to have a little breakfast. At the lunch counter, he started chatting up the waitress who took his order. A big container for pies sat on the counter. In the background was a slightly worn Coca-Cola machine. With the Coke and apple pie, the tableau had a feeling of Americana to it.

The Colonel was keeping busy as well. He often amused himself by playing tricks. Life was one big con game to him—con somebody or get conned; either way, it was good. If you put one over on somebody, it made your day. If you got conned, it was an education because you just added something to your own bag of tricks. In order to get the porter's attention, the Colonel held up two one-dollar bills, which was quite a nice tip in those days. Actually, it was a one-dollar bill folded over in such a way that it looked like he was holding up two.

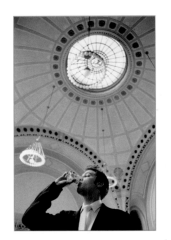

Flashing it in front of the porter's face, he said, "You see those musical instruments and those bags?" He told him we were going to Memphis on train so-and-so on track so-and-so. "Just bring them over there, and we'll see you later." With the help of another porter, the young man brought everything over to the other platform.

Later, as we got on the train, I watched the Colonel give the porter two quarters. Then he turned to Elvis with a self-satisfied grin on his face. That son of a gun, I thought. If that was the way he treated the porter, I had better watch my behind. I once asked him some time later why he never put a price on the playbills that were sold at the concerts. The Colonel replied, "Wertheimer," which was what he always called me, "you never want to put a price on anything. If you're in Vegas, you charge $2. If you're in a stadium, you charge a dime. Either way, you're making money." I was being tutored by the best.

We continued our journey on a very slow local train that felt like it covered no more than thirty miles an hour for the entire 400 miles to Memphis. Sitting nearby was a stuffed panda bear traveling on its own. It was never clear where this bear came from, although I suspected the Colonel planted it. Elvis held Panda Bear, who became another character on the train, on his hip and, looking very serious, decided to walk down the center aisle of the car. Strangers glanced up at this weird guy walking through the train with this big panda on his hip. Passing two women, an old lady, and an old man, he went all the way to the other end to a water fountain. With Panda still on his left hip, he pulled out a cone-shaped cup from the receptacle, squeezed it open and filled it with water—all with one hand. The whole time he didn't say a word to me. He completely ignored me, which really made me curious.

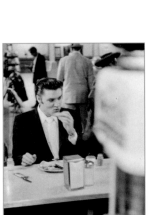

Elvis started back in the other direction until halfway down the aisle when he quickly turned to the left to two young ladies. "You coming to my concert tonight?"

"What concert?" they replied guardedly.

"At Russwood Park."

They still didn't recognize him. "Well, who are you?"

"I'm Elvis Presley."

The girls looked skeptical, so he pointed to me standing on top of some seats with my camera. "You see that photographer over there? Do you think he'd be taking my picture if I wasn't Elvis Presley?" Convinced that a photographer wouldn't be shooting pictures of just anyone, they loosened up and started chatting with Elvis about this and that. Pleased that I had caught the best part of the story, I wandered off back to my seat. A few minutes later, he returned to his and set Panda down next to him. Satisfied that he had converted yet another unbeliever, Elvis settled in to read an Archie and Veronica comic book.

Inching westward, the train hugged the border of Georgia before dipping into Alabama, stop-

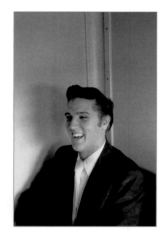

ping for lunch in Sheffield. On the platform in Sheffield, there was a middle-aged woman selling items like fried chicken, snow cones and cigarettes. After lunch and a short nap, Elvis went back to reading his comic book. Junior just sat in some sort of dreamlike state in the seat across from Elvis. Junior also slipped into a nap, and Panda served as his cushion.

Standing in the aisle opposite Elvis, I decided to shoot some pictures from my waist to see how candid the results would be. Up to now, I was always pulling the camera up to my face, giving him a chance to prepare for the image that was going to be captured. For a moment, he appeared deep in thought with his hand up to his head. People always believed that Elvis had a clarinet in his lap, but in fact, they were magazines that were a bit out of focus. I got one of my better pictures then, the one I still consider my Rembrandt shot. When I developed the film, a portrait of both his inner and outer self emerged. The light coming in from the train window lit one side of his face, while his hand created deep shadows on the other side. I called that particular shot "Going Home." (p. 152)

I n the last stretch of the trip, Elvis went into the washroom, a sort of anteroom to the bathroom. In those days, you could relax there and have a cigarette while the porter brought you a Coke and some candy. Elvis was a storyteller, and in this room he decided to indulge by telling a funny story. All the other musicians were there; at his immediate left were Scotty and Bill Black, and DJ and Junior were somewhere nearby. He animated his story by changing facial expressions, sticking his jaw out and looking like Mussolini, clutching his hands, putting two fingers up to his mouth and laughing. I kept shooting Elvis and a rather bored-looking Scotty. Apparently, that wasn't the first time they heard that story, but out of politeness, they would sit through each telling. I forgot what it was about, but it made Elvis laugh and laugh while everybody else sat around deadpan.

Fully awake now towards the end of this long and tedious train ride, Elvis began freshening up. He unbuttoned his fly and tucked his shirt into his pants. I was still clicking away as he stood there with his fly open. This time, he got a little annoyed. He never actually said, "Don't shoot," but he did stare me down as he zipped up his pants. I boldly stood my ground and kept shooting as he washed his hands and combed his hair. There were no paper towels so he had to shake off the water before putting his jacket on.

We hadn't reached Memphis yet but he headed toward one of the exits. Someone quickly handed him the acetate cuts of the recording session. I wasn't sure what all the commotion was about so I continued observing. The Colonel finally had roused himself from his nap and was talking to the train conductor, who got on the phone to the engineer. "We have somebody who wants to get off the train. Can we make a short stop at White Station?"

The Colonel approached Elvis. "Don't forget to give your folks my regards."

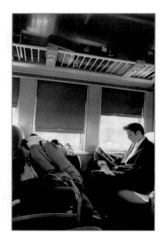

What was going on? The train came to a stop and I noticed a small sign with the word "White" on it go by. Feeling like a dumb hick from New York, I thought that maybe that was where white people got off the train. I wasn't sure what to expect down south.

It turned out that White, Tennessee was a small town right outside of Memphis. That stop was closer to Elvis's home on Audubon Drive than the main terminal in Memphis. With only the records, no luggage or instruments, he hopped off the train and headed down a grassy knoll towards the sidewalk of this little town. Between telephone poles and Cadillacs, Elvis stopped to ask a black woman on the street for directions and then turned to wave to us on the train. As the train started moving, I quickly figured that I was better off taking pictures of what was going on in front of me instead of jumping off the train and following Elvis. If I had stopped to collect my bags and all of my equipment, I would have missed what was probably one of the last times he could just walk down the street like an ordinary guy.

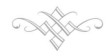

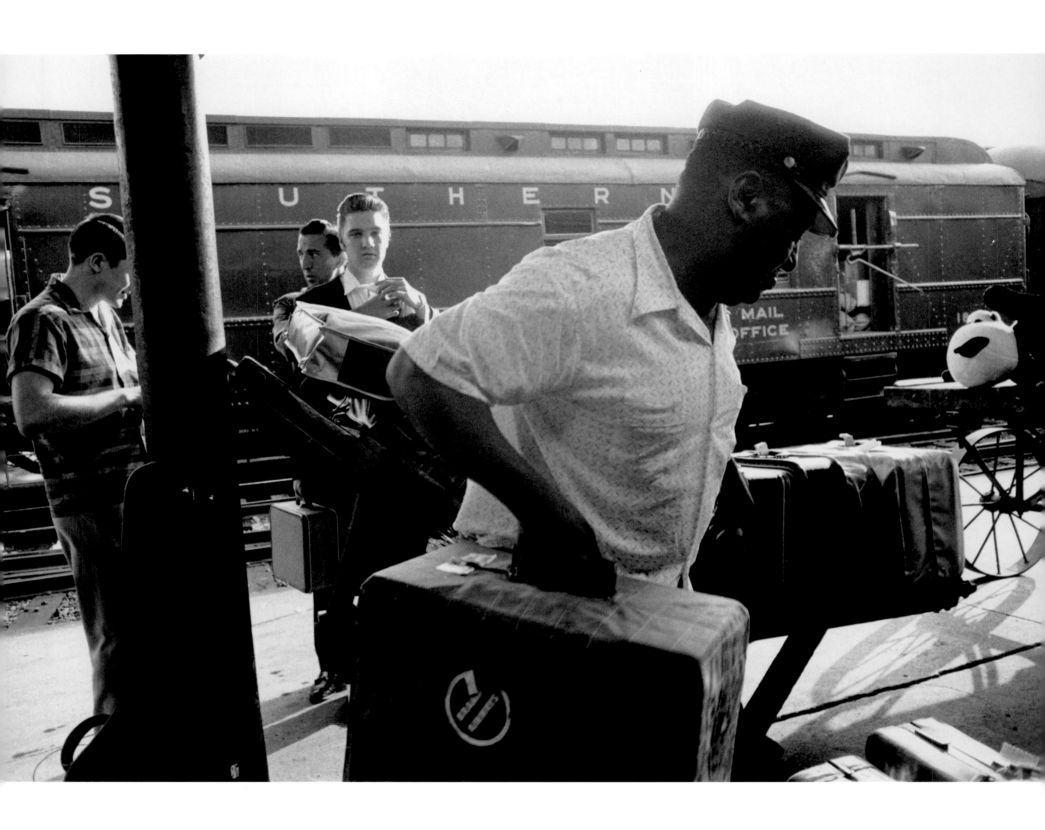

159

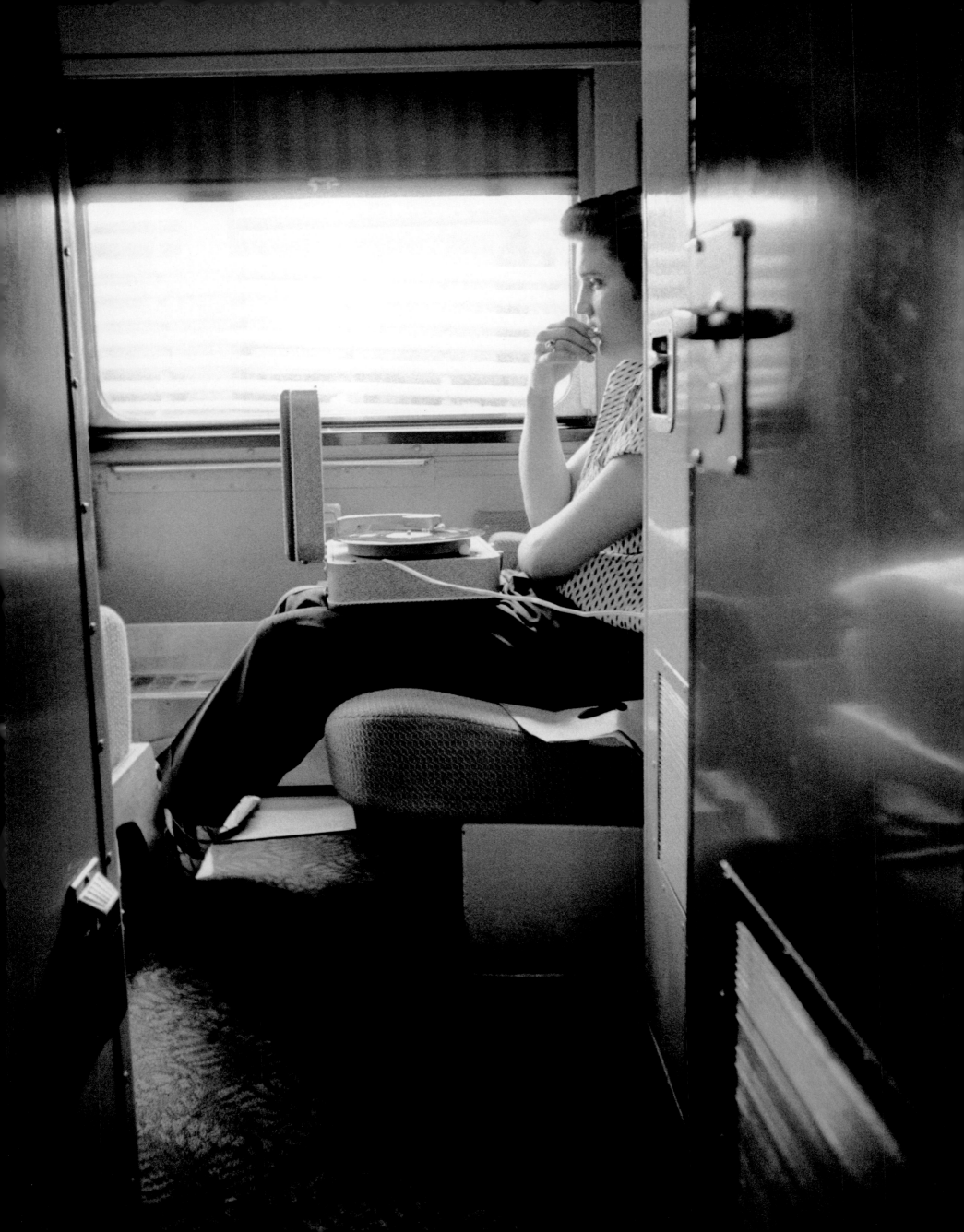

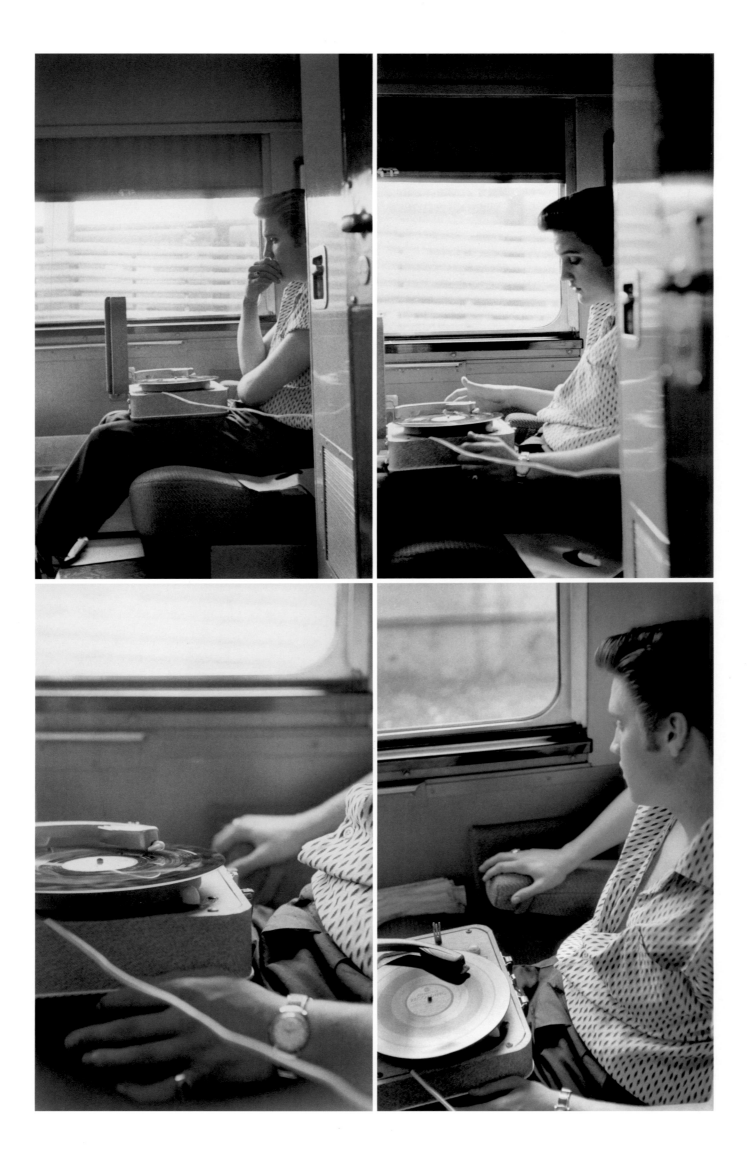

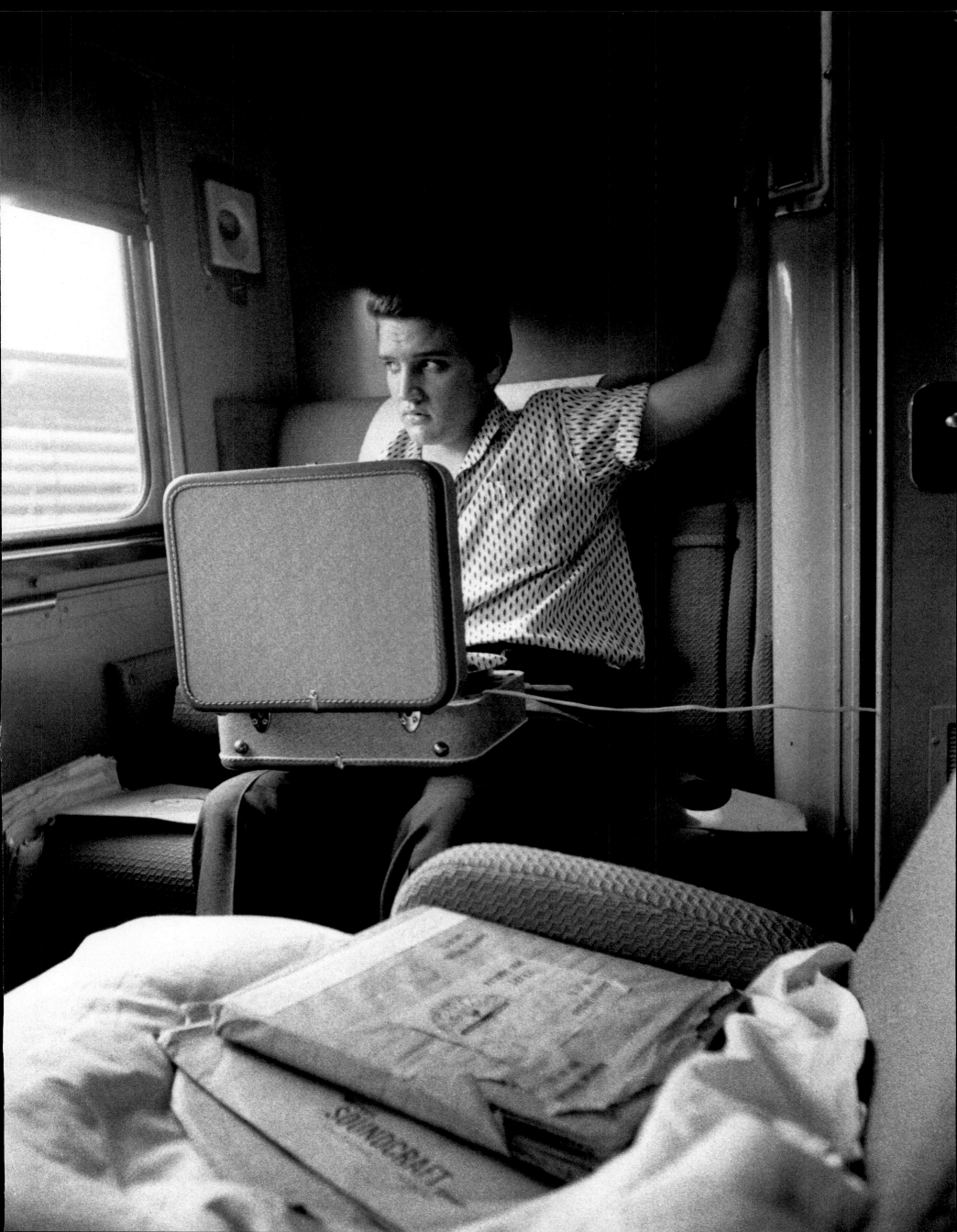

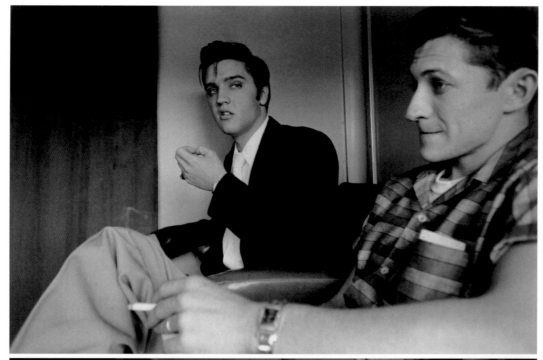

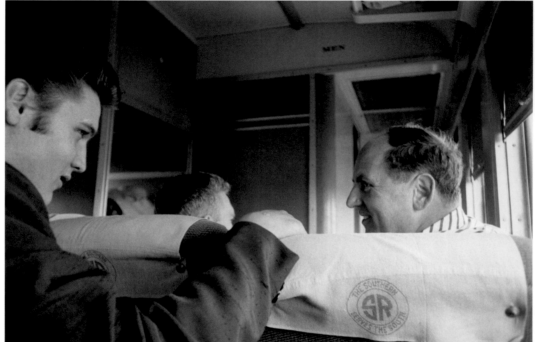

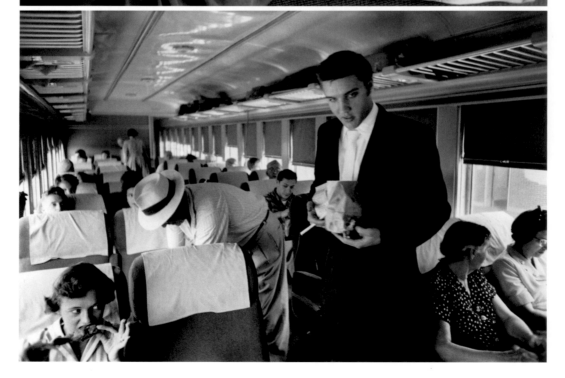

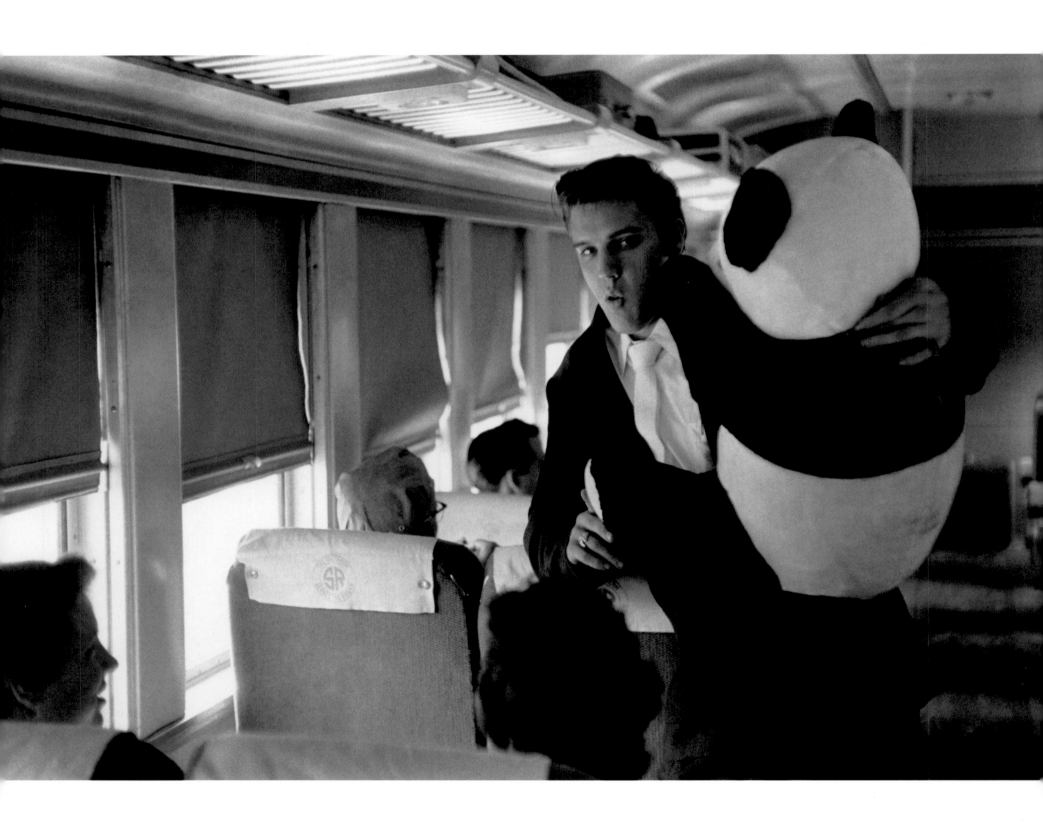

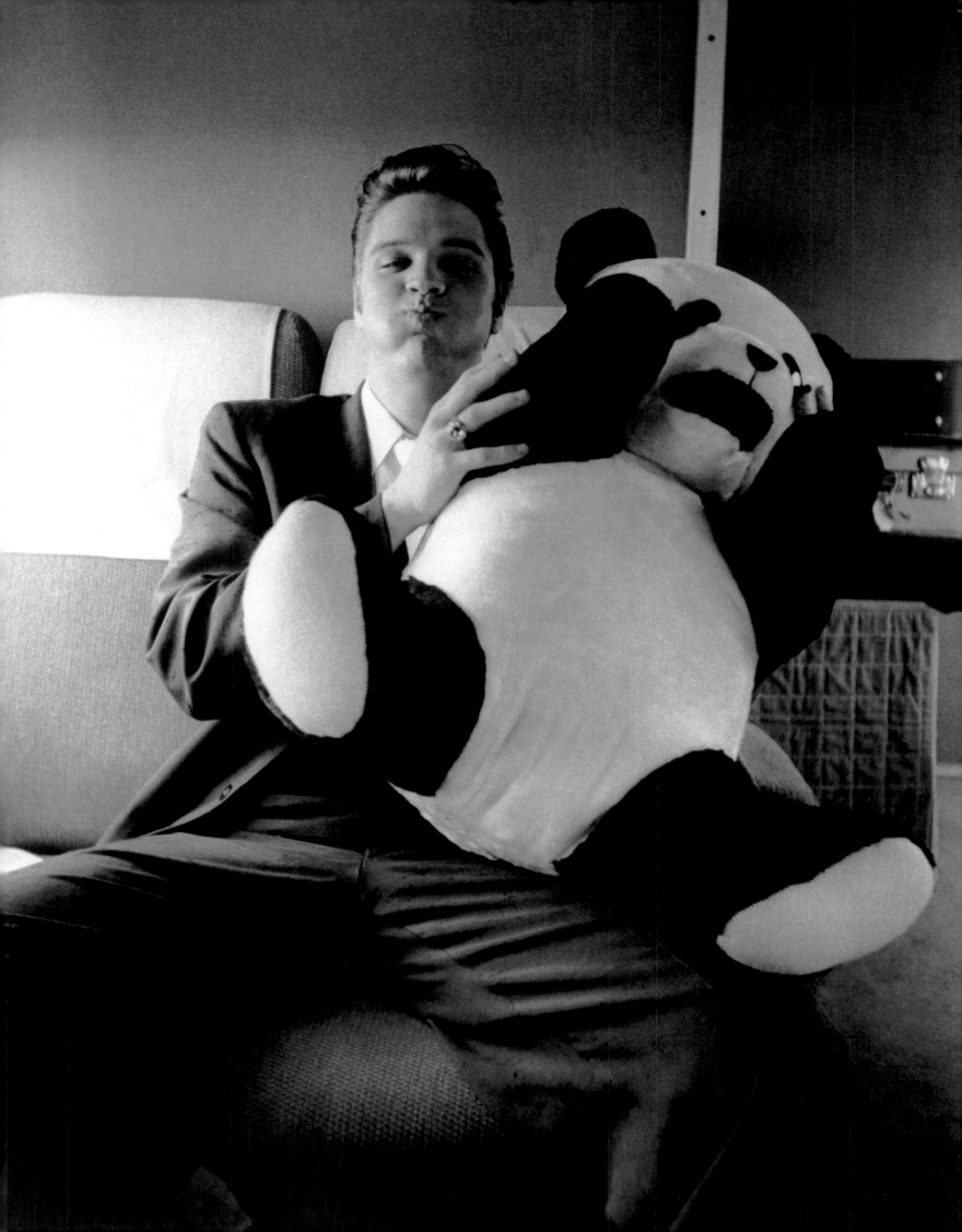

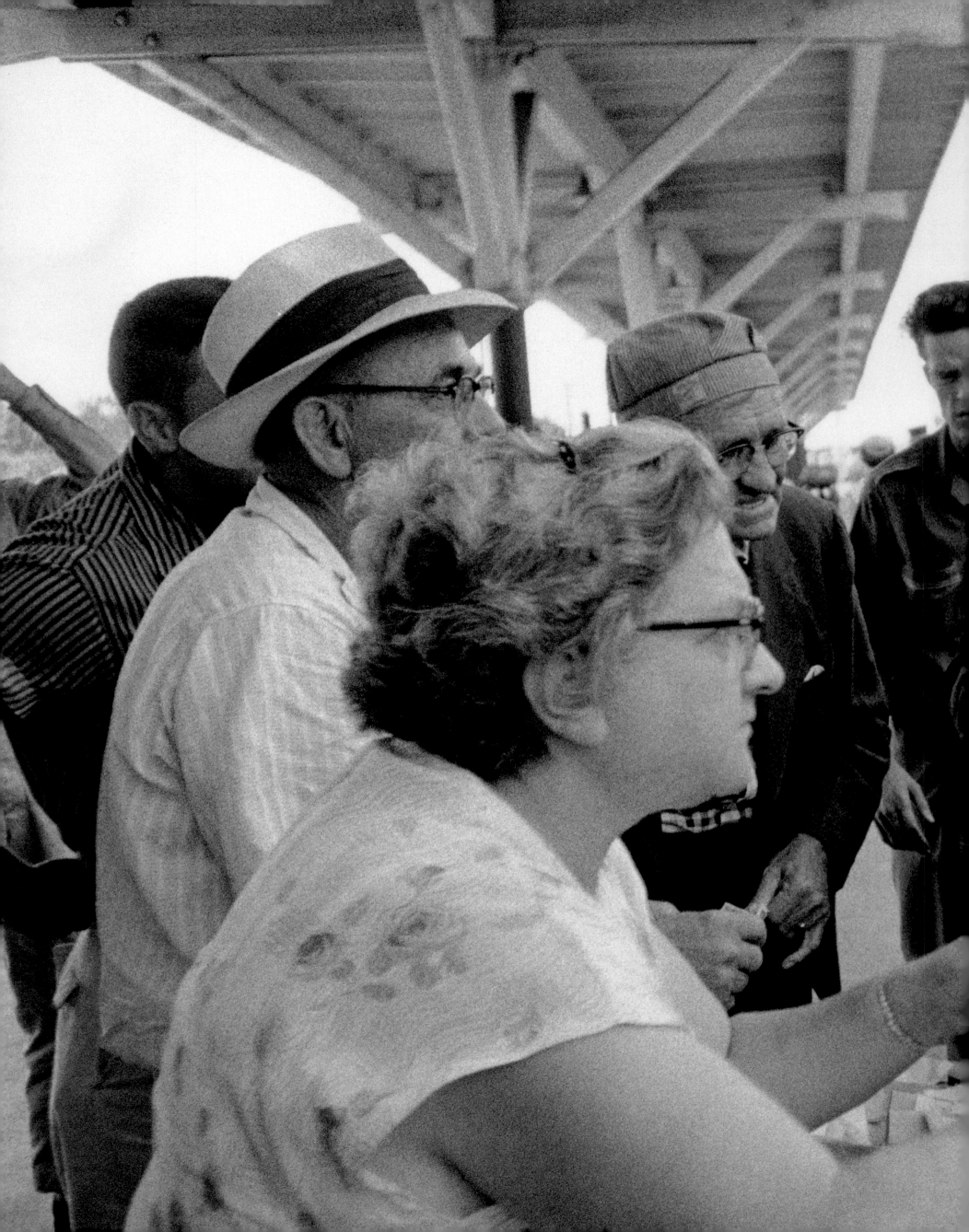

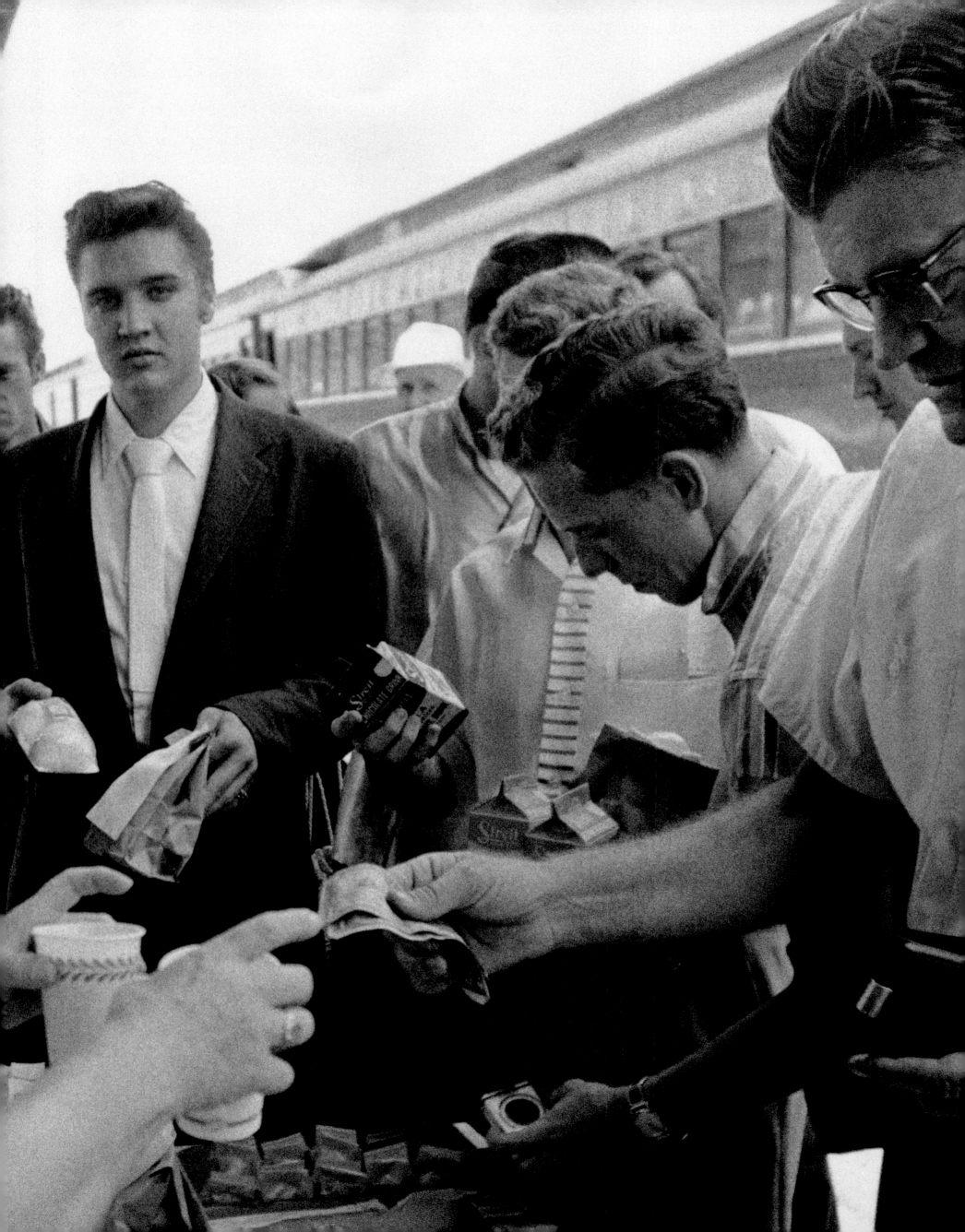

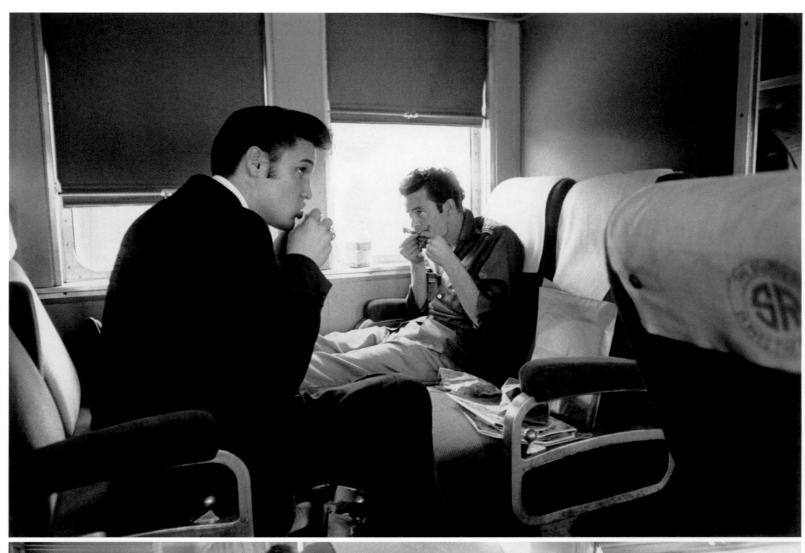

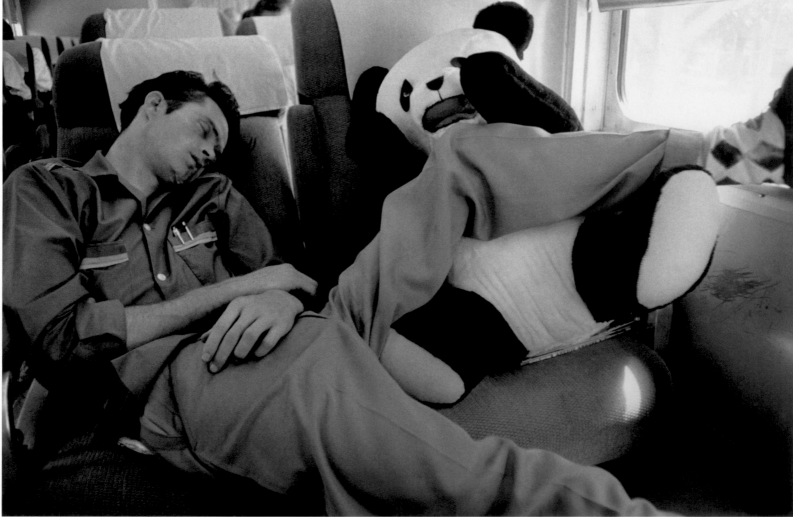

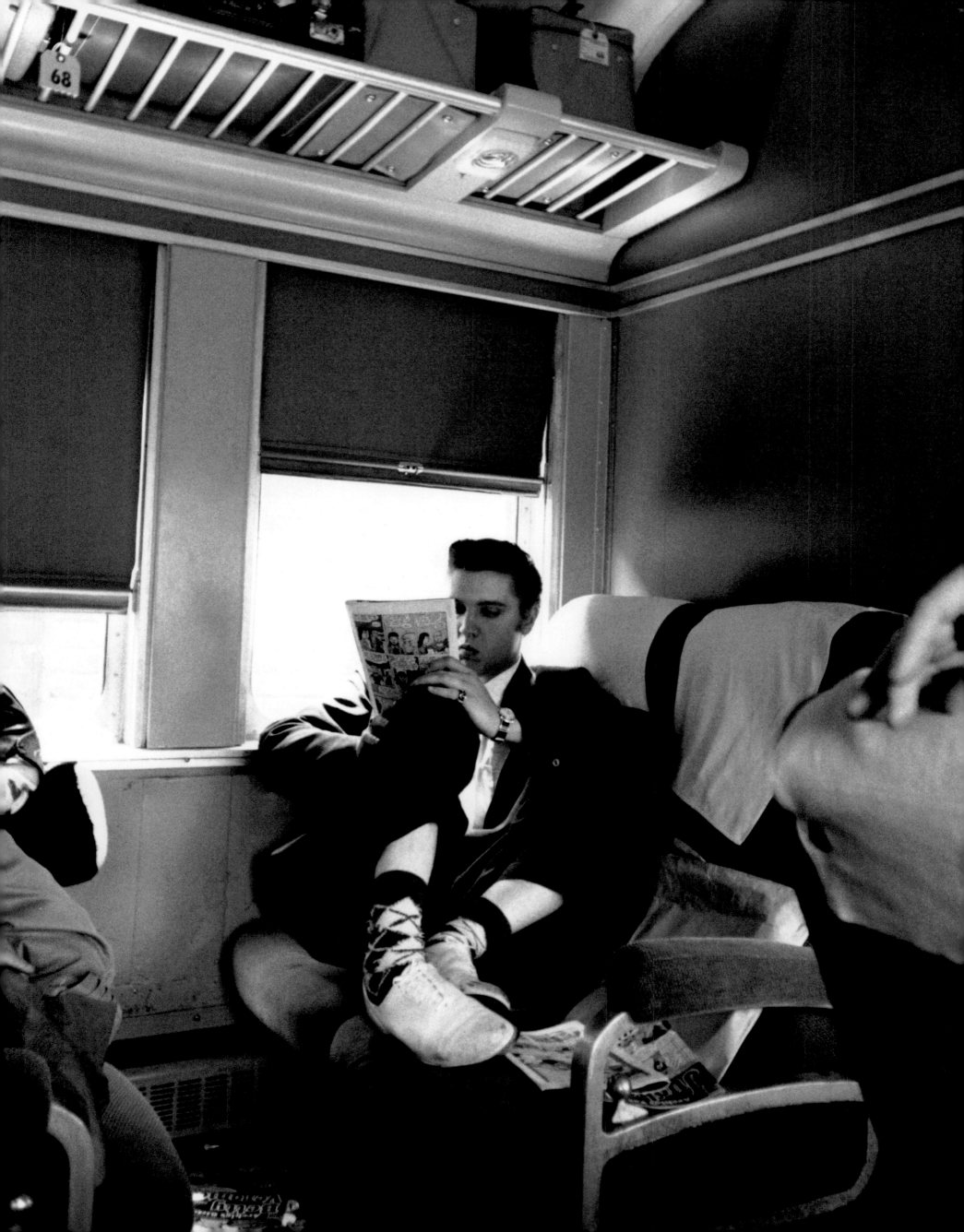

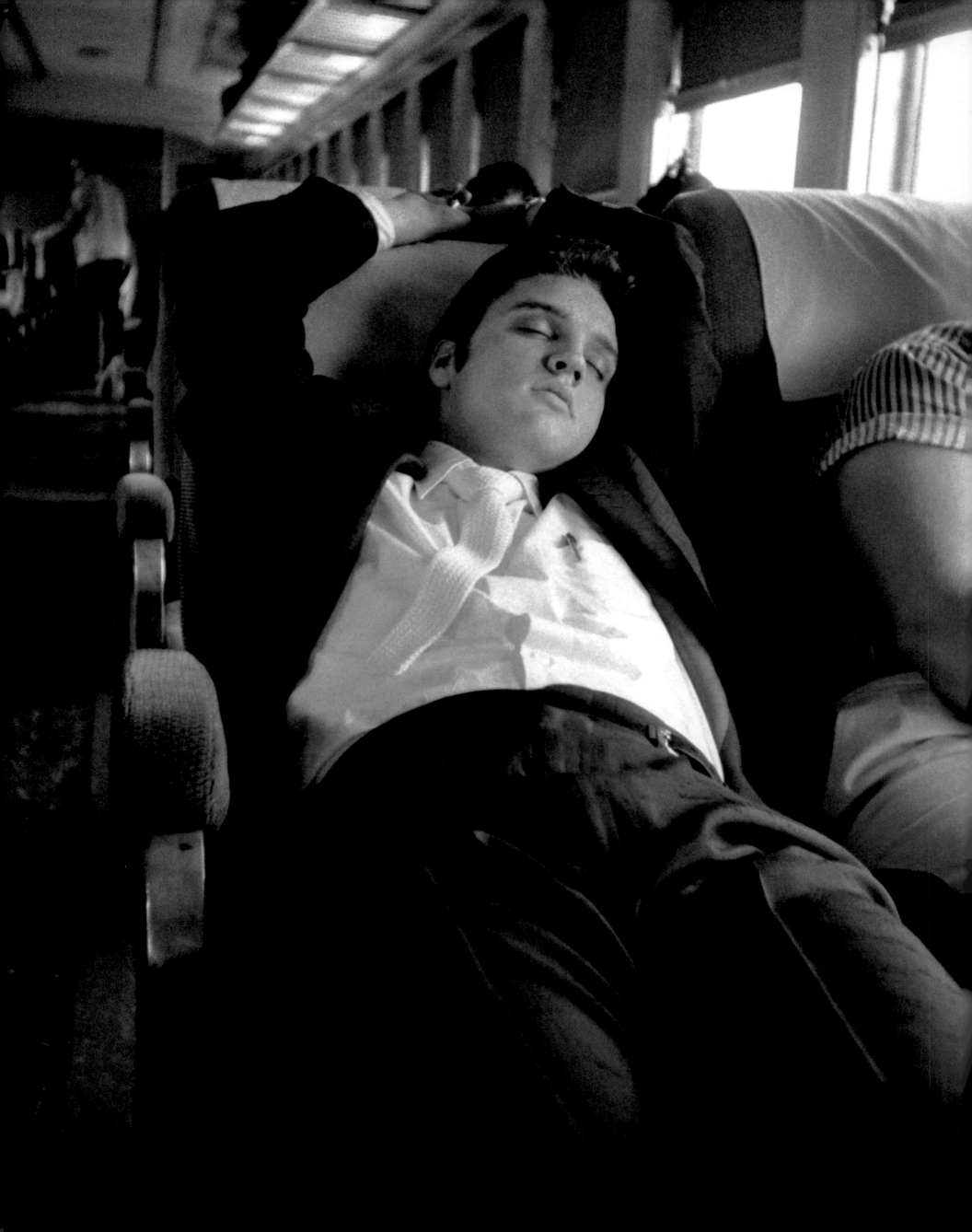

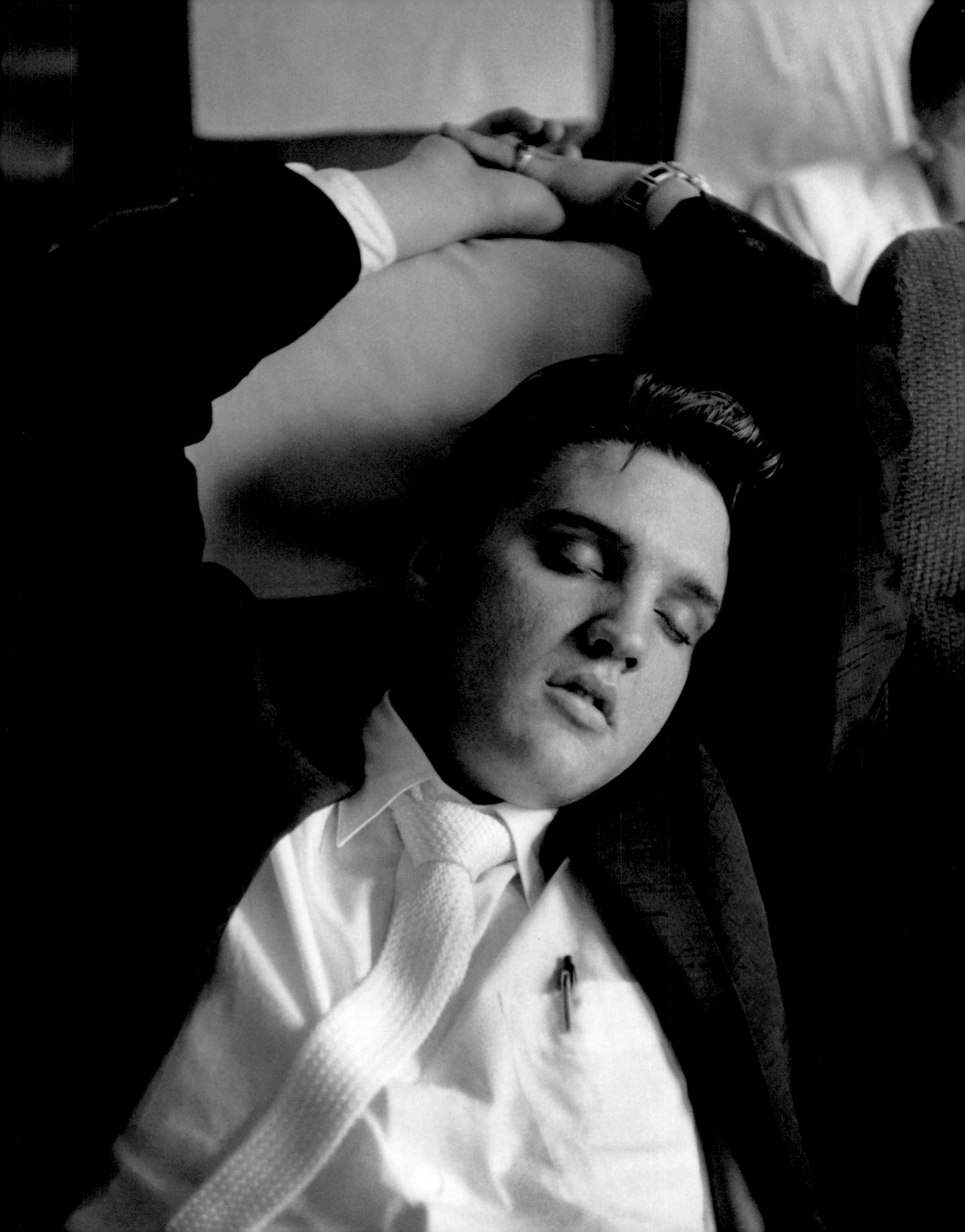

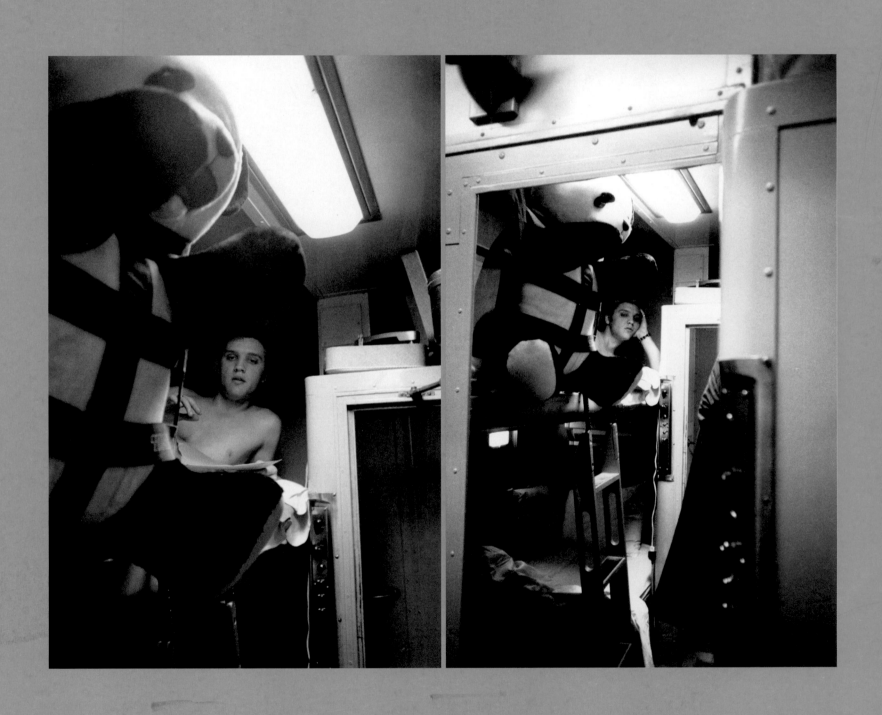

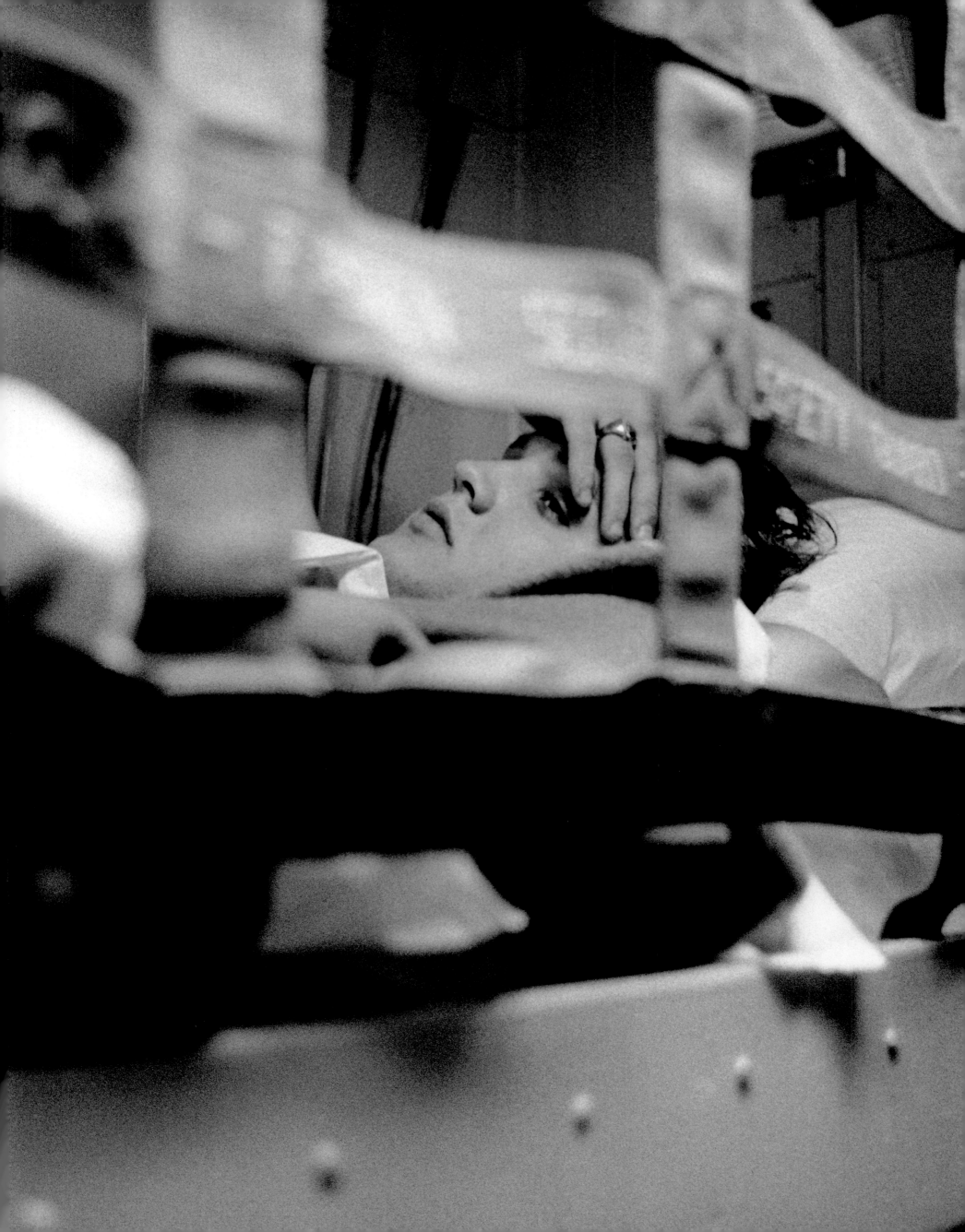

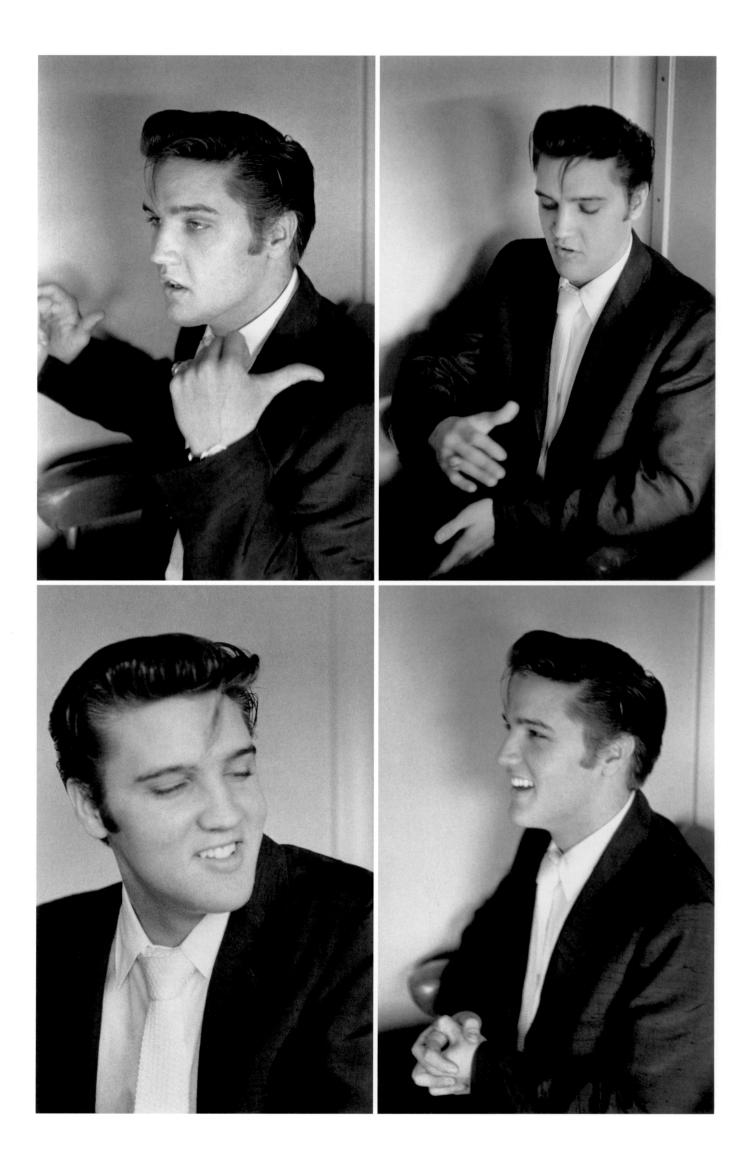

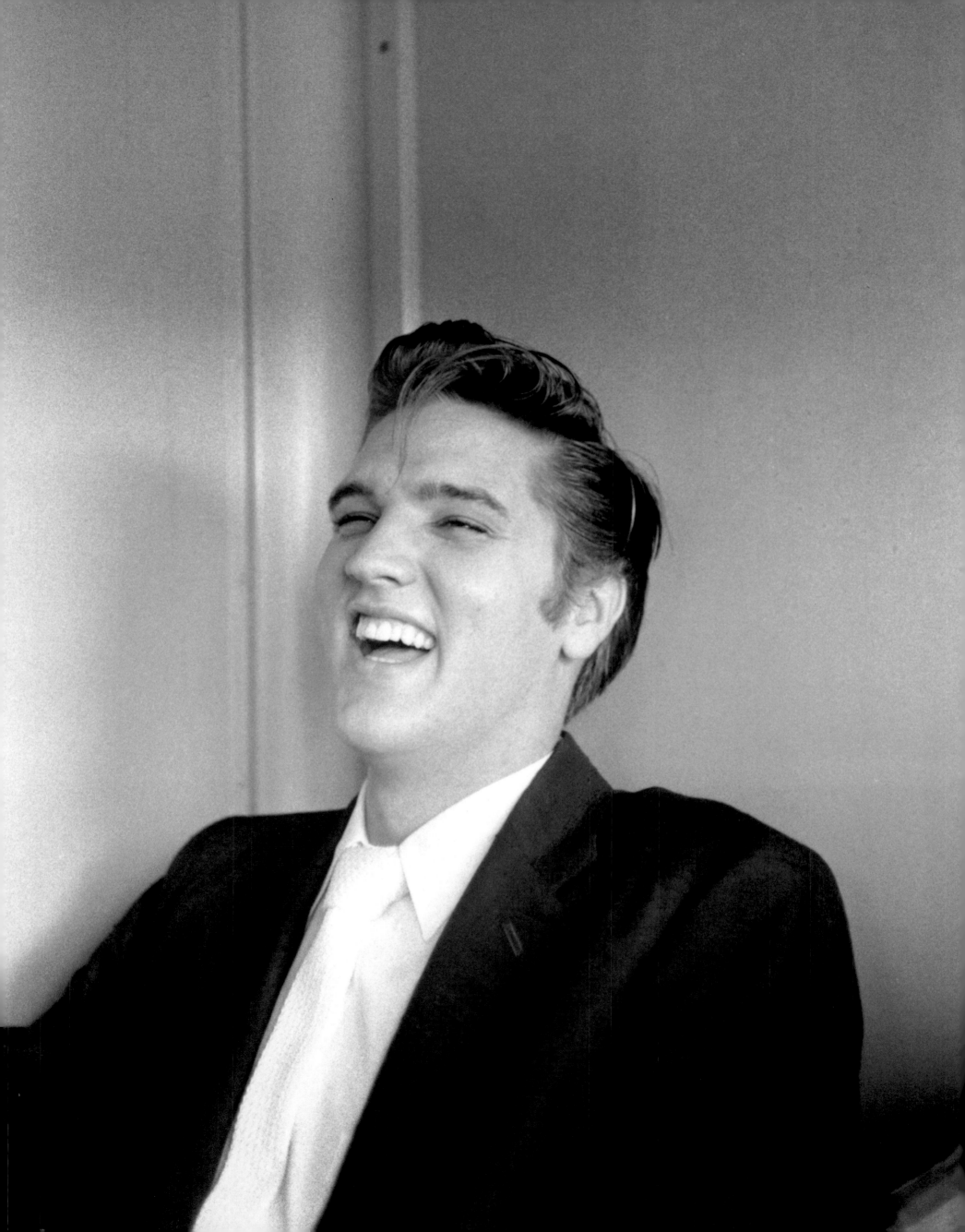

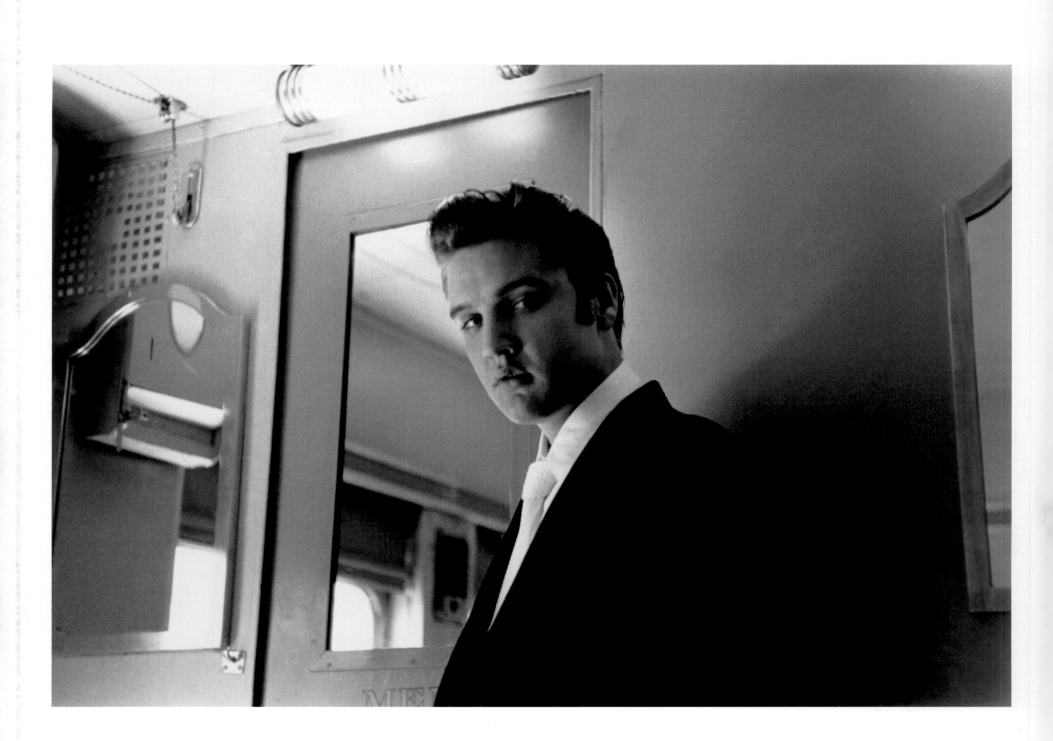

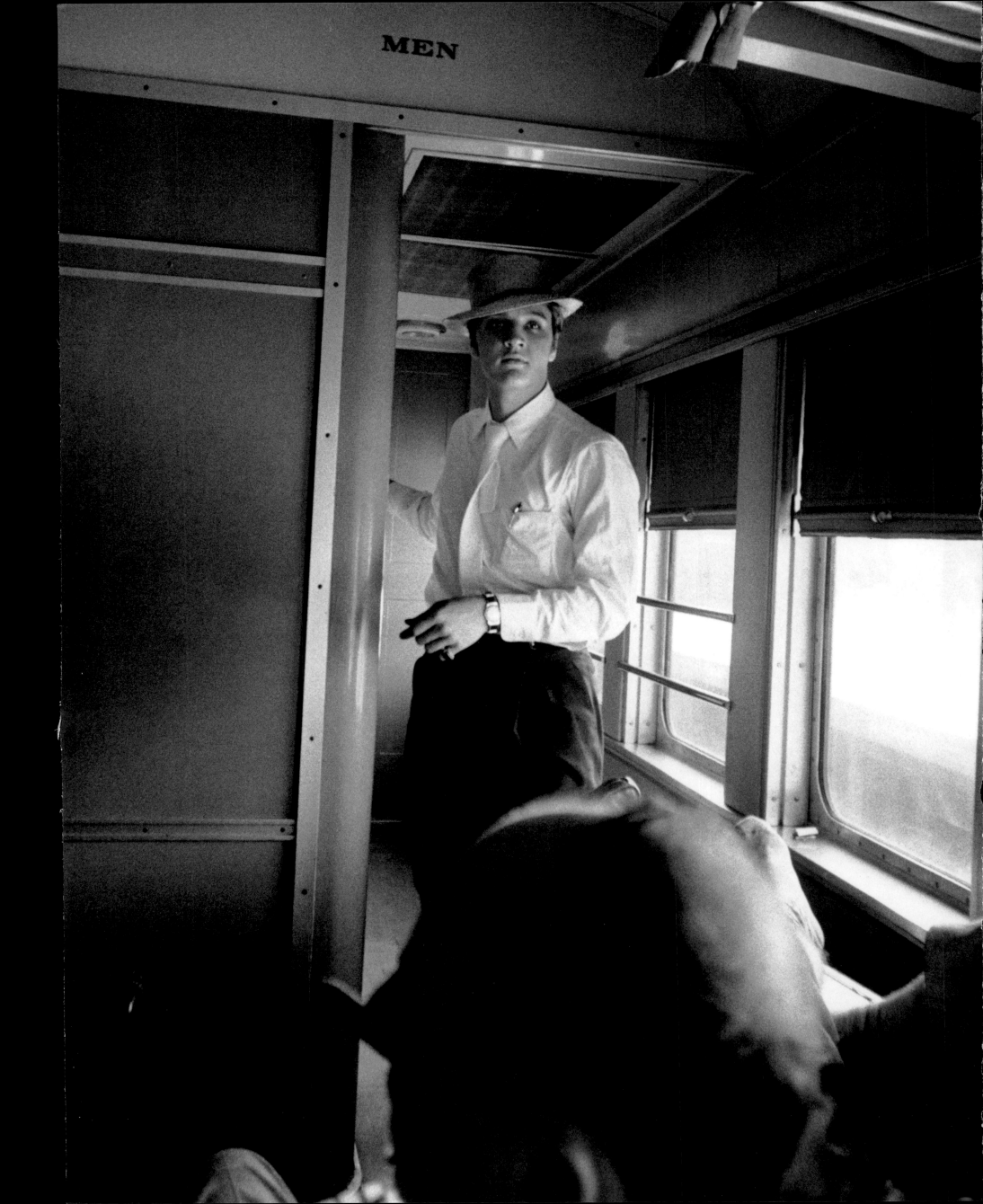

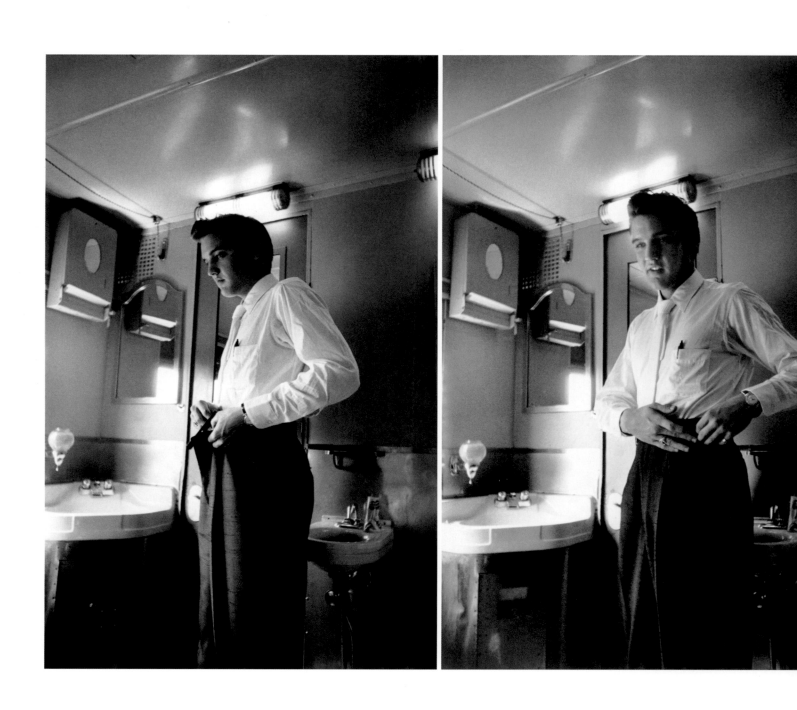

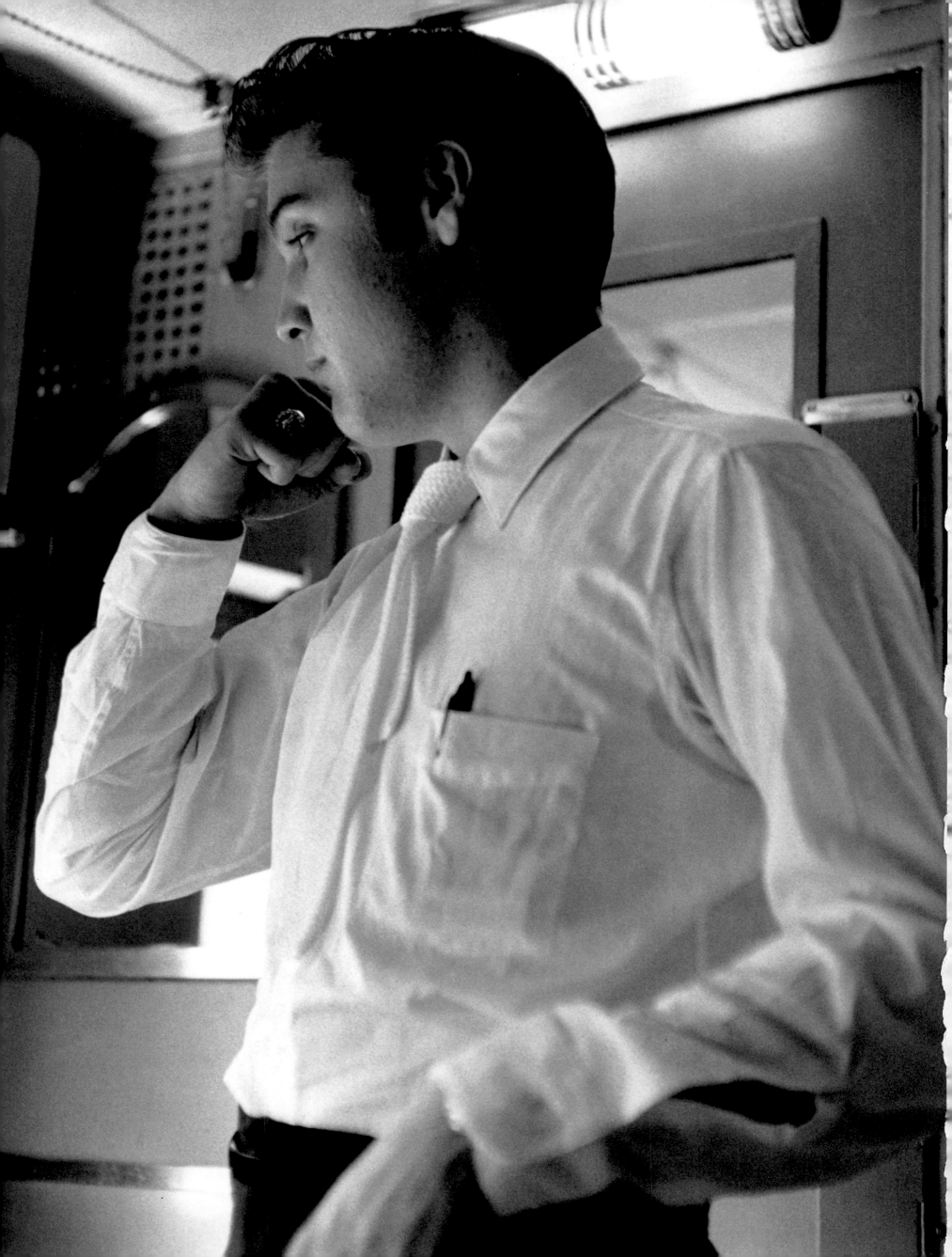

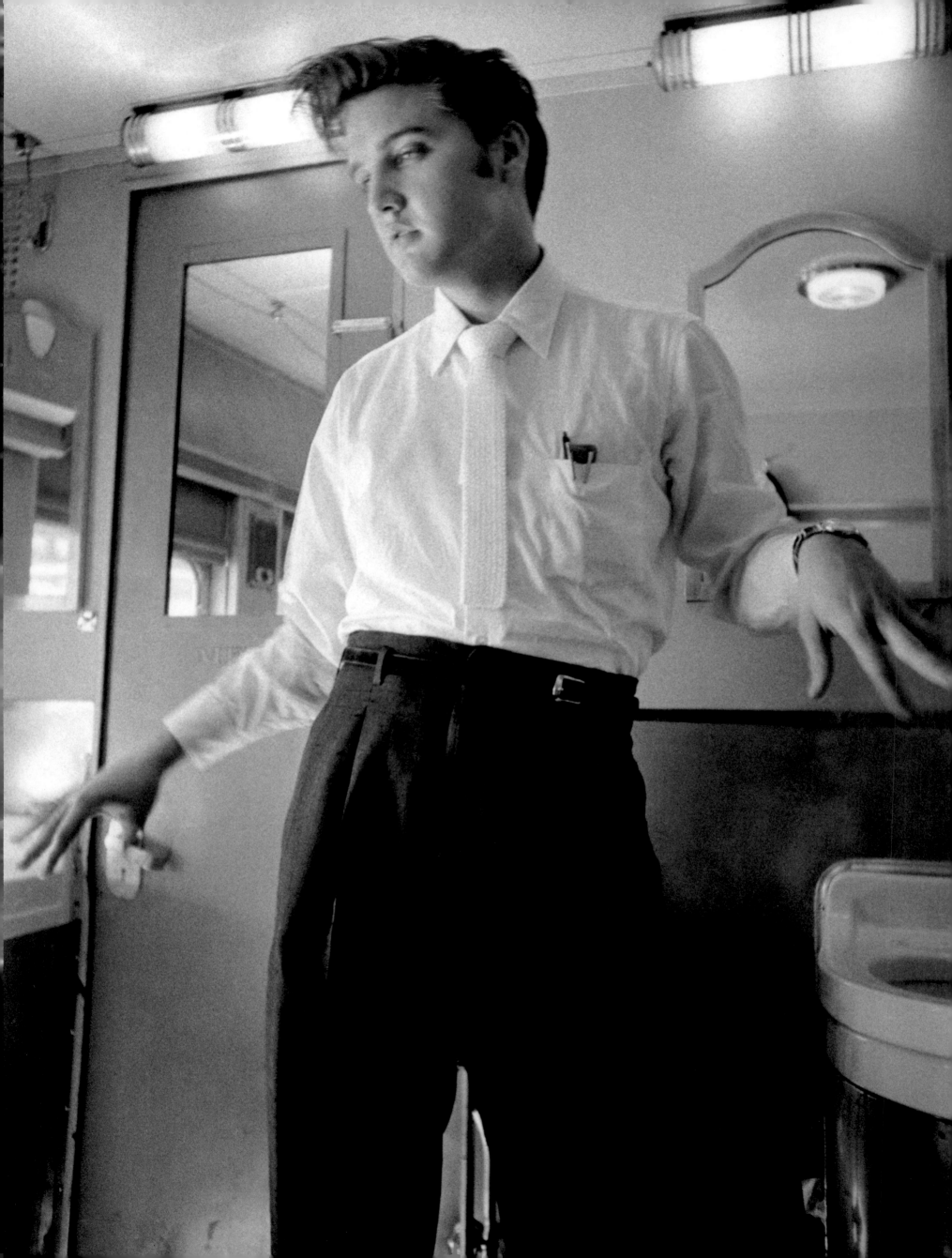

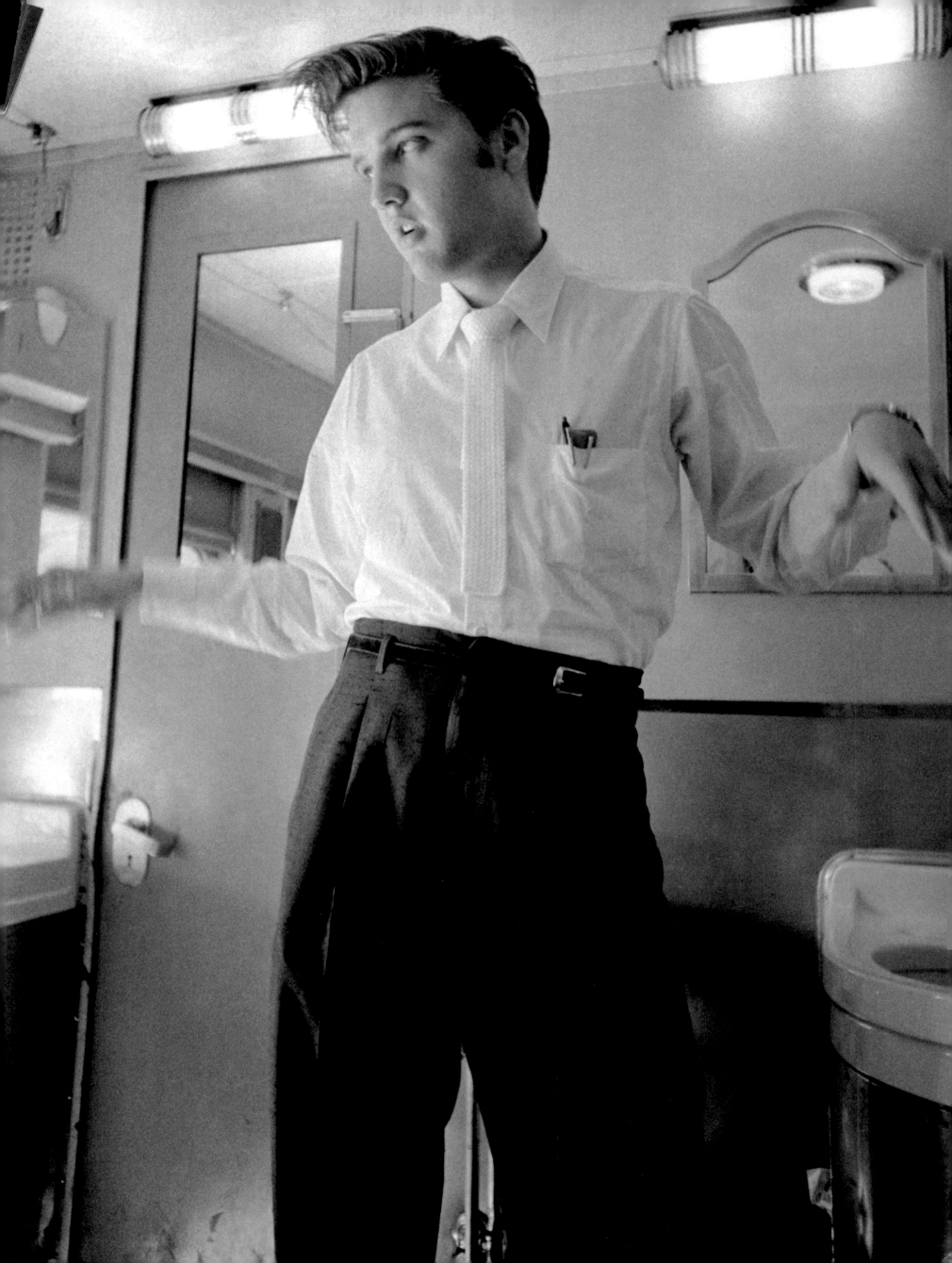

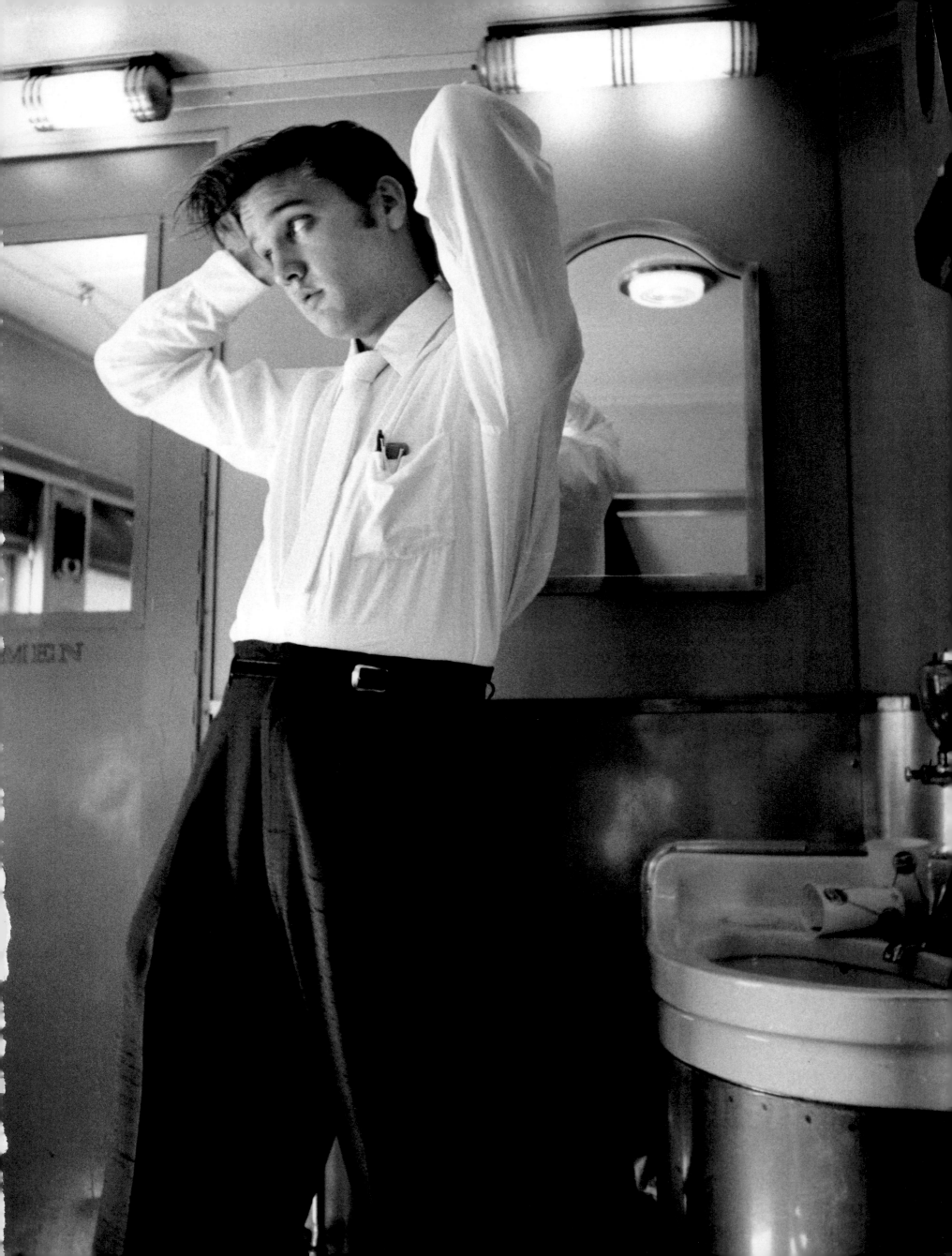

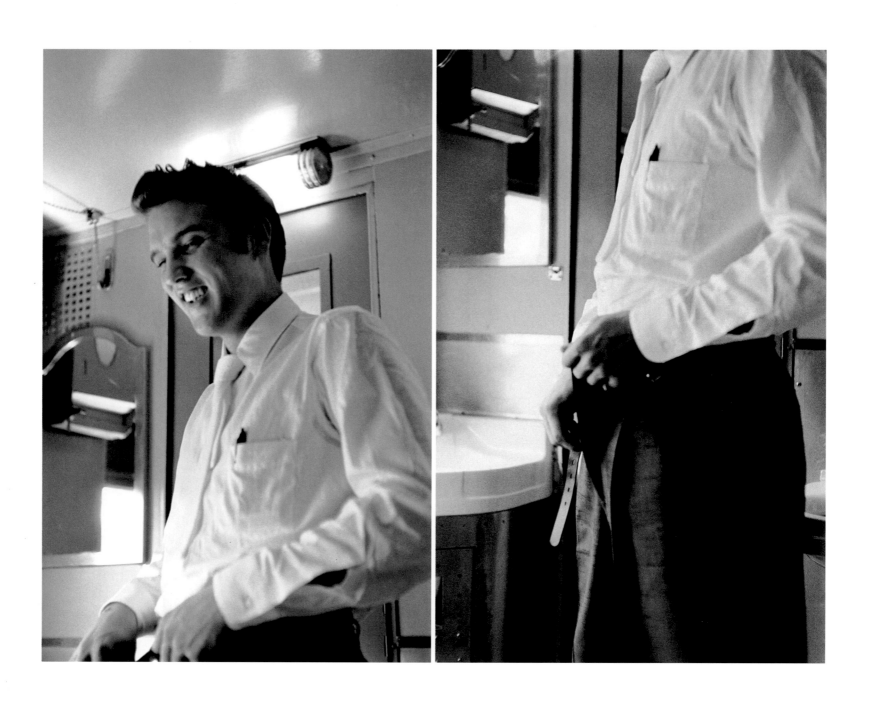

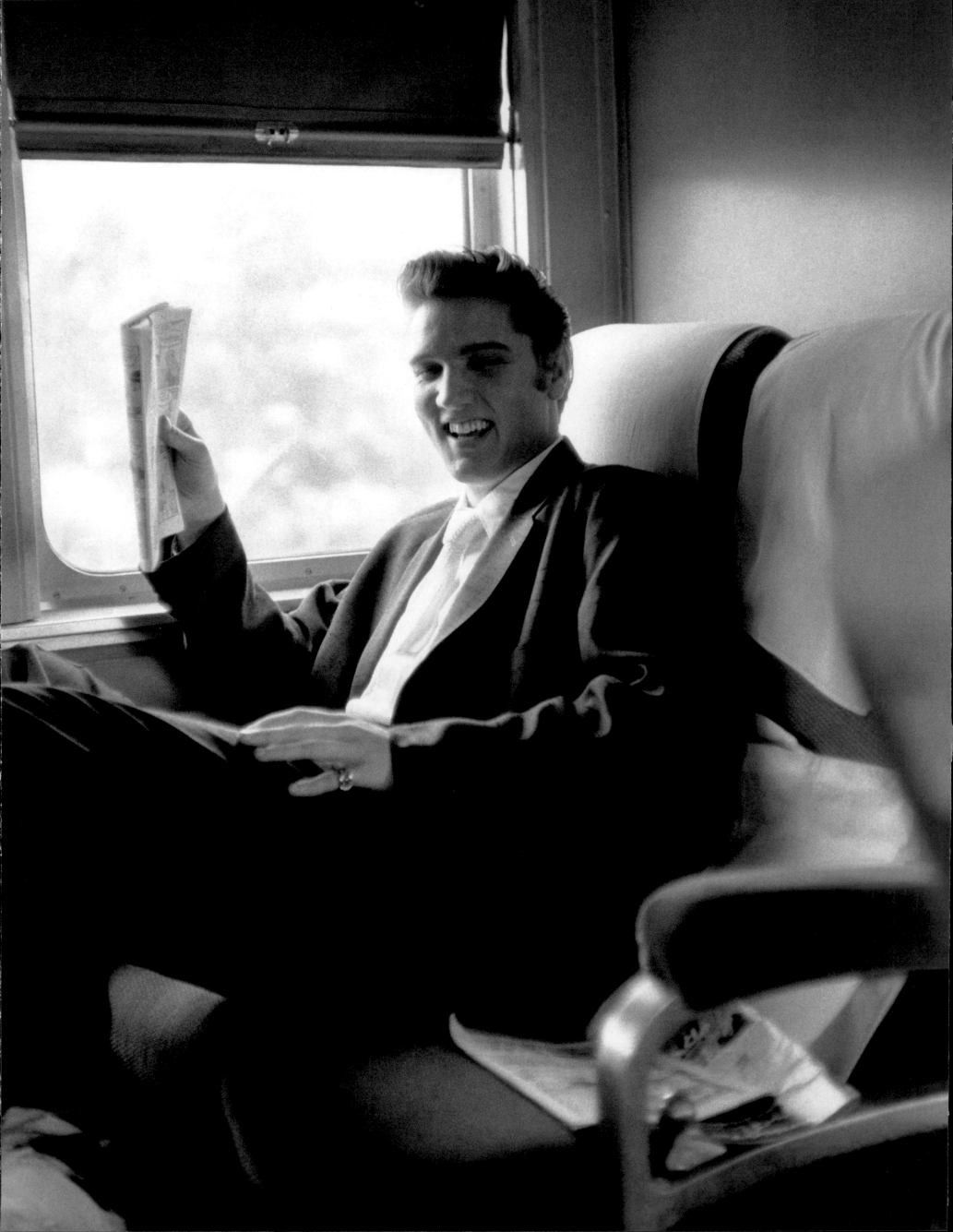

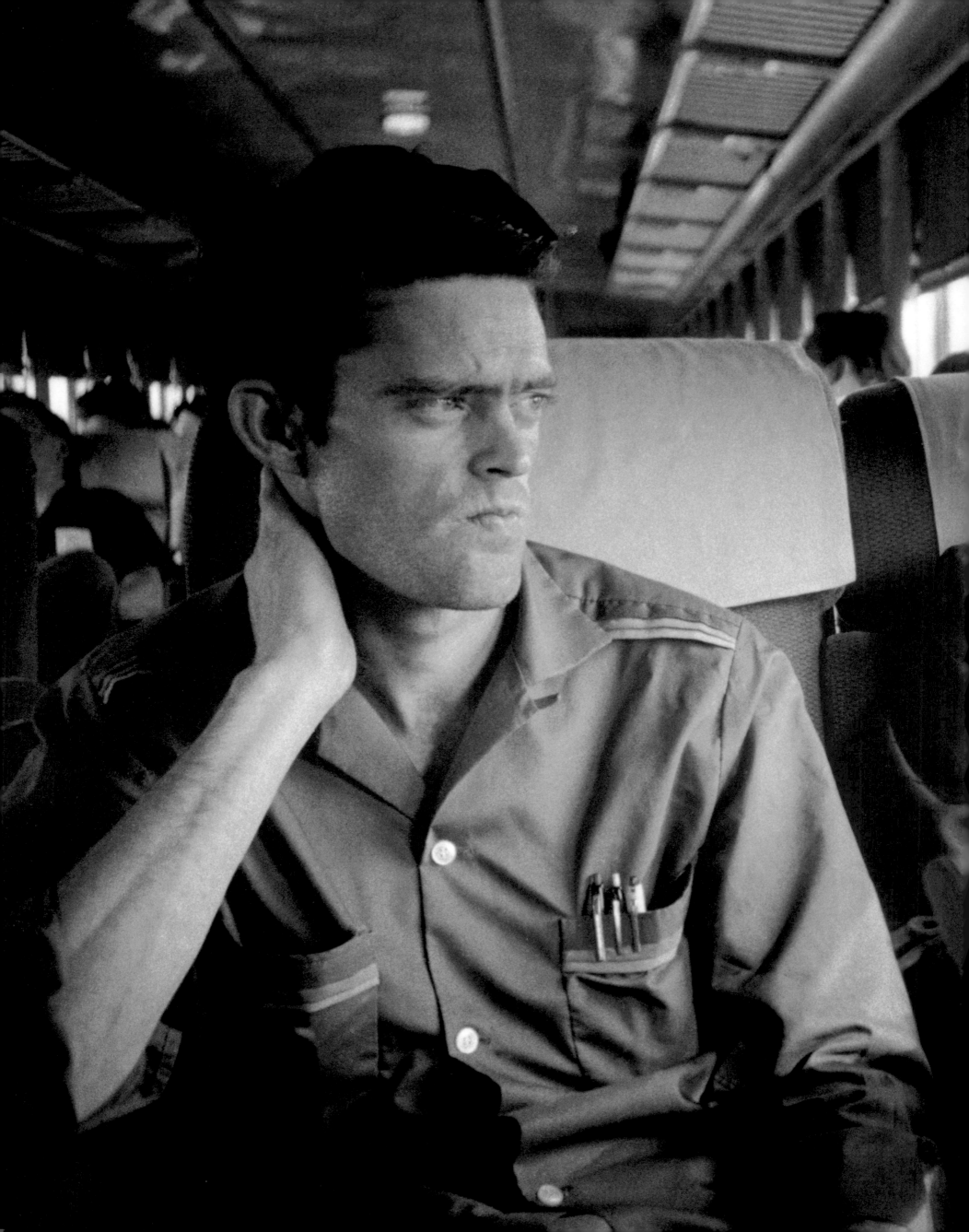

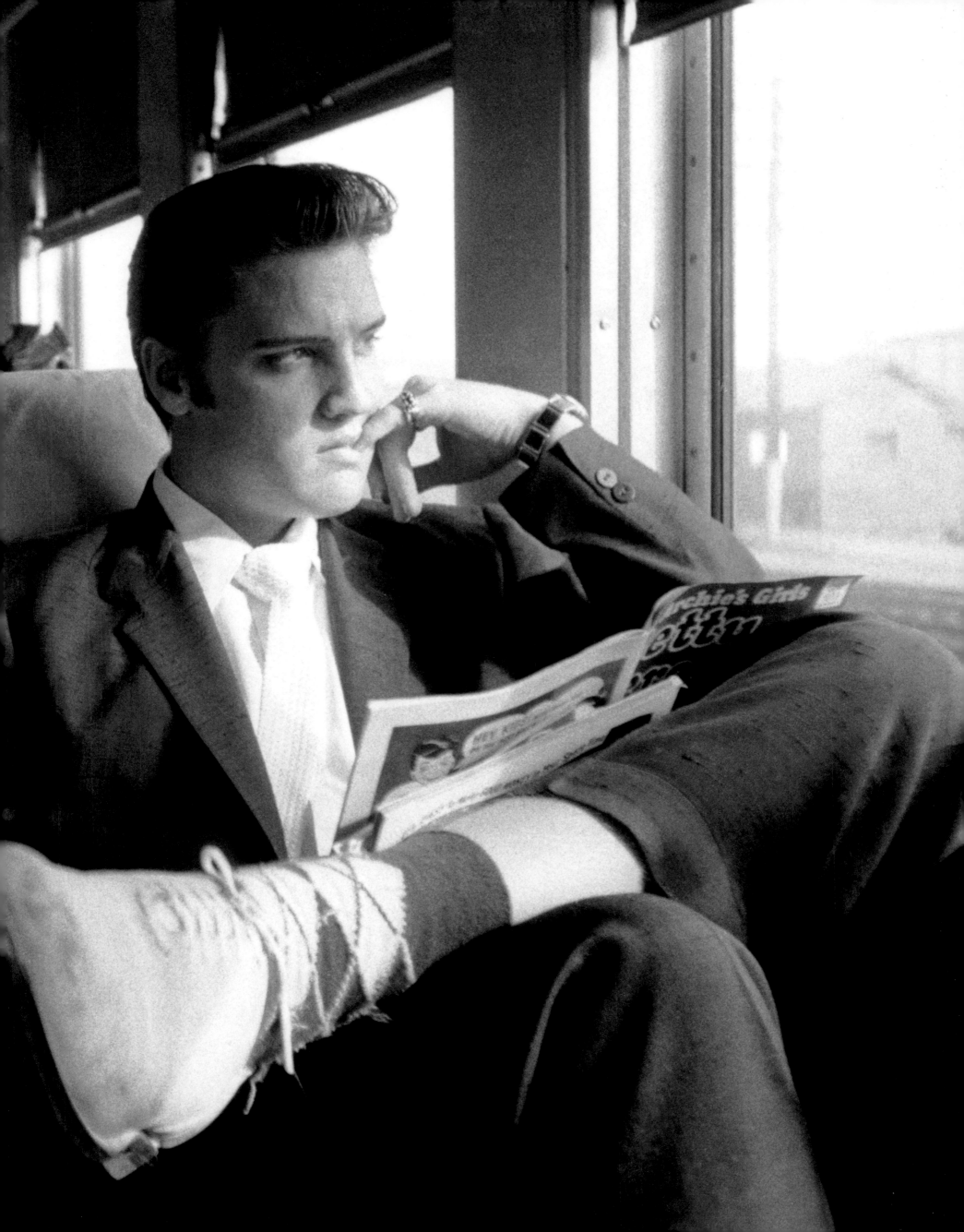

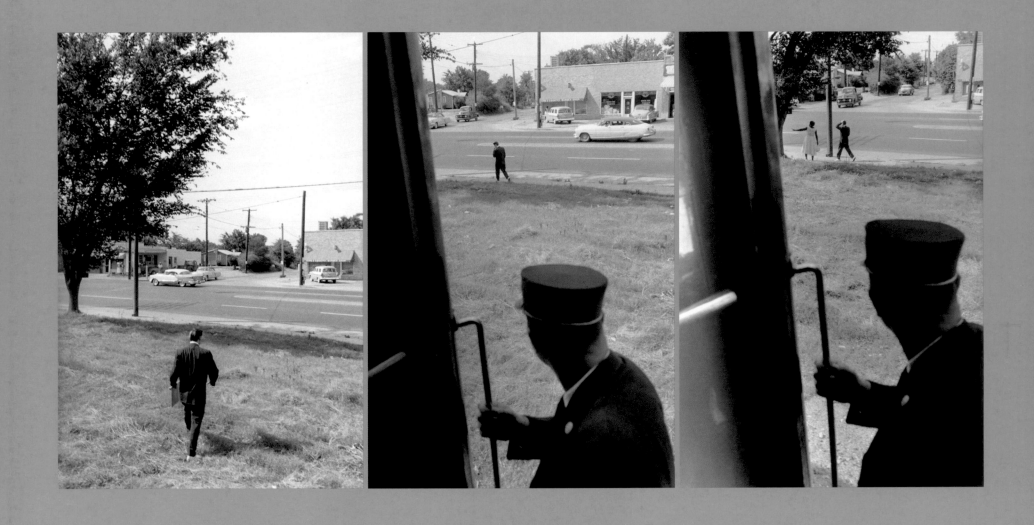

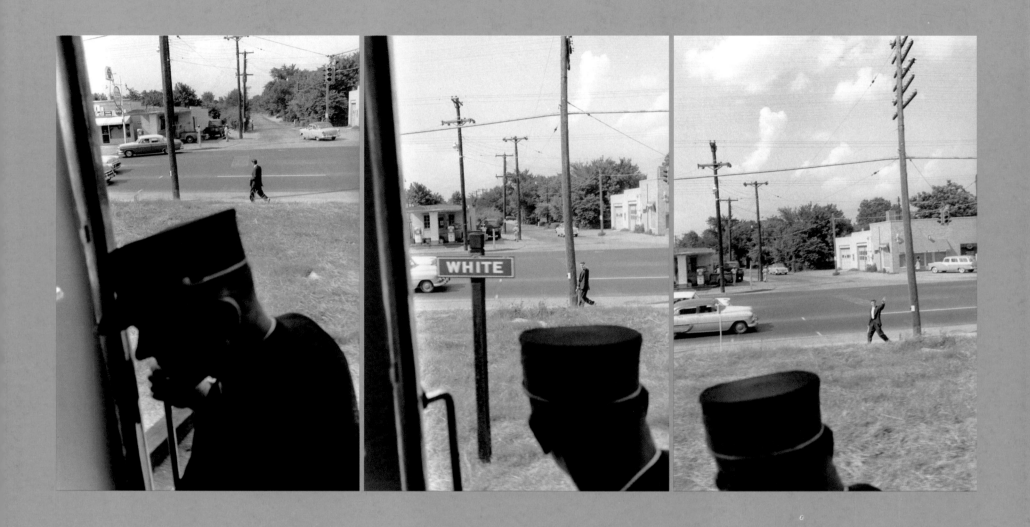

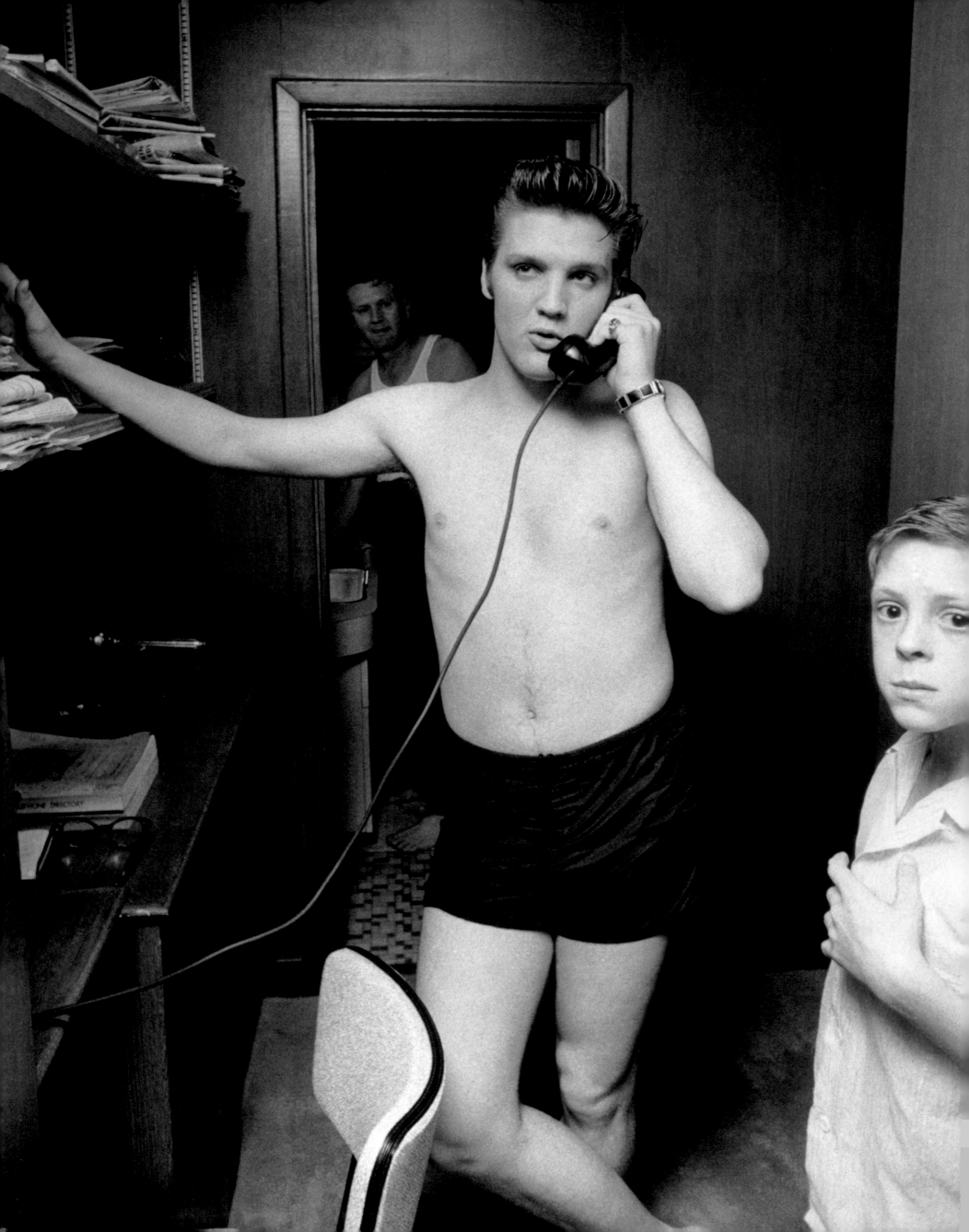

CHAPTER VII

HOME SWEET HOME

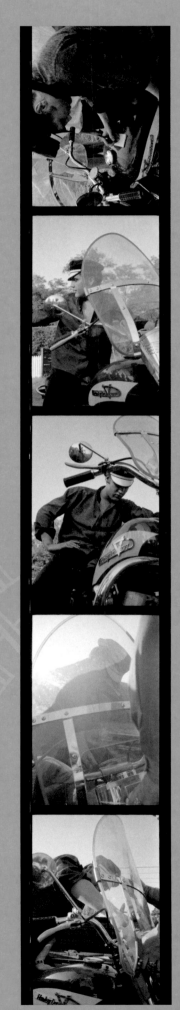

HOME SWEET HOME

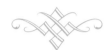

"**T**AKE ME TO 1034 AUDUBON DRIVE," I told the driver as soon as I got off at the main terminal in Memphis. Turning into a suburban residential area with ranch-style homes lining the streets, the cab pulled up to Elvis's home where a group of mostly teenage girls in dresses (no jeans here either) congregated on the front lawn. I worked my way through the crowd of people and rang the doorbell. A young lady opened the door and I explained that I had come down on the train with Elvis.

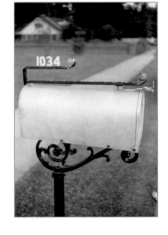

Once inside, I noticed an older woman in a housedress (p. 201). I walked up to her and introduced myself. "Hello. My name is Alfred Wertheimer, and I've been photographing Elvis. I assume you're Gladys Presley, Elvis's mother."

"Yes, I am."

"I'm going to be photographing for the rest of the day. Would you mind if I put my camera bag and my jacket down somewhere?"

"Make yourself at home." I thanked her and set my things down. It was a hot day so I left my jacket there too.

By the time I arrived at the house, Elvis was changing into what I called his Marlon Brando outfit. He wanted to go out for a ride on his motorcycle while there was still daylight. Coming out of his room, he threw me a "Hi" and went into the kitchen to talk to his mother. Then he disappeared into the backyard. With two Nikons loaded with 35-millimeter film slung around my neck, I followed him.

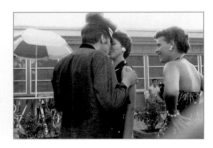

Girls dressed in their Sunday best were gathered in the carport area, watching as Elvis went down to a shed where he stored his Harley. He and his cousins, Bobby Smith, Billy Smith, and Gene Smith, rolled it out. (Smith was Gladys's maiden name.) Elvis got on the motorcycle but it wouldn't turn over. It kicked, sputtered, and fell silent. Vernon Presley, his father (p. 213), got down on his hands and knees to check the carburetor. No good. Of course, the girls didn't mind having Elvis stuck there. The guys, on the other hand, were dismayed.

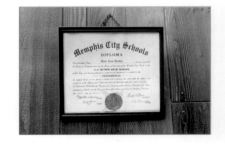

While the bike was being looked at, Elvis signed a few autographs on the gas tank for the girls. Then it occurred to him. He unscrewed the cap and found that there was no gas in the tank. "Hey, fellas. Somebody get me some gas."

One of his cousins ran off and came back with a small jerry can. They poured about a quart in the tank and, sure enough, the motorcycle kicked over and started to purr. Waving the girls off to the side, he slowly drove over the little grassy mound to his patio. He got off and walked the motorcycle through another crowd of girls and down the driveway. More girls stopped him near the street to take pictures with him in his cap with the star on it.

"Anybody want a ride?" Of course, everybody wanted a ride. A twelve-year-old boy hopped on the back and Elvis took off down the street. The rest of the crowd hung around waiting for the star to return.

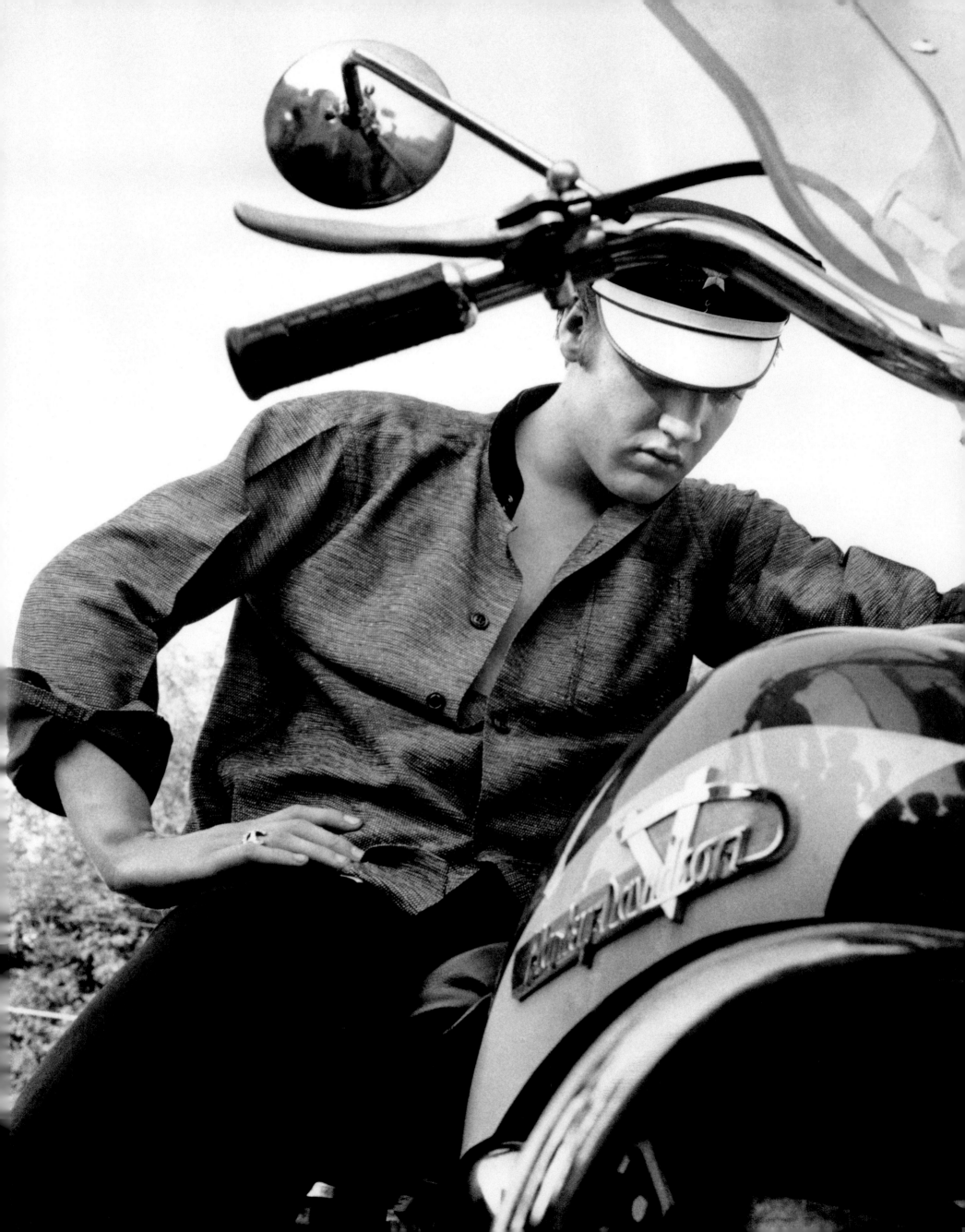

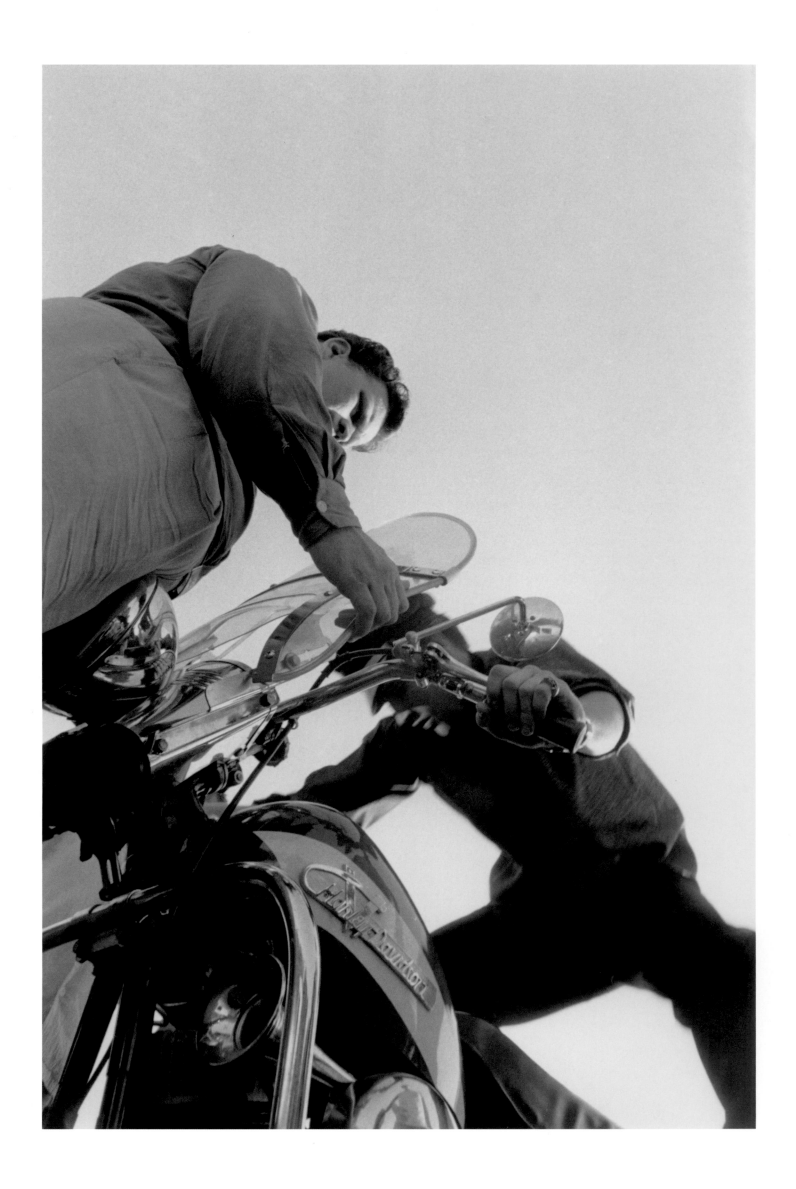

About ten minutes later, the motorcycle reappeared from the other direction and pulled into the driveway. The kid jumped off. Another round of photos was taken and then a girl got on. After the second ride, I said, "You know, I think we can get some really good pictures if you'd take me around the block. While you're driving, I'll take some photographs." He thought it was a good idea too so I hopped on.

Being a New Yorker and never having set foot in the South before, I figured that a Memphis block was like a New York block. A couple hundred yards this way, a couple hundred yards that way, and we'd be back in no time. We took the right turn out of the driveway. I had my Nikon with a wide-angle lens, which ended up not being wide enough. All of sudden, I was moving at forty miles per hour, holding on for dear life. How was I going to take pictures at this speed? Not only that, how was I going to do it leaning over Elvis's shoulder with one arm stretched out as far as possible? It all worked in my imagination, except that I had the wrong lens and my arms weren't long enough. This proved impossible to do alone. What I really needed was a moving vehicle running parallel to us about ten feet away with another cameraman shooting us.

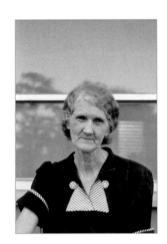

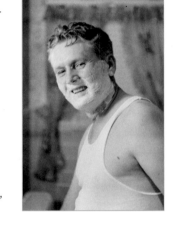

I still did what I could and hoped for the best. I had half a roll of film in the camera. We were halfway around this so-called block, which went a mile in one direction and two in the other, when the motorcycle started sputtering. That quart was practically gone. Elvis managed to get off the main street into an area with a couple of convenience stores but no gas station. A little worried, I said, "We've got to get to Russwood Stadium tonight, Elvis. What are we going to do?"

He didn't seem the least bit concerned. Cool as a cucumber, he remarked, "Just wait, you'll see." It was as if he had some sort of script that I hadn't read yet.

Within minutes, a woman in a car pulled up. She assessed the situation and got out of the car.

"We need some gas. I ran out."

He didn't have to tell her who he was. She knew already and was eager to be helpful. She got back into her car and drove away. Cynical New Yorker that I was, I asked, "How do you know she'll come back?"

"She'll come back."

"He's so trusting," I thought. Sure enough, the woman returned ten minutes later, a jerry can of gas in hand. I asked if he needed some money to pay for the gas.

"No, I don't need any money." Once he filled the tank and started up the motor, he walked over to her car, leaned in and gave her a kiss on the cheek. Then he went around the car to the passenger side and gave her baby girl a kiss. With that, the woman drove away happy.

If I had used my head, I would have remembered that none of the stores would be open that day. It was the Fourth of July. After burning up half a roll trying to get those motorcycle shots, I ran out of film. I had an empty camera and no film with all this taking place. Those were some of the best shots that I never got. I could have kicked myself in the butt.

"Okay, hop on the back." I swung my leg around and hung on to his waist, empty cameras around my neck.

We were much later than expected when we pulled into the driveway. He rode right by his mother and stopped the motorcycle.

"Are you all right, son?" she asked.

"Yeah, I'm fine, Mom." No explanation. No nothing. She must have been used to it.

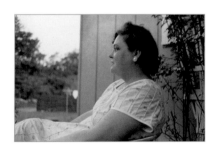

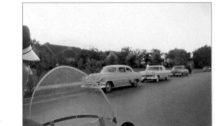

A week later when I finally developed that half-roll I shot on the back of Elvis's Harley, I saw the tip of Elvis's cap, part of his nose, and some houses in the background. I didn't get a single complete shot of him, nor was there a single frame of me with Elvis anywhere. In my whole journey with Elvis, I didn't get a single picture of us together. In spite of the hundreds of girls I watched posing for pictures with him, I was too proud to ask someone else to take just one photograph of Elvis and me.

Back at the house, his father, his Uncle Travis and Bobby Smith were drinking Pepsis on the patio, enjoying the hot summer afternoon. Once Elvis got home, it was time for a swim. The family had just moved into that house a couple of months earlier. Already on their way to becoming a middle-class family, the Presleys were the only ones in the neighborhood to have a large pool in the backyard. But the pool was still under construction. The valves weren't working properly so an ordinary garden hose was hooked up to the kitchen sink and ran all the way across the lawn. The water had been gushing out for six hours, filling the deep end up to only about three feet. This turned out to be a lucky break for me.

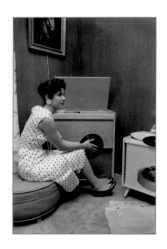

Elvis wanted to cool off anyway after the long train trip and his motorcycle ride. He ran into the house and changed into his bathing suit for a swim. Since the shallow end was empty and the water was only waist-high in the deep end, I could take the chance and get down to eye-level, or rather water-level, to shoot Elvis and his family horsing around in the pool without ruining my cameras. I asked Gladys for a bathing suit and she very kindly loaned me one.

While horsing around, he suddenly raised his hands up in the air and shouted, "Hey, hold it fellas. Stop."

"Ma! Ma!" he yelled. Elvis had forgotten to take off his watch. Gladys came up to the side of the pool, dried it off on her dress, and reassured him that it was still working.

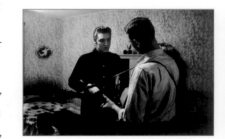

Then it was straight into horseplay with water spraying all over the place. I was the silent bather, trying to keep a safe distance because they were really pummeling each other. It was worth the risk of potentially destroying my equipment though. I was catching glimpses of where Elvis came from, where he felt relaxed and safe.

Tired of swimming, he went back inside to change. Since he was in the shower, I asked Gladys if I could photograph around the house. She didn't mind at all so I shot whatever was around me. Snooping around Elvis's bedroom like a reporter, I saw the socks on the floor and the guitar along the wall. I quickly snapped the clothes inside his closet. Walking down a corridor, I stopped in front of his high school diploma and plaques from various magazines proclaiming Elvis to be the most likely to do this and to be that. His gold record for "Heartbreak Hotel" was already up on the wall. On a table, I came across a photo album. I wanted to take a few snapshots of the some of the family photos for possible use in a magazine, so I went back to Mrs. Presley to ask her permission. She figured that if someone was interested enough in her son to publish photographs and help his career, then it was okay.

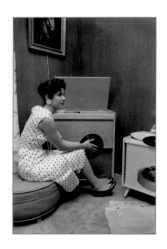

I must admit that I took full advantage of the situation. I set up the photo album on a chair and used my strobe unit to bounce light off the ceiling. I didn't want to take the chance of missing these by relying on available light. Here was Elvis as a young boy and as a teenager. There he was with his date, Dixie Lock, at his high school prom. Meanwhile, I realized that there was an old lady in the room, who turned out to be Elvis's grandmother, Minnie May Presley (p. 197). A young girl in a white dress with black polka dots was also there, waiting for Elvis. She happened to be Barbara Hearn, a former high school sweetheart. When he finished his shower, I put the photo album back where I found it.

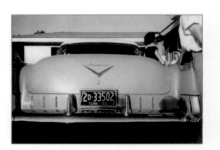

Elvis came out of his room shirtless, just wearing his pants and a pair of socks. In the corner, underneath a painted copy of an Elvis photograph that his mother liked so much, was a console with a record player. He walked up to it, put on one of the acetate disks and flopped down in a stuffed chair near the door. Barbara sat close to the wall, next to the record player. He wanted her to hear it, but he also was listening just as intently as he had on the train coming down. They sat there quietly, focusing on the music. When all the discs had been played, Elvis looked up and she told him how nice the songs were. Then he tried to kiss her, but he had his shirt off and she seemed quite prim. Perhaps she didn't think kissing like that was proper. Besides, Grandma was in the room.

Elvis put the music back on again, wanting to see how it would feel to dance to it. He took Barbara's hand, and pulled her towards him. "Hound Dog," the liveliest of the three songs, played as he swung her around. It was an odd scene, with a half-naked man in his socks dancing with this girl dressed to the hilt and not a hair out of place.

Showtime was quickly approaching though, so Elvis went back into his room to finish dressing. While Cousin Bobby tuned Elvis's guitar, I had to get myself ready as well. I reloaded my cameras and prepared to tackle the concert that night.

Many years later, I realized how fortunate I had been. Apart from the crowds on the lawn, it really was just a pleasant day with a regular family whose son had just returned home for a summer holiday. Through my camera, I joined a neighborhood full of friendly folk. I saw a mother happy to see her boy and a boy giving his mother a kiss. Elvis had come home.

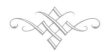

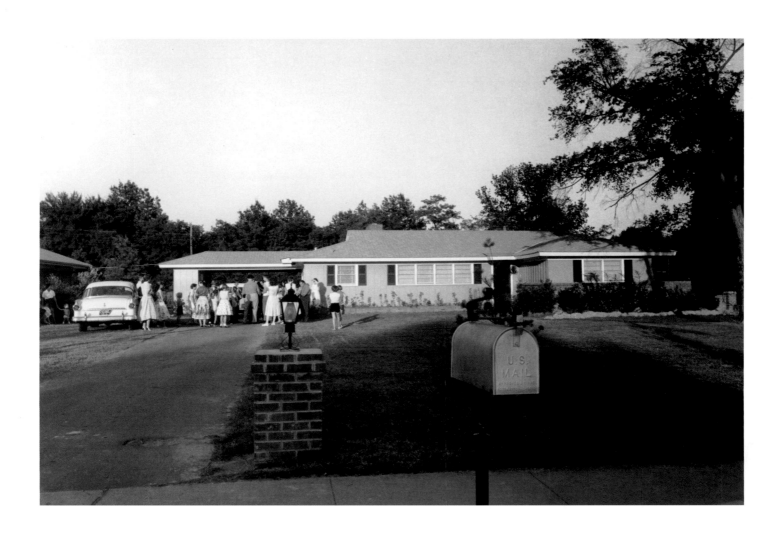

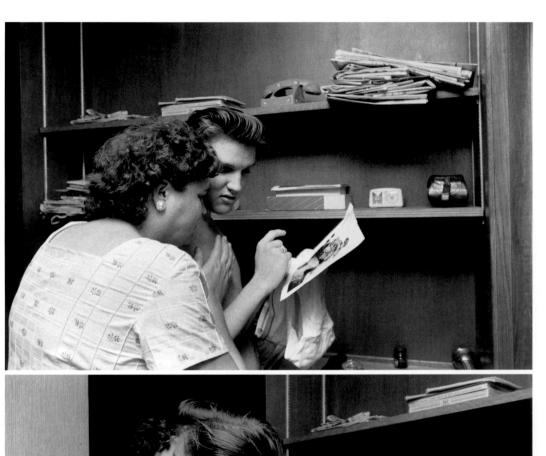

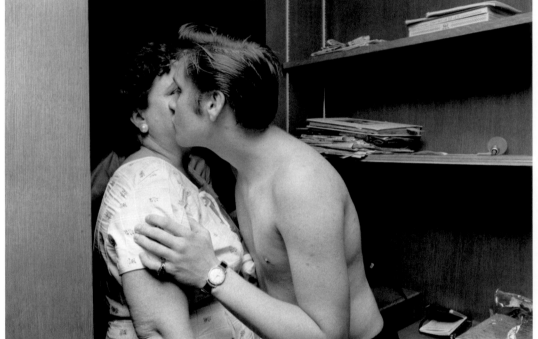

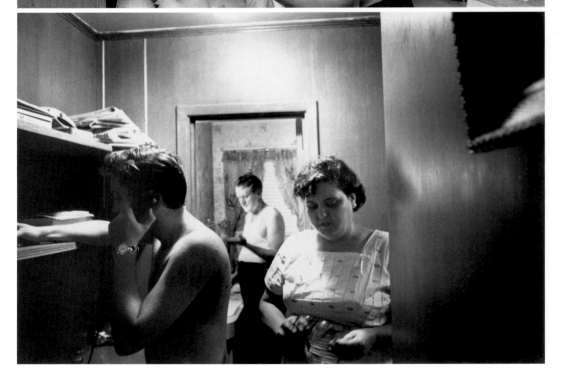

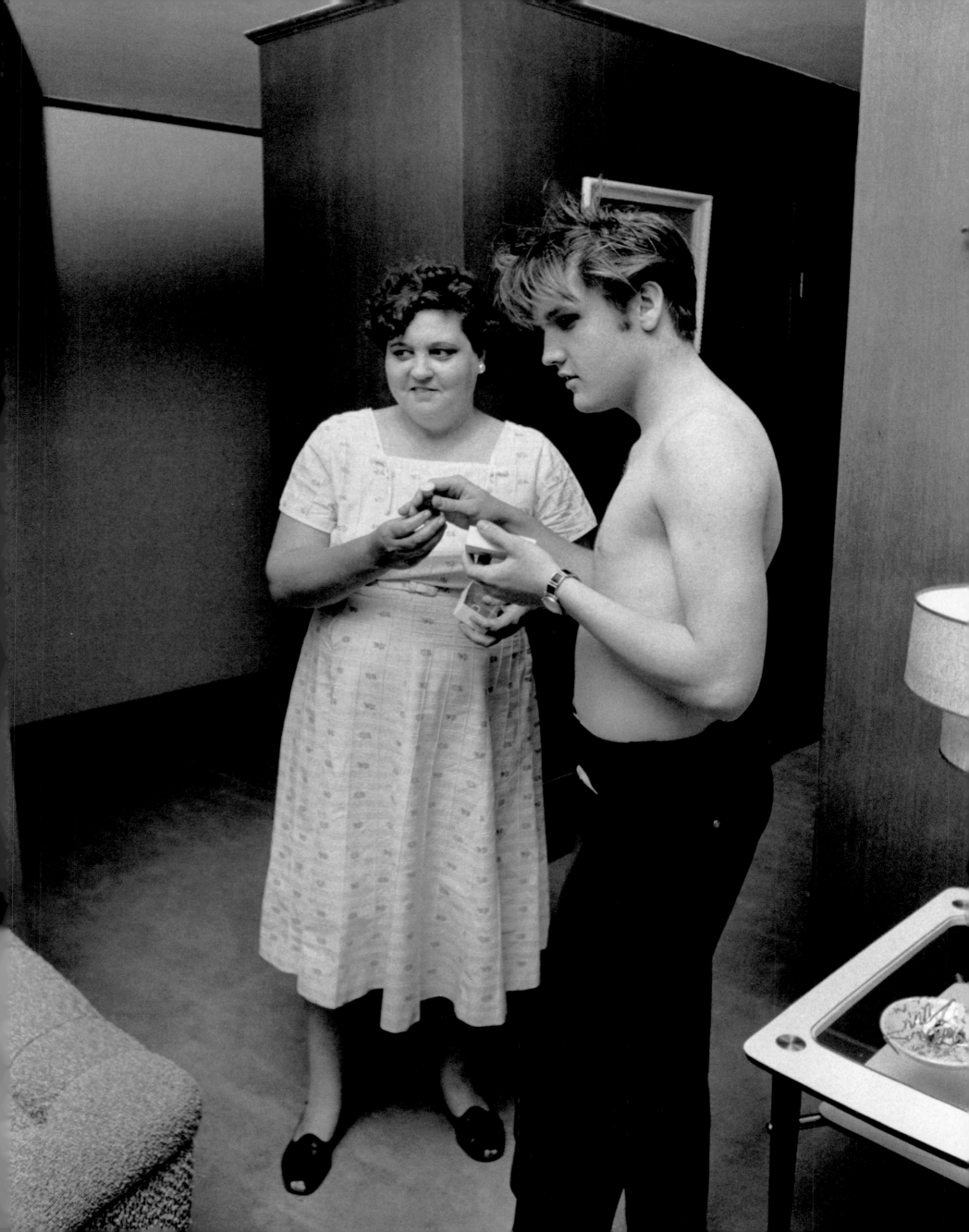

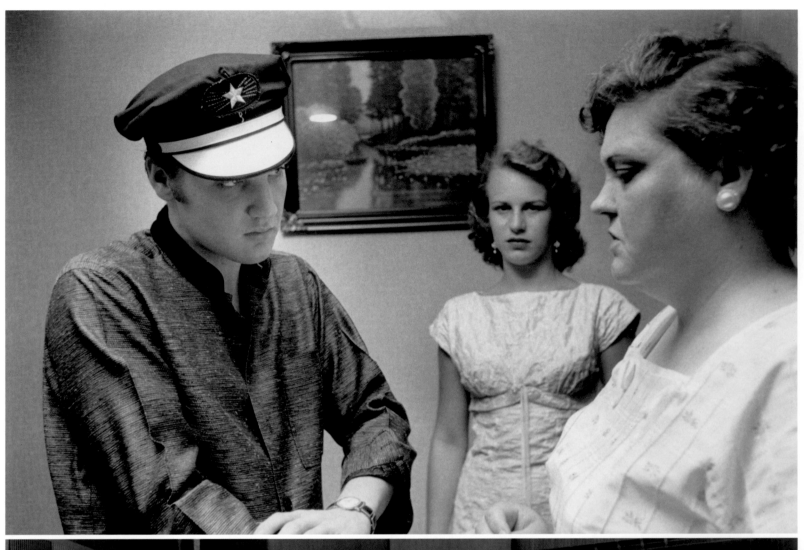
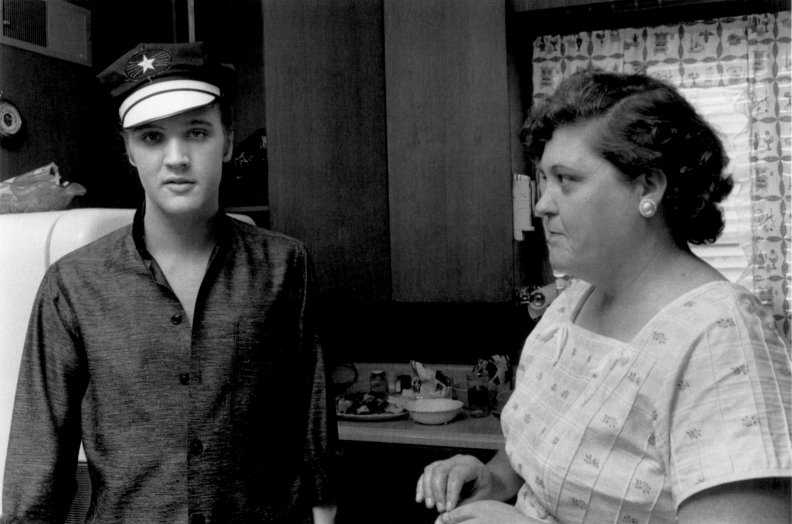

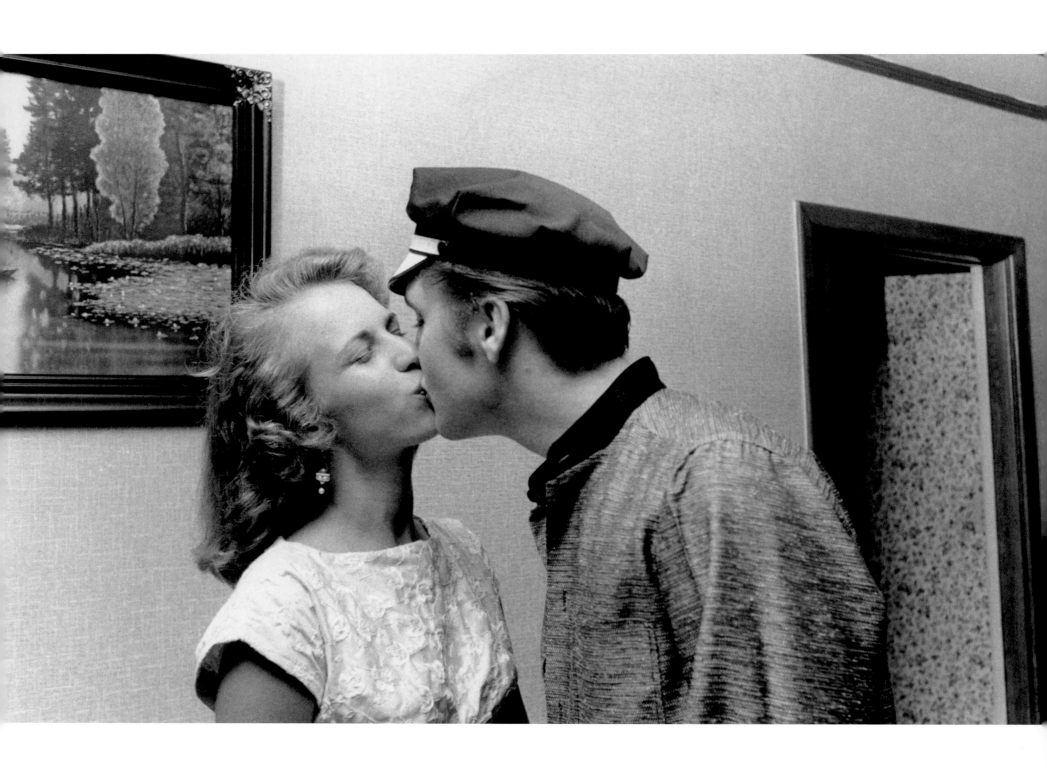

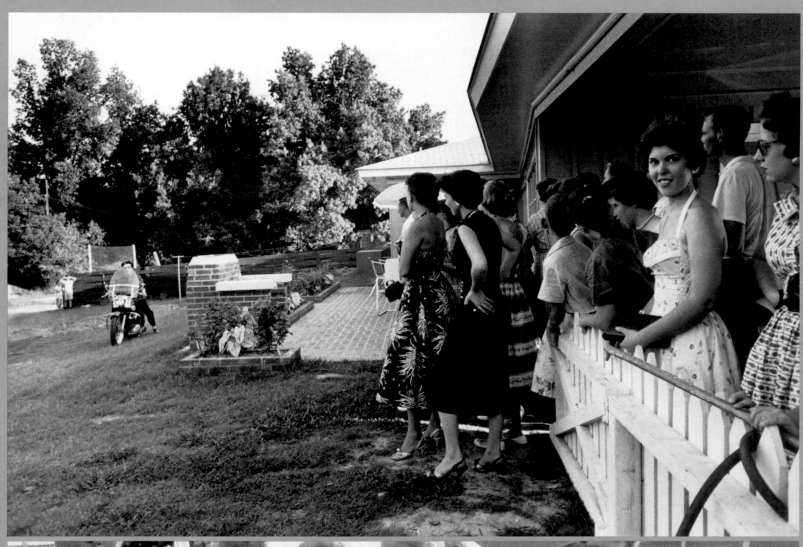

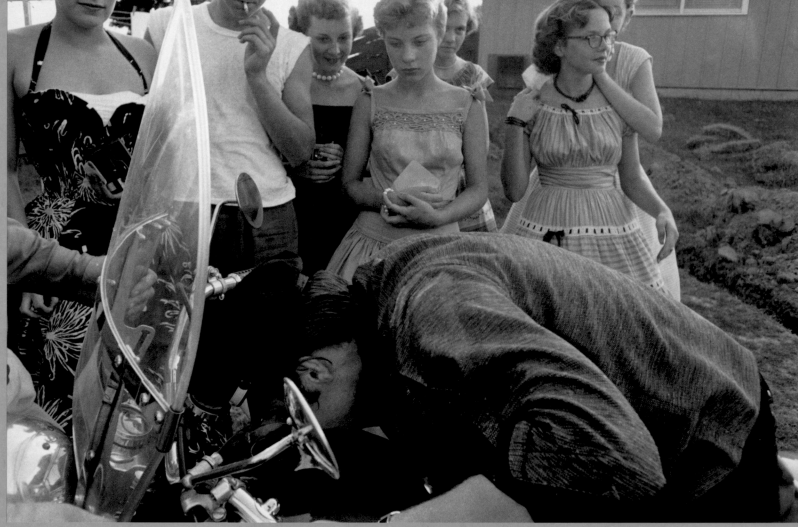

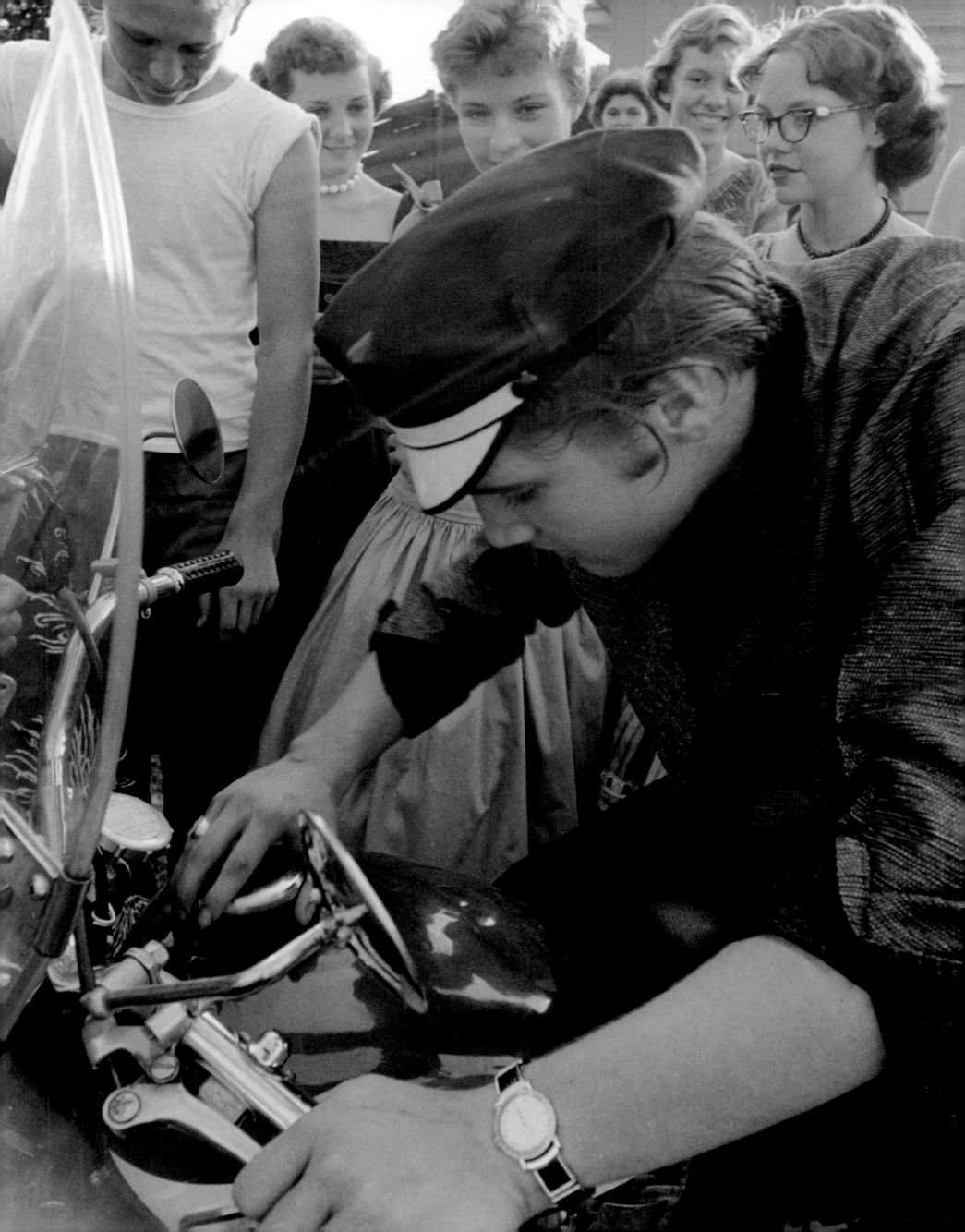

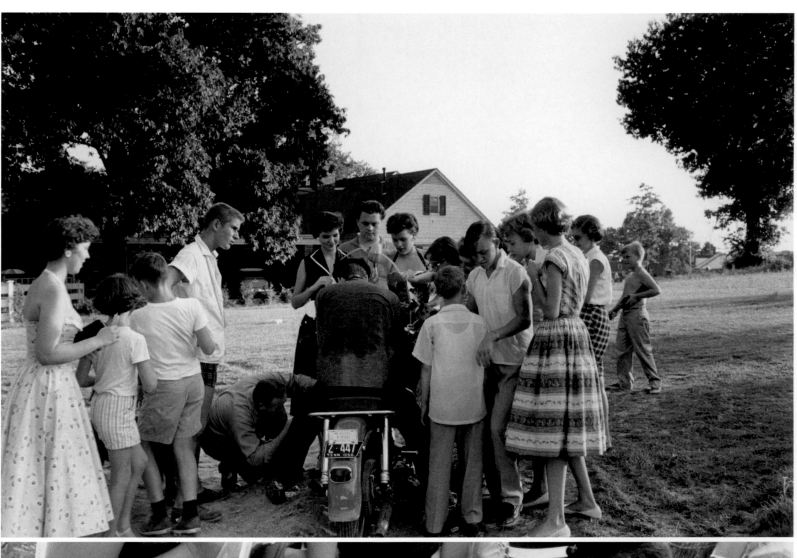

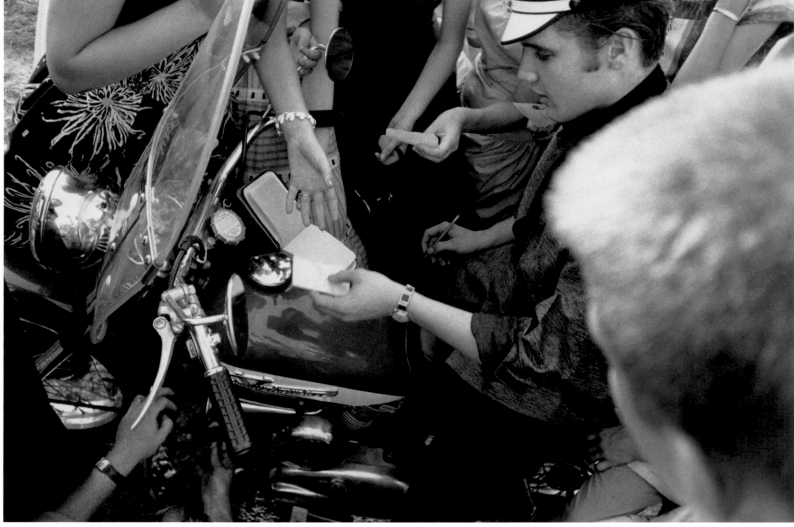

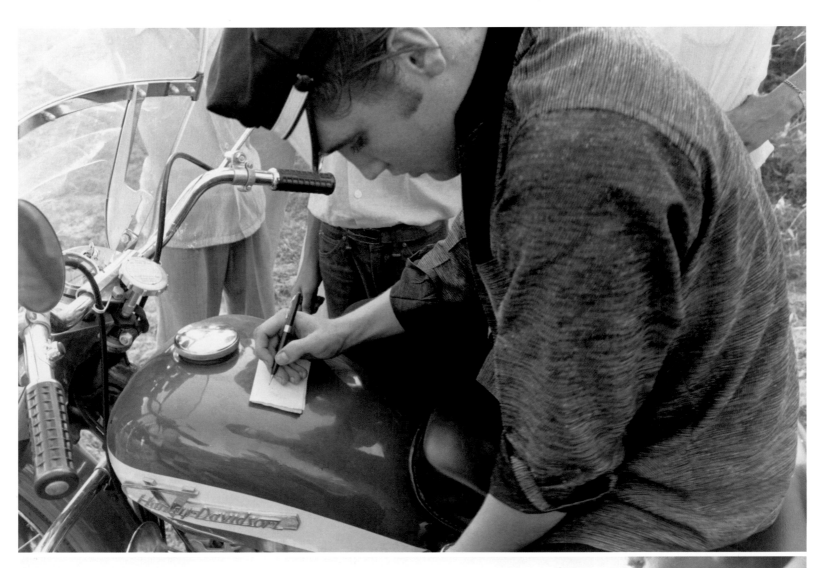

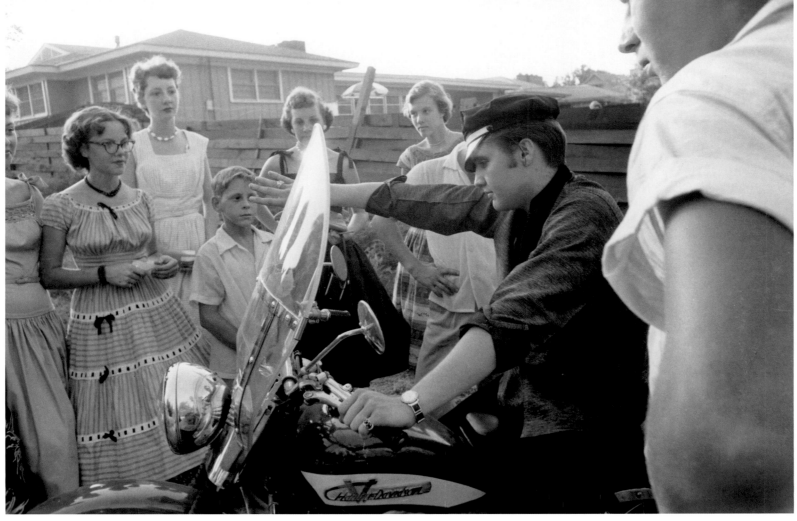

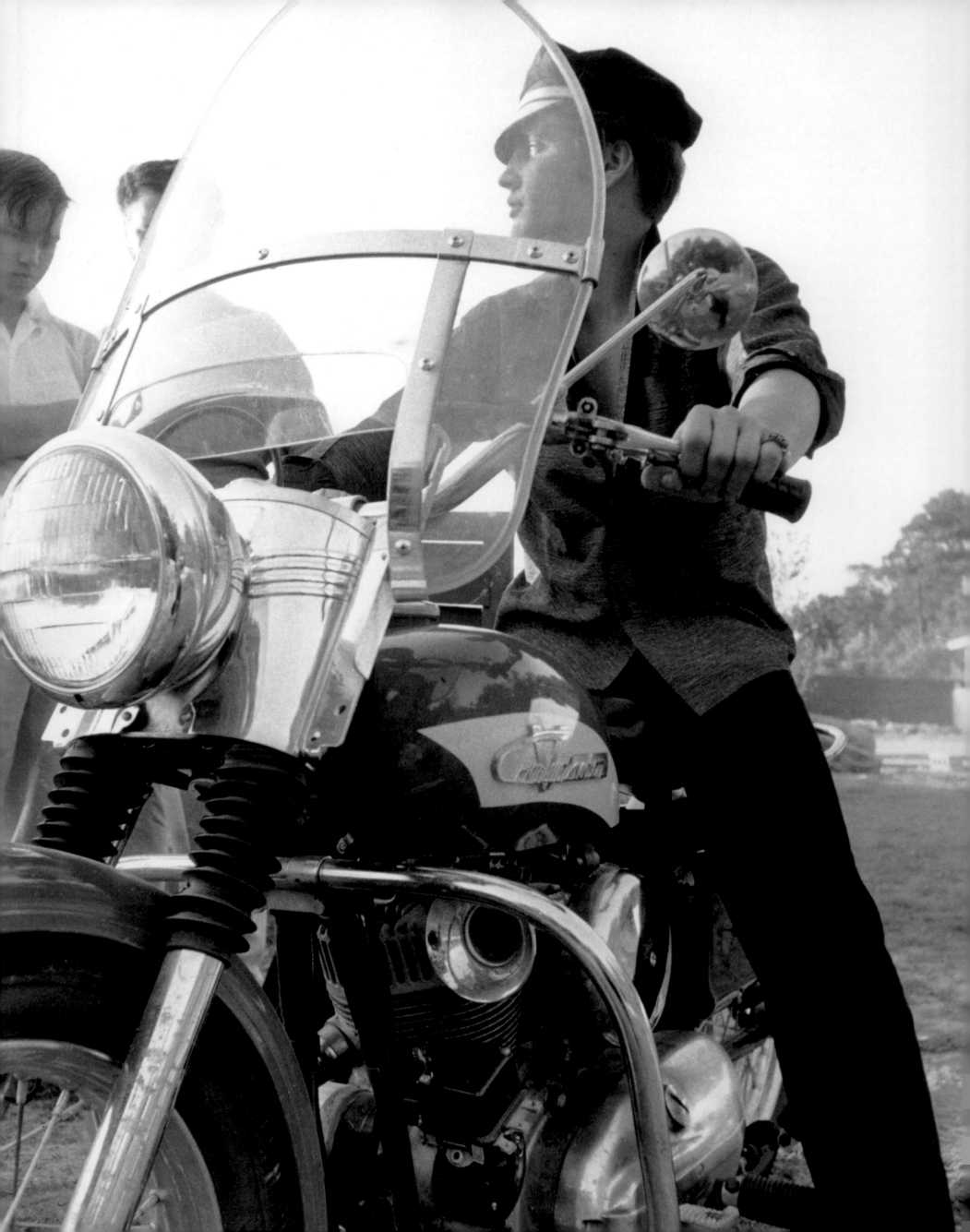

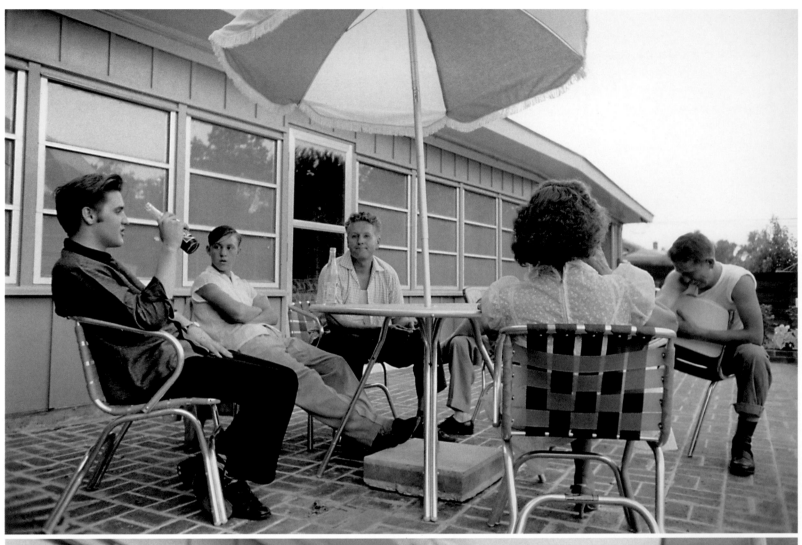

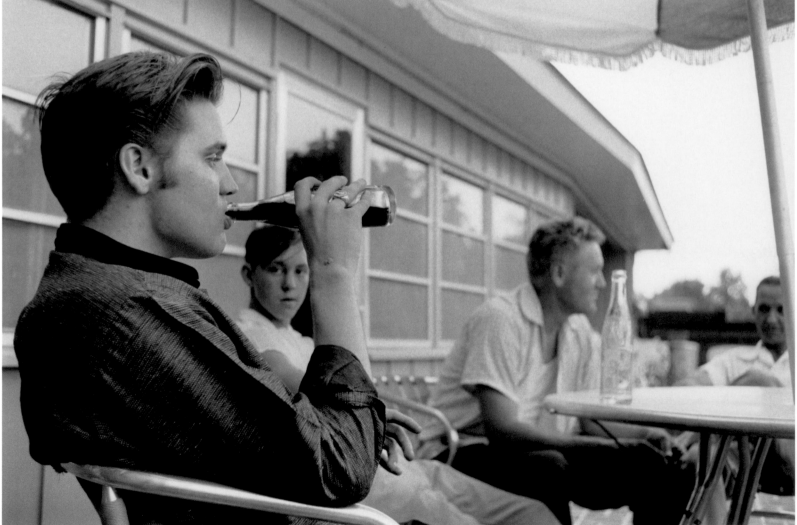

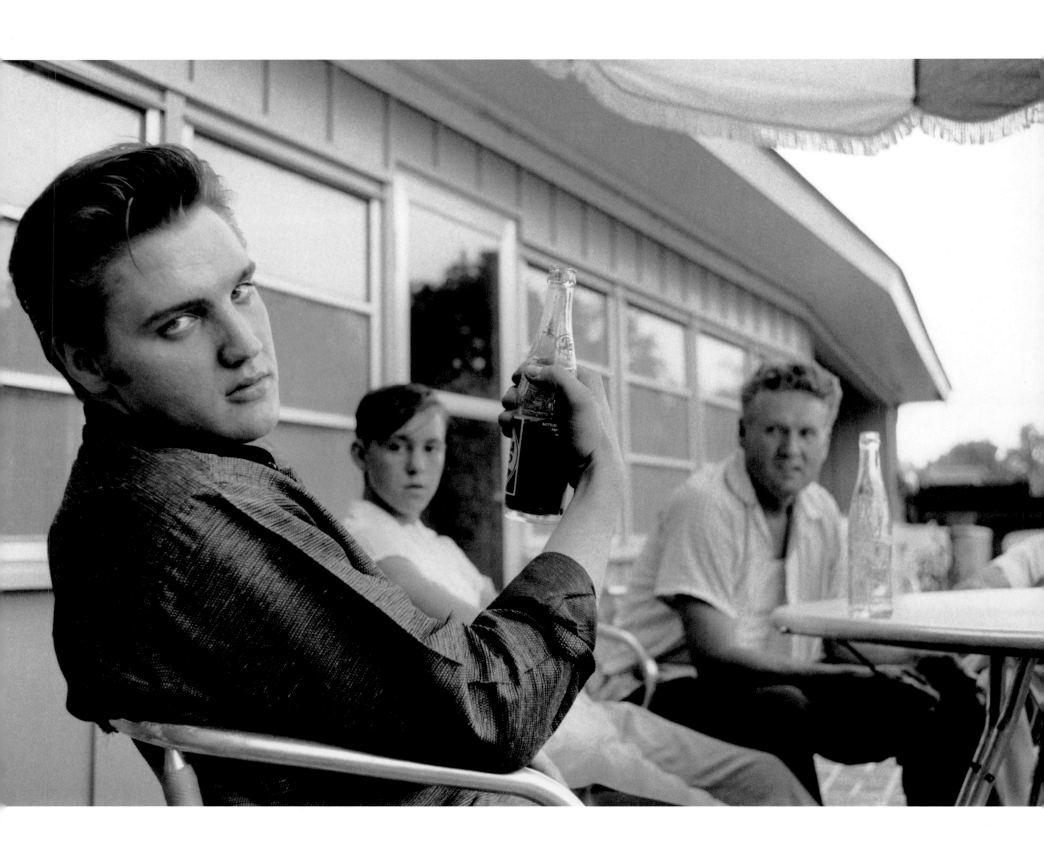

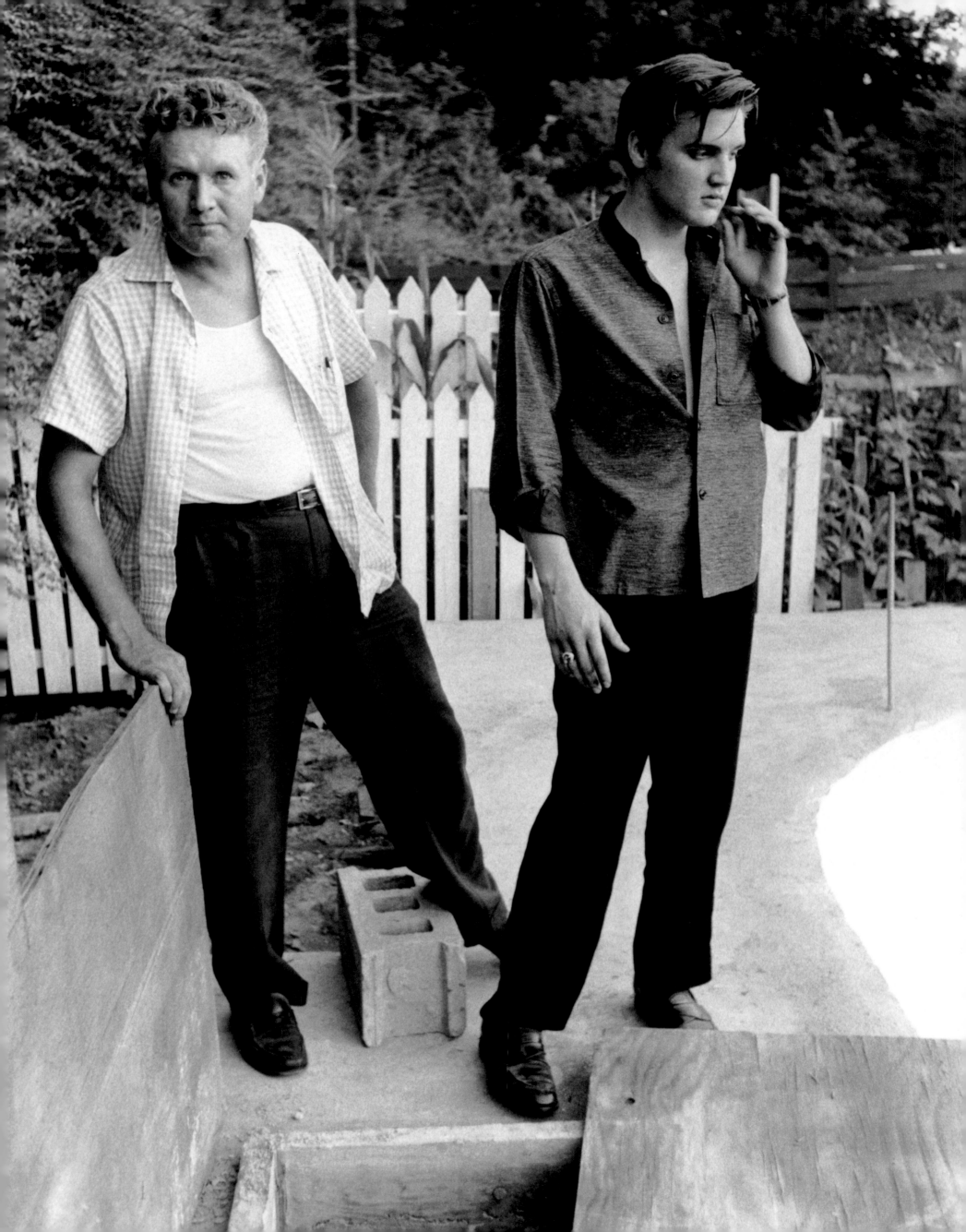

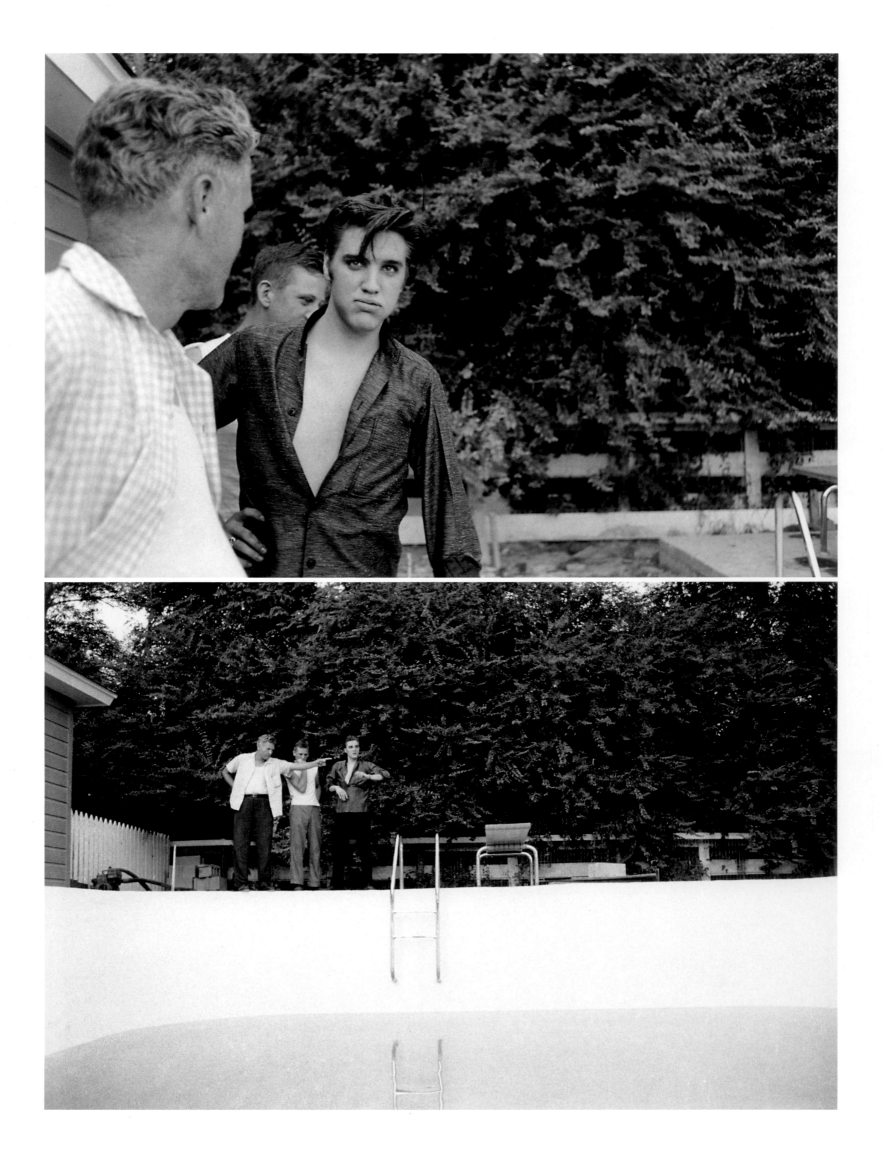

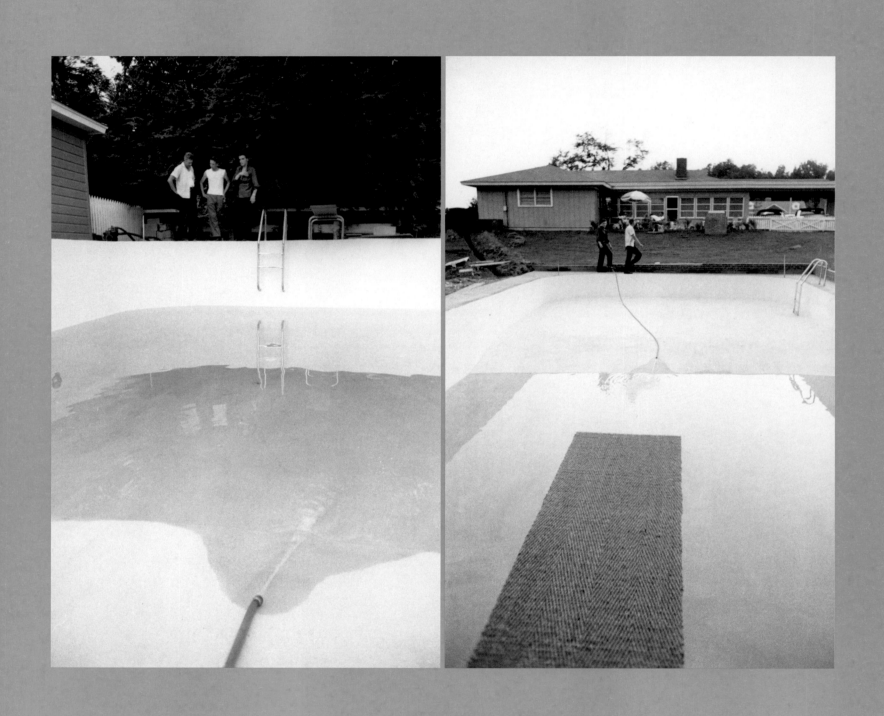

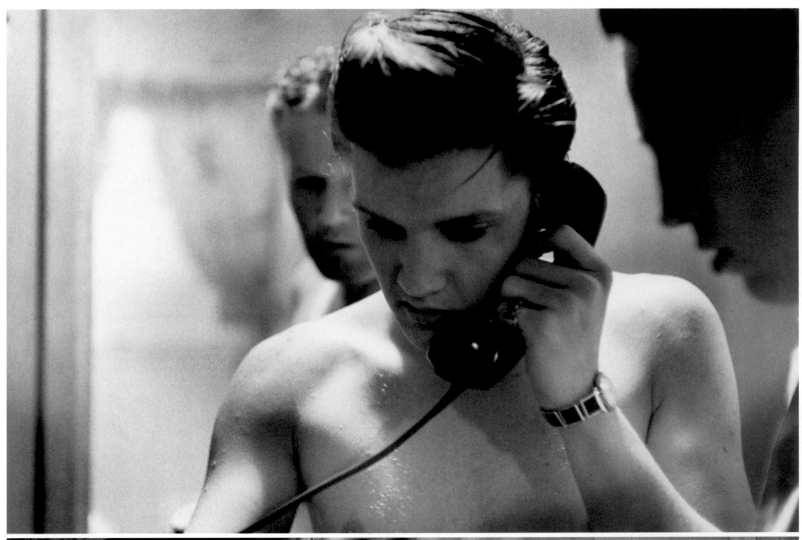

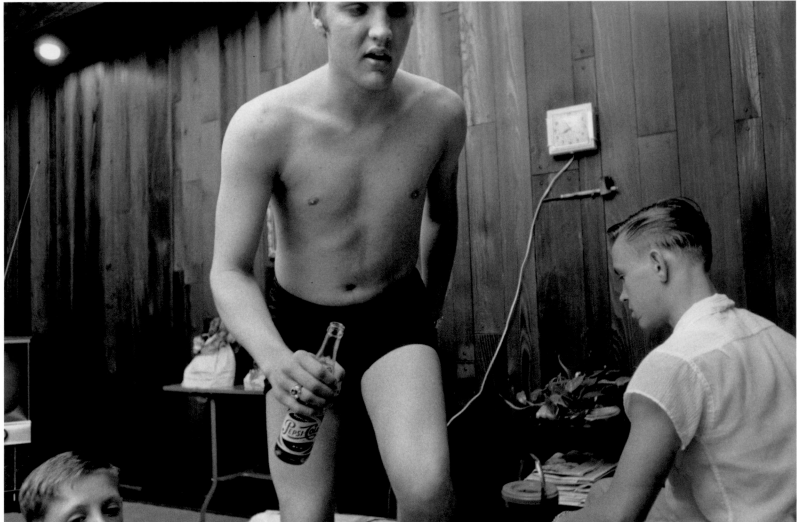

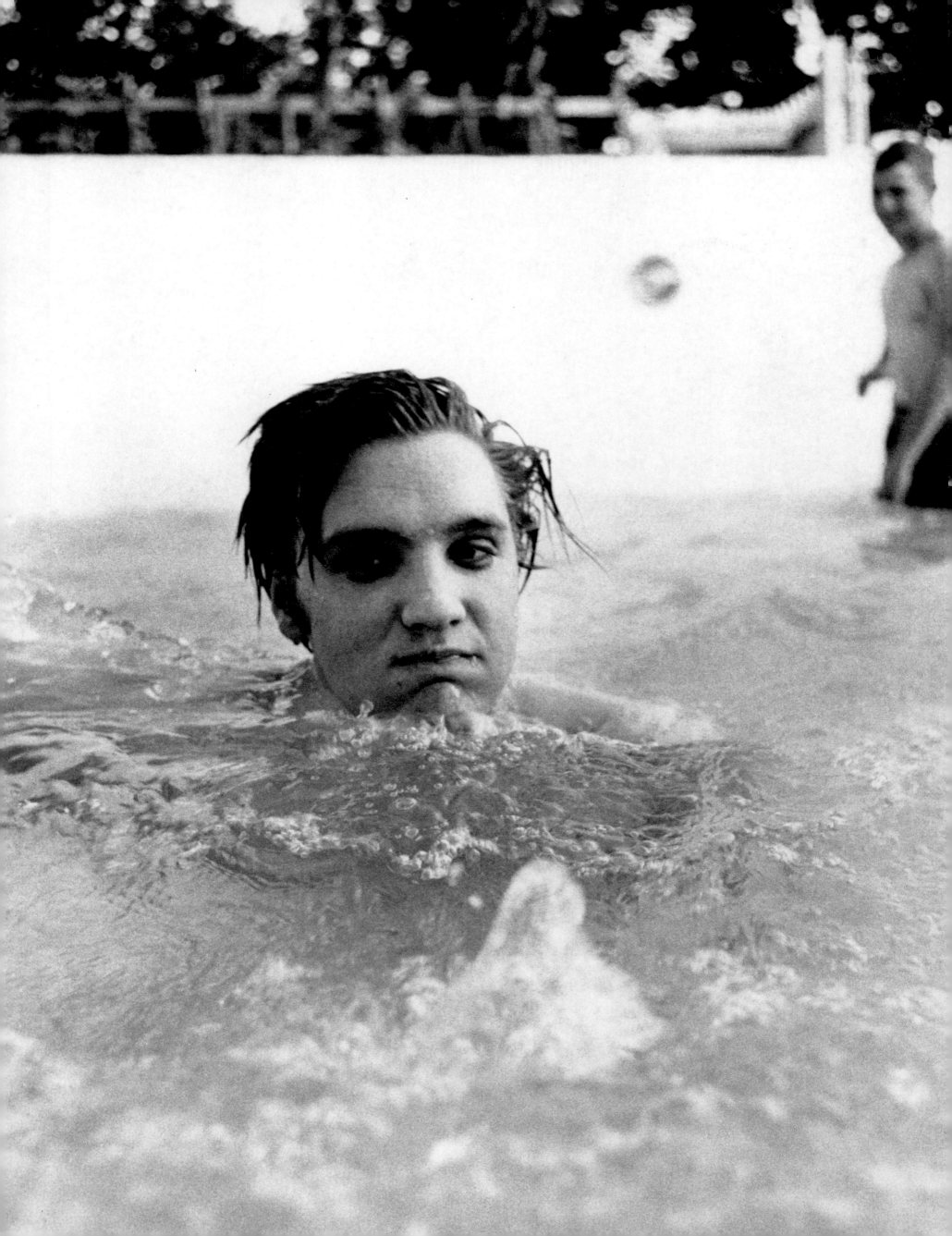

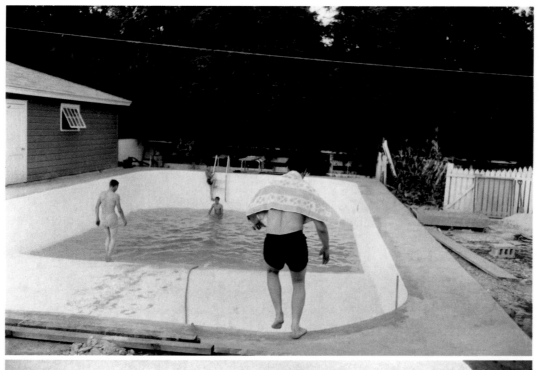

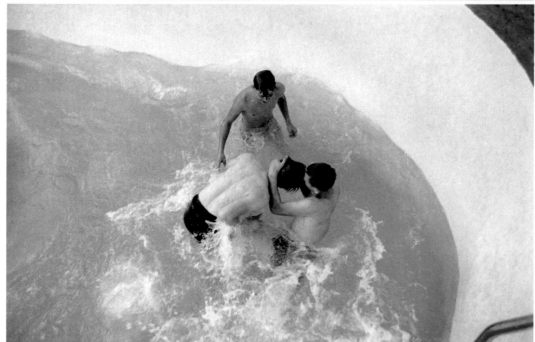

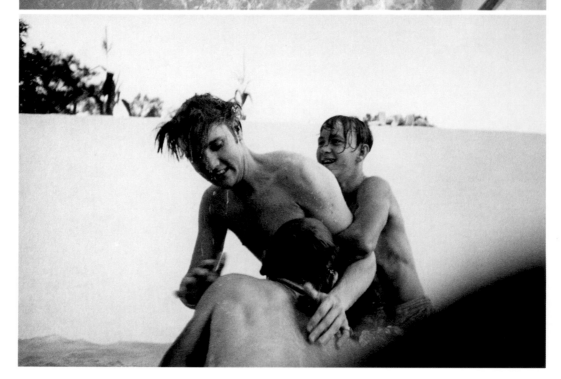

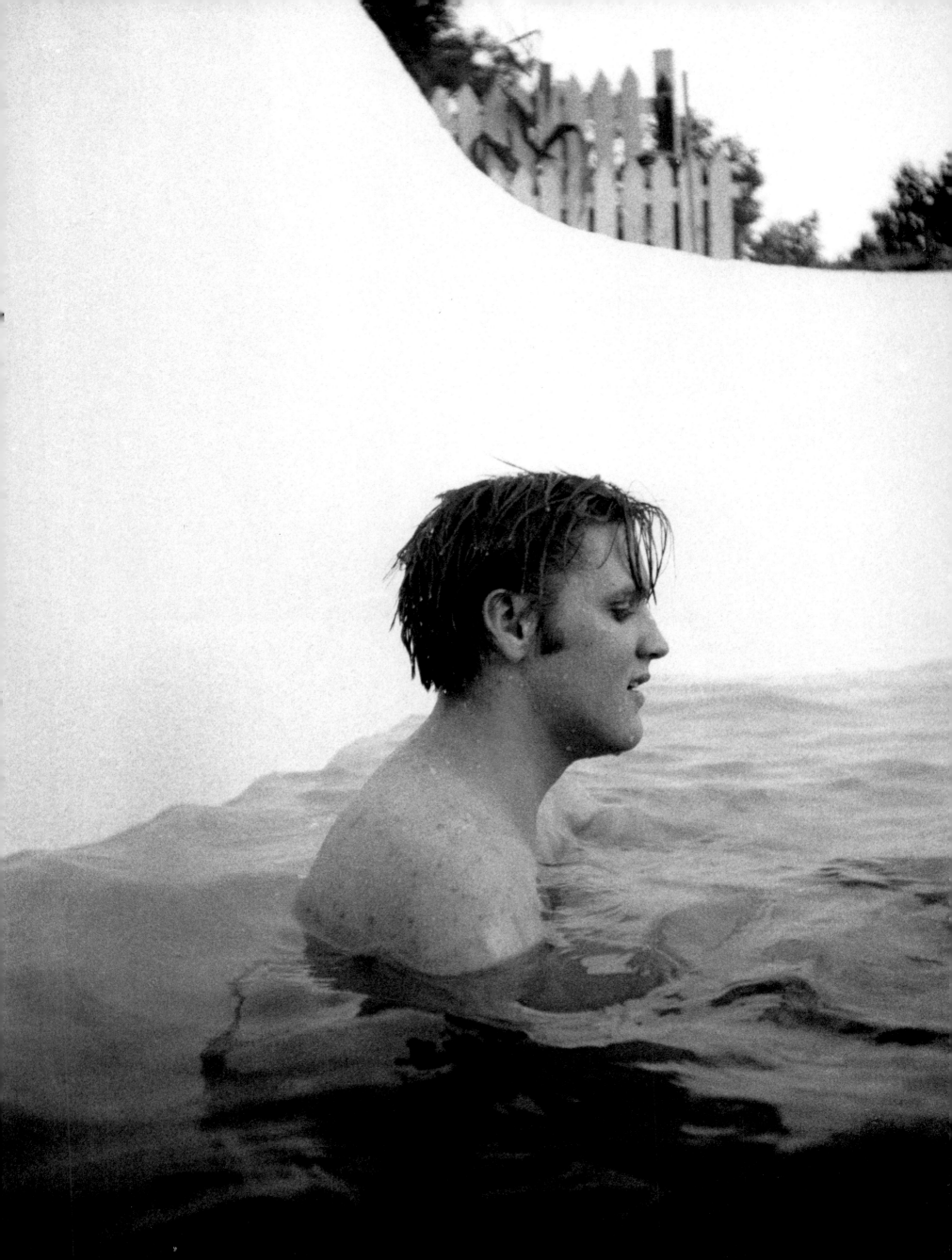

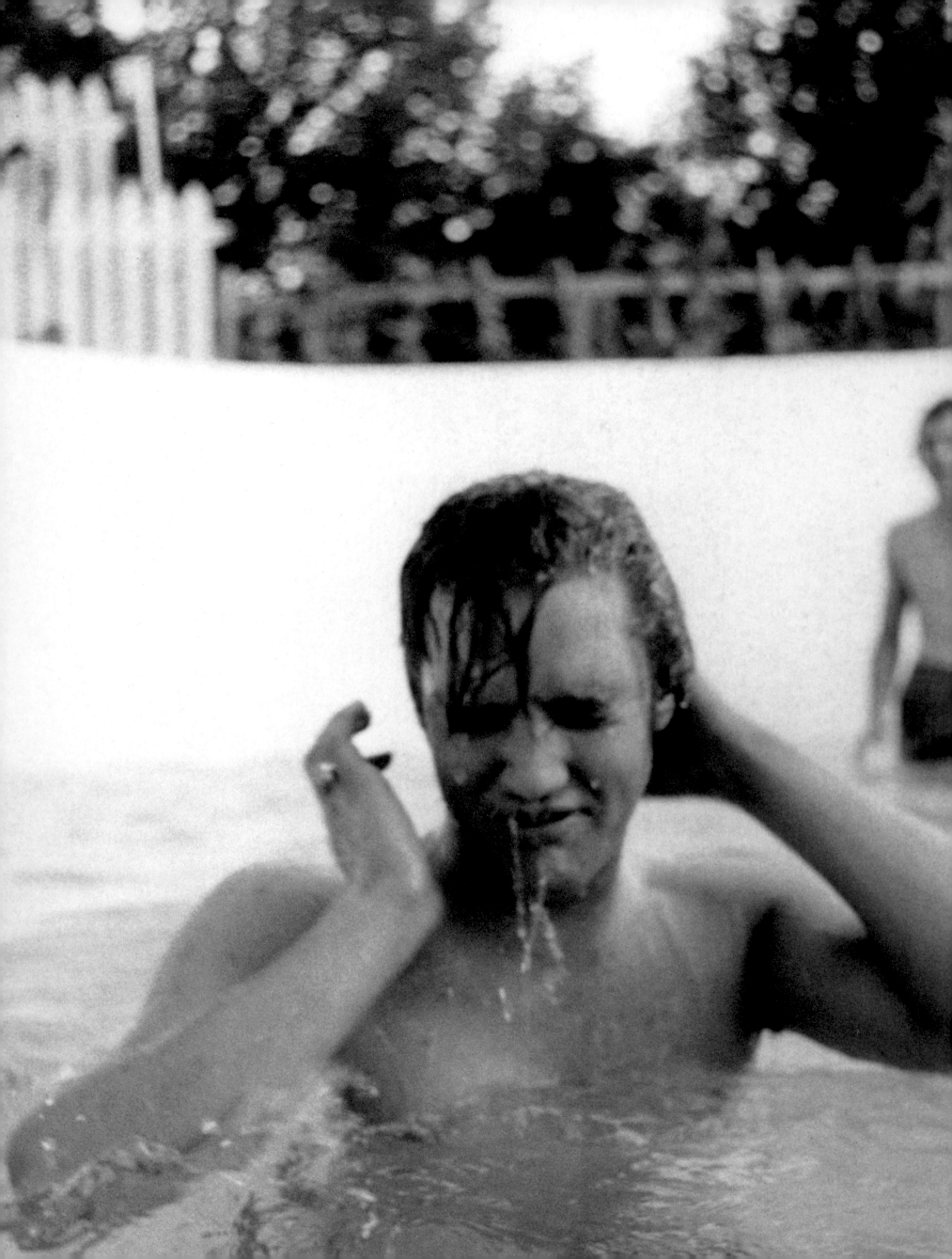

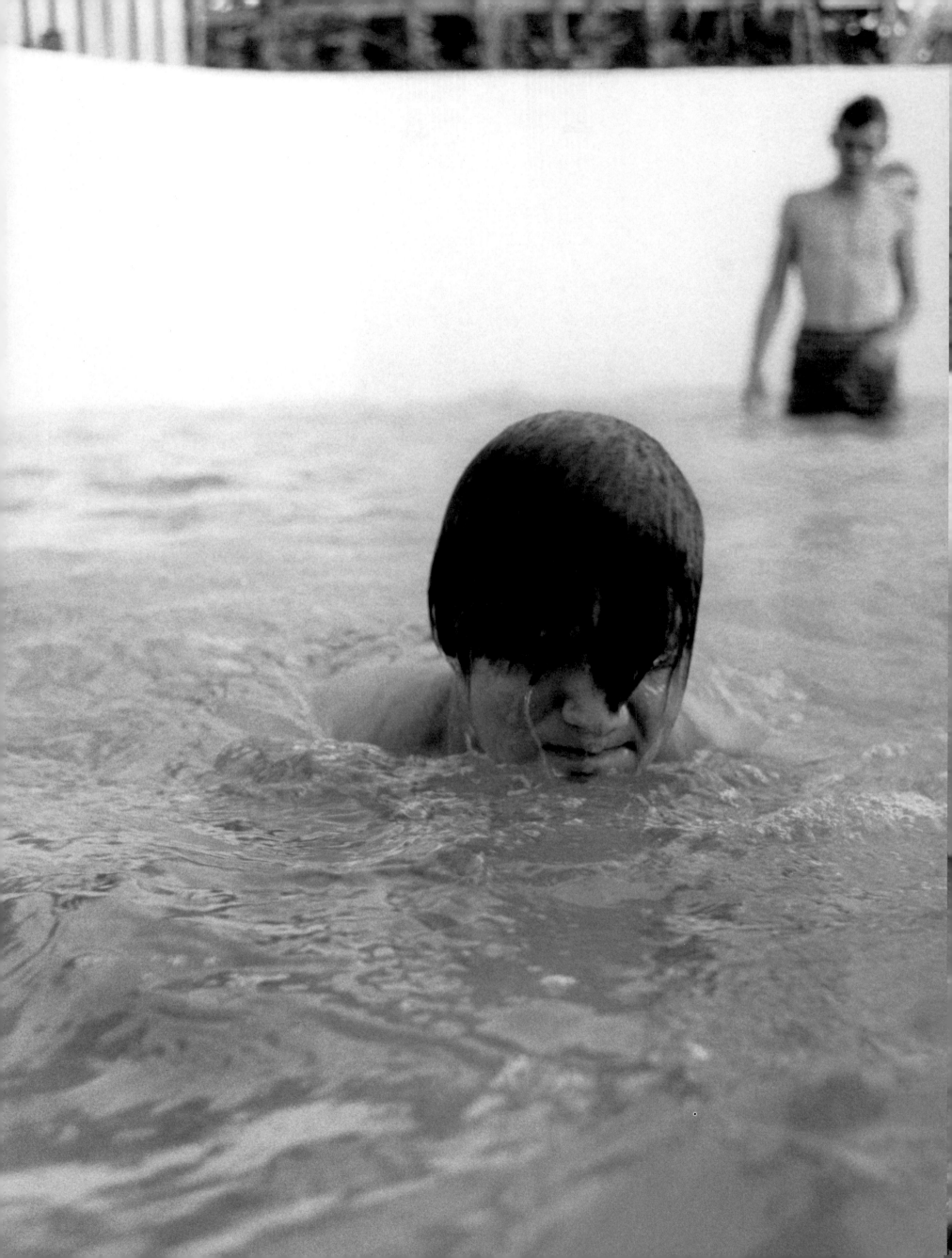

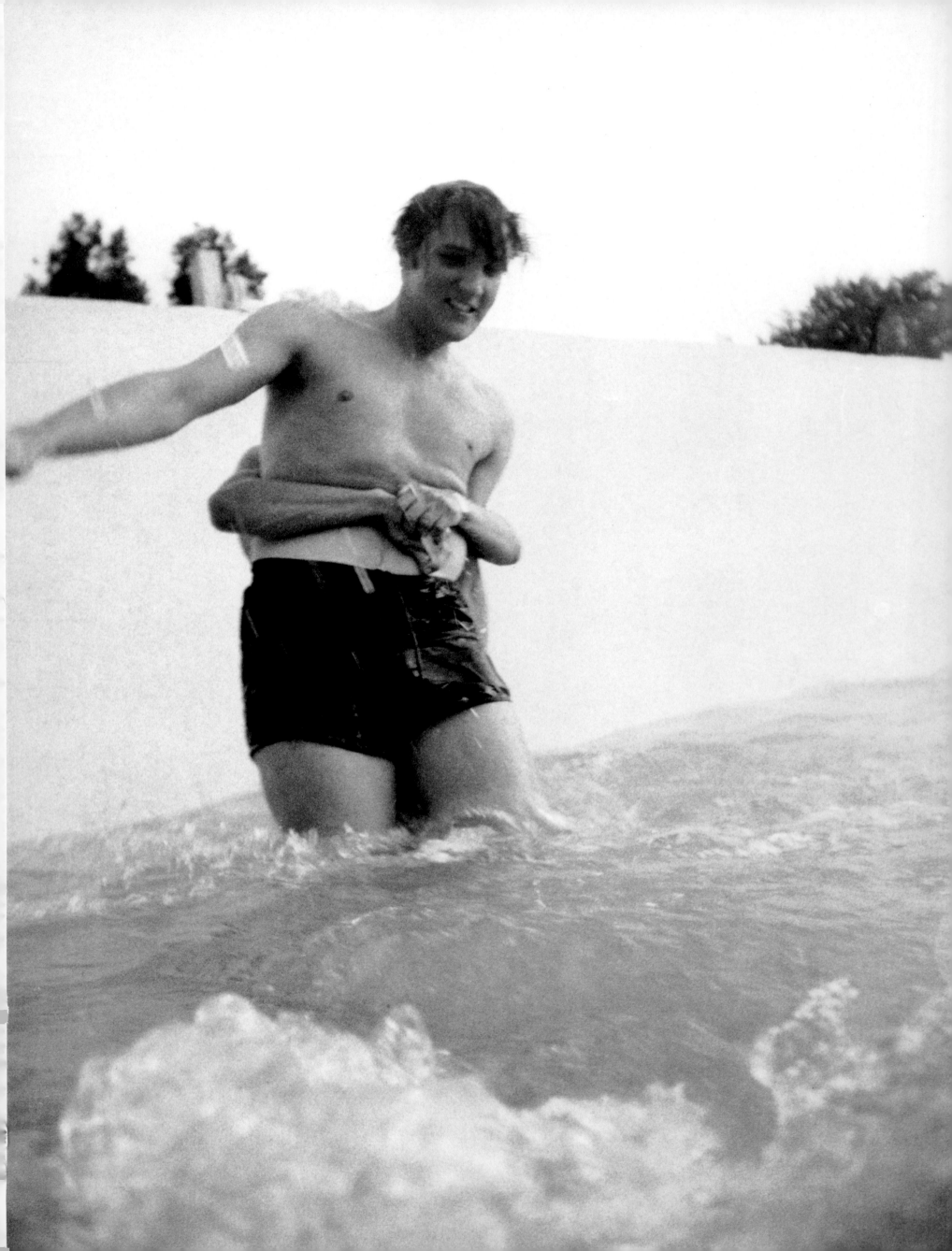

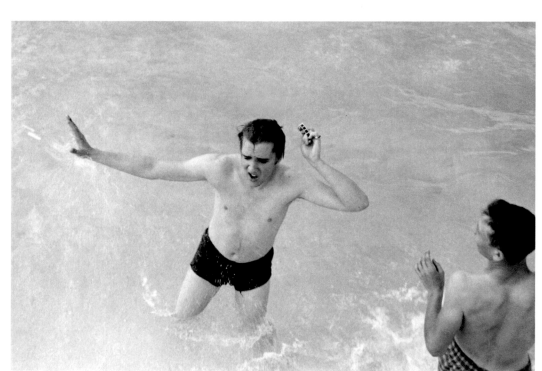

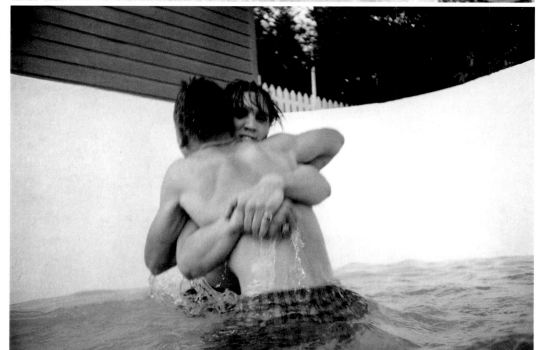

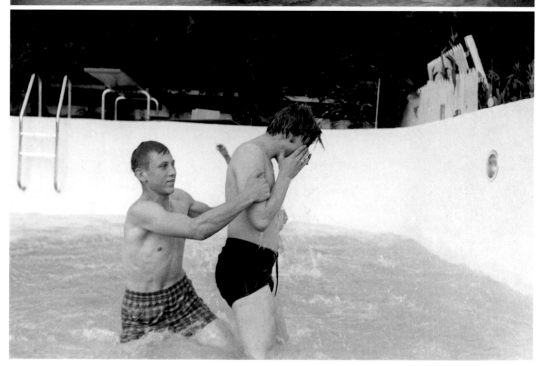

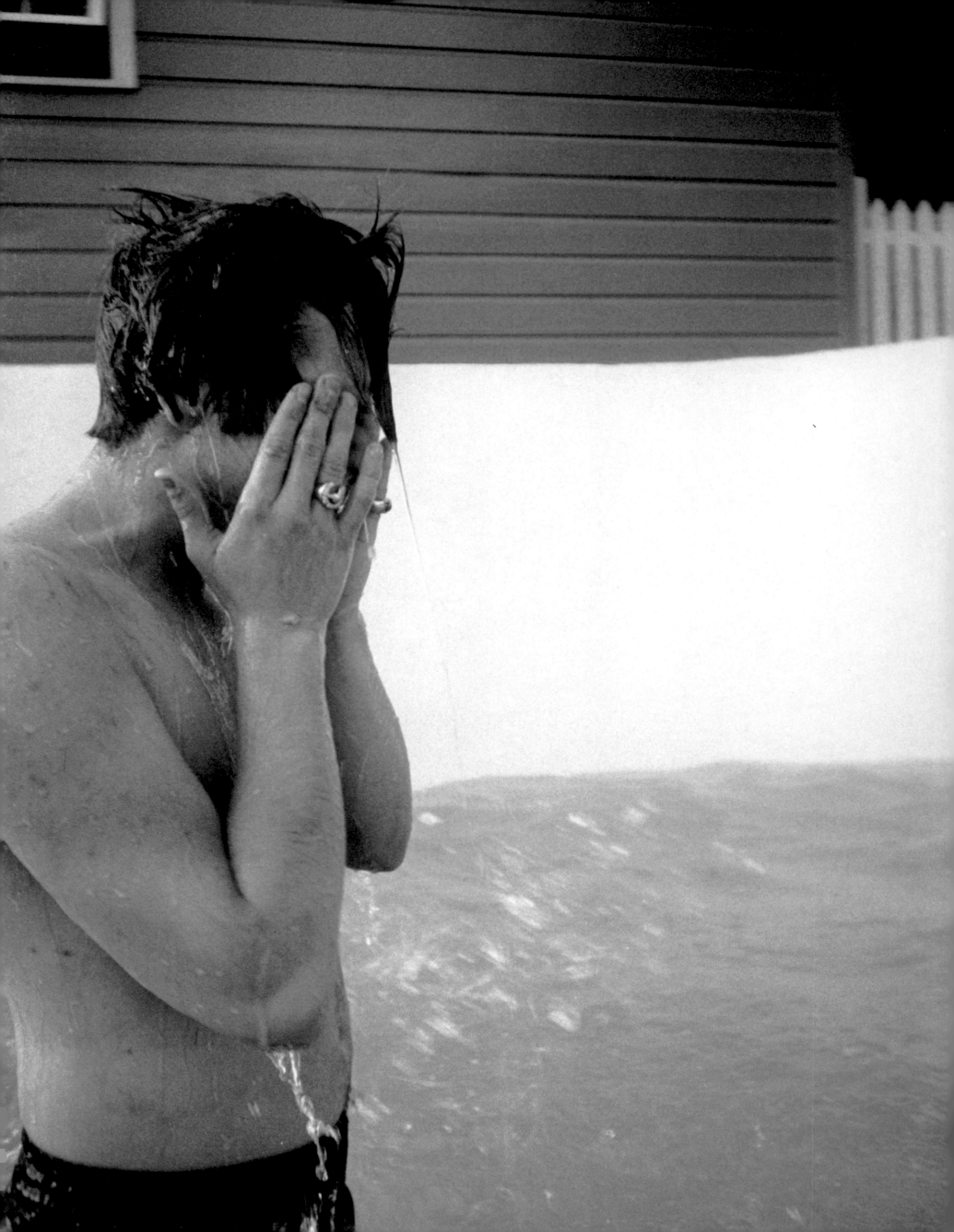

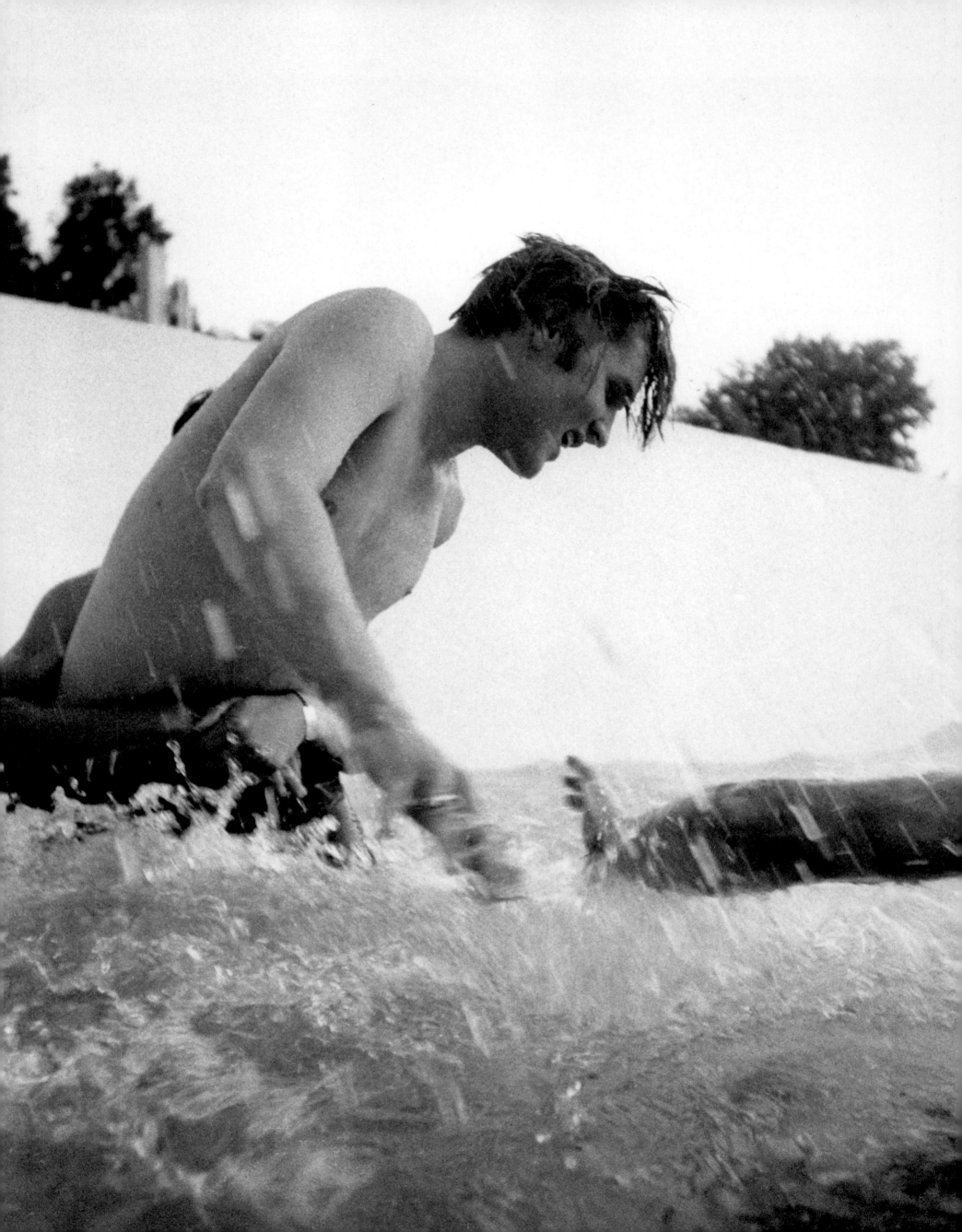

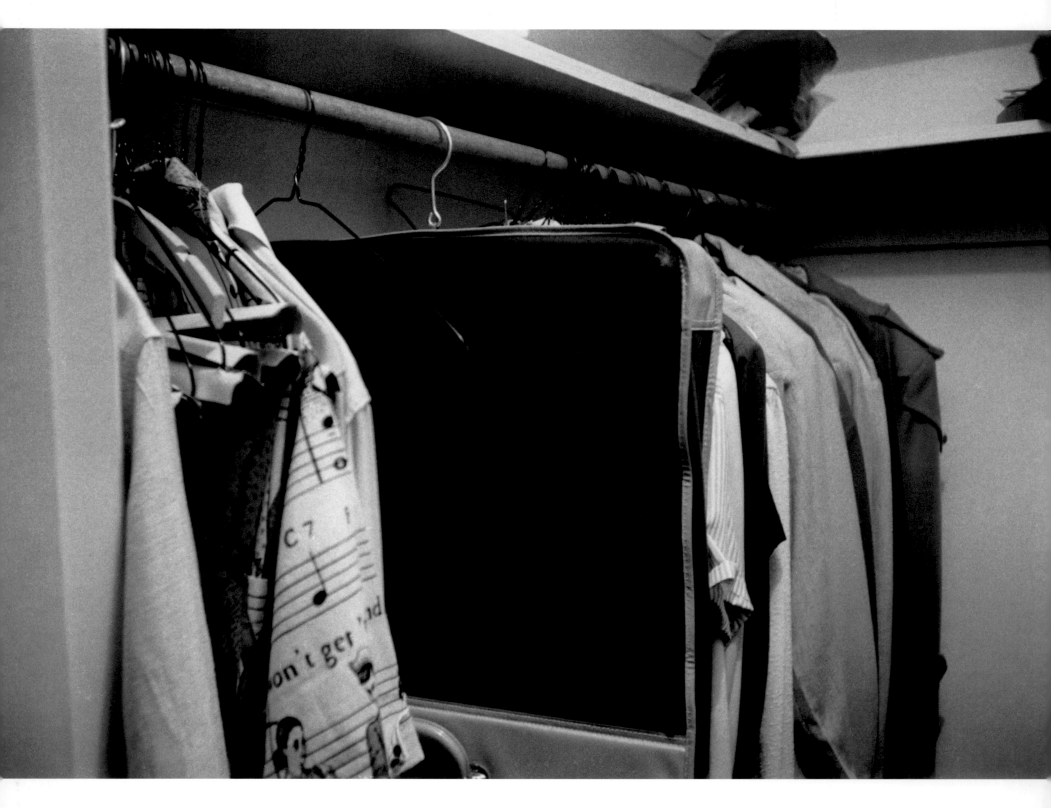

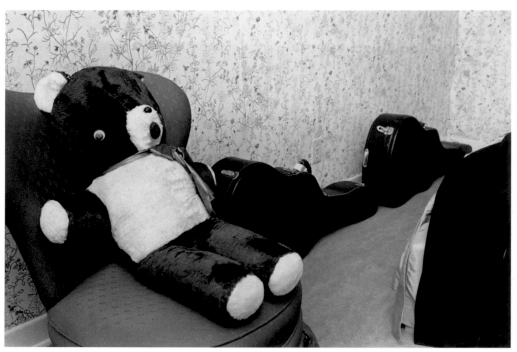

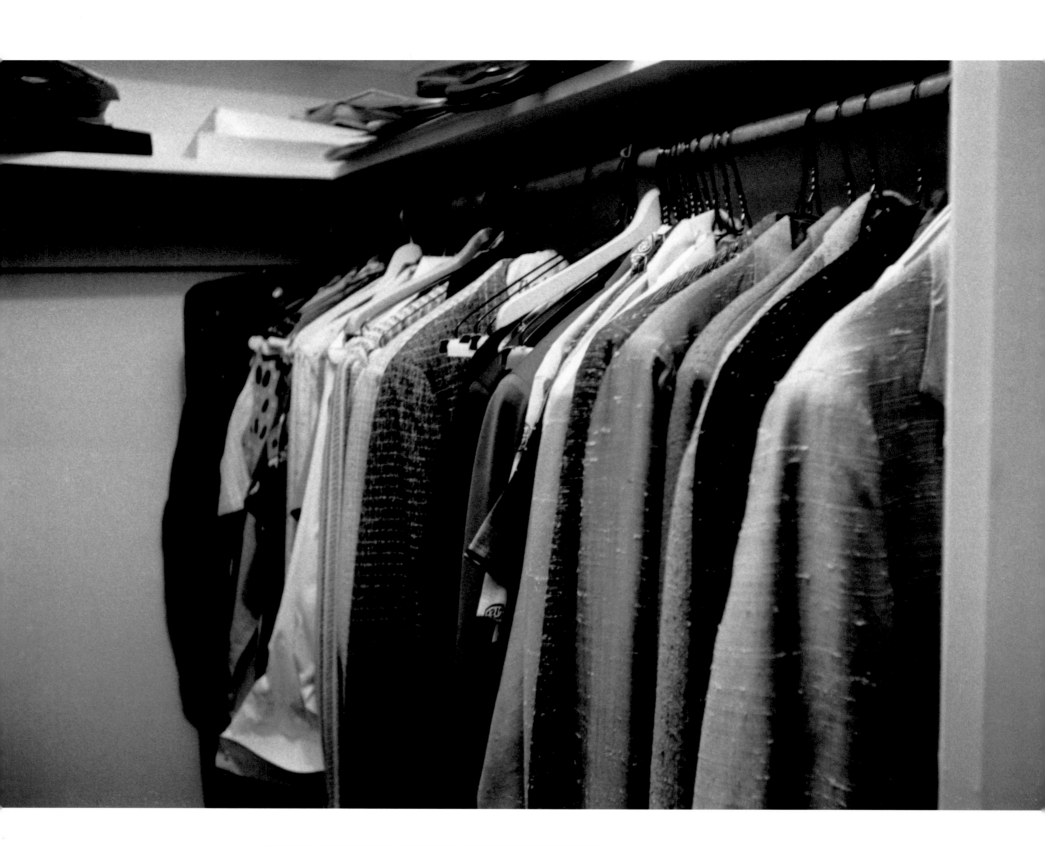

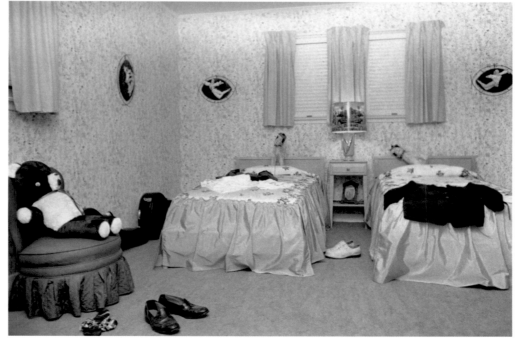

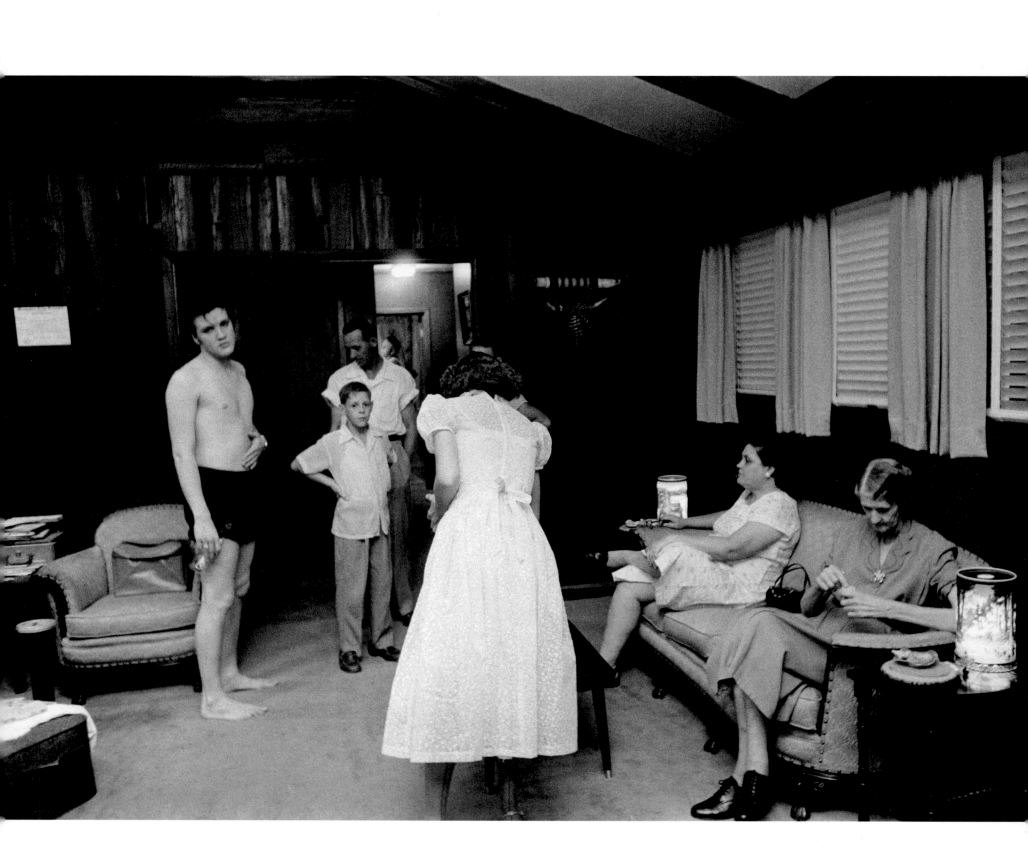

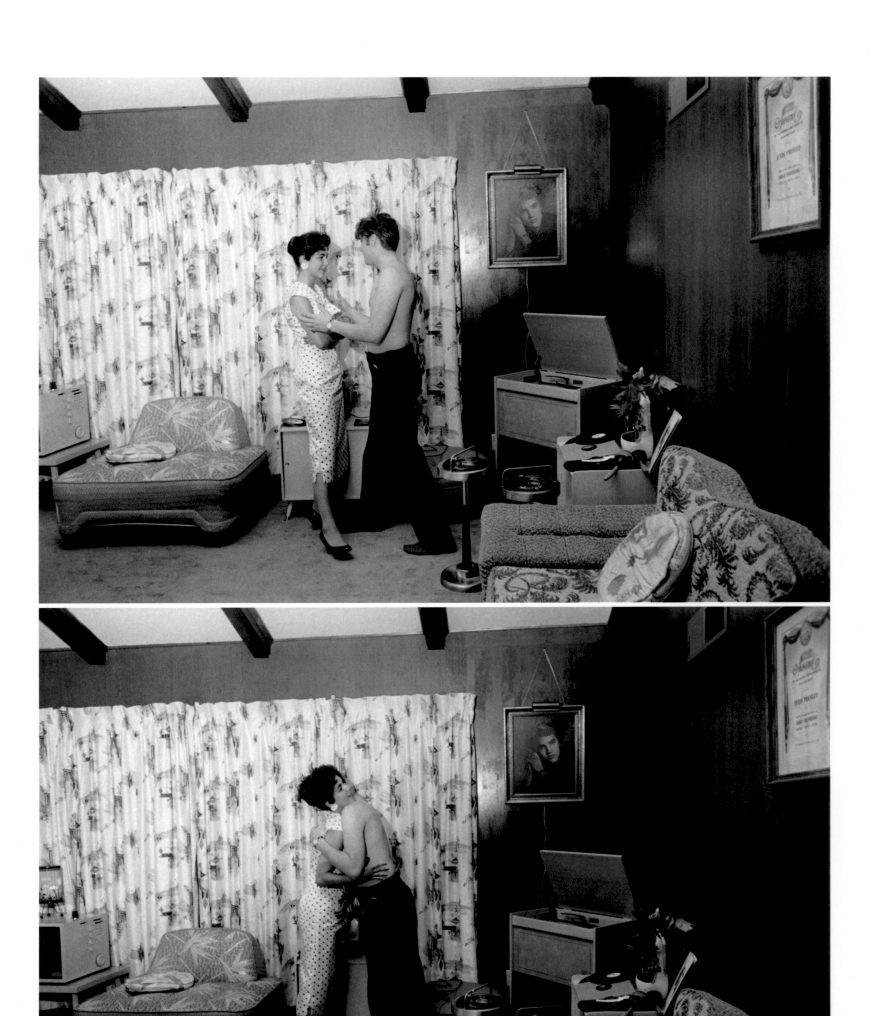

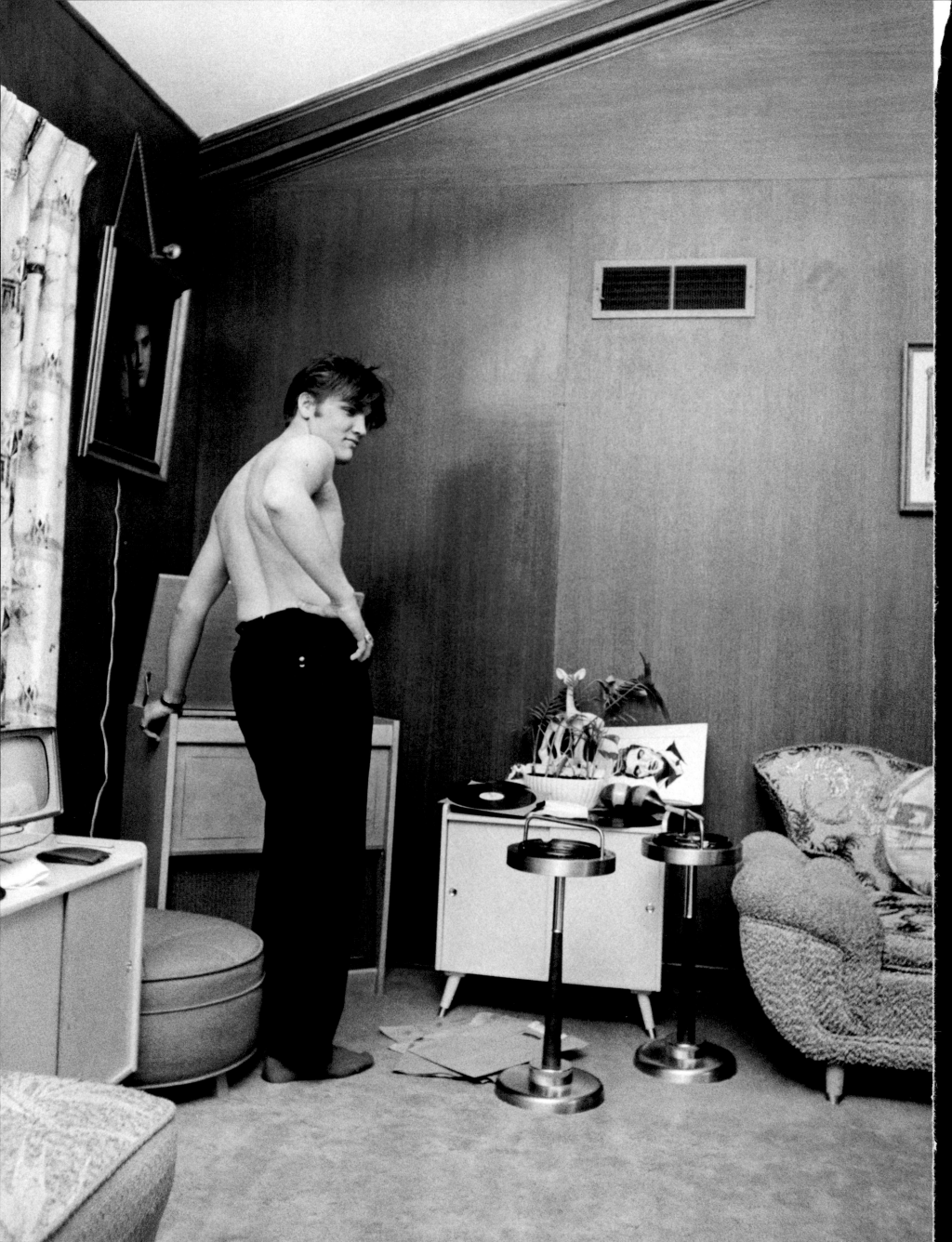

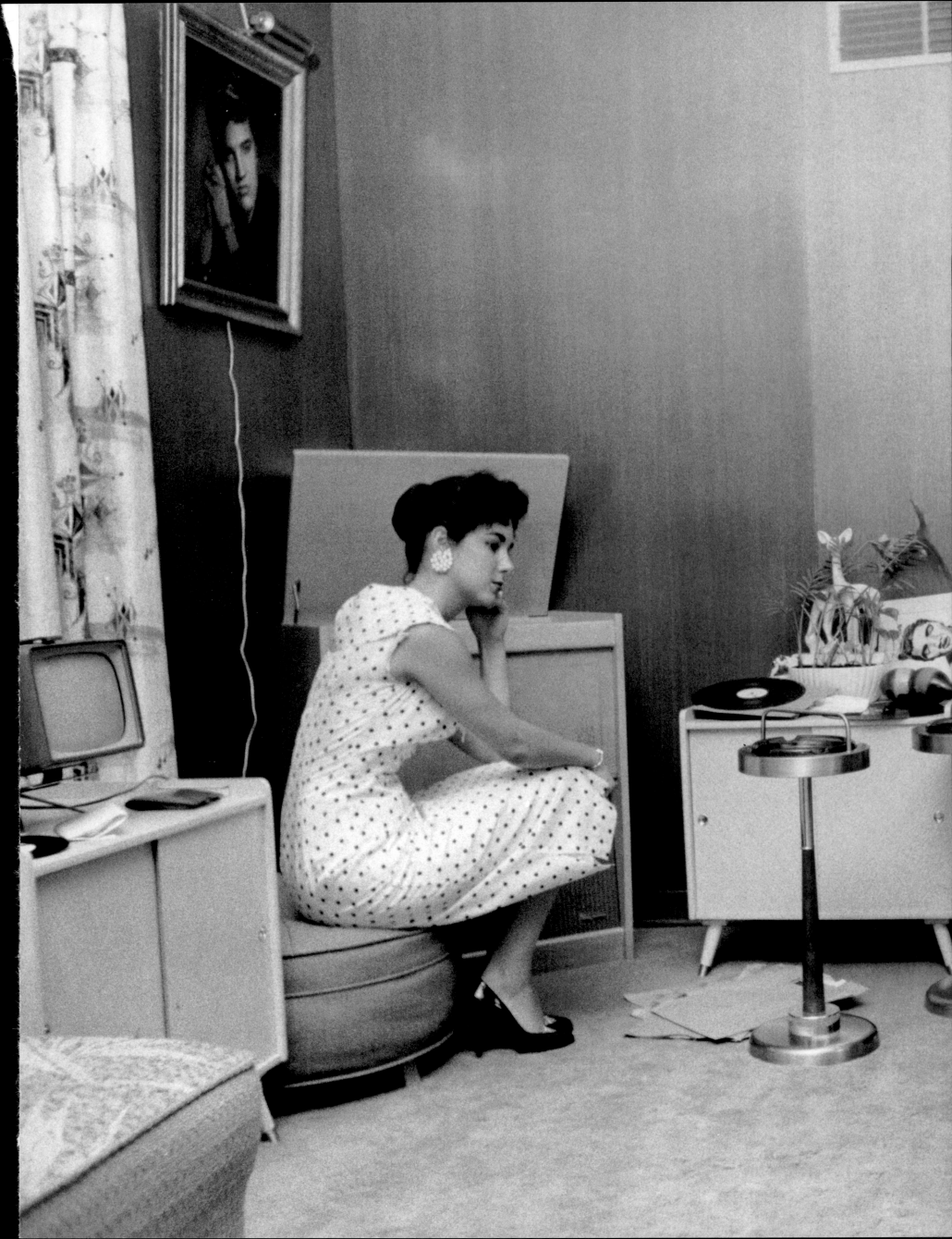

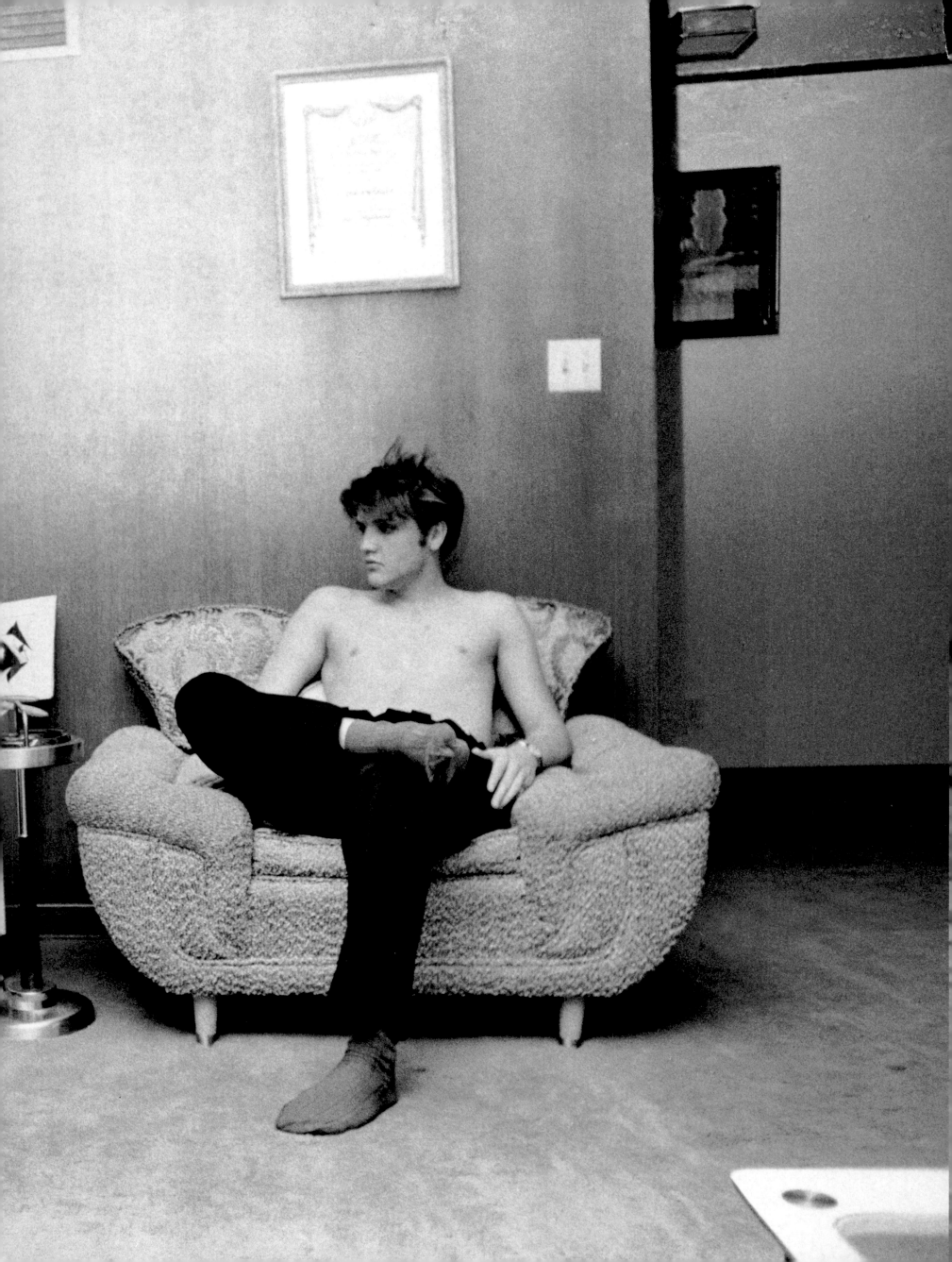

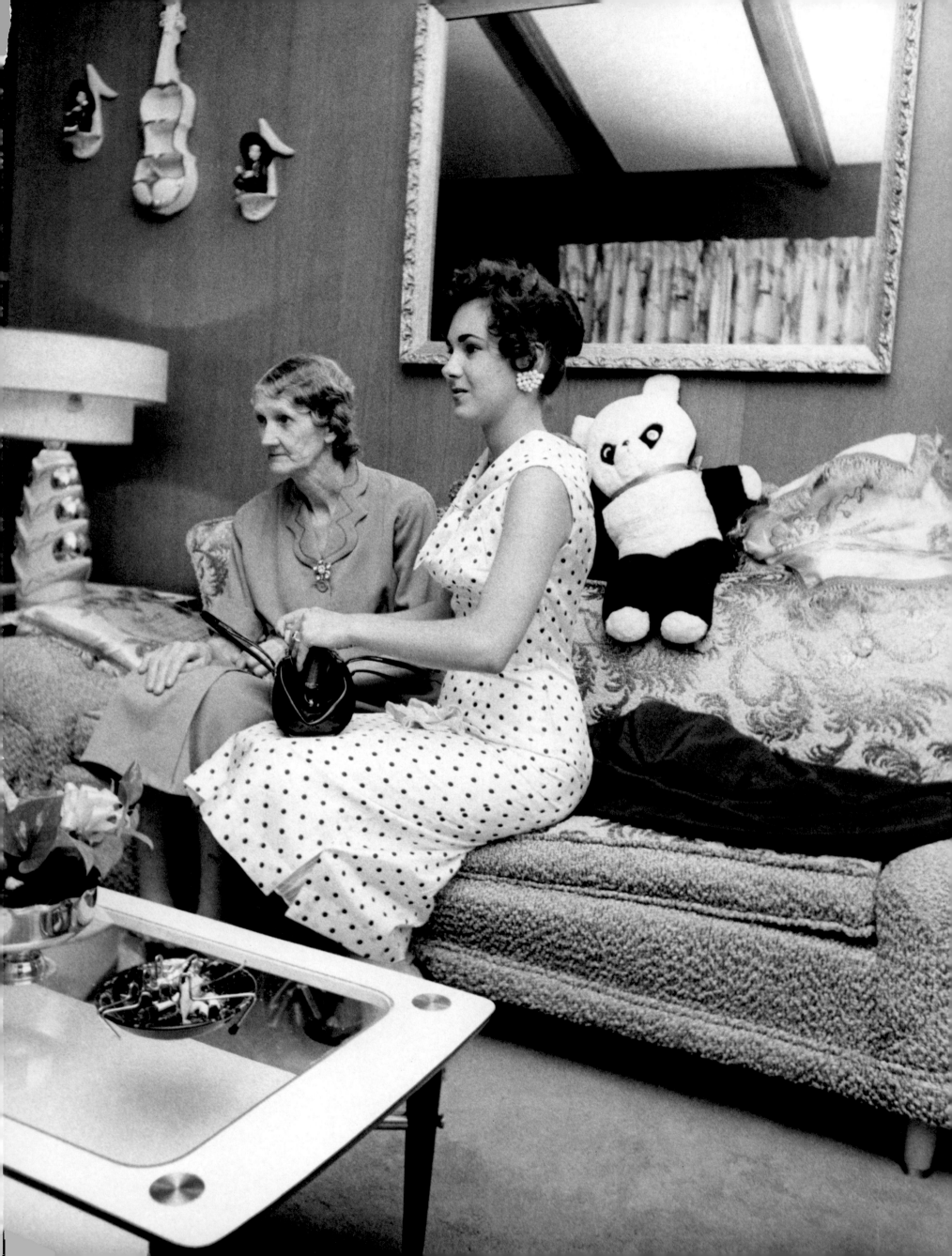

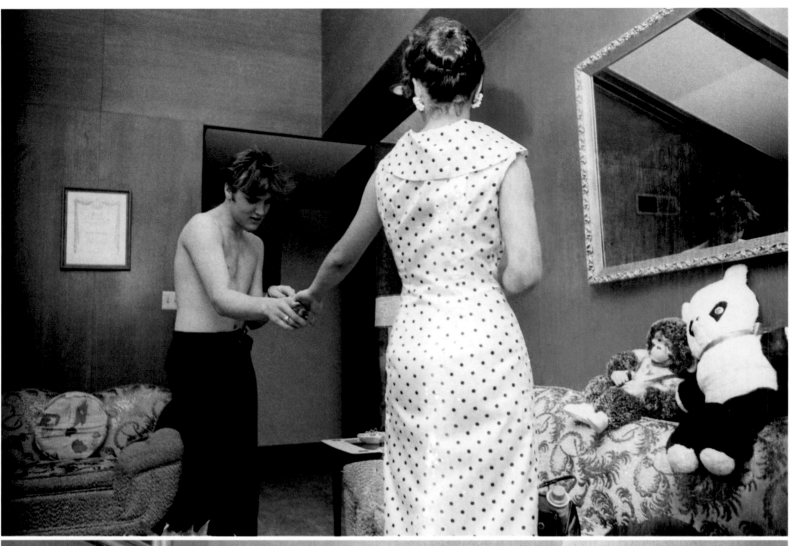
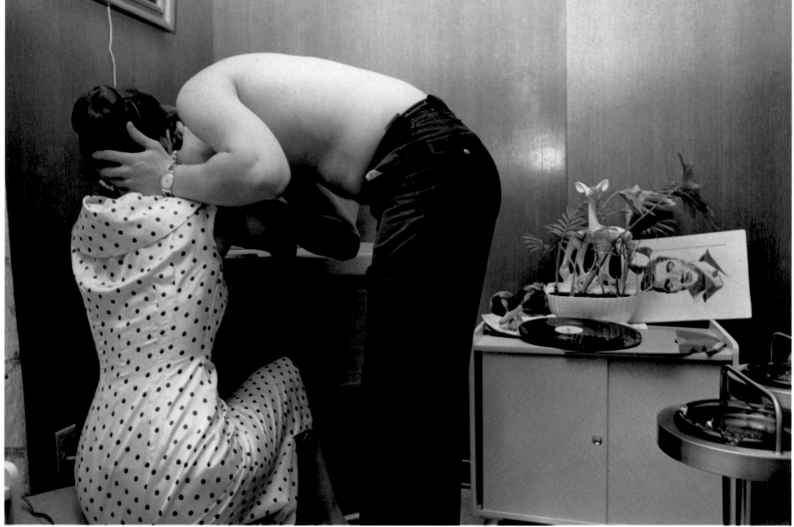

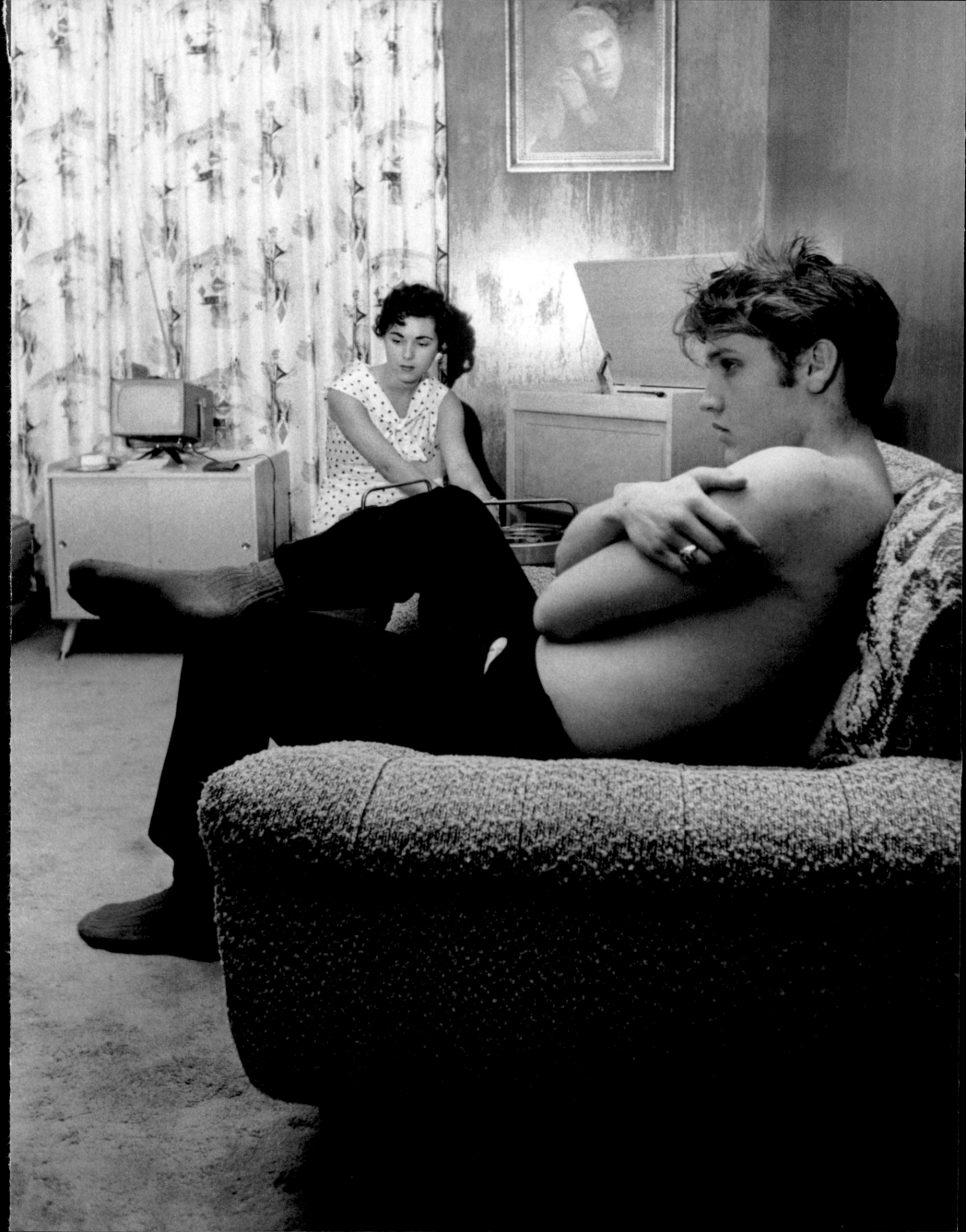

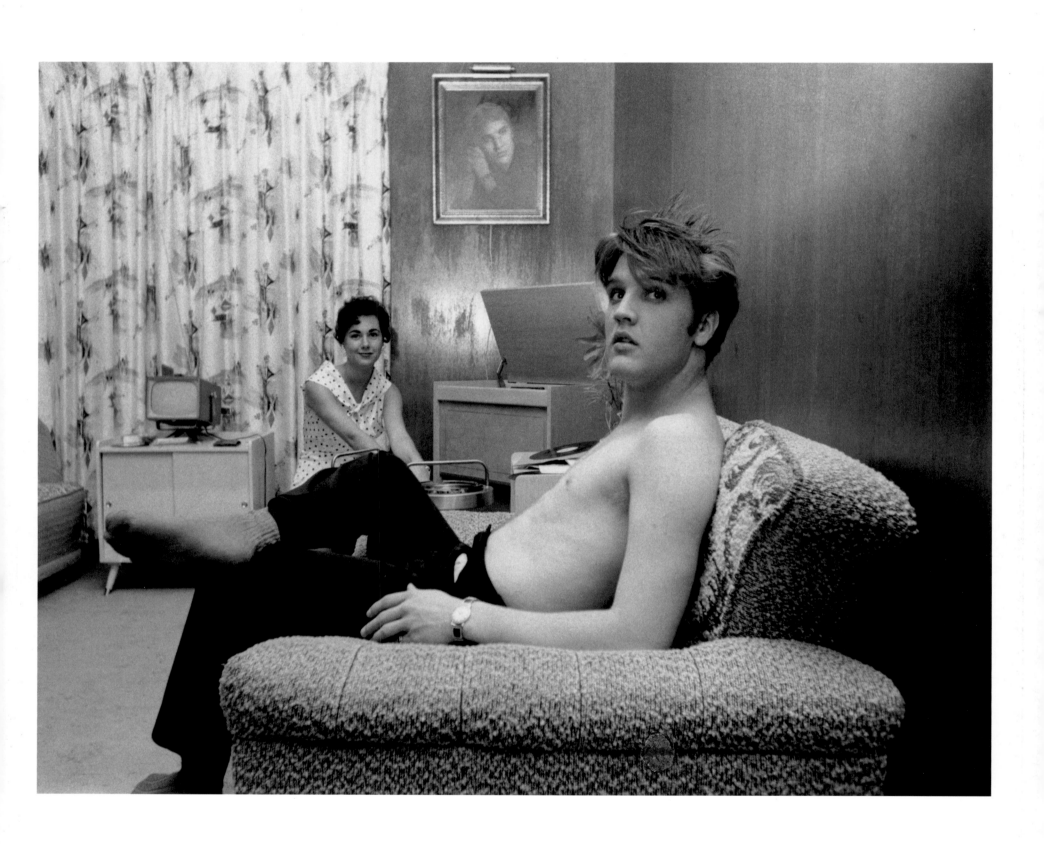

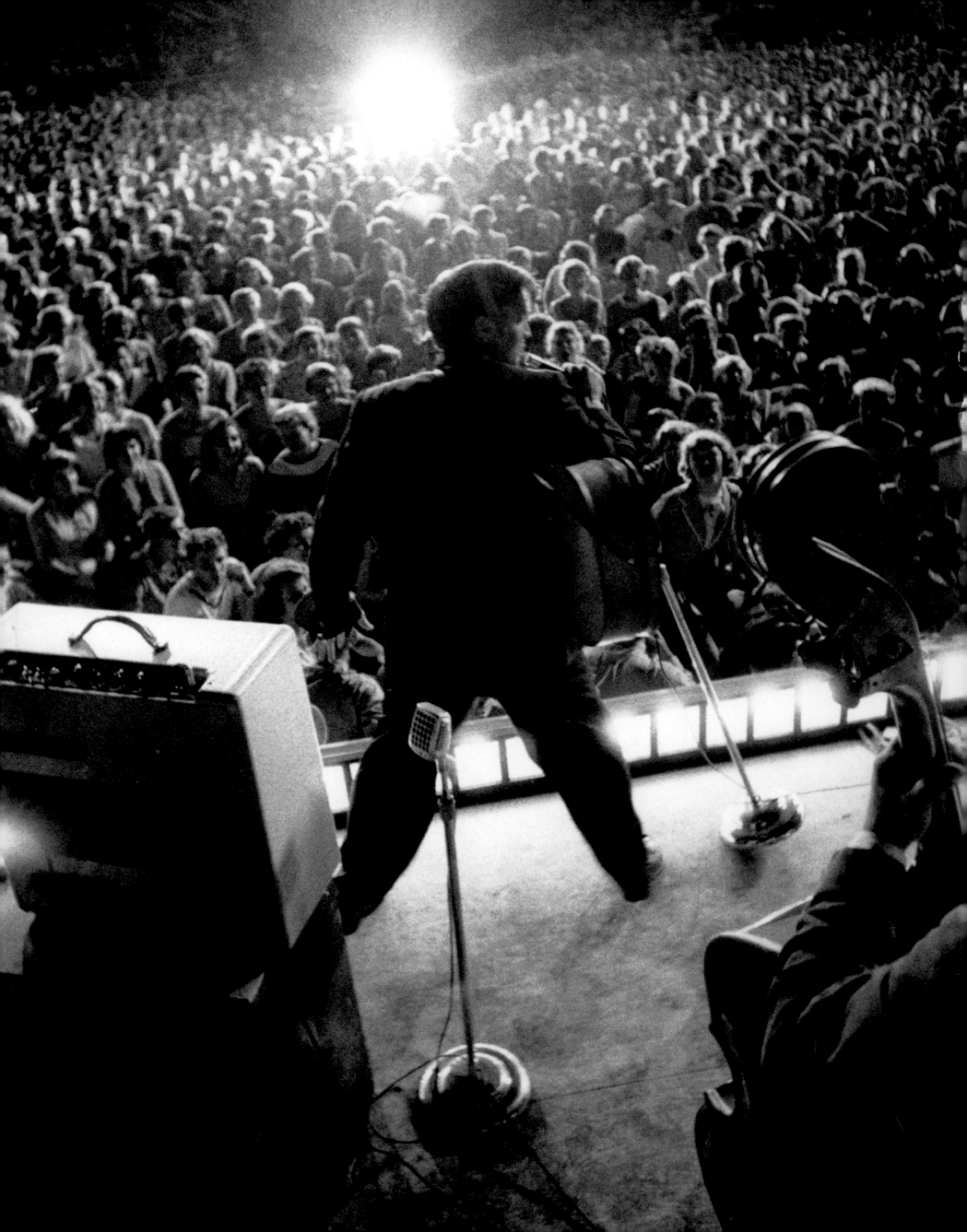

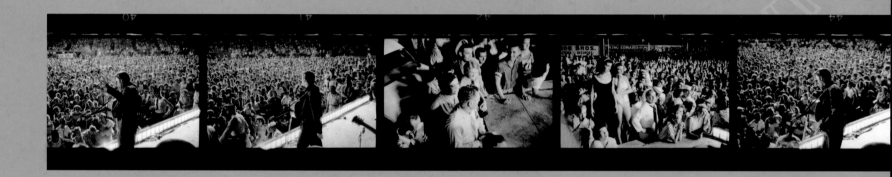

CHAPTER VIII

RUSSWOOD PARK

MEMPHIS

RUSSWOOD PARK
MEMPHIS

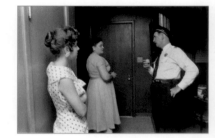

BLACK SHIRT, BLACK PANTS, BLACK SHOES, AND A BLACK BELT. Elvis was putting it all together for his hometown audience when the doorbell rang. The Colonel stood outside, cigar in one hand and a pad of paper in the other. After paying his respects to Mrs. Presley, he went straight to Elvis's bedroom to review the evening's itinerary. Another doorbell ring. The sheriff had arrived to escort Elvis to Russwood Park.

We climbed into the sheriff's black-and-white police car, which was parked out front. The others would follow shortly afterward in another car. Elvis sat in between the Colonel and the sheriff while I had the prisoner's seat in the back. As we wound through rural country roads, I could see nothing in the darkness surrounding us and had no sense of where we were going. Yet the image framed directly before me held my interest. The Colonel was wearing his hat with the feather, Elvis's hair was combed perfectly, and the sheriff's hat sat on top of a very straight, clean-cut neck. I wanted to take a nice wide-angle shot from my perspective in the back seat, but in order to get anything, I needed to use a strobe unit. The idea of using a flashing strobe light in the middle of the sheriff's car didn't seem particularly wise. I could see us veering off and crashing somewhere in the pitch-black night, but I decided to take my chances anyway. I held the strobe up and released the shutter once. Relieved that no one seemed startled or upset, I took only that single shot. The sheriff knew I was a photographer and the other two were used to my being on the wall, so to speak, but I didn't push my luck.

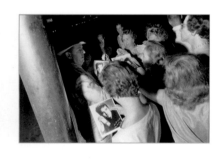

Waiting at the stadium was a police escort comprised of four or five officers and the Navy Shore Patrol, which had cordoned off a path to the stage. Stationed in Memphis, the Shore Patrol was called in to help maintain order. I walked mostly backward about ten feet ahead of the group so that I could stop and shoot Elvis moving through a surging crowd trying to get as close as possible to him. As we approached the stage, you could hear the people and feel their anticipation. Looking out, I saw banks of floodlights shining down from the bleachers onto the packed outfield and infield of this old baseball stadium. Gladys and Vernon, Elvis's Uncle Travis, his grandmother Minnie May, and Barbara had been escorted already to a special VIP area near the stage.

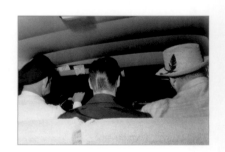

In a tier above the stage, house musicians were arranged to accompany the other acts. This was where I positioned myself for a bird's-eye view of the scene. I could see the Colonel surrounded by some of his cronies. Instead of watching the show, he appeared deep in thought. The Colonel was always thinking, always making hay out of the present while figuring out the next move. During the concert, he kept a stack of prints in front of him. At one point, I looked over to see a bunch of women crowding around him reaching out for them. He handed each of them a photograph and collected money in return, which he put it in his pocket. Some time later, I questioned him about that. He explained quite logically that if you gave things away for free, they would be put away and forgotten. People appreciated things they paid for, so they'd get a lot more mileage out of them that way. It was another lesson from the man who certainly had his own particular idea of how the world worked.

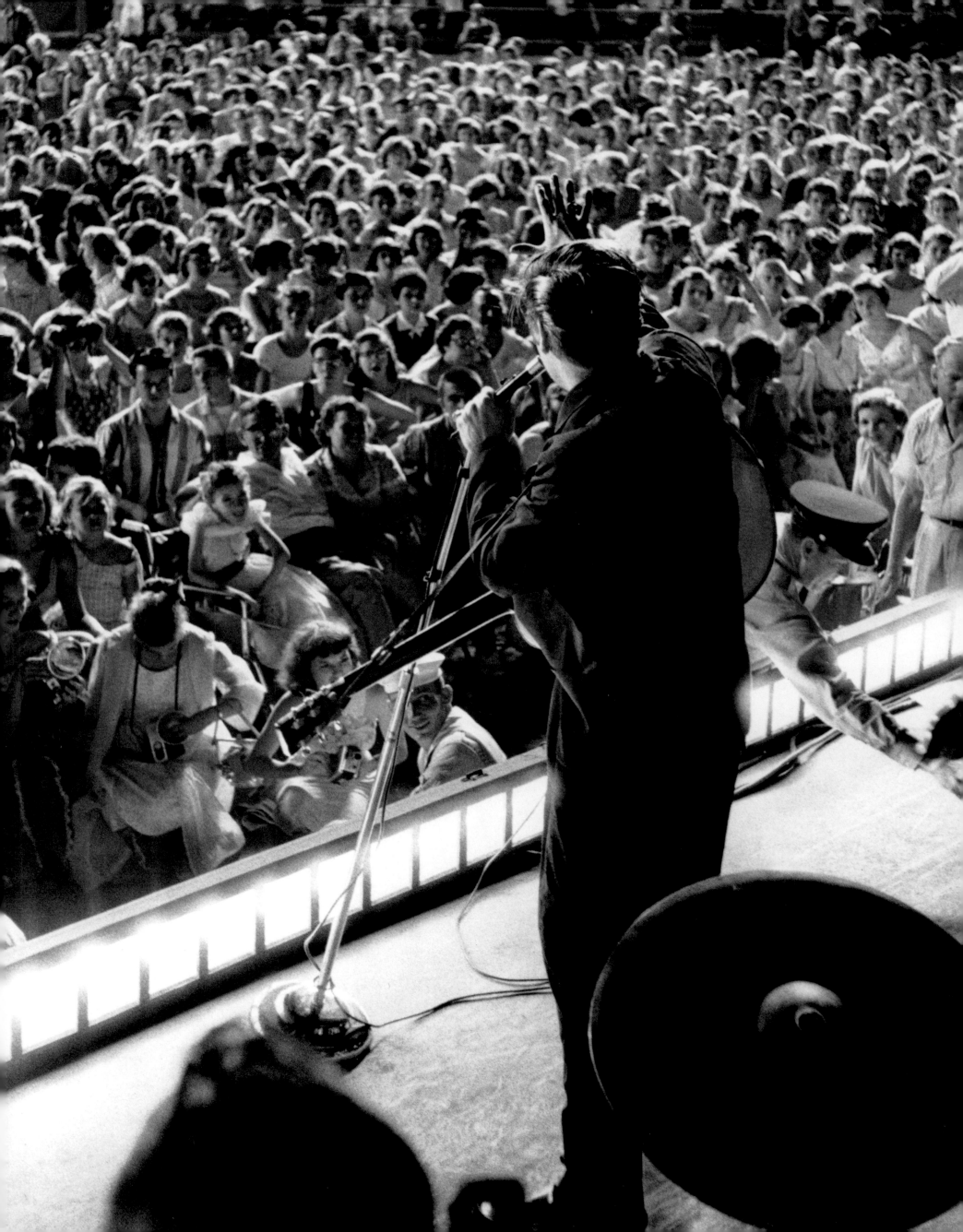

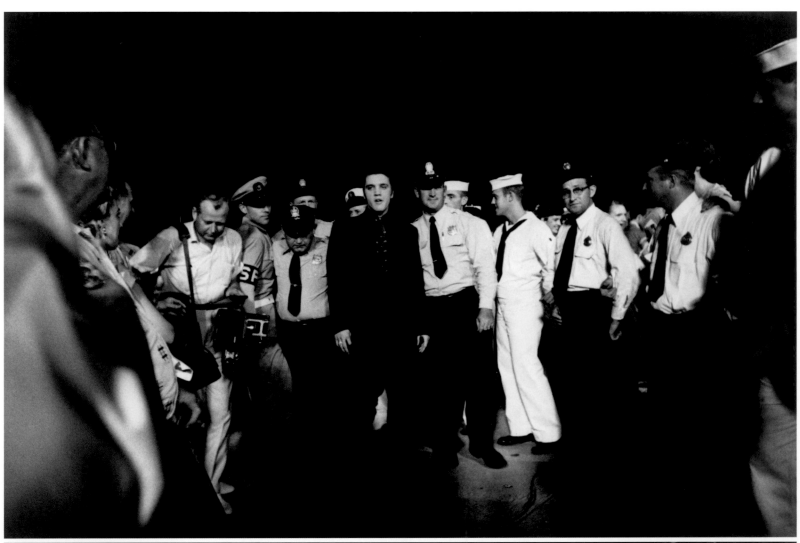

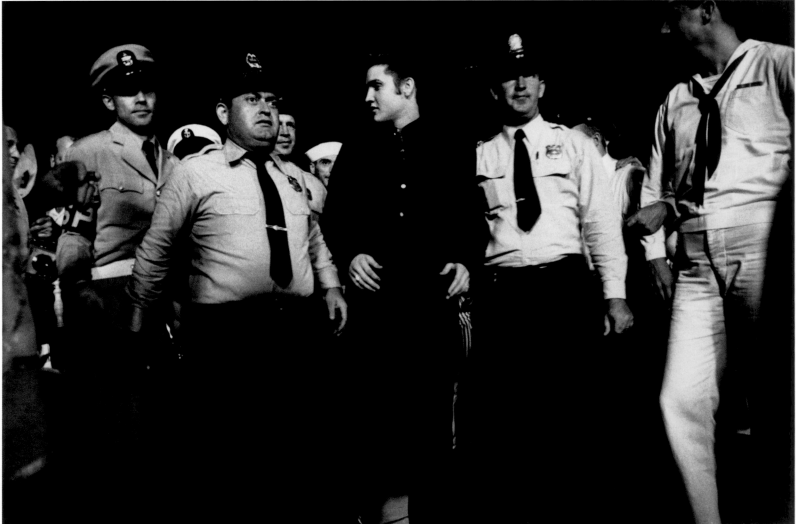

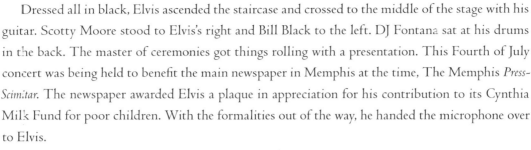

Dressed all in black, Elvis ascended the staircase and crossed to the middle of the stage with his guitar. Scotty Moore stood to Elvis's right and Bill Black to the left. DJ Fontana sat at his drums in the back. The master of ceremonies got things rolling with a presentation. This Fourth of July concert was being held to benefit the main newspaper in Memphis at the time, The Memphis *Press-Scimitar*. The newspaper awarded Elvis a plaque in appreciation for his contribution to its Cynthia Milk Fund for poor children. With the formalities out of the way, he handed the microphone over to Elvis.

Since Elvis had been seen just three days earlier on *The Steve Allen Show*, where he was tightly scripted into a tuxedo singing to a hound dog, he started this night's performance off with a statement.

"Tonight, you're going to see what the real Elvis Presley is all about."

Before you knew it, he was gyrating all over the stage in his signature way. The audience loved it. Thousands of people screamed and hollered for their hometown boy who had made it in the big time. Elvis felt good that night, and so did I.

After shooting about ten frames from a certain position, I usually felt as if I had gotten what I wanted and could move on. Of course, this was based on pure speculation and trust in my own judgment. I wouldn't know what was in my camera until I got back to my studio. To set the frames during this concert, I had a lot of information to think through and a measure of faith that my choices would work out. I got a few horizontals of Elvis, the musicians and the huge sea of fans. I decided to take a few verticals, as well. The spotlights were bright and I was shooting at them, but I wanted to capture the feeling of this place, from Elvis in the lower third of the frame, moving up to the lights in the bleachers, I realized that this was a large stadium.

Although flashbulbs were going off constantly during the performance, I knew they wouldn't affect my still shots. Except for one. Someone in the audience directly in line with Elvis was taking pictures, probably using a Kodak Brownie Box camera with a flash gun attached. When I developed the film, I discovered a shot of Elvis with a magnificent spray of light in front of him. Not strong enough to reach the stage, the flash in the audience highlighted the backs of about thirty rows of heads as well. That random flash was in perfect sync with my shutter opening as I took the picture of Elvis performing. When I saw that photograph, it represented for me this entire experience and was better than anything I had done previously or would do later. Instead of ruining the frame, this unexpected lucky moment gave me "Starburst." (p. 238)

Once he finished his songs, Elvis left the stage. I was still up high and shooting down on the scene. The Shore Patrol and local police were holding the crowd back as he headed straight for a waiting patrol car. I remember a sign at the far end of the stadium advertising the Memphis Steam Laundry that read, "If you hit this sign, you get $1,000." No one, not even Joe DiMaggio, could hit a ball that far. As a photographer though, I had gotten lucky. I did hit that sign.

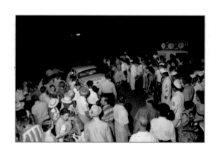

Elvis was driven slowly out of the stadium. Within a few minutes, I found myself standing alone with all of my belongings. Hopping on a night train, I went back up north, back to New York where my journey had begun.

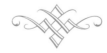

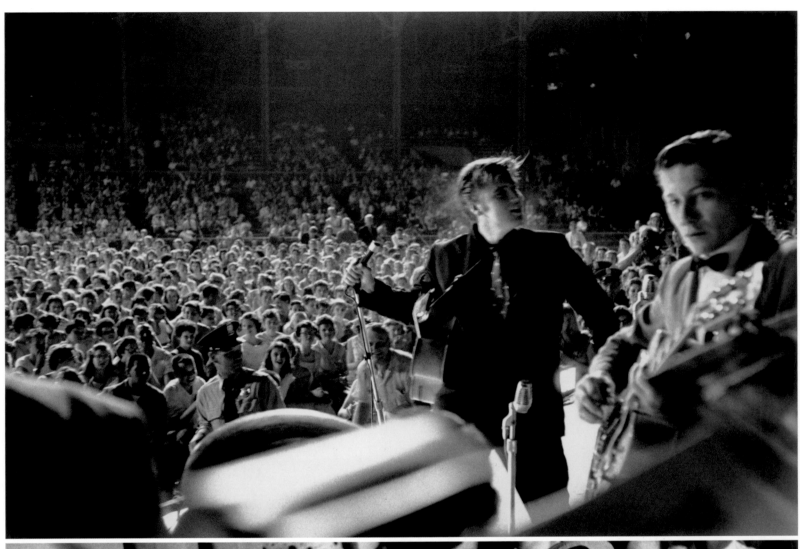

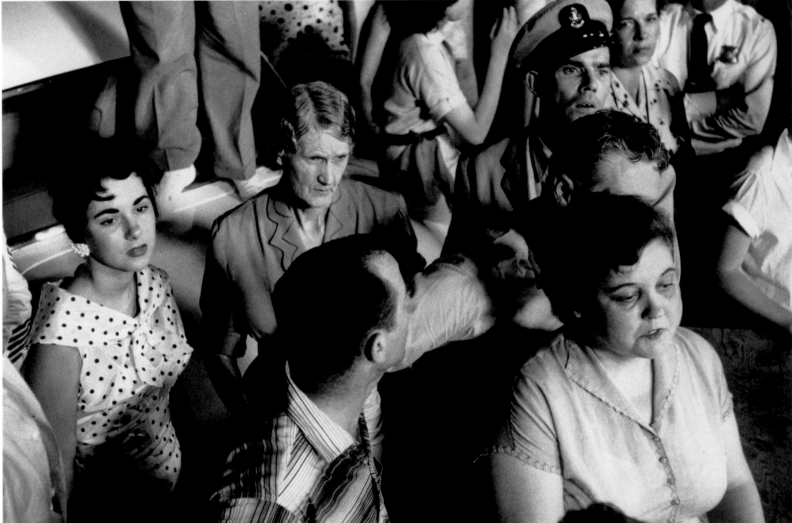

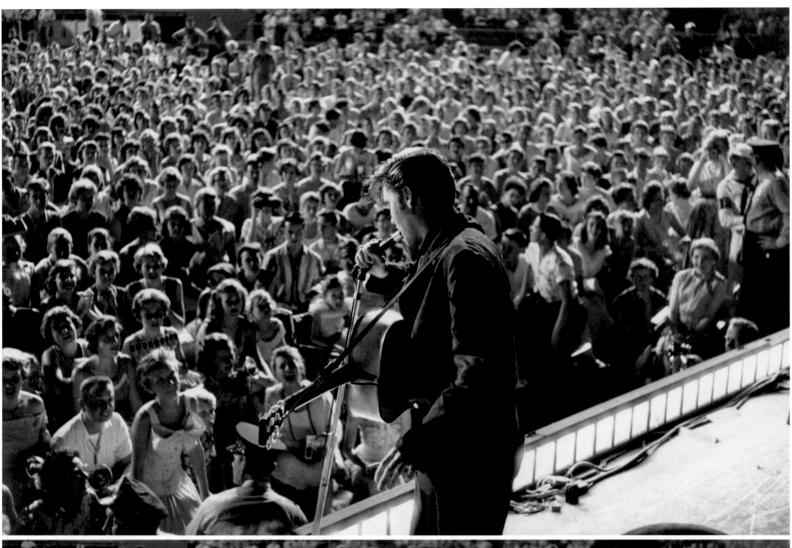

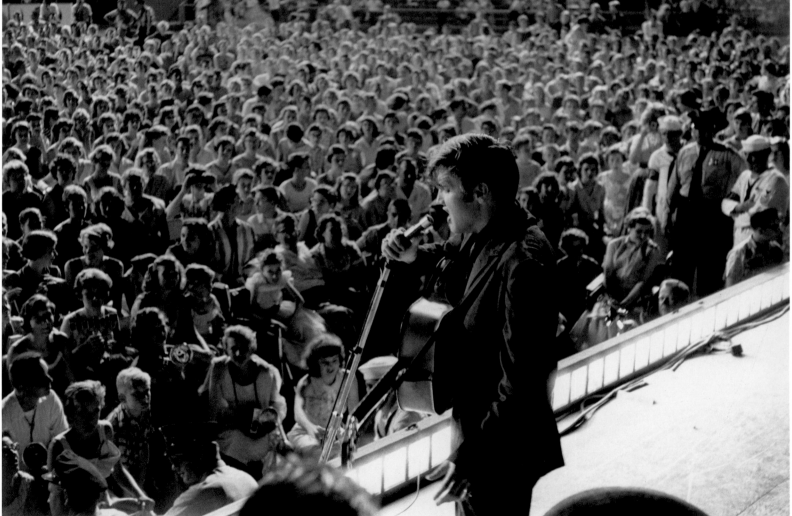

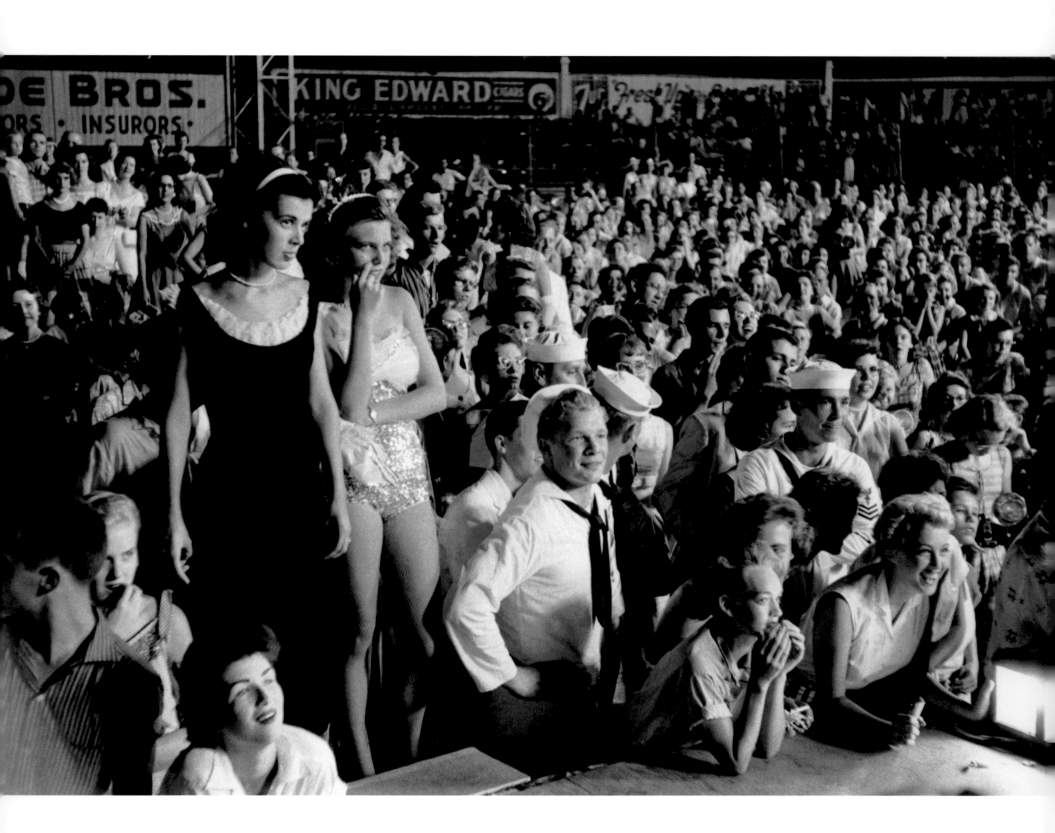

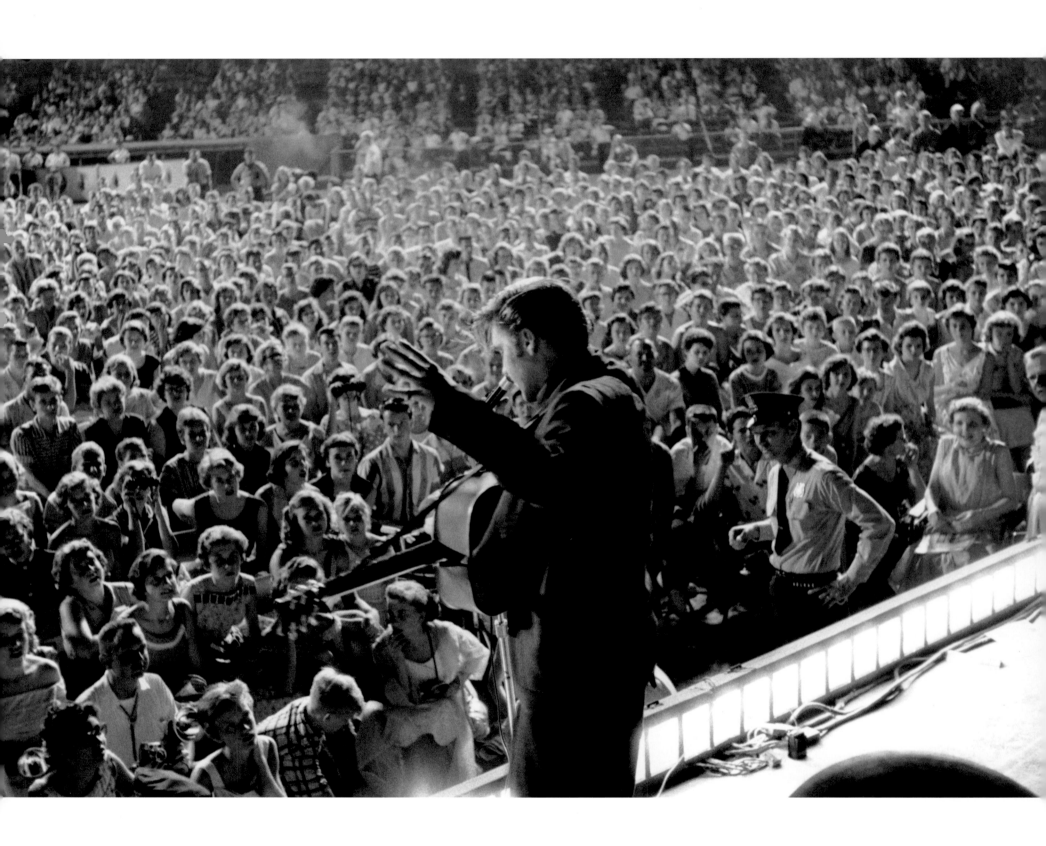

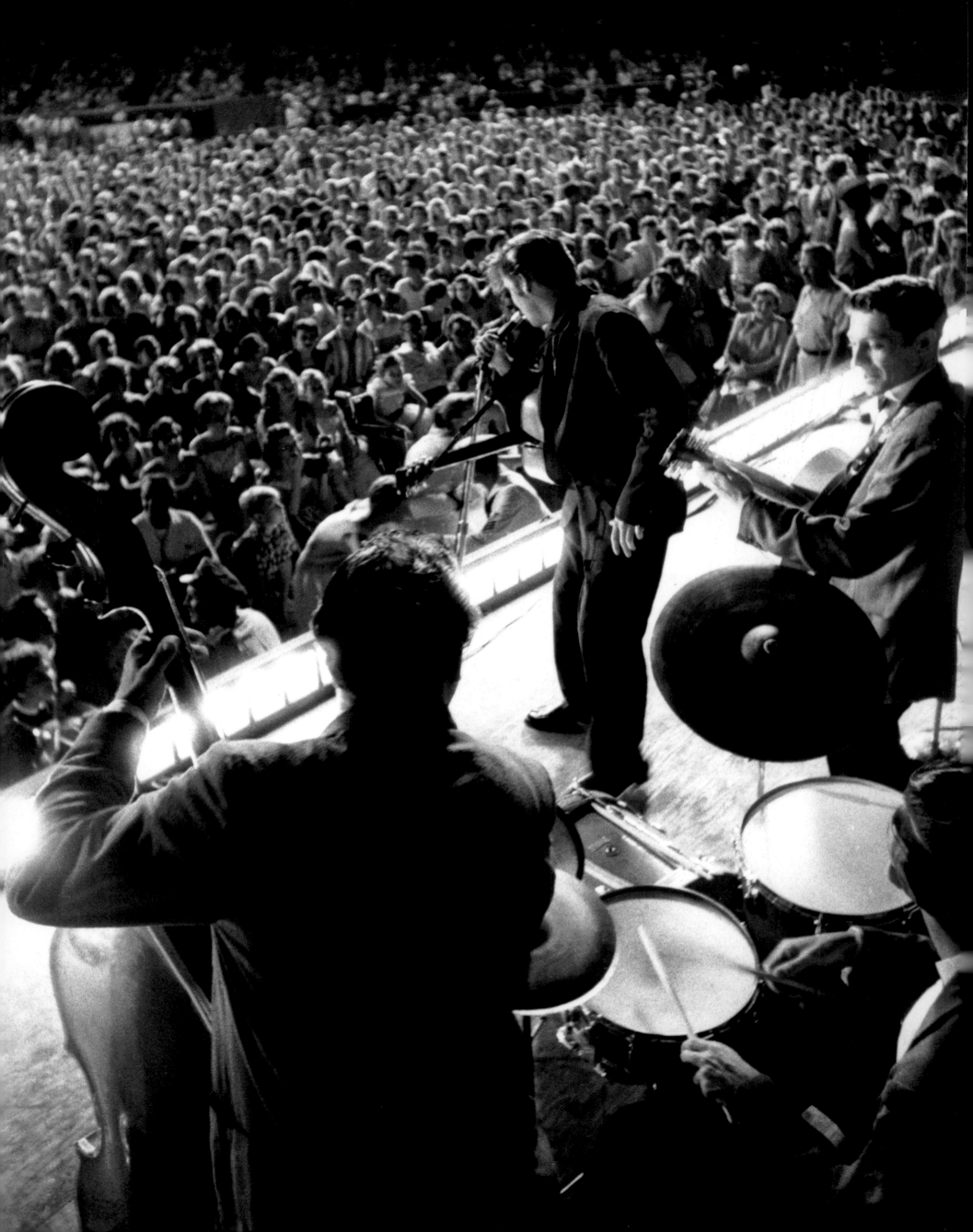

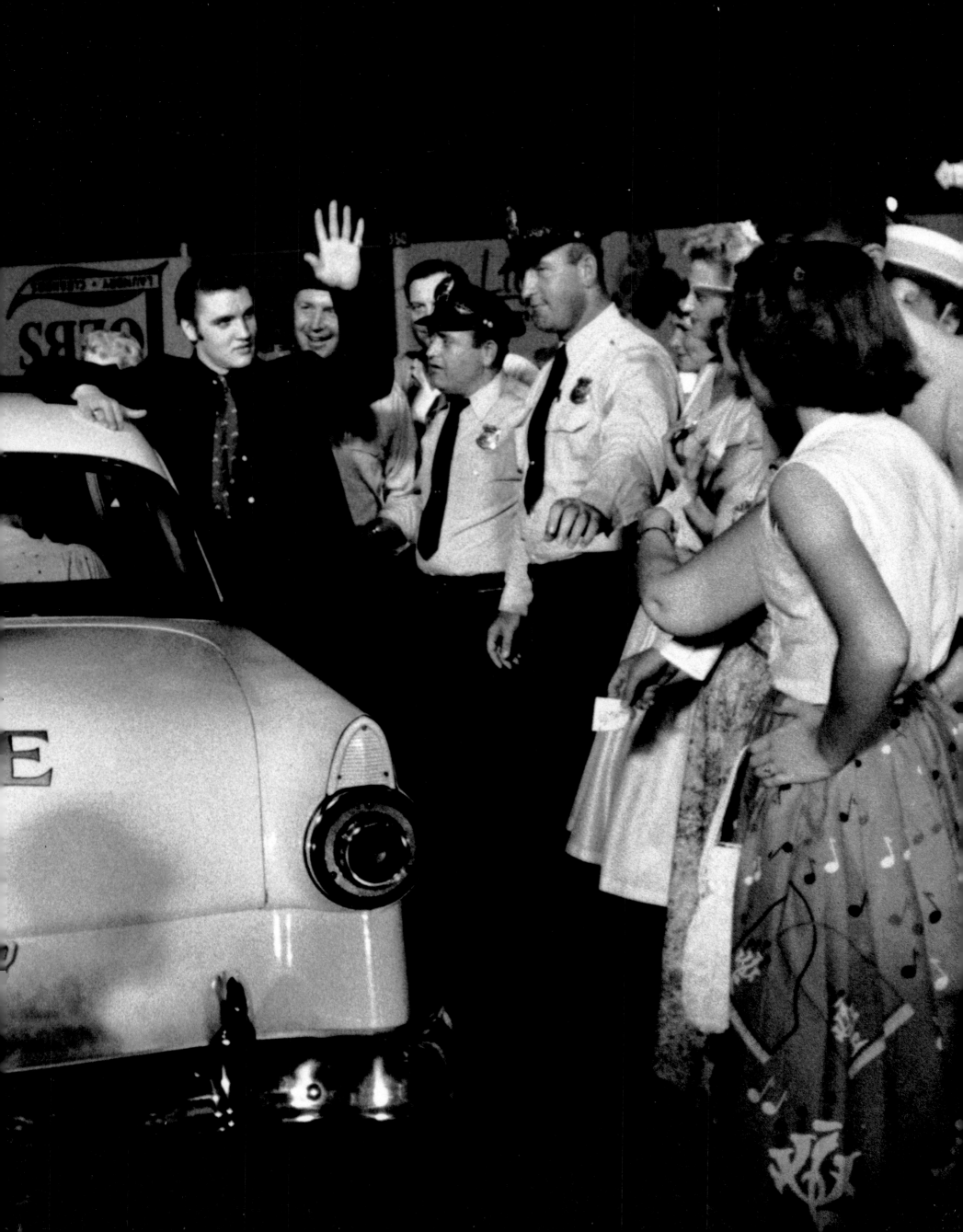

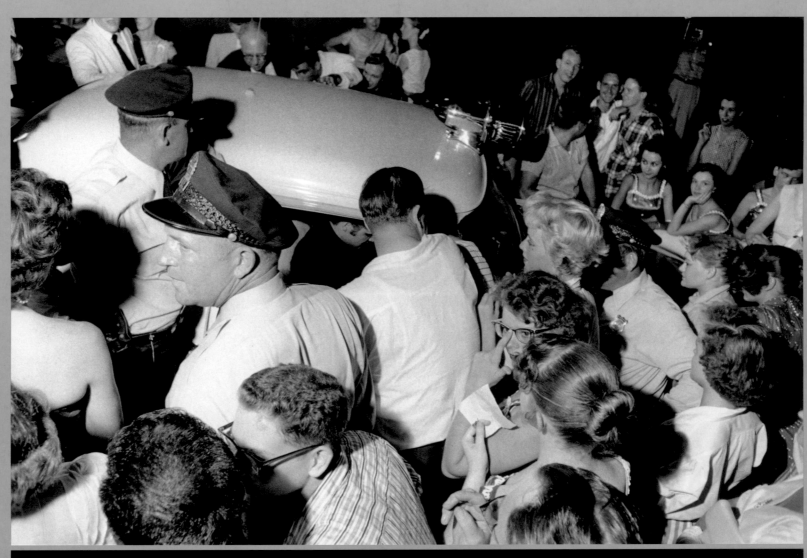
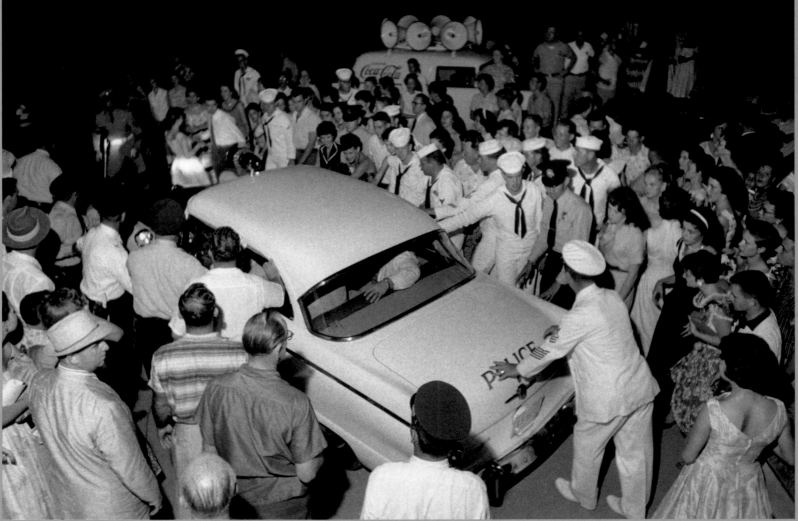

from the author This project is largely due to the creative vision of Chris Murray, Govinda Gallery, Washington, DC. My publisher, Raoul Goff, CEO of Insight Editions/Palace Press, for his faith and dedicated follow-through in making this project meet the highest industry standards. Peter Guralnick whose talent with words is simply amazing—a true artist. Barbara Genetin, my designer at Insight Editions/Palace Press. Milciades and Ana Buritica for keeping my home in order and being my right hand throughout the last 12 years. Spiro Carras, filmmaker, my guru, mentor and guide in the world of cyberspace. Lynda Gregory for sticking by me "brick by brick" and Diane Kantzoglou, "snip by snip". Georgina Galanis for being there and taking care of business as it was needed. Yetish Yetish for his talent in bringing these Elvis photographs to life from the original negatives. Elektra Carras, April Walsh and Ashley Walsh, my invaluable summer interns.

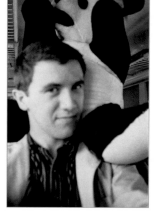

Katy and Julius Wertheimer, my beloved parents. Pamela Wertheimer and Heidi Wohlfeld, my nieces. The Wohlfeld Family. Henry and Renee Wertheimer. Josephine Kress and Therese Schevtchenko with whom I shared many years of friendship and love. Paul Schutzer, my personal friend and studio colleague for his prophetic insight about Elvis in 1956 and for introducing me to Ann Fulchino. Ann Fulchino of RCA Victor Publicity Department who first introduced me to Elvis. Colonel Thomas A. Parker, Elvis's manager, who even remembered my last name and how to pronounce it. Charlie Reiche, a master printer who was my mentor in the darkroom at Scope Associates. Roland Mitchell for his friendship and conscientious darkroom printing talent. Monetta Sleet and G. Marshall Wilson, photographers. Howard Leichman, my west coast friend Tom Palumbo who gave me my first job as his assistant running a fashion photography studio. Milton Newborn of Topix, my first photography agent.

Gladys Presley for being so hospitable, opening her personal scrapbook to be photographed and giving me one of Elvis's bathing suits so I could take photos inside the family pool. Scotty Moore and DJ Fontana, who continue to make music at the Peabody Hotel in Memphis. Steve Sholes, A&R man for RCA Victor who allowed me full access to the "Hound Dog" and Don't Be Cruel" recording session on July 2, 1956.

Carol F. Butler, Kelly C. Hill and Susan M. Sherwood of Elvis Presley Enterprises, Inc. Robert FX Sillerman for his entrepreneurial spirit and vision. My agents, Robert Pledge and Jeffrey Smith of Contact Press Images for international magazine sales of Elvis photos from the Wertheimer Collection. Barbara Cox of Photokunst, Staley Wise Gallery, Cooper Union, my alma mater and Mani's Food Market in NYC for its always fresh produce.

The many artists, filmmakers, photographers and musicians that crossed my horizon and influenced me with their impressive work. Most of all, thank you to Elvis, for letting me get so close.

—Alfred Wertheimer

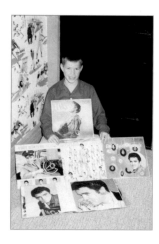

from the editor First and foremost, I want to thank Alfred Wertheimer for his trust and support in my efforts to present his wonderful photos of Elvis Presley through exhibitions and this publication. Al is a dear friend whom I greatly admire and whose company is always such a pleasure to me. Thank you, Alfred. To my friend and publishing partner, Raoul Goff, who shared my dream for this book from the very beginning. Raoul's commitment to quality in design and printing is an inspiration to me. To my assistant Carol Huh whose contribution to this book has been invaluable. Carol helped me every step of the way in bringing together *Elvis at 21*. Her expert copyediting, organization of materials, and good advice kept me steady and on time. My deep appreciation to Peter Guralnick for his preface to this book. Peter's book on Elvis, *Last Train to Memphis*, is the best biography of a musical artist I have ever read. Peter is a true gentleman whose books are an important contribution to our cultural legacy. To my brother Matthew, who first played Elvis's 45rpm records for me. To my Mom who didn't enjoy Elvis very much, but sure loved me...and to my Dad who would be proud of this book. To Carlotta Hester, whose encouragement, love, and kindness keeps me happy. To David Murray who went with me on my first visit to Sun Studios in Memphis, Tennessee. To Michael Meyer for his hospitality in New York City while I was working on this book. His generosity and enthusiasm helped me get the job done. To Richard Harrington whose appreciation for, and support of, my projects has always meant so much to me. To Ned Rifkin for his friendship and vision. To Chris Bruce and Bob Santelli for their interest in Al Wertheimer's photography. To Sam Phillips, and Scotty, Bill, and DJ. To Lisa Marie Presley for a dance with you in L.A. that I will always remember. Your music rocks. And most of all to Elvis, who turned me on and set me free.

—Chris Murray

colophon

The body of this book was set in Centaur, an exquisite, classical
font originally designed by Bruce Rogers for the Metropolitan Museum of New York
in 1914. The forms are based on those of the Renaissance printer Nicolas Jenson.

Display type was set in Trajan, a font designed for Adobe in 1989 by noted type designer
Carol Twombly, to echo the style of the chiseled writings of the Romans during the first century AD.

This book was printed using a quadtone process employing four layers of ink:
two blacks, a special warm gray, and a metallic pewter. A dry-trapped spot gloss varnish
was used to preserve the density of the original prints.

Publisher and Creative Director: Raoul Goff
Executive Directors: Michael Madden, Peter Beren
Art Director: Iain Morris
Designers: Raoul Goff, Barbara Genetin
Coordinating Editor: Carol Huh
Executive Editor: Mariah Bear
Production Manager: Lisa Bartlett
Studio Production & Press Supervision: Noah Potkin

Insight Editions
17 Paul Drive
San Rafael, CA 94903
(415) 526-1370
www.insighteditions.com

Library of Congress Cataloging-in-Publication Data available.

ISBN 1-933784-01-6
Limited Edition ISBN 1-933784-11-13

Palace Press International, in association with Global ReLeaf, will plant two trees for each tree used in the
manufacturing of this book. Global ReLeaf is an international campaign by American Forests, the nation's oldest
non-profit conservation organization and a world leader in planting tress for environmental restoration.

Alfred Wertheimer's photographs are represented by
Govinda Gallery
1227 34th Street, NW
Washington, DC 20007
www.govindagallery.com
Printed in China by Palace Press International

10 9 8 7 6 5 4 3 2 1

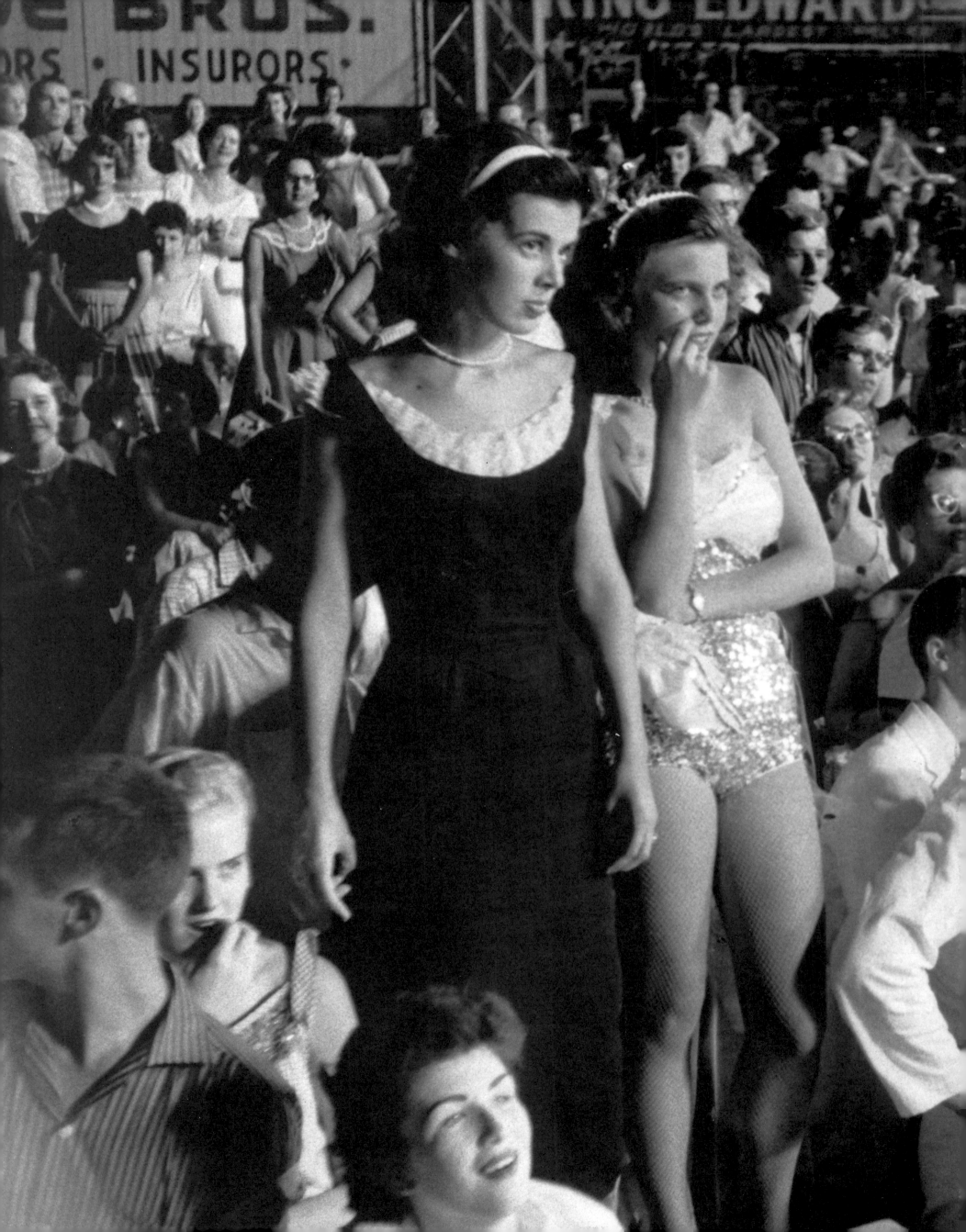